Shojo Beat

Kaze Hikaru

11

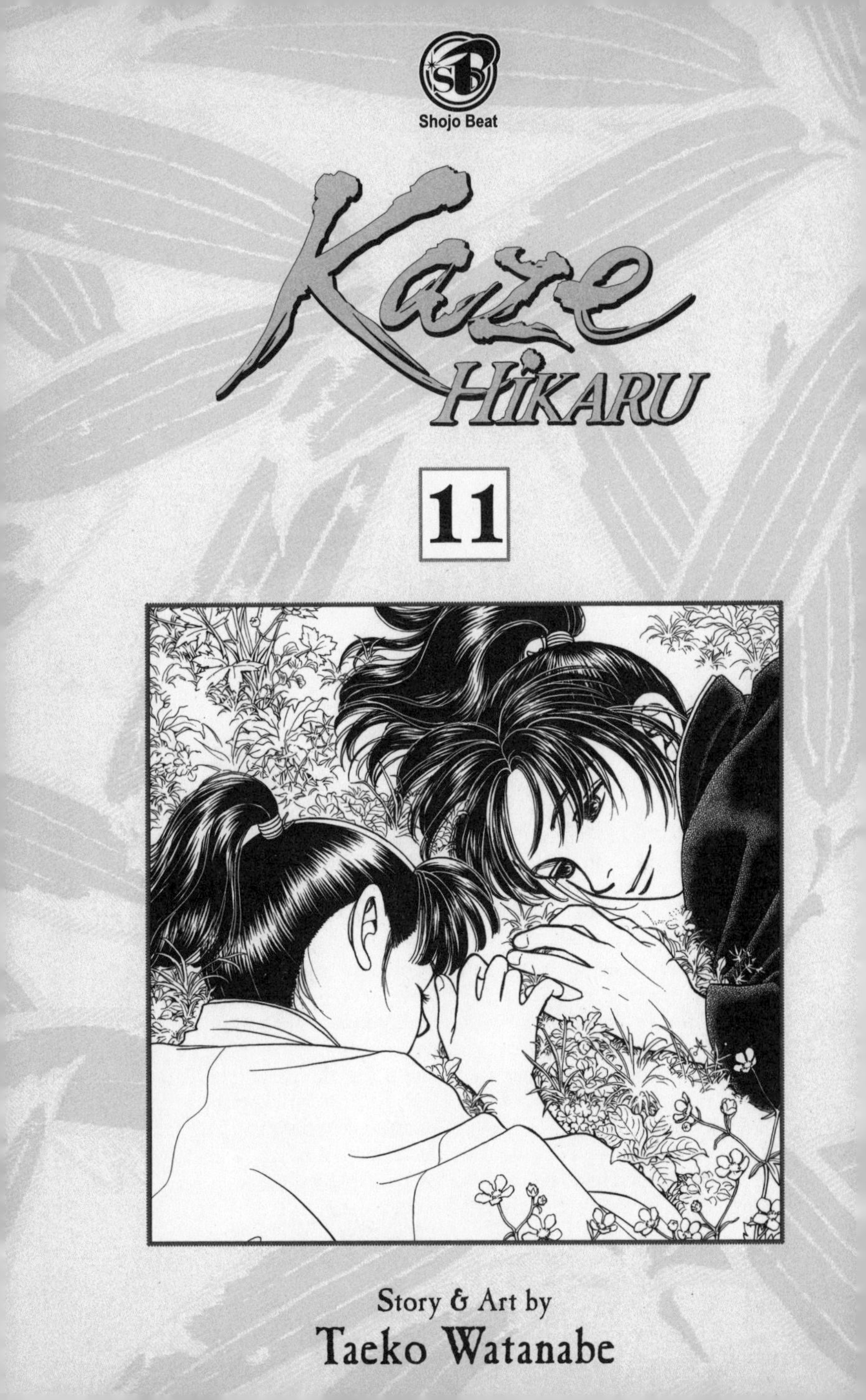

Story & Art by

Taeko Watanabe

Contents

Story Thus Far

It is the end of the Bakufu era, the 3rd year of Bunkyu (1863) in Kyoto. The Shinsengumi is a band of warriors formed to protect the Shogun.

Tominaga Sei, the daughter of a former Bakufu bushi, joined the Shinsengumi disguised as a boy by the name of Kamiya Seizaburo to avenge her father and brother. She has continued her training under the only person in the Shinsengumi who knows her true identity, Okita Soji, and she aspires to become a true *bushi*.

The Shinsengumi prove their worth through their success in the Ikedaya Affair and the *Kinmon no Hen*. After receiving orders from the Bakufu for the group to expand, Kondo returns from a recruiting trip to Edo with strong allies, including Ito Kashitaro and his men. Ito is warmly welcomed by the men, although he immediately falls for both Hijikata and Seizaburo. During this critical time for the Shinsengumi, Seizaburo finds young Mabo orphaned by the war and changed almost beyond recognition!!

Characters

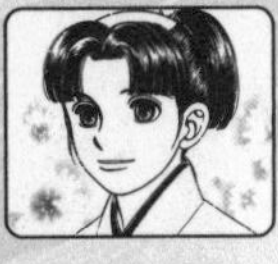

Tominaga Sei

She disguises herself as a boy to enter the Mibu-Roshi. She trains under Soji, aspiring to become a true *bushi*. But secretly, she is in love with Soji.

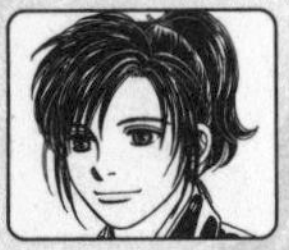

Okita Soji

Assistant vice captain of the Shinsengumi, and licensed master of the Ten'nen Rishin-Ryu. He supports the troop alongside Kondo and Hijikata and guides Seizaburo with a kind yet firm hand.

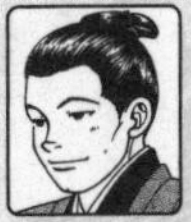

Kondo Isami

Captain of the Shinsengumi and fourth grandmaster of the Ten'nen Rishin-ryu. A passionate, warm and well-respected leader.

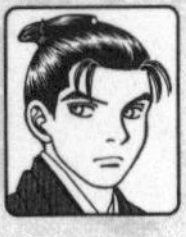

Hijikata Toshizo

Vice captain of the Shinsengumi. He commands both the group and himself with a rigid strictness. He is also known as the "Oni vice captain."

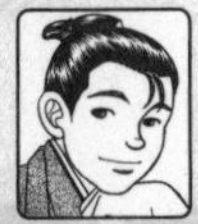

Yamanami Keisuke

Vice captain of the Shinsengumi. A master of the Hokushin Itto-Ryu, he is kind and well learned.

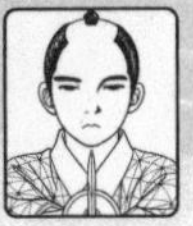

Saito Hajime

Assistant vice captain. He was a friend of Sei's older brother. Sei is attached to him in place of her lost brother.

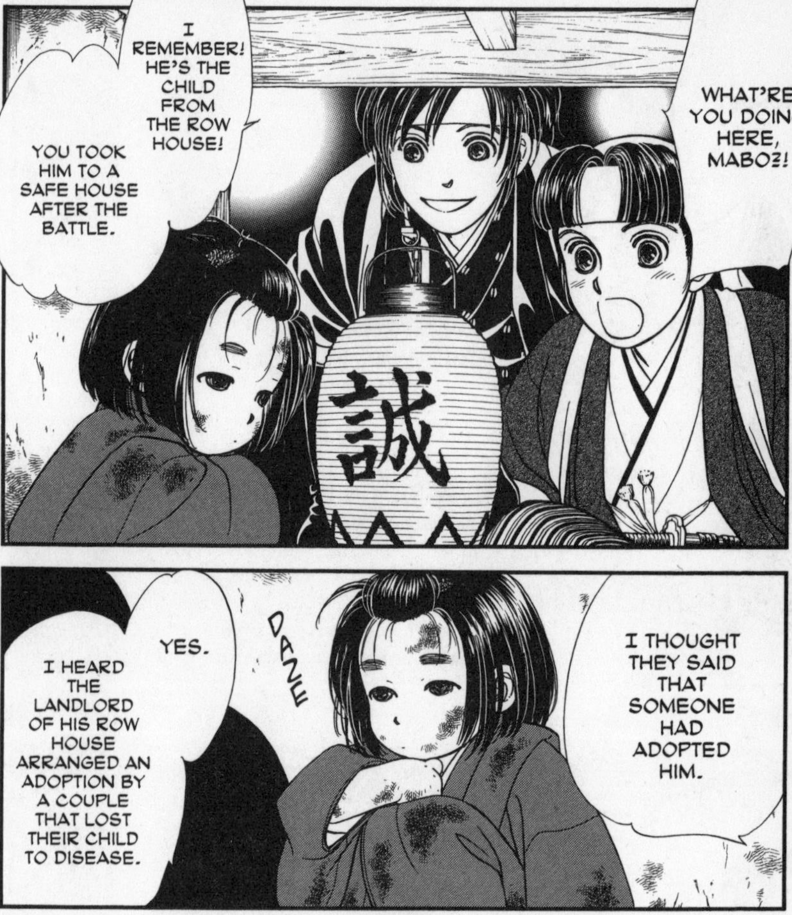
WHAT'RE YOU DOING HERE, MABO?!
I REMEMBER! HE'S THE CHILD FROM THE ROW HOUSE!
YOU TOOK HIM TO A SAFE HOUSE AFTER THE BATTLE.
I THOUGHT THEY SAID THAT SOMEONE HAD ADOPTED HIM.
DAZE
YES.
I HEARD THE LANDLORD OF HIS ROW HOUSE ARRANGED AN ADOPTION BY A COUPLE THAT LOST THEIR CHILD TO DISEASE.

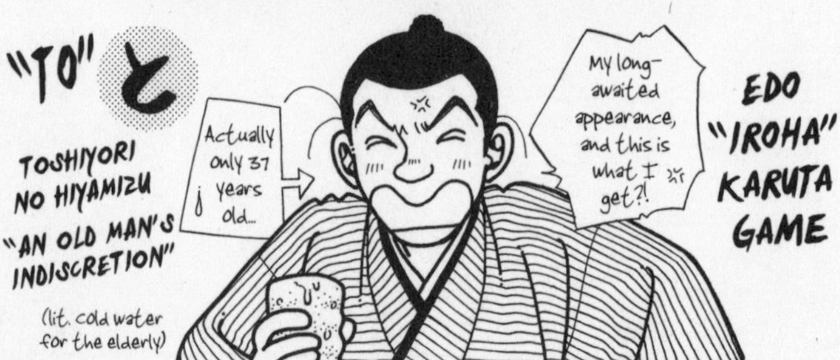
EDO "IROHA" KARUTA GAME
My long-awaited appearance, and this is what I get?!
Actually only 37 years old...
"TO" と
TOSHIYORI NO HIYAMIZU
"AN OLD MAN'S INDISCRETION"
(lit. cold water for the elderly)

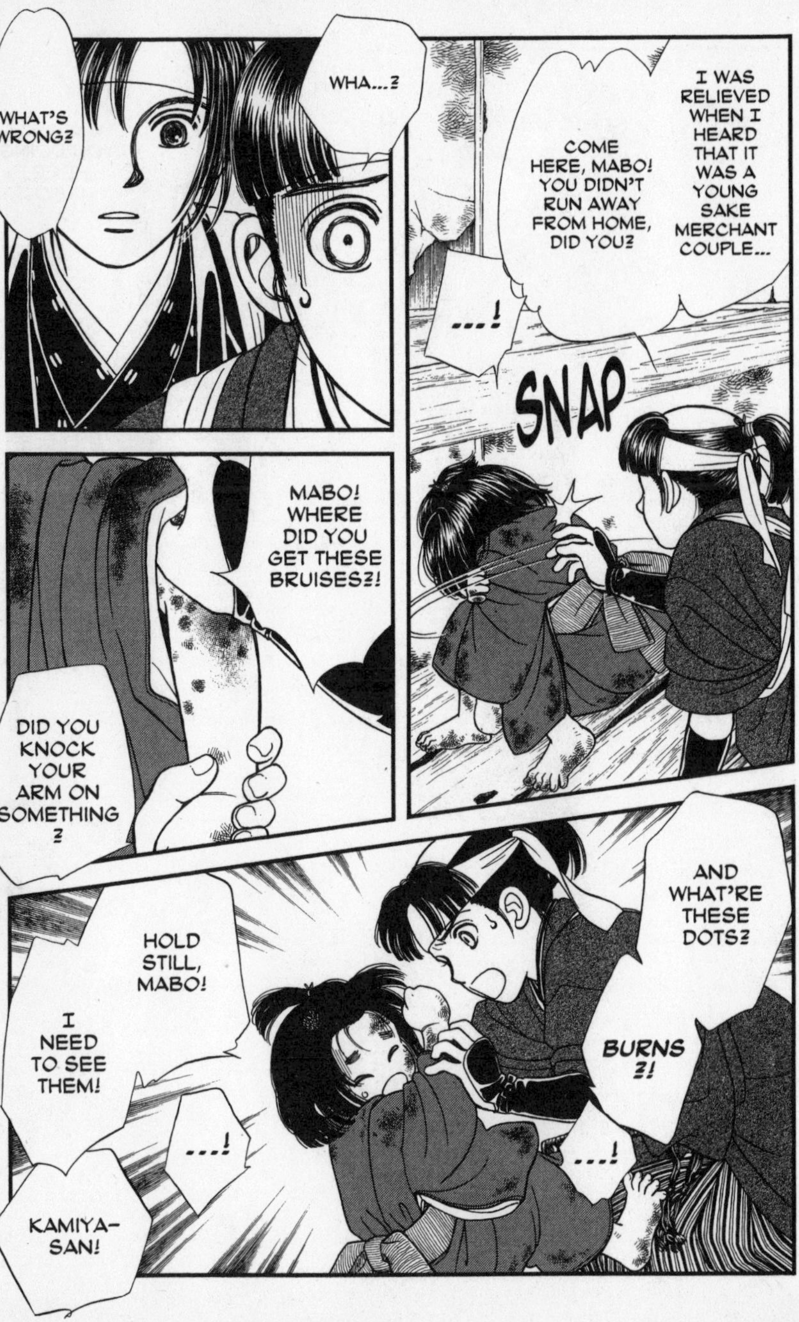
I WAS RELIEVED WHEN I HEARD THAT IT WAS A YOUNG SAKE MERCHANT COUPLE...
COME HERE, MABO! YOU DIDN'T RUN AWAY FROM HOME, DID YOU?
...!
SNAP
WHA...?
WHAT'S WRONG?
MABO! WHERE DID YOU GET THESE BRUISES?!
DID YOU KNOCK YOUR ARM ON SOMETHING?
AND WHAT'RE THESE DOTS?
BURNS?!
...!
HOLD STILL, MABO!
I NEED TO SEE THEM!
...!
KAMIYA-SAN!

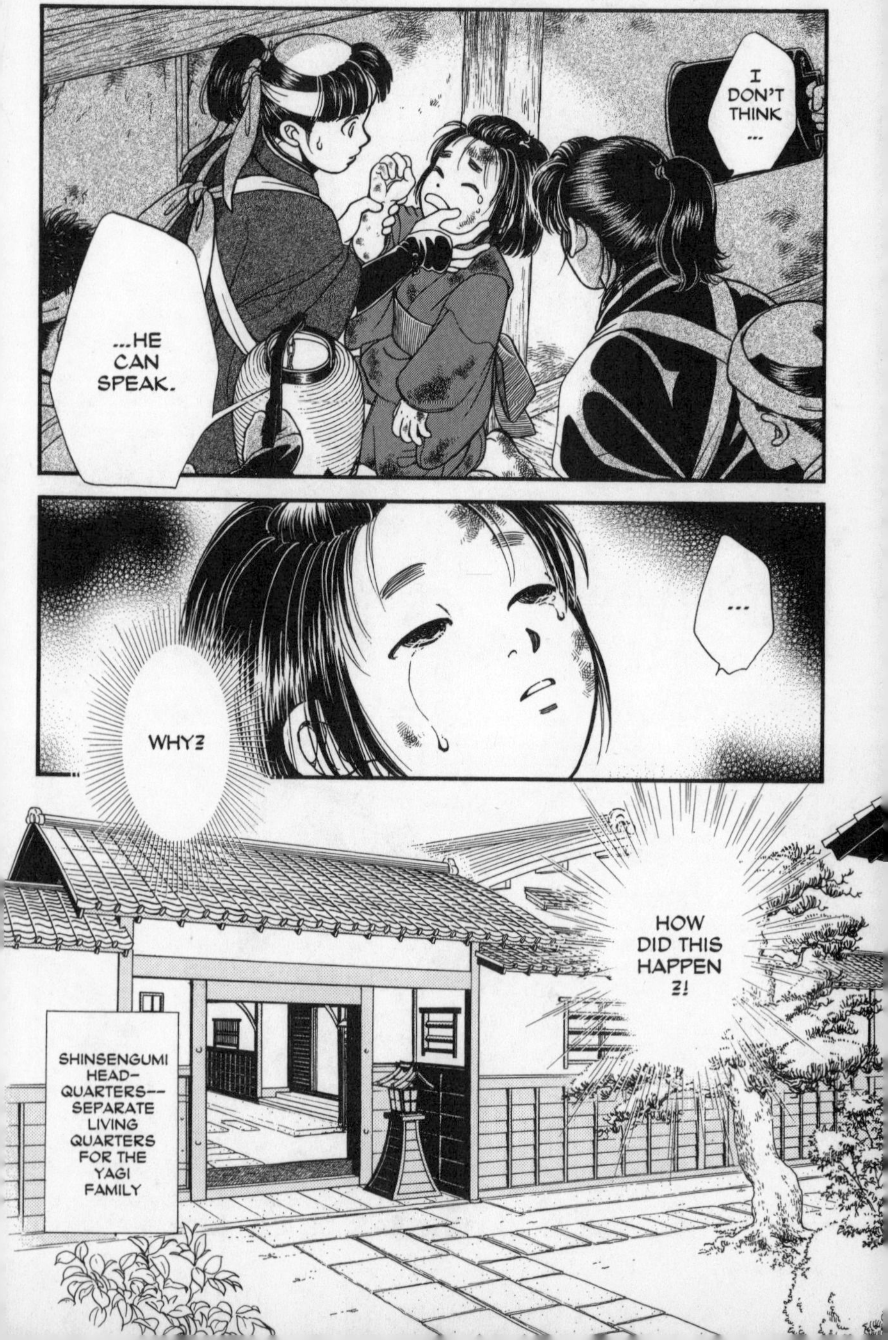
I DON'T THINK ...
...HE CAN SPEAK.
...
WHY?
HOW DID THIS HAPPEN?!
SHINSENGUMI HEAD-QUARTERS--SEPARATE LIVING QUARTERS FOR THE YAGI FAMILY

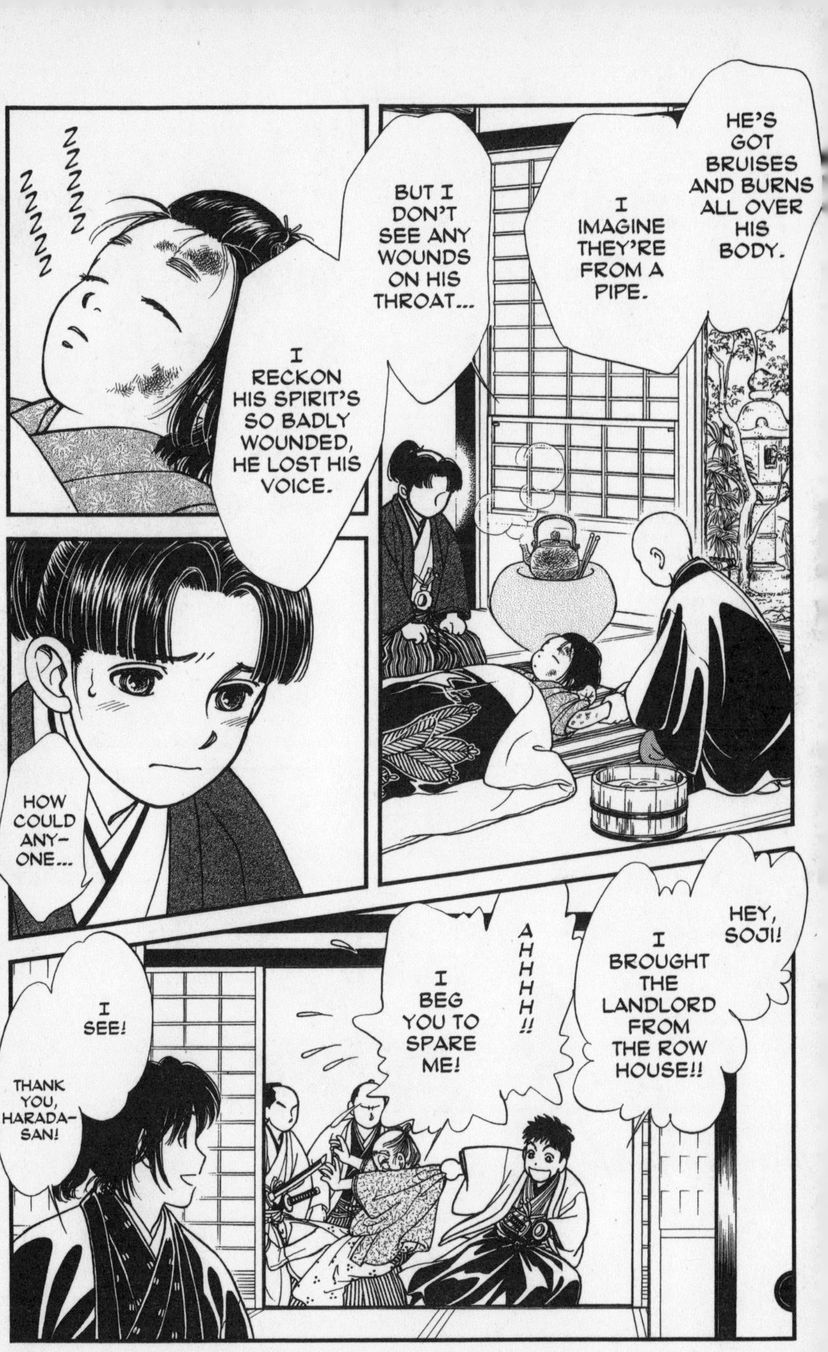
HE'S GOT BRUISES AND BURNS ALL OVER HIS BODY.
I IMAGINE THEY'RE FROM A PIPE.
BUT I DON'T SEE ANY WOUNDS ON HIS THROAT...
ZZZZZ ZZZZZ
I RECKON HIS SPIRIT'S SO BADLY WOUNDED, HE LOST HIS VOICE.
HOW COULD ANY-ONE...
HEY, SOJI!
I BROUGHT THE LANDLORD FROM THE ROW HOUSE!!
AHHHH!!
I BEG YOU TO SPARE ME!
I SEE!
THANK YOU, HARADA-SAN!

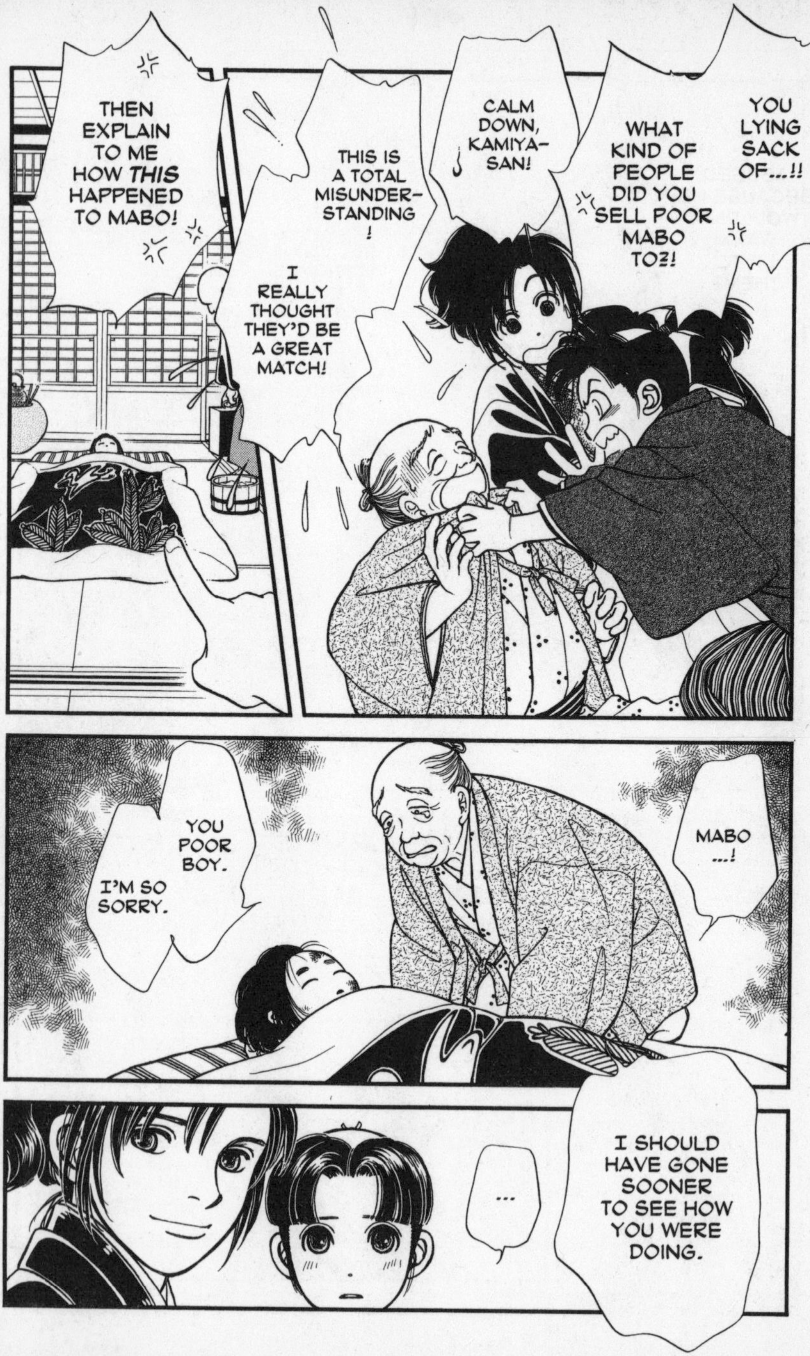
YOU LYING SACK OF...!!
WHAT KIND OF PEOPLE DID YOU SELL POOR MABO TO?!
CALM DOWN, KAMIYA-SAN!
THIS IS A TOTAL MISUNDERSTANDING!
I REALLY THOUGHT THEY'D BE A GREAT MATCH!
THEN EXPLAIN TO ME HOW *THIS* HAPPENED TO MABO!
MABO...!
YOU POOR BOY.
I'M SO SORRY.
I SHOULD HAVE GONE SOONER TO SEE HOW YOU WERE DOING.
...

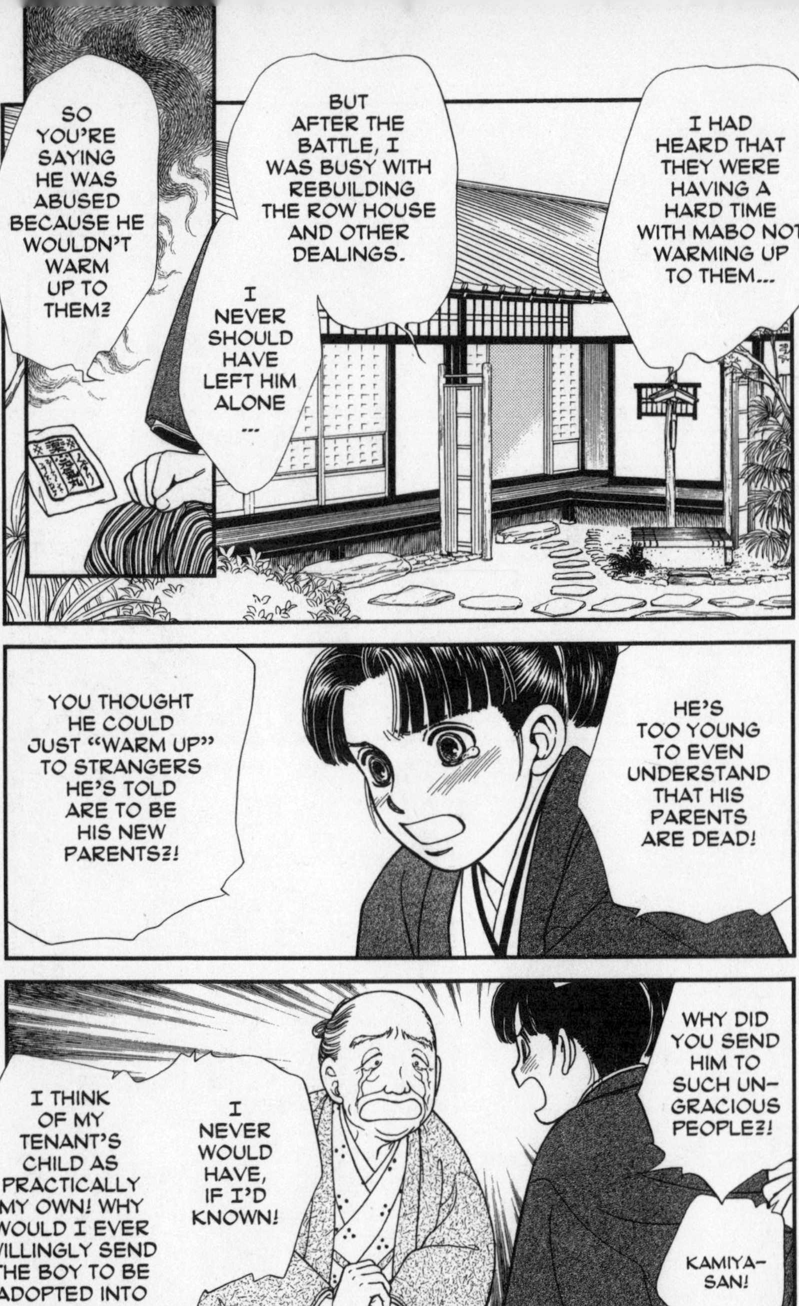
I HAD HEARD THAT THEY WERE HAVING A HARD TIME WITH MABO NOT WARMING UP TO THEM...
BUT AFTER THE BATTLE, I WAS BUSY WITH REBUILDING THE ROW HOUSE AND OTHER DEALINGS.
I NEVER SHOULD HAVE LEFT HIM ALONE...
SO YOU'RE SAYING HE WAS ABUSED BECAUSE HE WOULDN'T WARM UP TO THEM?
HE'S TOO YOUNG TO EVEN UNDERSTAND THAT HIS PARENTS ARE DEAD!
YOU THOUGHT HE COULD JUST "WARM UP" TO STRANGERS HE'S TOLD ARE TO BE HIS NEW PARENTS?!
WHY DID YOU SEND HIM TO SUCH UN-GRACIOUS PEOPLE?!
KAMIYA-SAN!
I NEVER WOULD HAVE, IF I'D KNOWN!
I THINK OF MY TENANT'S CHILD AS PRACTICALLY MY OWN! WHY WOULD I EVER WILLINGLY SEND THE BOY TO BE ADOPTED INTO MISERY?!

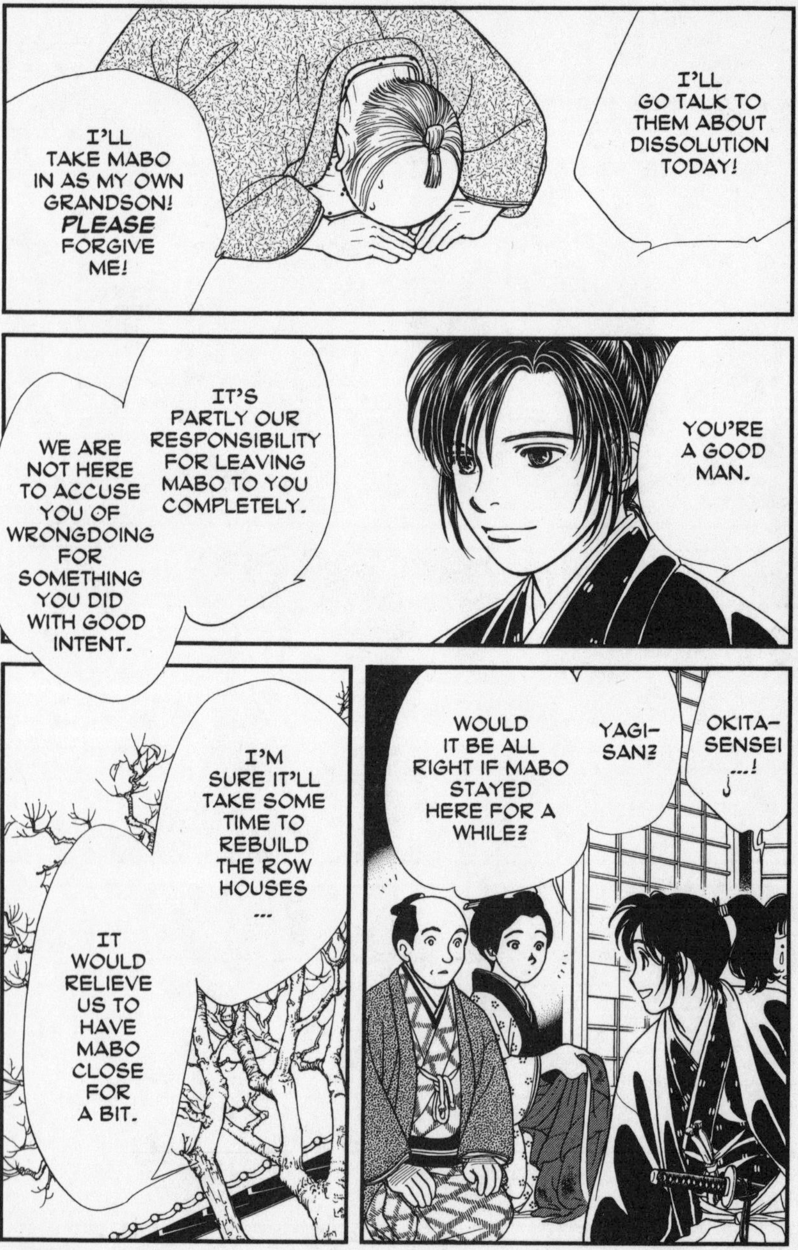
I'LL GO TALK TO THEM ABOUT DISSOLUTION TODAY!
I'LL TAKE MABO IN AS MY OWN GRANDSON! *PLEASE* FORGIVE ME!
YOU'RE A GOOD MAN.
IT'S PARTLY OUR RESPONSIBILITY FOR LEAVING MABO TO YOU COMPLETELY.
WE ARE NOT HERE TO ACCUSE YOU OF WRONGDOING FOR SOMETHING YOU DID WITH GOOD INTENT.
OKITA-SENSEI...!
YAGI-SAN?
WOULD IT BE ALL RIGHT IF MABO STAYED HERE FOR A WHILE?
I'M SURE IT'LL TAKE SOME TIME TO REBUILD THE ROW HOUSES...
IT WOULD RELIEVE US TO HAVE MABO CLOSE FOR A BIT.

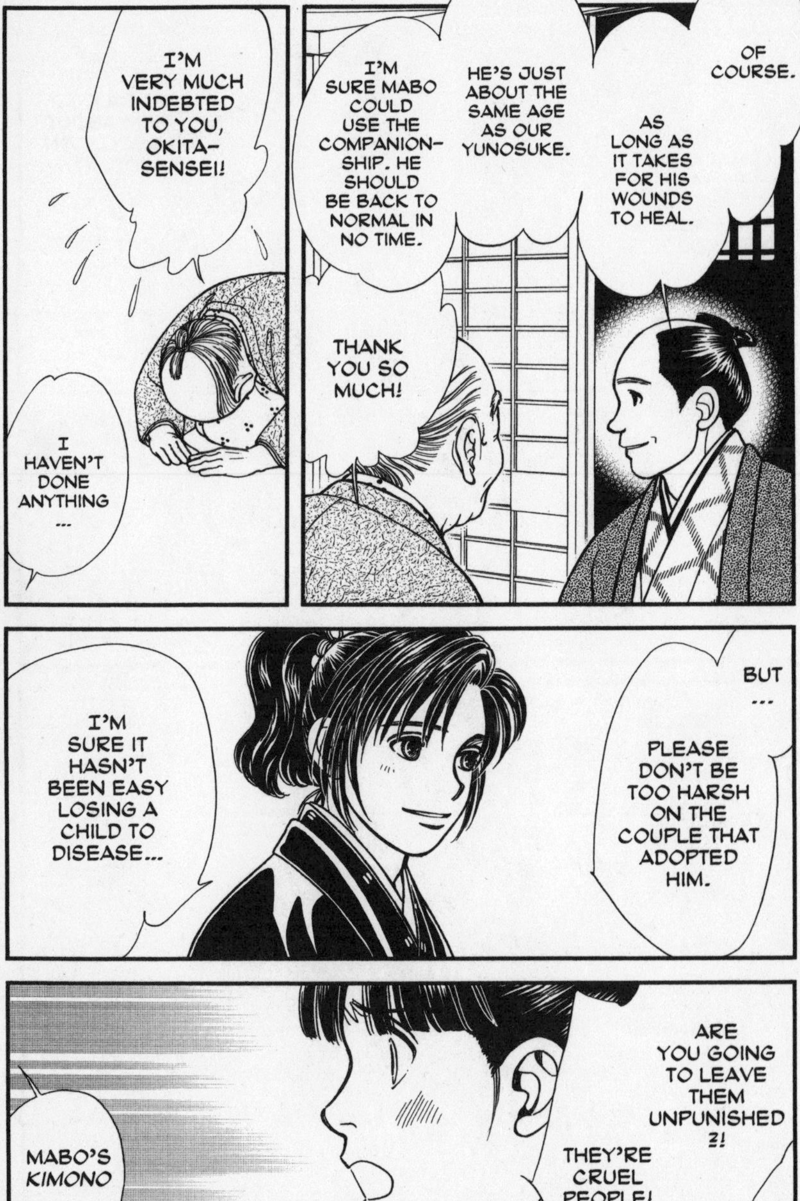

OF COURSE.
AS LONG AS IT TAKES FOR HIS WOUNDS TO HEAL.
HE'S JUST ABOUT THE SAME AGE AS OUR YUNOSUKE.
I'M SURE MABO COULD USE THE COMPANIONSHIP. HE SHOULD BE BACK TO NORMAL IN NO TIME.
THANK YOU SO MUCH!
I'M VERY MUCH INDEBTED TO YOU, OKITA-SENSEI!
I HAVEN'T DONE ANYTHING ...
BUT ...
PLEASE DON'T BE TOO HARSH ON THE COUPLE THAT ADOPTED HIM.
I'M SURE IT HASN'T BEEN EASY LOSING A CHILD TO DISEASE...
ARE YOU GOING TO LEAVE THEM UNPUNISHED ?!
THEY'RE CRUEL PEOPLE!
MABO'S KIMONO ...

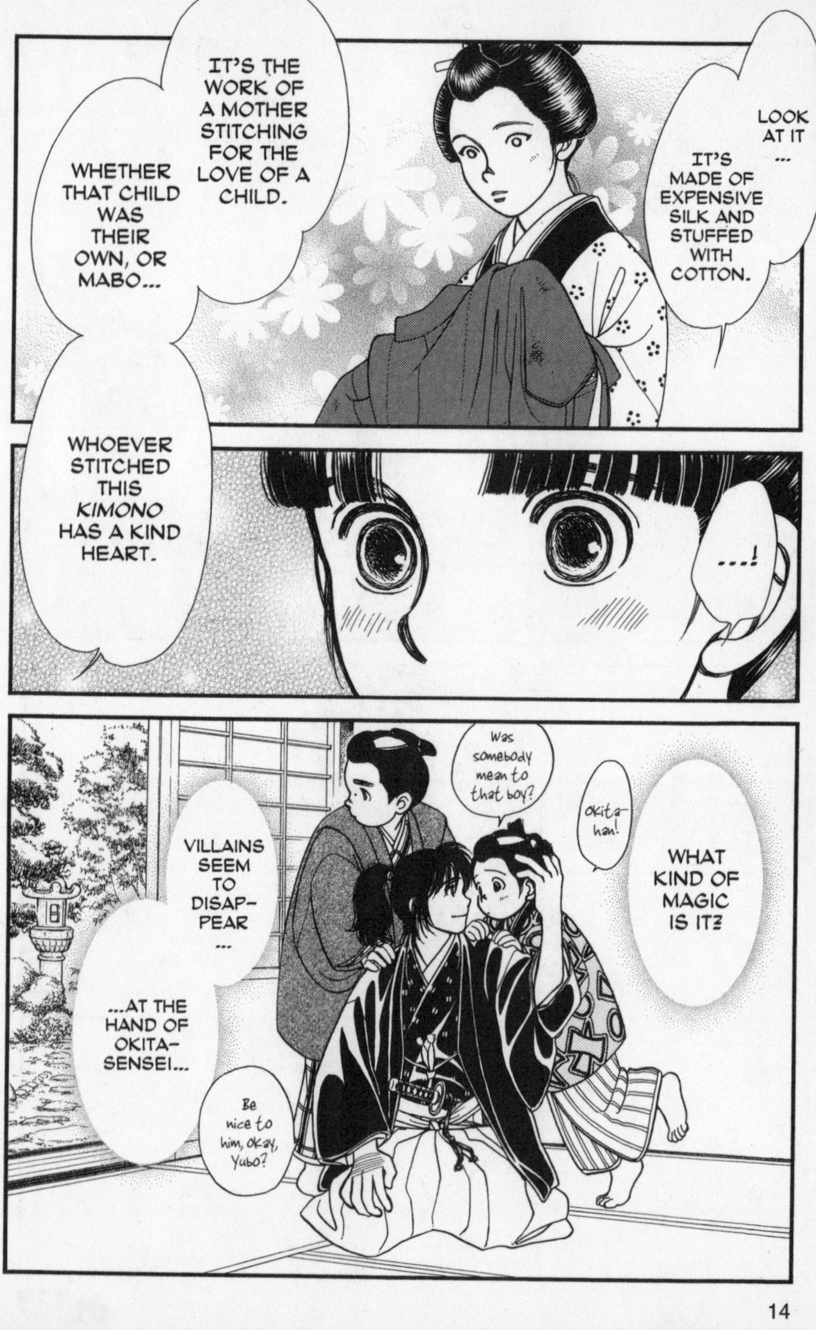
LOOK AT IT ... IT'S MADE OF EXPENSIVE SILK AND STUFFED WITH COTTON.
IT'S THE WORK OF A MOTHER STITCHING FOR THE LOVE OF A CHILD.
WHETHER THAT CHILD WAS THEIR OWN, OR MABO...
WHOEVER STITCHED THIS *KIMONO* HAS A KIND HEART.
...!
WHAT KIND OF MAGIC IS IT?
Okita-han!
Was somebody mean to that boy?
VILLAINS SEEM TO DISAPPEAR ...
...AT THE HAND OF OKITA-SENSEI...
Be nice to him, okay, Yubo?

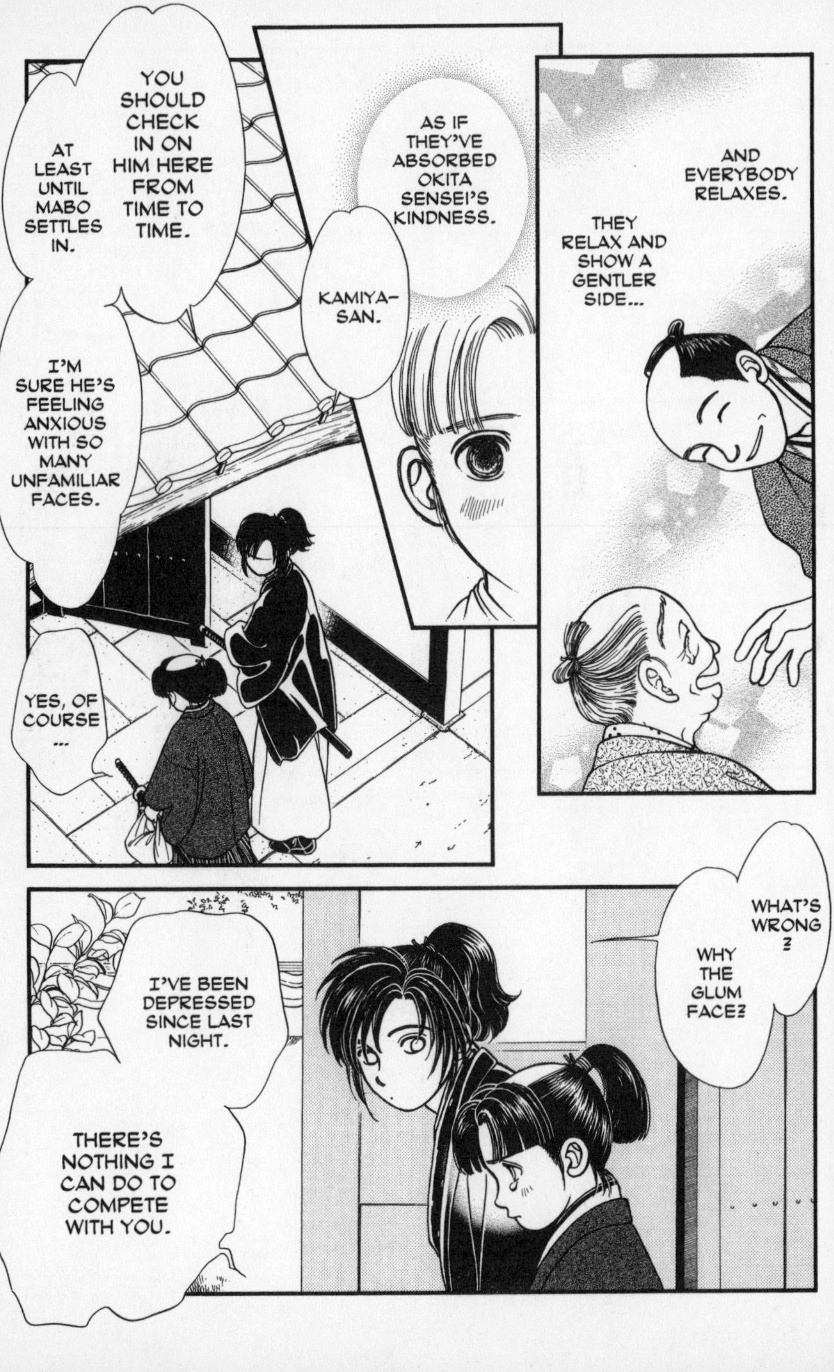
AND EVERYBODY RELAXES.
THEY RELAX AND SHOW A GENTLER SIDE...
AS IF THEY'VE ABSORBED OKITA SENSEI'S KINDNESS.
KAMIYA-SAN.
YOU SHOULD CHECK IN ON HIM HERE FROM TIME TO TIME.
AT LEAST UNTIL MABO SETTLES IN.
I'M SURE HE'S FEELING ANXIOUS WITH SO MANY UNFAMILIAR FACES.
YES, OF COURSE...
WHAT'S WRONG?
WHY THE GLUM FACE?
I'VE BEEN DEPRESSED SINCE LAST NIGHT.
THERE'S NOTHING I CAN DO TO COMPETE WITH YOU.

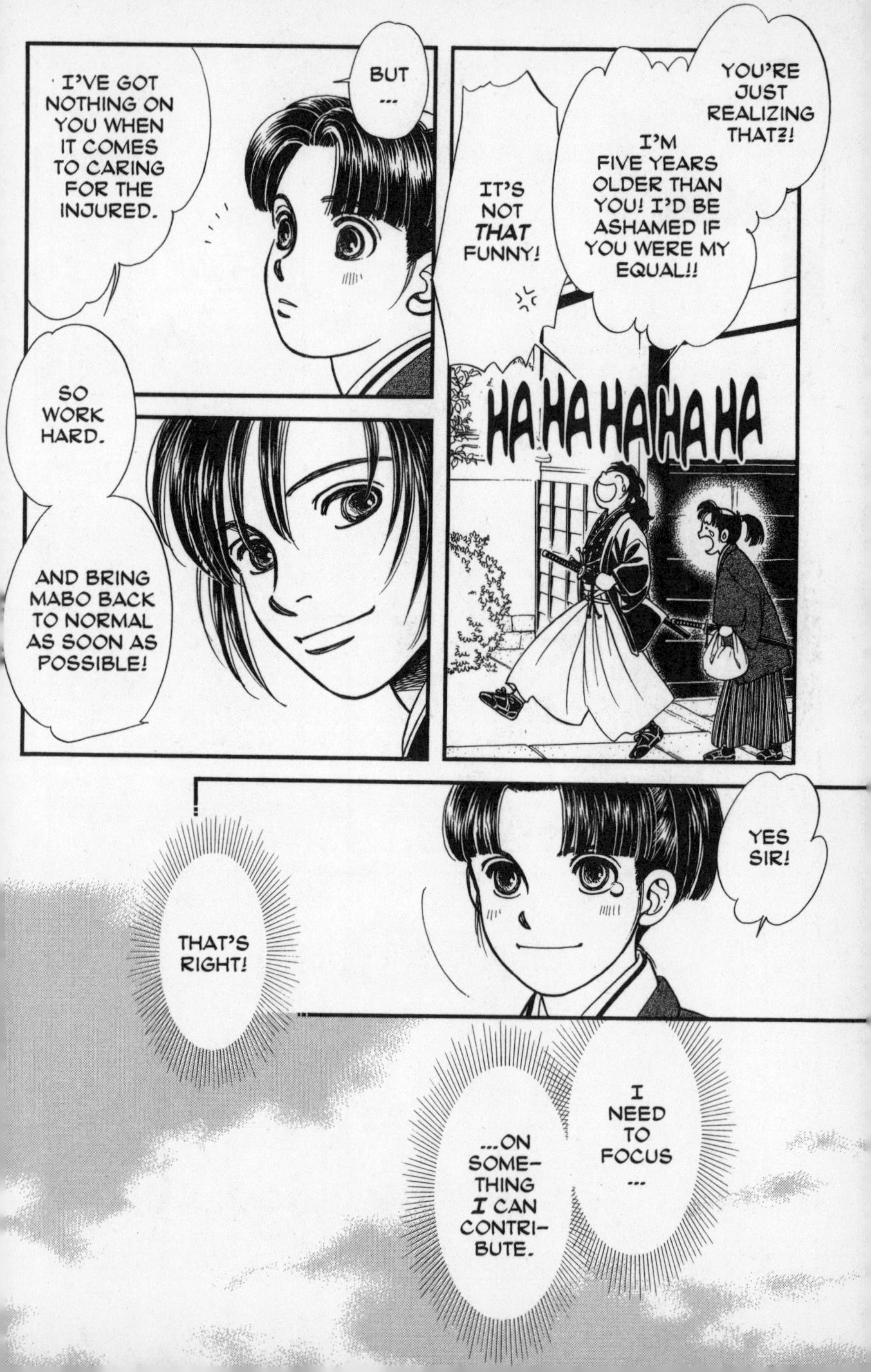
YOU'RE JUST REALIZING THAT?!
I'M FIVE YEARS OLDER THAN YOU! I'D BE ASHAMED IF YOU WERE MY EQUAL!!
IT'S NOT *THAT* FUNNY!
HA HA HA HA HA HA
BUT ...
I'VE GOT NOTHING ON YOU WHEN IT COMES TO CARING FOR THE INJURED.
SO WORK HARD.
AND BRING MABO BACK TO NORMAL AS SOON AS POSSIBLE!
YES SIR!
THAT'S RIGHT!
I NEED TO FOCUS ...
...ON SOME-THING *I* CAN CONTRI-BUTE.

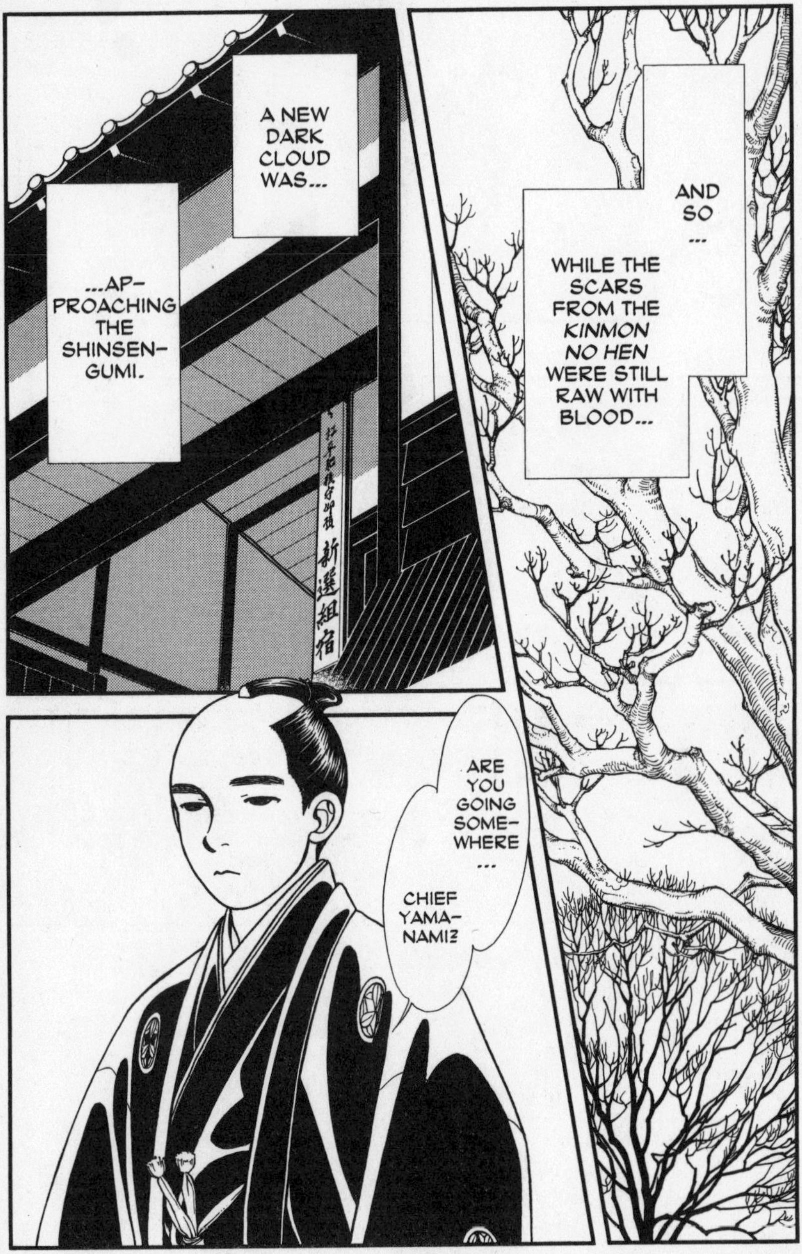
AND SO ...
WHILE THE SCARS FROM THE *KINMON NO HEN* WERE STILL RAW WITH BLOOD...
A NEW DARK CLOUD WAS...
...AP-PROACHING THE SHINSEN-GUMI.
新選組宿
ARE YOU GOING SOME-WHERE ...
CHIEF YAMA-NAMI?

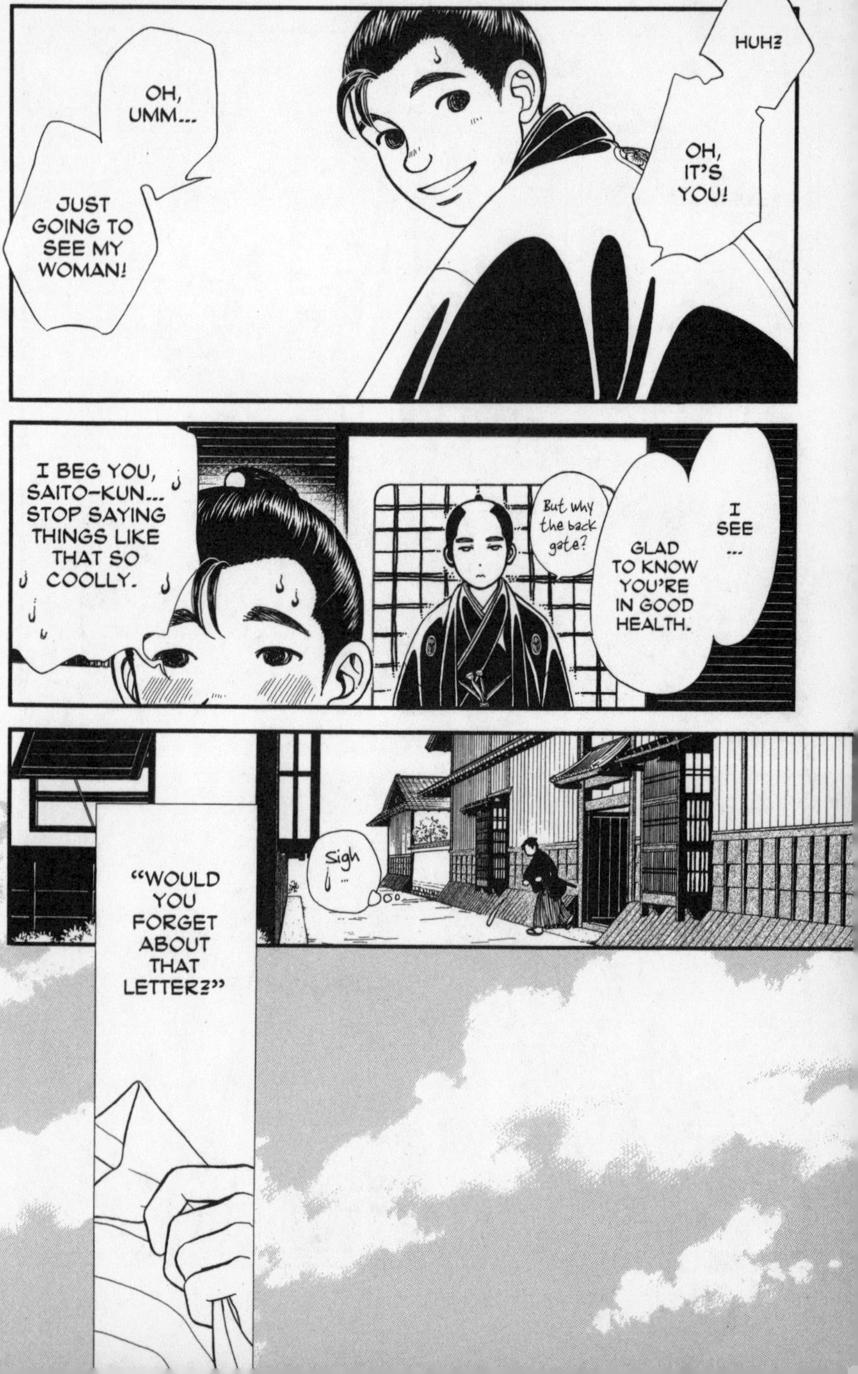
HUH?
OH, IT'S YOU!
OH, UMM...
JUST GOING TO SEE MY WOMAN!
I SEE...
GLAD TO KNOW YOU'RE IN GOOD HEALTH.
But why the back gate?
I BEG YOU, SAITO-KUN... STOP SAYING THINGS LIKE THAT SO COOLLY.
Sigh...
"WOULD YOU FORGET ABOUT THAT LETTER?"

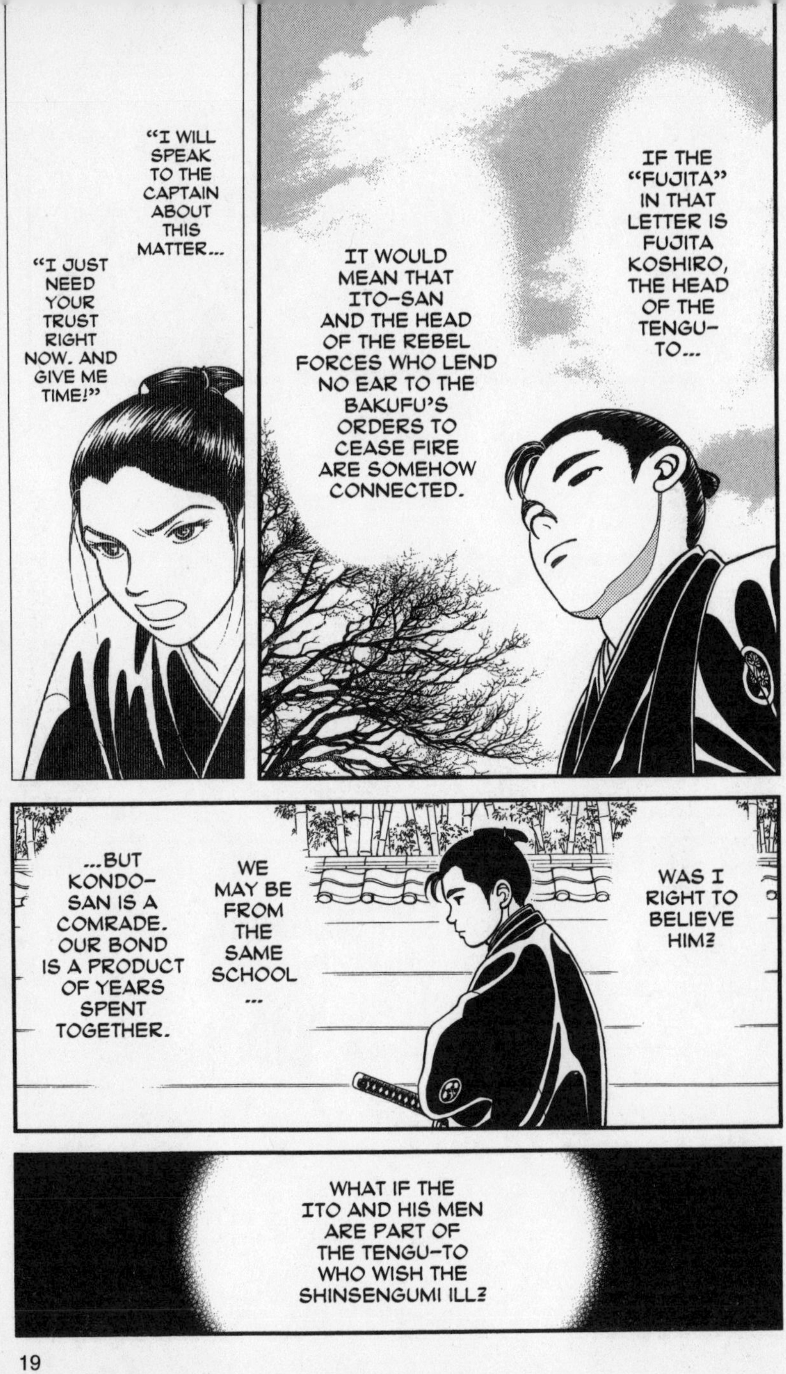
IF THE "FUJITA" IN THAT LETTER IS FUJITA KOSHIRO, THE HEAD OF THE TENGU-TO...
IT WOULD MEAN THAT ITO-SAN AND THE HEAD OF THE REBEL FORCES WHO LEND NO EAR TO THE BAKUFU'S ORDERS TO CEASE FIRE ARE SOMEHOW CONNECTED.
"I WILL SPEAK TO THE CAPTAIN ABOUT THIS MATTER...
"I JUST NEED YOUR TRUST RIGHT NOW. AND GIVE ME TIME!"
WAS I RIGHT TO BELIEVE HIM?
WE MAY BE FROM THE SAME SCHOOL...
...BUT KONDO-SAN IS A COMRADE. OUR BOND IS A PRODUCT OF YEARS SPENT TOGETHER.
WHAT IF THE ITO AND HIS MEN ARE PART OF THE TENGU-TO WHO WISH THE SHINSENGUMI ILL?

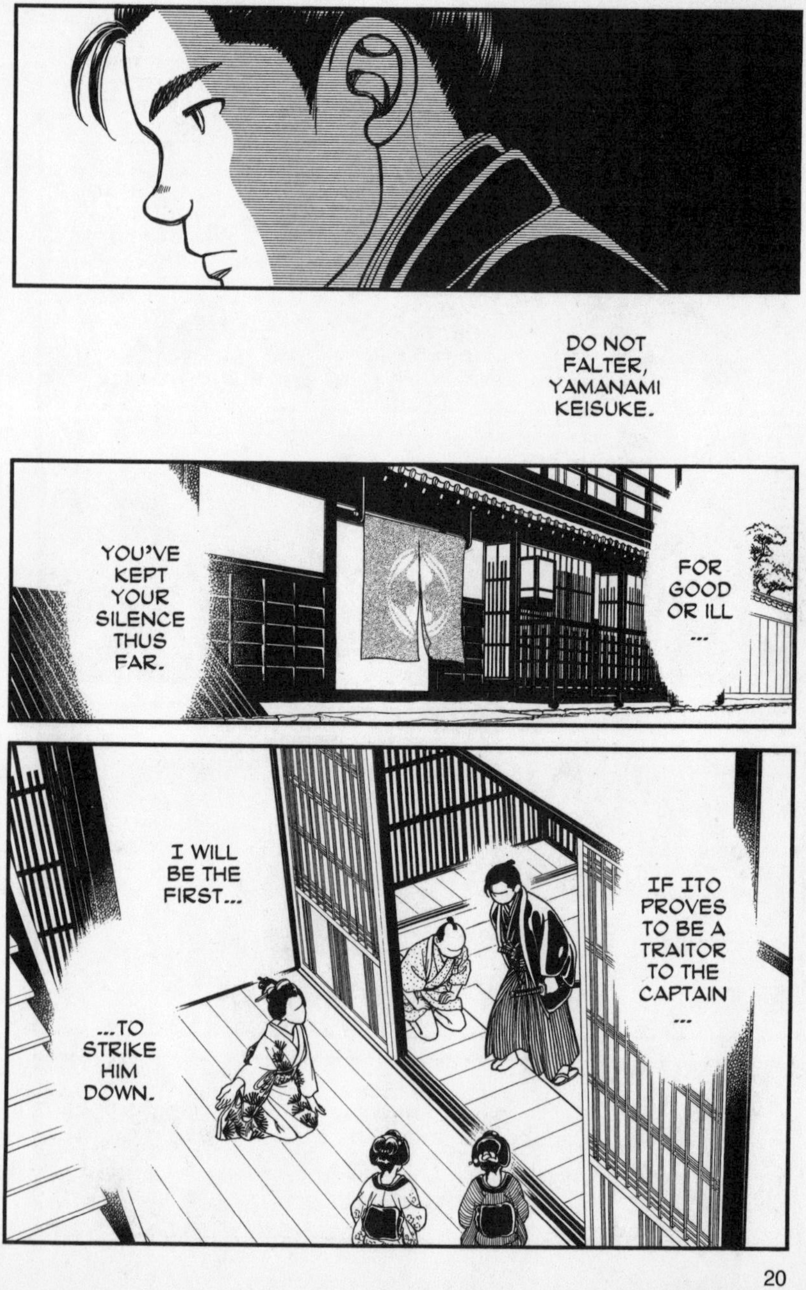
DO NOT FALTER, YAMANAMI KEISUKE.
FOR GOOD OR ILL ...
YOU'VE KEPT YOUR SILENCE THUS FAR.
IF ITO PROVES TO BE A TRAITOR TO THE CAPTAIN ...
I WILL BE THE FIRST...
...TO STRIKE HIM DOWN.

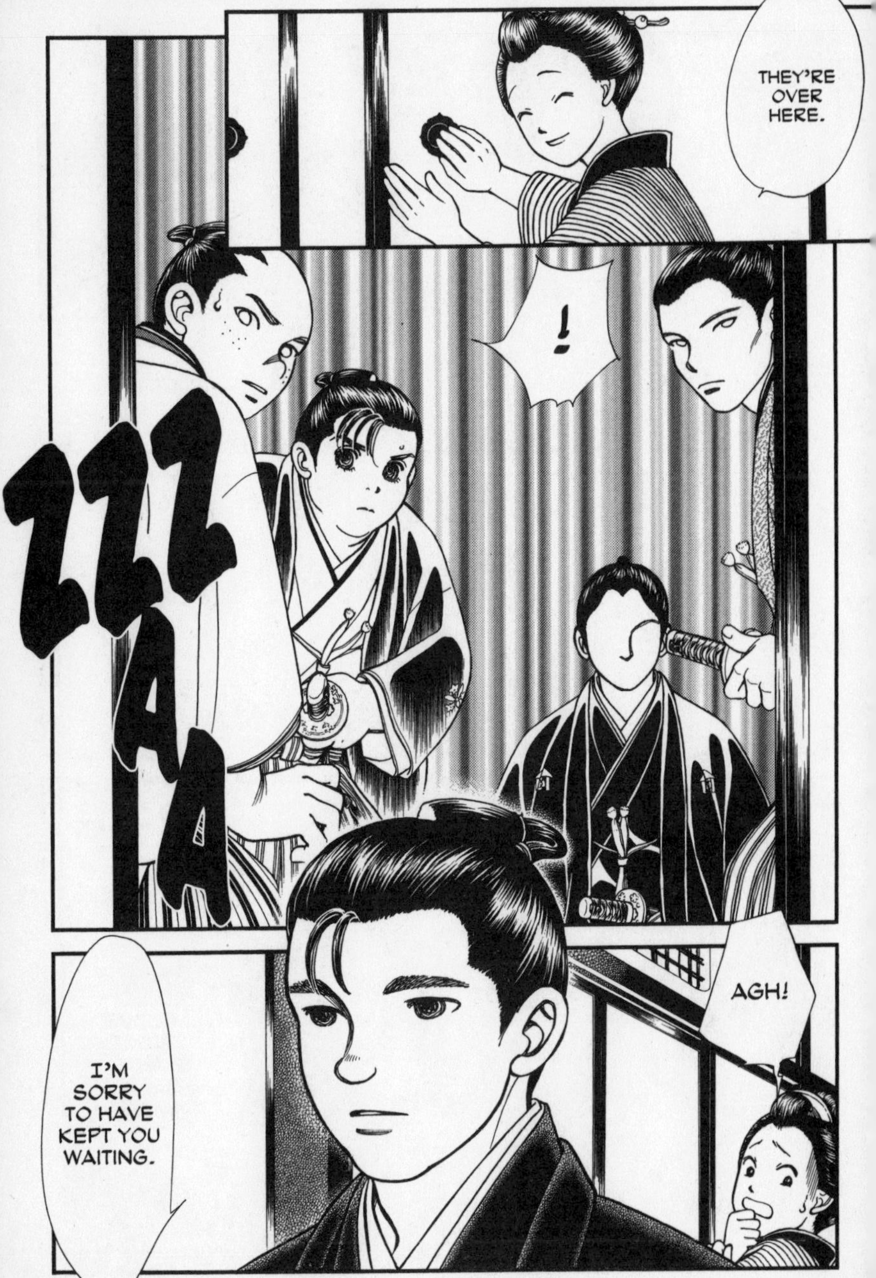
THEY'RE OVER HERE.
!
ZZZAAA
AGH!
I'M SORRY TO HAVE KEPT YOU WAITING.

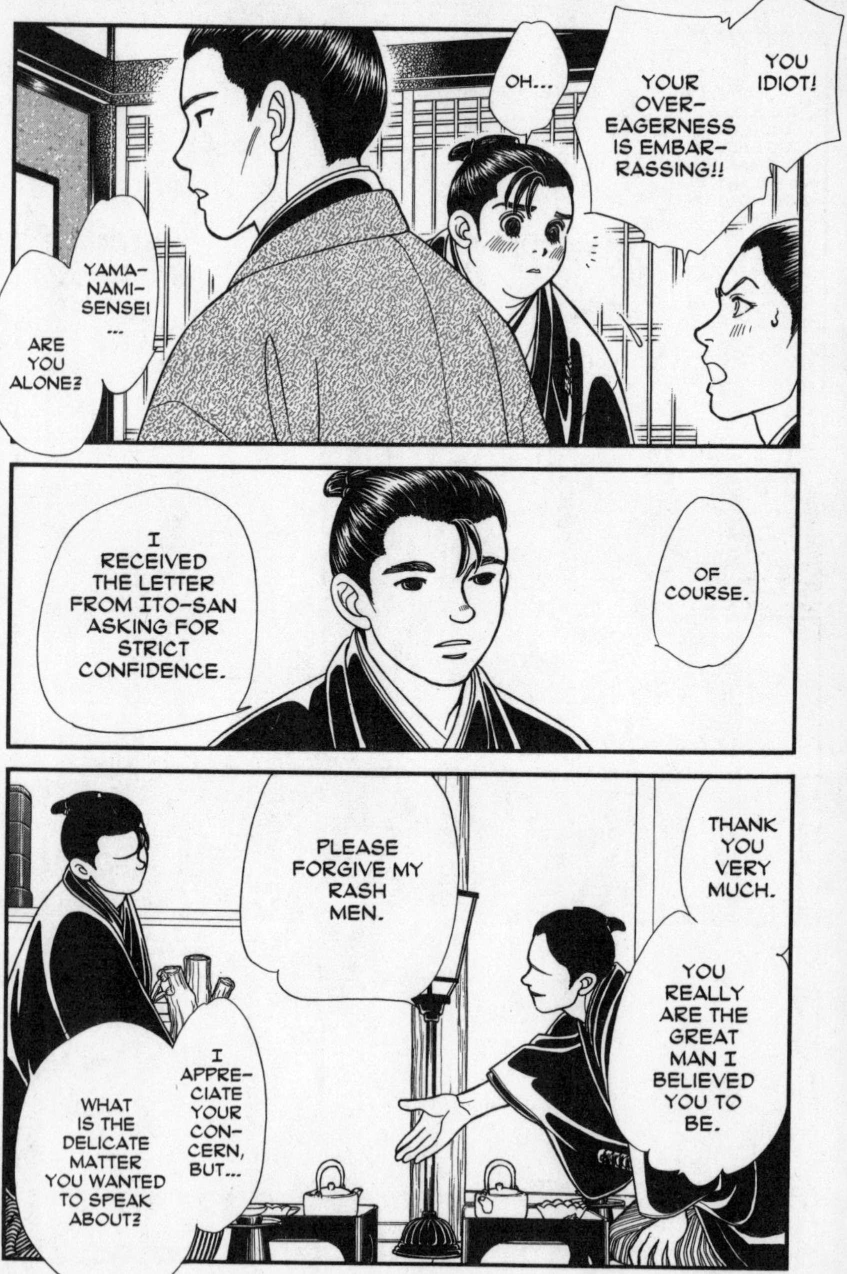
YOU IDIOT!
YOUR OVER-EAGERNESS IS EMBARRASSING!!
OH...
...
YAMANAMI-SENSEI ... ARE YOU ALONE?
OF COURSE.
I RECEIVED THE LETTER FROM ITO-SAN ASKING FOR STRICT CONFIDENCE.
THANK YOU VERY MUCH.
YOU REALLY ARE THE GREAT MAN I BELIEVED YOU TO BE.
PLEASE FORGIVE MY RASH MEN.
I APPRECIATE YOUR CONCERN, BUT...
WHAT IS THE DELICATE MATTER YOU WANTED TO SPEAK ABOUT?

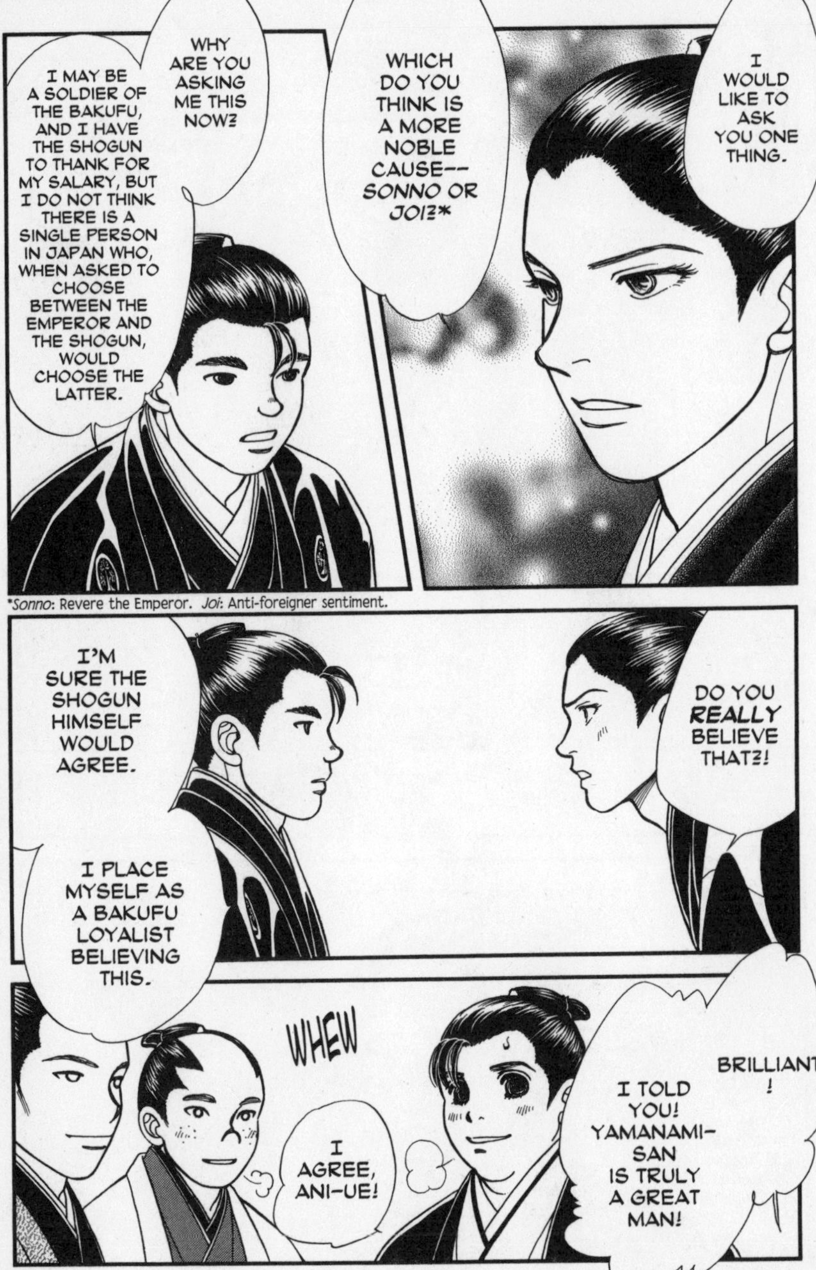
I WOULD LIKE TO ASK YOU ONE THING.
WHICH DO YOU THINK IS A MORE NOBLE CAUSE-- SONNO OR JOI?!*
WHY ARE YOU ASKING ME THIS NOW?
I MAY BE A SOLDIER OF THE BAKUFU, AND I HAVE THE SHOGUN TO THANK FOR MY SALARY, BUT I DO NOT THINK THERE IS A SINGLE PERSON IN JAPAN WHO, WHEN ASKED TO CHOOSE BETWEEN THE EMPEROR AND THE SHOGUN, WOULD CHOOSE THE LATTER.
DO YOU ***REALLY*** BELIEVE THAT?!
I'M SURE THE SHOGUN HIMSELF WOULD AGREE.
I PLACE MYSELF AS A BAKUFU LOYALIST BELIEVING THIS.
BRILLIANT!
I TOLD YOU! YAMANAMI-SAN IS TRULY A GREAT MAN!
WHEW
I AGREE, ANI-UE!

*_Sonno_: Revere the Emperor. _Joi_: Anti-foreigner sentiment.

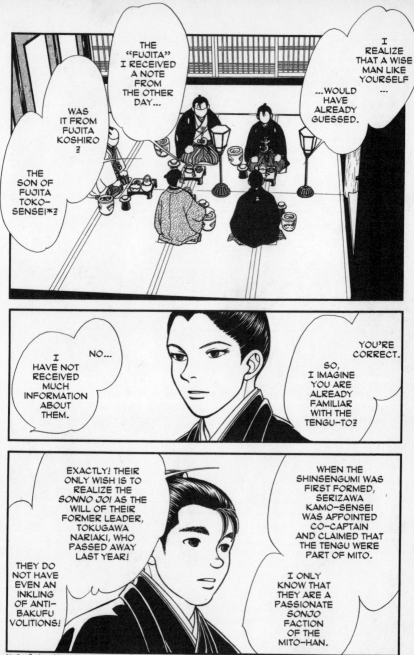

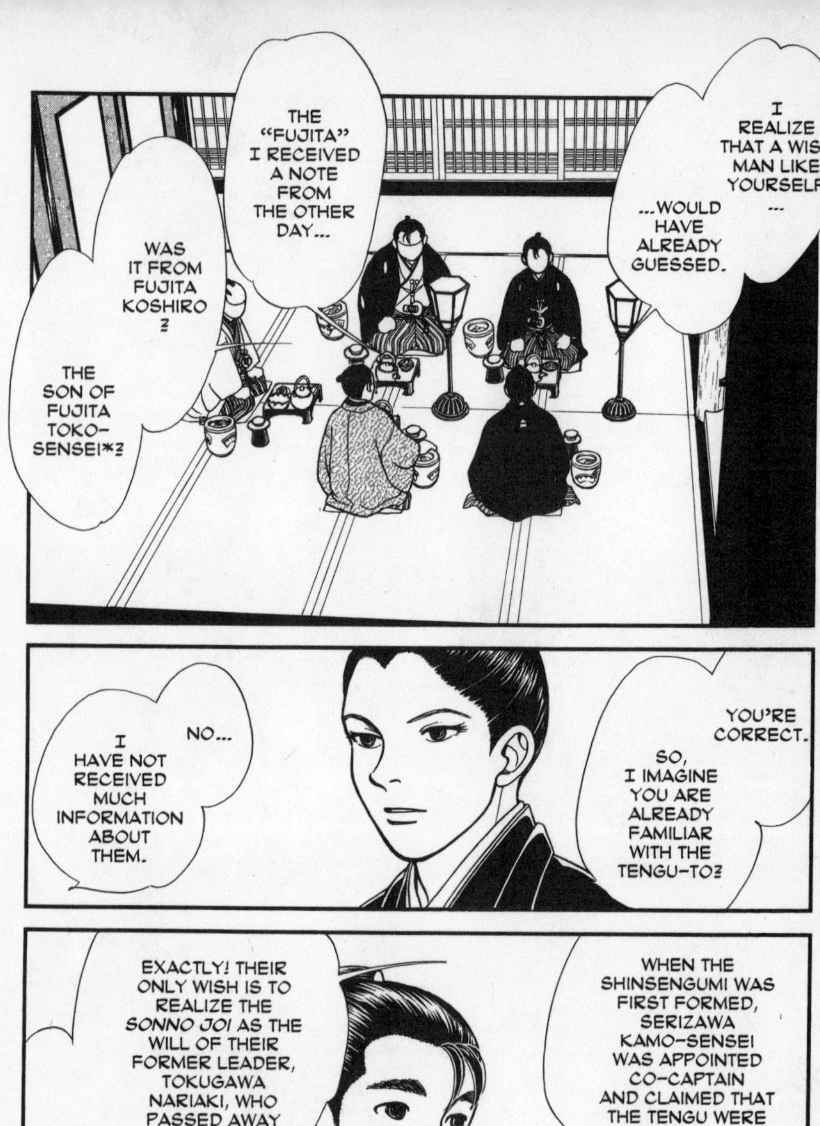
I REALIZE THAT A WISE MAN LIKE YOURSELF ---
...WOULD HAVE ALREADY GUESSED.
THE "FUJITA" I RECEIVED A NOTE FROM THE OTHER DAY...
WAS IT FROM FUJITA KOSHIRO?
THE SON OF FUJITA TOKO-SENSEI*?
YOU'RE CORRECT.
SO, I IMAGINE YOU ARE ALREADY FAMILIAR WITH THE TENGU-TO?
NO...
I HAVE NOT RECEIVED MUCH INFORMATION ABOUT THEM.
WHEN THE SHINSENGUMI WAS FIRST FORMED, SERIZAWA KAMO-SENSEI WAS APPOINTED CO-CAPTAIN AND CLAIMED THAT THE TENGU WERE PART OF MITO.
I ONLY KNOW THAT THEY ARE A PASSIONATE *SONJO* FACTION OF THE MITO-HAN.
EXACTLY! THEIR ONLY WISH IS TO REALIZE THE *SONNO JOI* AS THE WILL OF THEIR FORMER LEADER, TOKUGAWA NARIAKI, WHO PASSED AWAY LAST YEAR!
THEY DO NOT HAVE EVEN AN INKLING OF ANTI-BAKUFU VOLITIONS!

*A Confucian philosopher and soldier of the Mito-han who greatly influenced the *Sonno Joi* (Revere the emperor, expel the foreigners) philosophy.

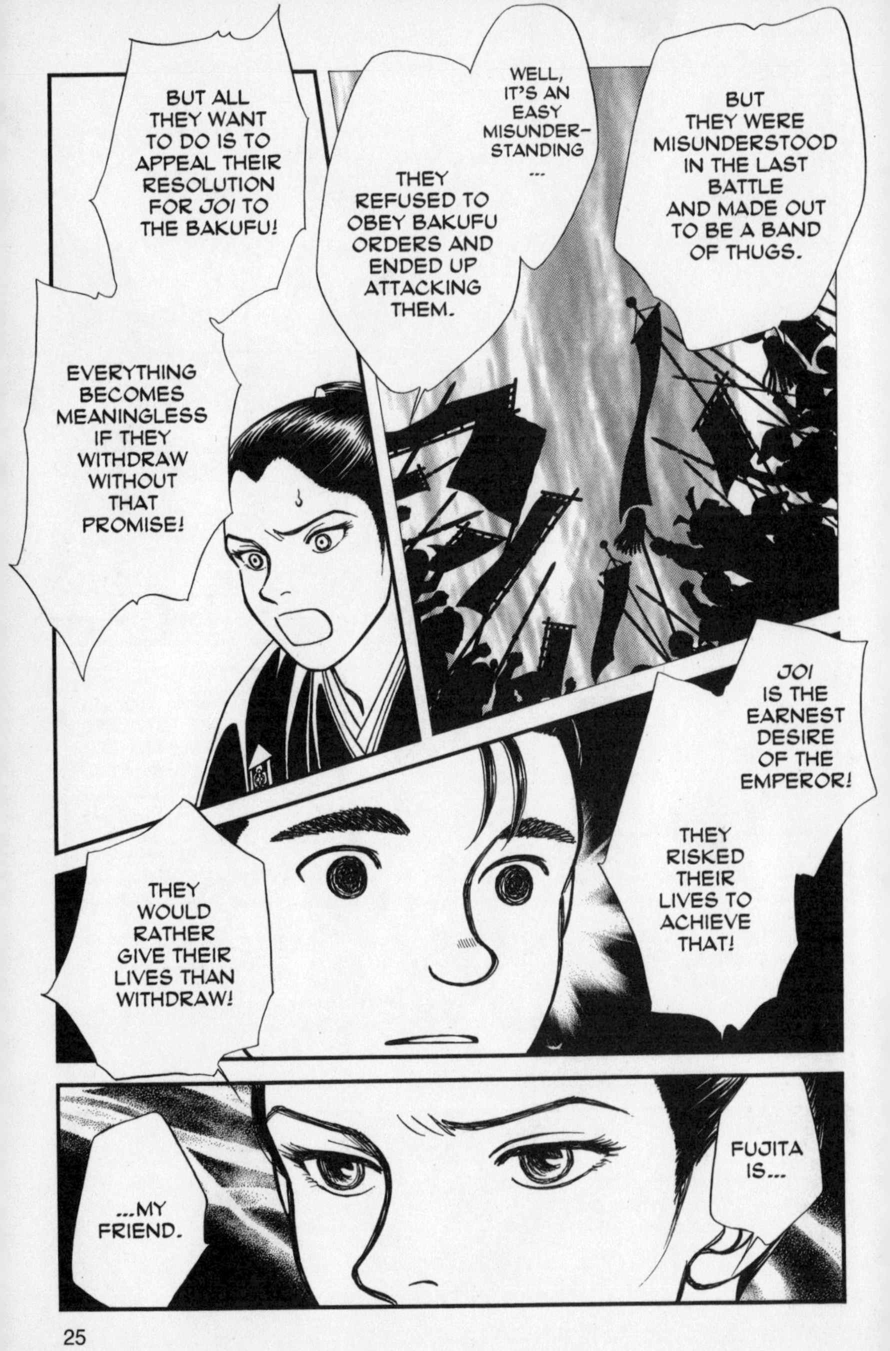
BUT THEY WERE MISUNDERSTOOD IN THE LAST BATTLE AND MADE OUT TO BE A BAND OF THUGS.
WELL, IT'S AN EASY MISUNDER-STANDING ...
THEY REFUSED TO OBEY BAKUFU ORDERS AND ENDED UP ATTACKING THEM.
BUT ALL THEY WANT TO DO IS TO APPEAL THEIR RESOLUTION FOR *JOI* TO THE BAKUFU!
EVERYTHING BECOMES MEANINGLESS IF THEY WITHDRAW WITHOUT THAT PROMISE!
JOI IS THE EARNEST DESIRE OF THE EMPEROR!
THEY RISKED THEIR LIVES TO ACHIEVE THAT!
THEY WOULD RATHER GIVE THEIR LIVES THAN WITHDRAW!
FUJITA IS...
...MY FRIEND.

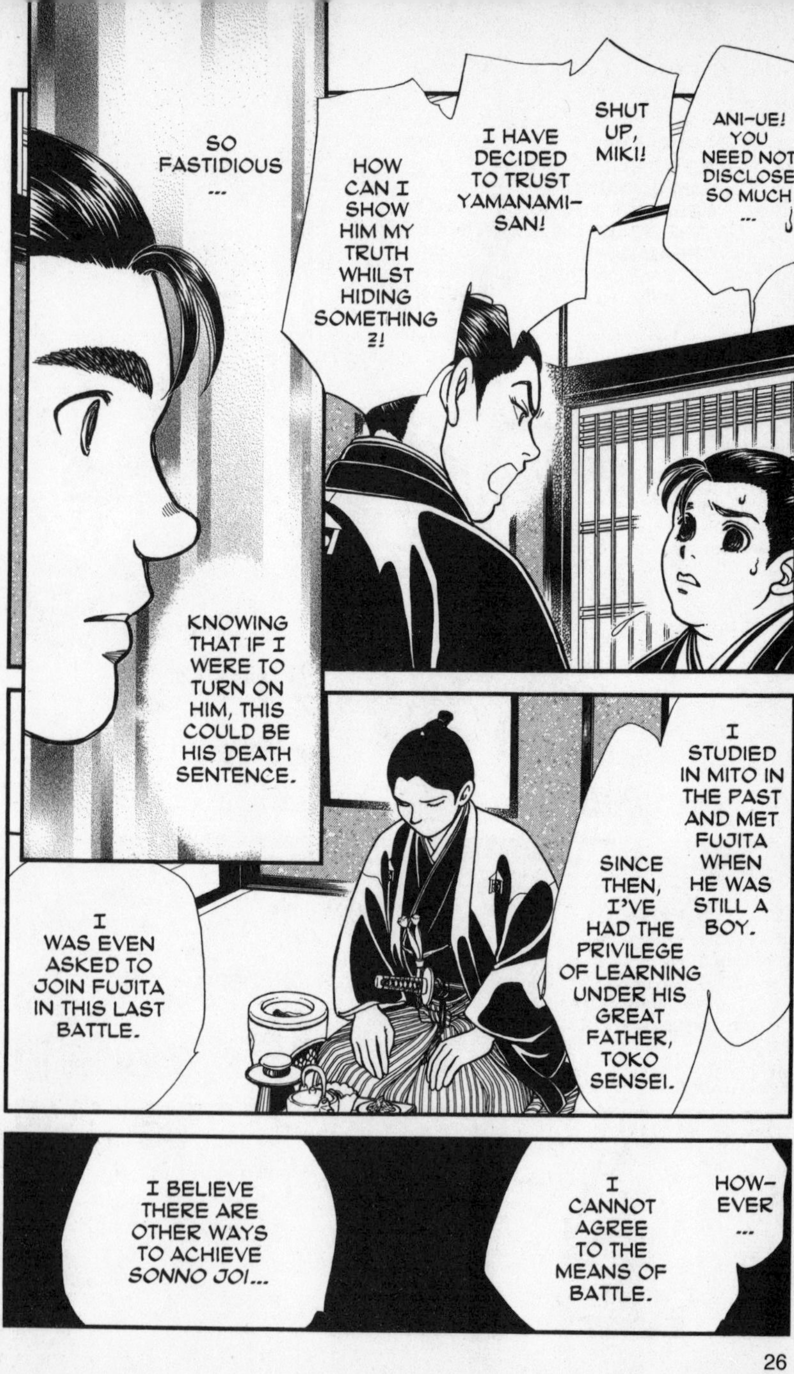
ANI-UE! YOU NEED NOT DISCLOSE SO MUCH ...
SHUT UP, MIKI!
I HAVE DECIDED TO TRUST YAMANAMI-SAN!
HOW CAN I SHOW HIM MY TRUTH WHILST HIDING SOMETHING ?!
SO FASTIDIOUS ...
KNOWING THAT IF I WERE TO TURN ON HIM, THIS COULD BE HIS DEATH SENTENCE.
I STUDIED IN MITO IN THE PAST AND MET FUJITA WHEN HE WAS STILL A BOY.
SINCE THEN, I'VE HAD THE PRIVILEGE OF LEARNING UNDER HIS GREAT FATHER, TOKO SENSEI.
I WAS EVEN ASKED TO JOIN FUJITA IN THIS LAST BATTLE.
HOW-EVER ...
I CANNOT AGREE TO THE MEANS OF BATTLE.
I BELIEVE THERE ARE OTHER WAYS TO ACHIEVE SONNO JOI...

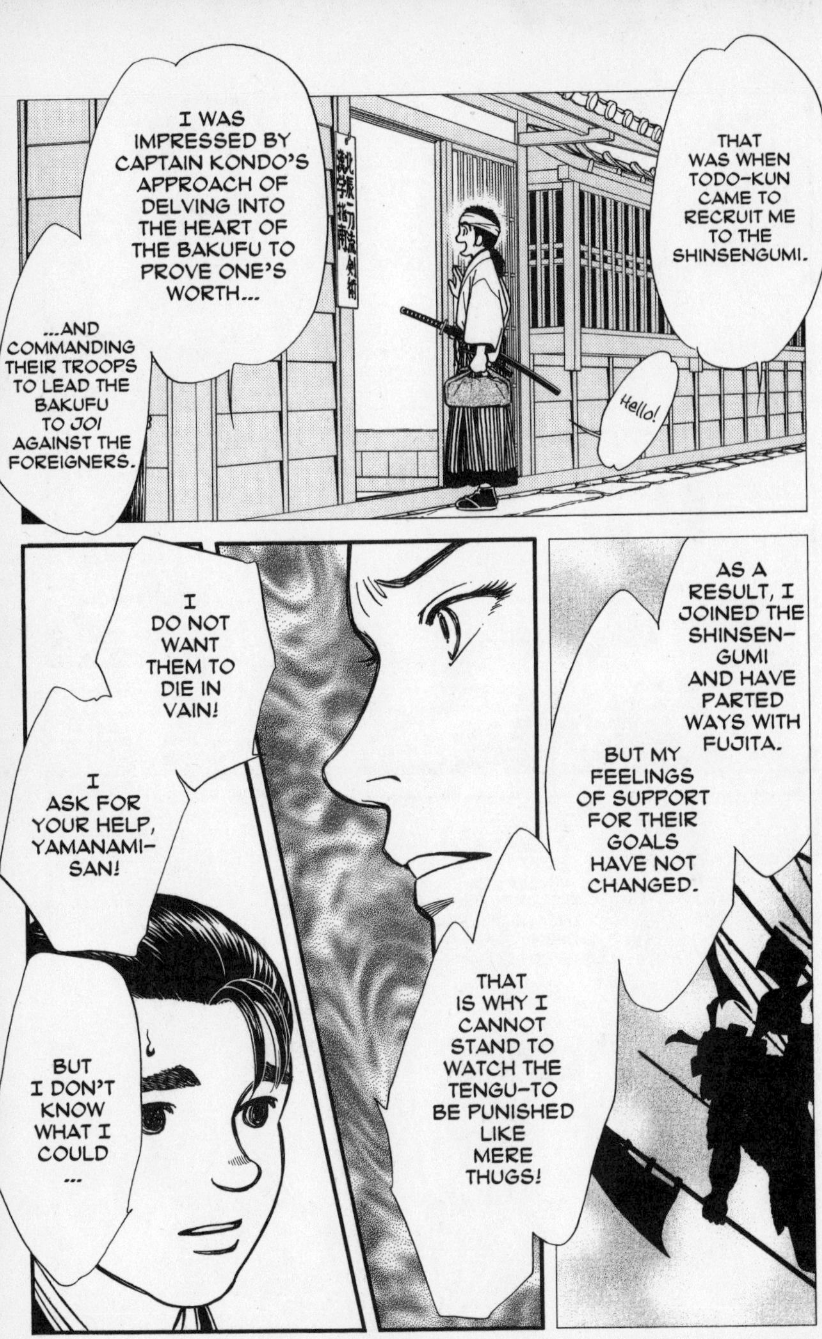

THAT WAS WHEN TODO-KUN CAME TO RECRUIT ME TO THE SHINSENGUMI.
Hello!
I WAS IMPRESSED BY CAPTAIN KONDO'S APPROACH OF DELVING INTO THE HEART OF THE BAKUFU TO PROVE ONE'S WORTH...
...AND COMMANDING THEIR TROOPS TO LEAD THE BAKUFU TO *JOI* AGAINST THE FOREIGNERS.
AS A RESULT, I JOINED THE SHINSEN-GUMI AND HAVE PARTED WAYS WITH FUJITA.
BUT MY FEELINGS OF SUPPORT FOR THEIR GOALS HAVE NOT CHANGED.
THAT IS WHY I CANNOT STAND TO WATCH THE TENGU-TO BE PUNISHED LIKE MERE THUGS!
I DO NOT WANT THEM TO DIE IN VAIN!
I ASK FOR YOUR HELP, YAMANAMI-SAN!
BUT I DON'T KNOW WHAT I COULD ...

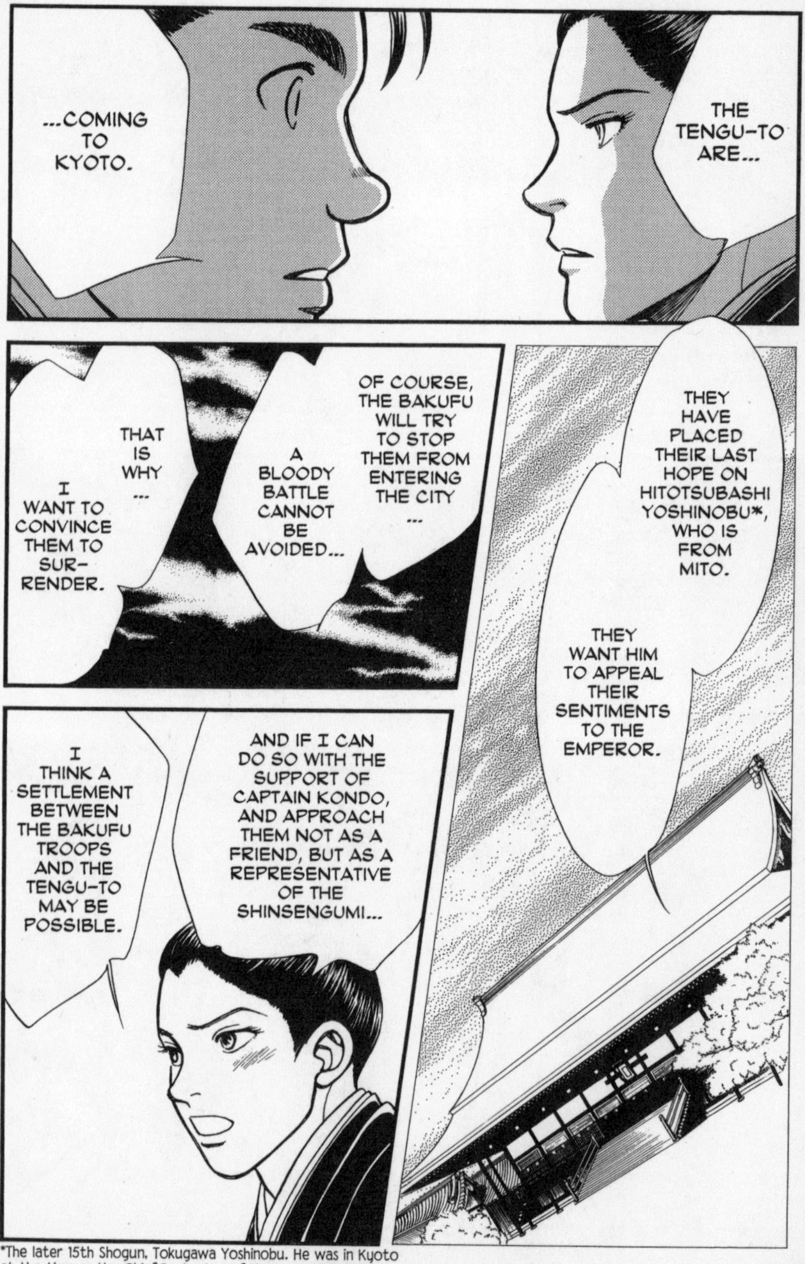

THE TENGU-TO ARE...
...COMING TO KYOTO.
THEY HAVE PLACED THEIR LAST HOPE ON HITOTSUBASHI YOSHINOBU*, WHO IS FROM MITO.
THEY WANT HIM TO APPEAL THEIR SENTIMENTS TO THE EMPEROR.
OF COURSE, THE BAKUFU WILL TRY TO STOP THEM FROM ENTERING THE CITY ...
A BLOODY BATTLE CANNOT BE AVOIDED...
THAT IS WHY ...
I WANT TO CONVINCE THEM TO SUR-RENDER.
AND IF I CAN DO SO WITH THE SUPPORT OF CAPTAIN KONDO, AND APPROACH THEM NOT AS A FRIEND, BUT AS A REPRESENTATIVE OF THE SHINSENGUMI...
I THINK A SETTLEMENT BETWEEN THE BAKUFU TROOPS AND THE TENGU-TO MAY BE POSSIBLE.

*The later 15th Shogun, Tokugawa Yoshinobu. He was in Kyoto at the time as the Chief Protector of the Imperial Palace.

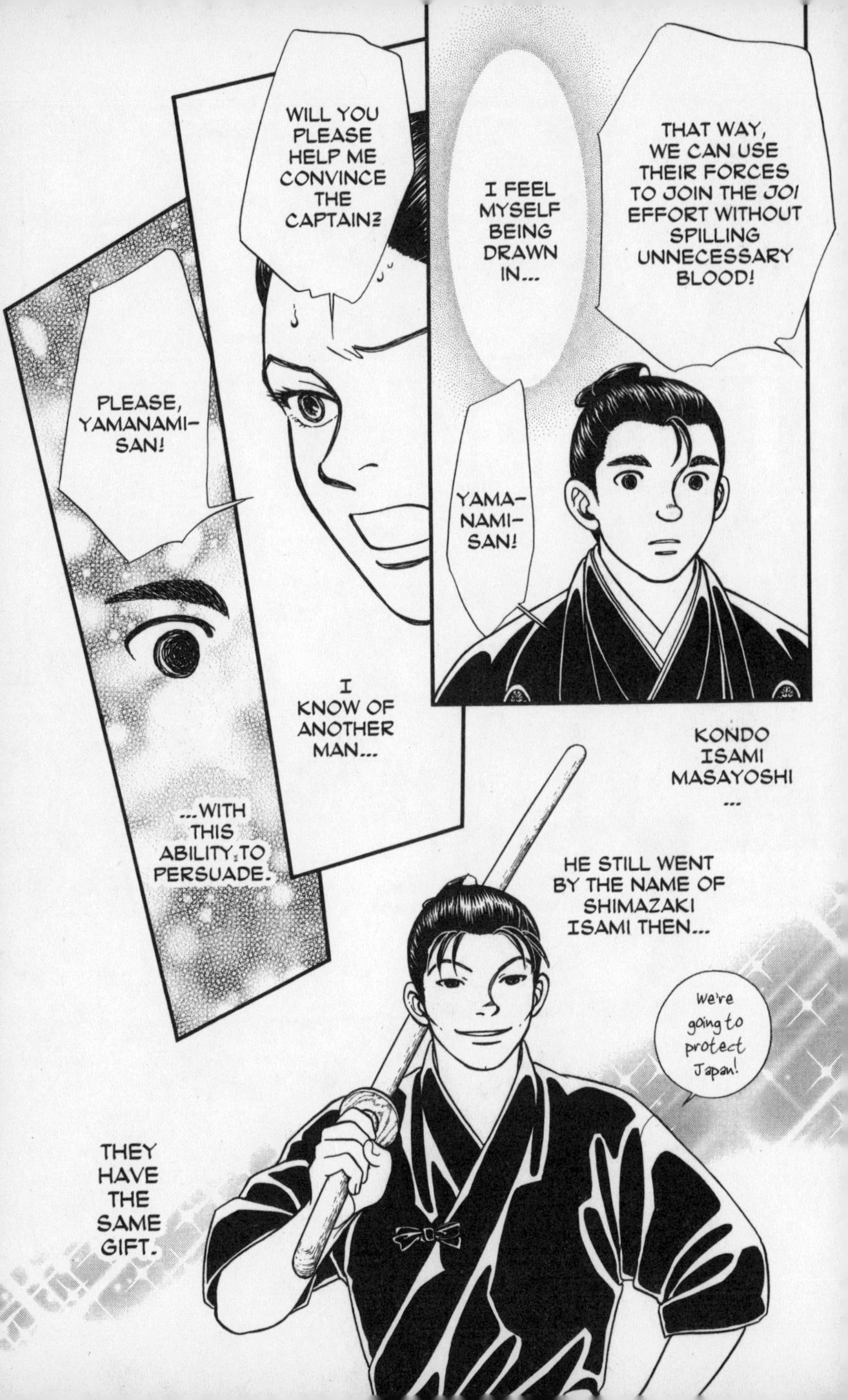
THAT WAY, WE CAN USE THEIR FORCES TO JOIN THE *JOI* EFFORT WITHOUT SPILLING UNNECESSARY BLOOD!
I FEEL MYSELF BEING DRAWN IN...
YAMANAMI-SAN!
WILL YOU PLEASE HELP ME CONVINCE THE CAPTAIN?
PLEASE, YAMANAMI-SAN!
I KNOW OF ANOTHER MAN...
...WITH THIS ABILITY TO PERSUADE.
KONDO ISAMI MASAYOSHI...
HE STILL WENT BY THE NAME OF SHIMAZAKI ISAMI THEN...
We're going to protect Japan!
THEY HAVE THE SAME GIFT.

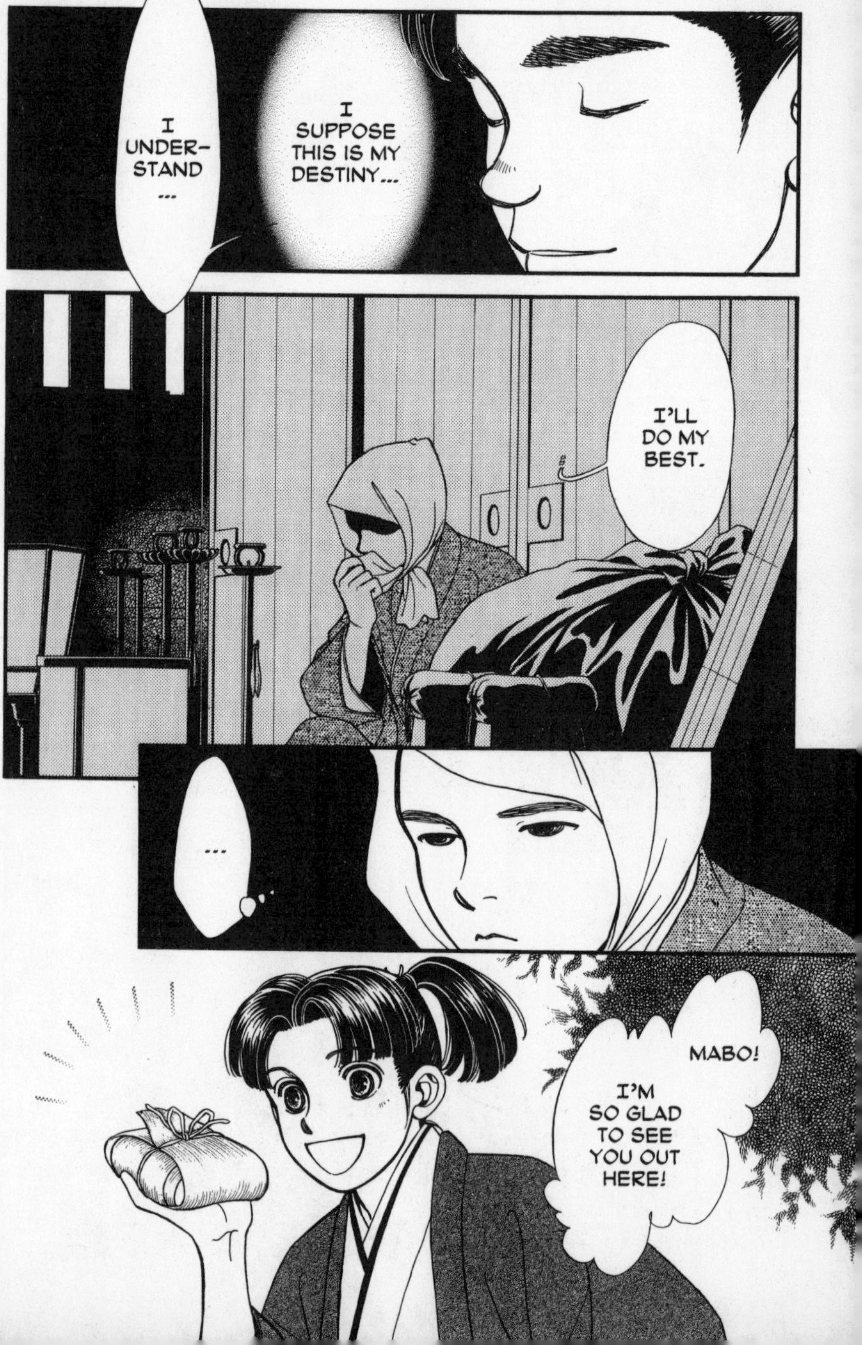
I SUPPOSE THIS IS MY DESTINY...
I UNDER-STAND ...
I'LL DO MY BEST.
...
MABO!
I'M SO GLAD TO SEE YOU OUT HERE!

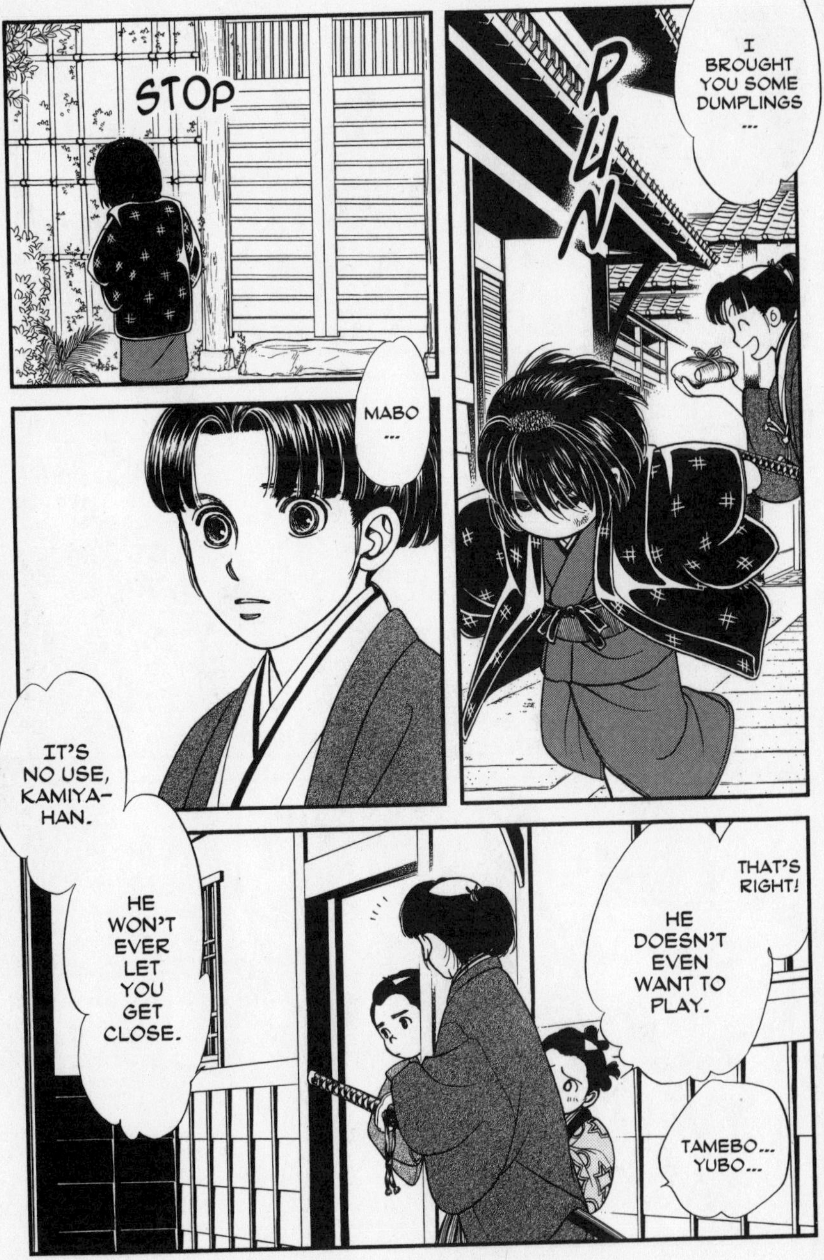
I BROUGHT YOU SOME DUMPLINGS ...
RUN
STOP
MABO ...
IT'S NO USE, KAMIYA-HAN.
HE WON'T EVER LET YOU GET CLOSE.
THAT'S RIGHT!
HE DOESN'T EVEN WANT TO PLAY.
TAMEBO... YUBO...

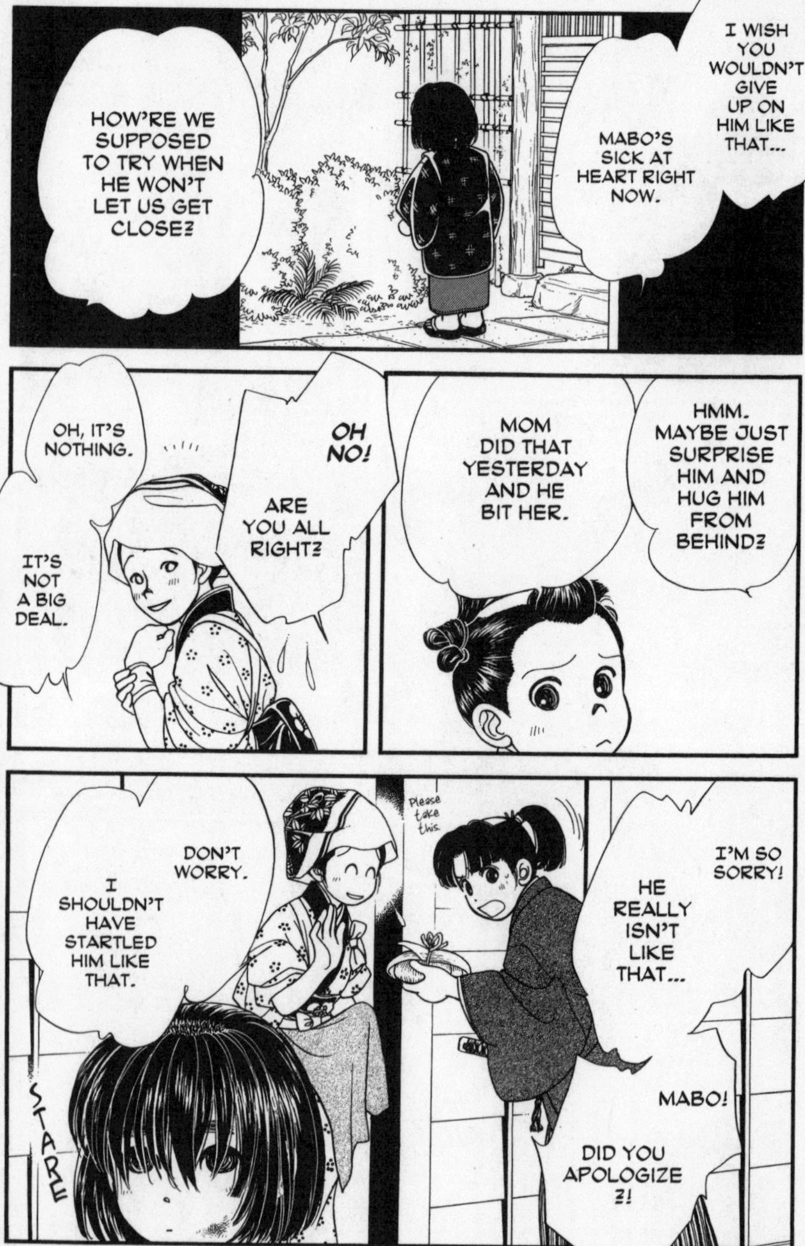
I WISH YOU WOULDN'T GIVE UP ON HIM LIKE THAT...
MABO'S SICK AT HEART RIGHT NOW.
HOW'RE WE SUPPOSED TO TRY WHEN HE WON'T LET US GET CLOSE?
HMM. MAYBE JUST SURPRISE HIM AND HUG HIM FROM BEHIND?
MOM DID THAT YESTERDAY AND HE BIT HER.
OH NO!
ARE YOU ALL RIGHT?
OH, IT'S NOTHING.
IT'S NOT A BIG DEAL.
I'M SO SORRY!
HE REALLY ISN'T LIKE THAT...
MABO!
DID YOU APOLOGIZE?!
Please take this.
DON'T WORRY.
I SHOULDN'T HAVE STARTLED HIM LIKE THAT.
STARE

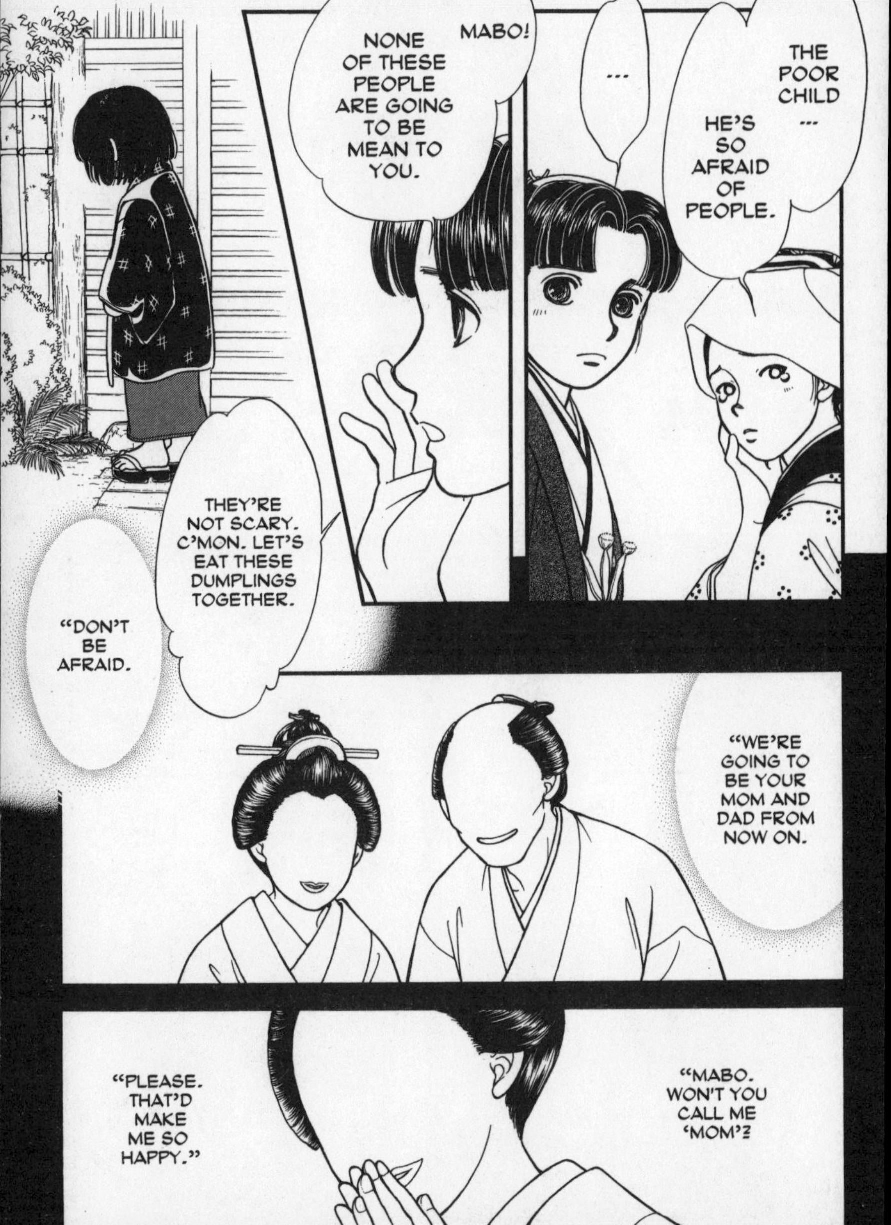
THE POOR CHILD ---
HE'S SO AFRAID OF PEOPLE.

MABO!
NONE OF THESE PEOPLE ARE GOING TO BE MEAN TO YOU.
THEY'RE NOT SCARY. C'MON. LET'S EAT THESE DUMPLINGS TOGETHER.
"DON'T BE AFRAID.
"WE'RE GOING TO BE YOUR MOM AND DAD FROM NOW ON.
"MABO. WON'T YOU CALL ME 'MOM'?
"PLEASE. THAT'D MAKE ME SO HAPPY."

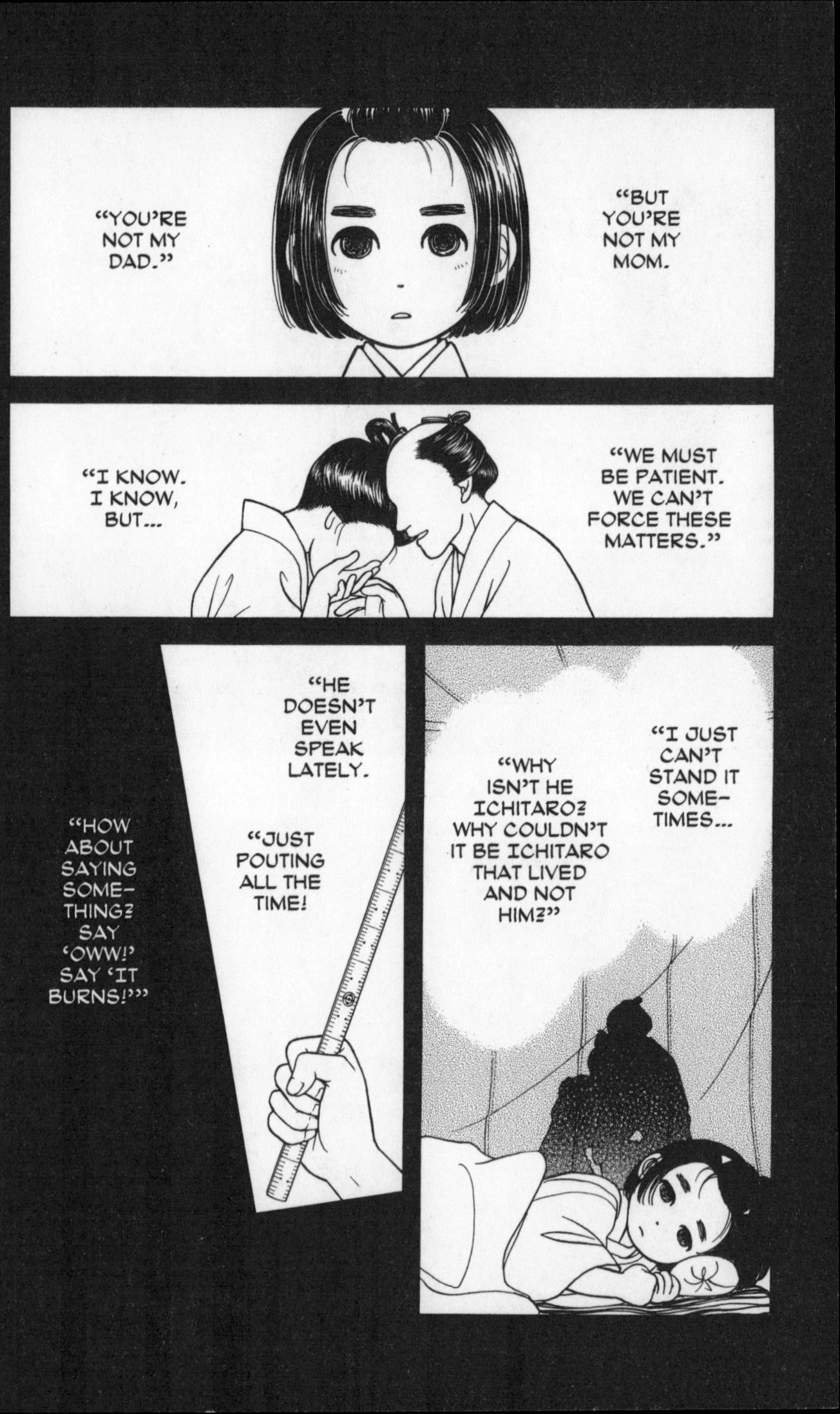
"BUT YOU'RE NOT MY MOM.
"YOU'RE NOT MY DAD."
"WE MUST BE PATIENT. WE CAN'T FORCE THESE MATTERS."
"I KNOW. I KNOW, BUT...
"I JUST CAN'T STAND IT SOME-TIMES...
"WHY ISN'T HE ICHITARO? WHY COULDN'T IT BE ICHITARO THAT LIVED AND NOT HIM?"
"HE DOESN'T EVEN SPEAK LATELY.
"JUST POUTING ALL THE TIME!
"HOW ABOUT SAYING SOME-THING? SAY 'OWW!' SAY 'IT BURNS!'"

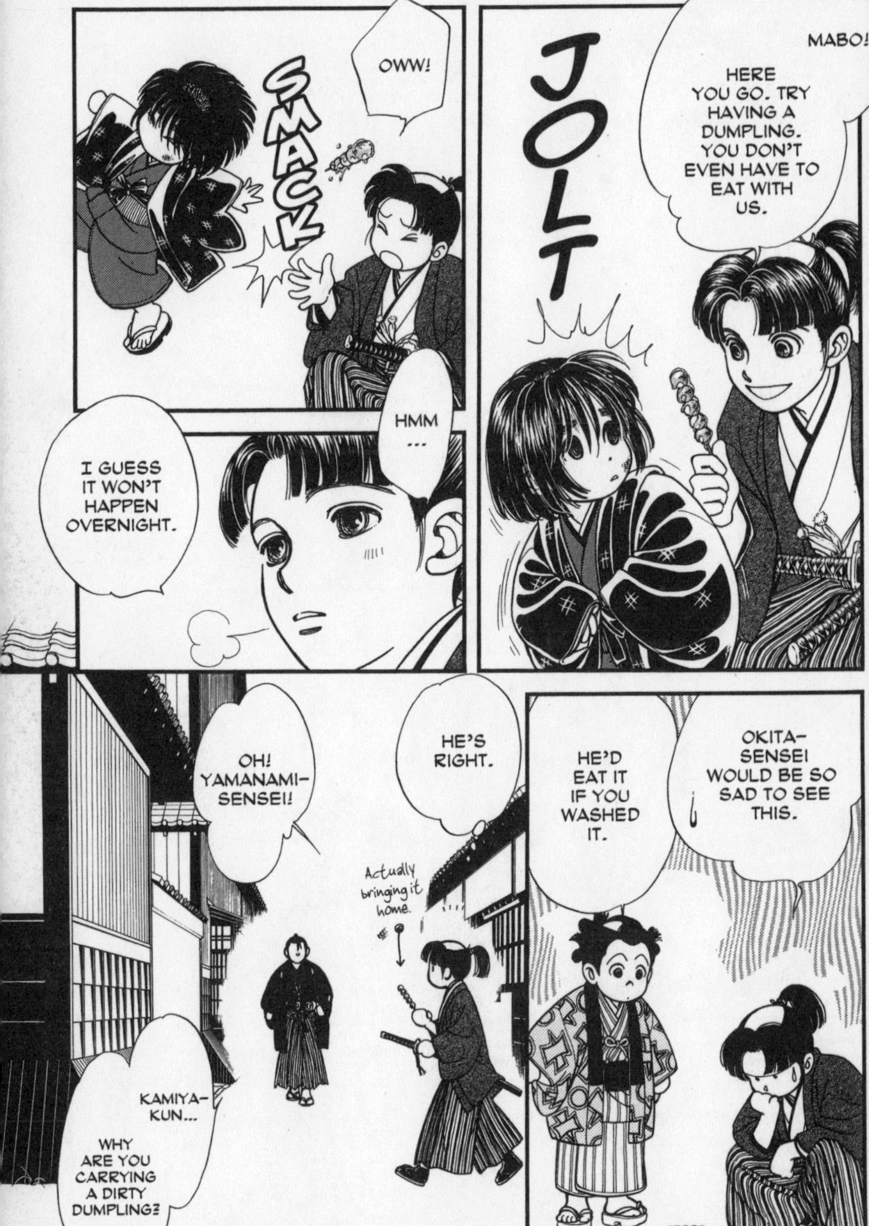
MABO!
HERE YOU GO. TRY HAVING A DUMPLING. YOU DON'T EVEN HAVE TO EAT WITH US.
JOLT
OWW!
SMACK
HMM ---
I GUESS IT WON'T HAPPEN OVERNIGHT.
OKITA-SENSEI WOULD BE SO SAD TO SEE THIS.
HE'D EAT IT IF YOU WASHED IT.
HE'S RIGHT.
Actually bringing it home.
OH! YAMANAMI-SENSEI!
KAMIYA-KUN...
WHY ARE YOU CARRYING A DIRTY DUMPLING?

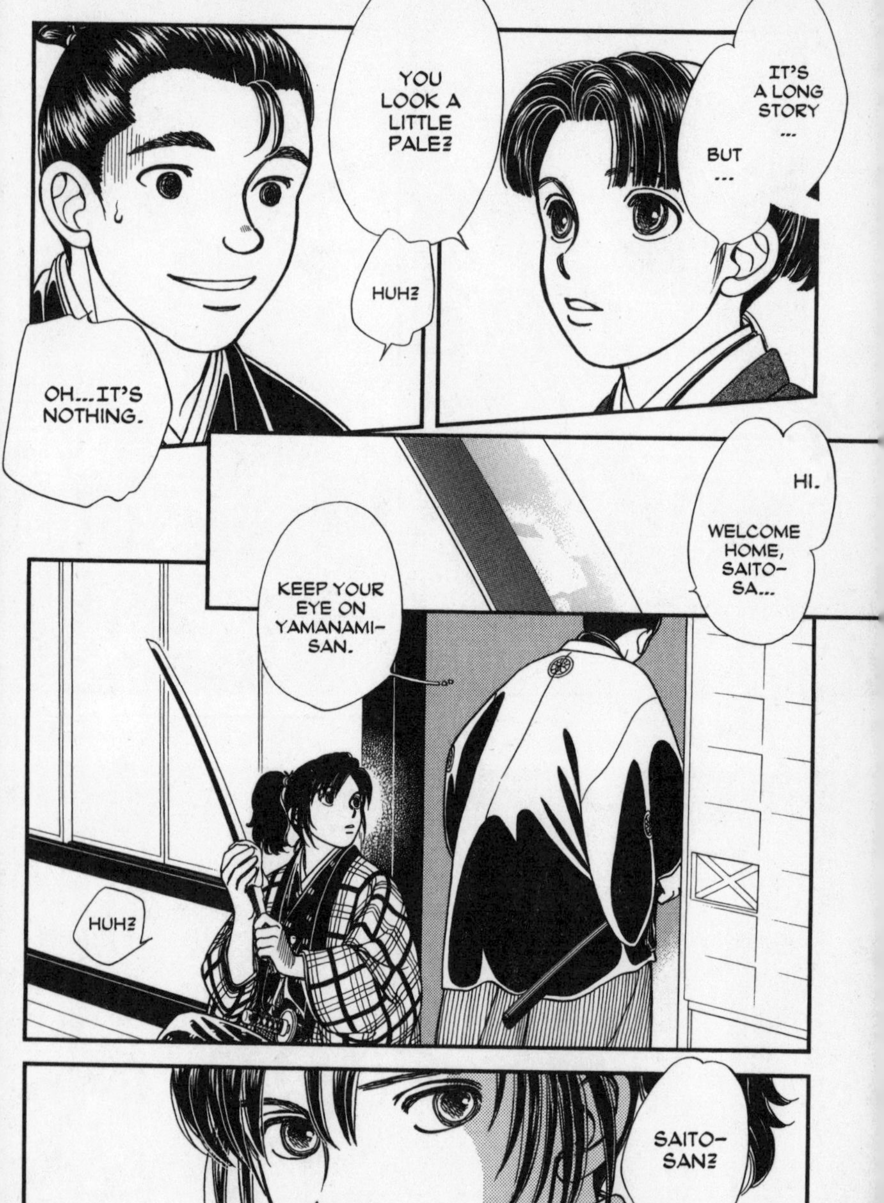
IT'S A LONG STORY ... BUT ...
YOU LOOK A LITTLE PALE?
HUH?
OH...IT'S NOTHING.
HI.
WELCOME HOME, SAITO-SA...
KEEP YOUR EYE ON YAMANAMI-SAN.
HUH?
SAITO-SAN?

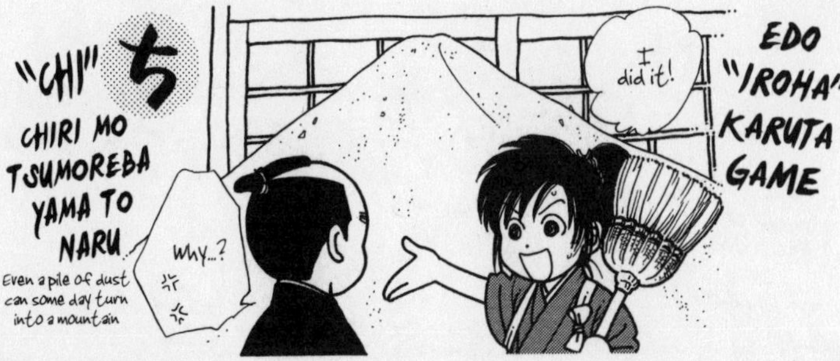
EDO
"IROHA"
KARUTA
GAME
"CHI" ち
CHIRI MO
TSUMOREBA
YAMA TO
NARU
Even a pile of dust
can some day turn
into a mountain
I did it!
Why...?

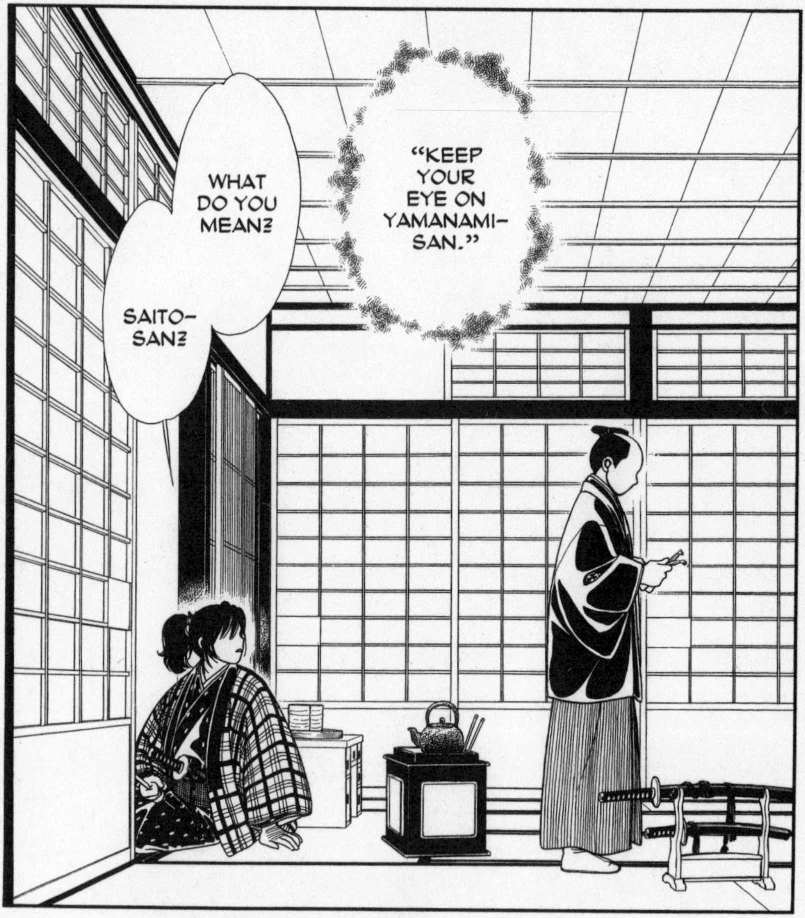
"KEEP YOUR EYE ON YAMANAMI-SAN."
WHAT DO YOU MEAN?
SAITO-SAN?

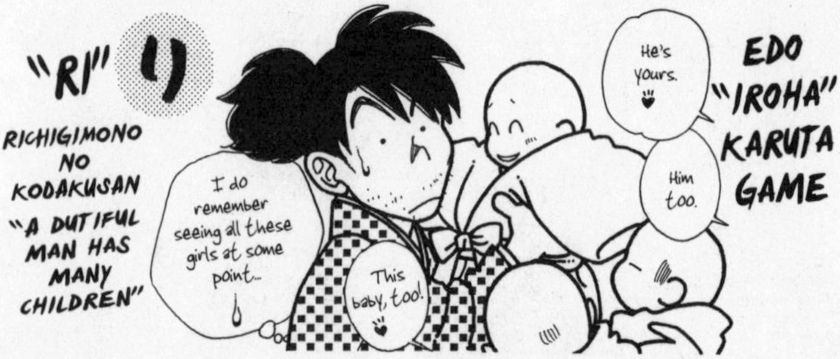
EDO "IROHA" KARUTA GAME
He's yours.
Him too.
This baby, too!
I do remember seeing all these girls at some point...
"RI" り
RICHIGIMONO NO KODAKUSAN
"A DUTIFUL MAN HAS MANY CHILDREN"

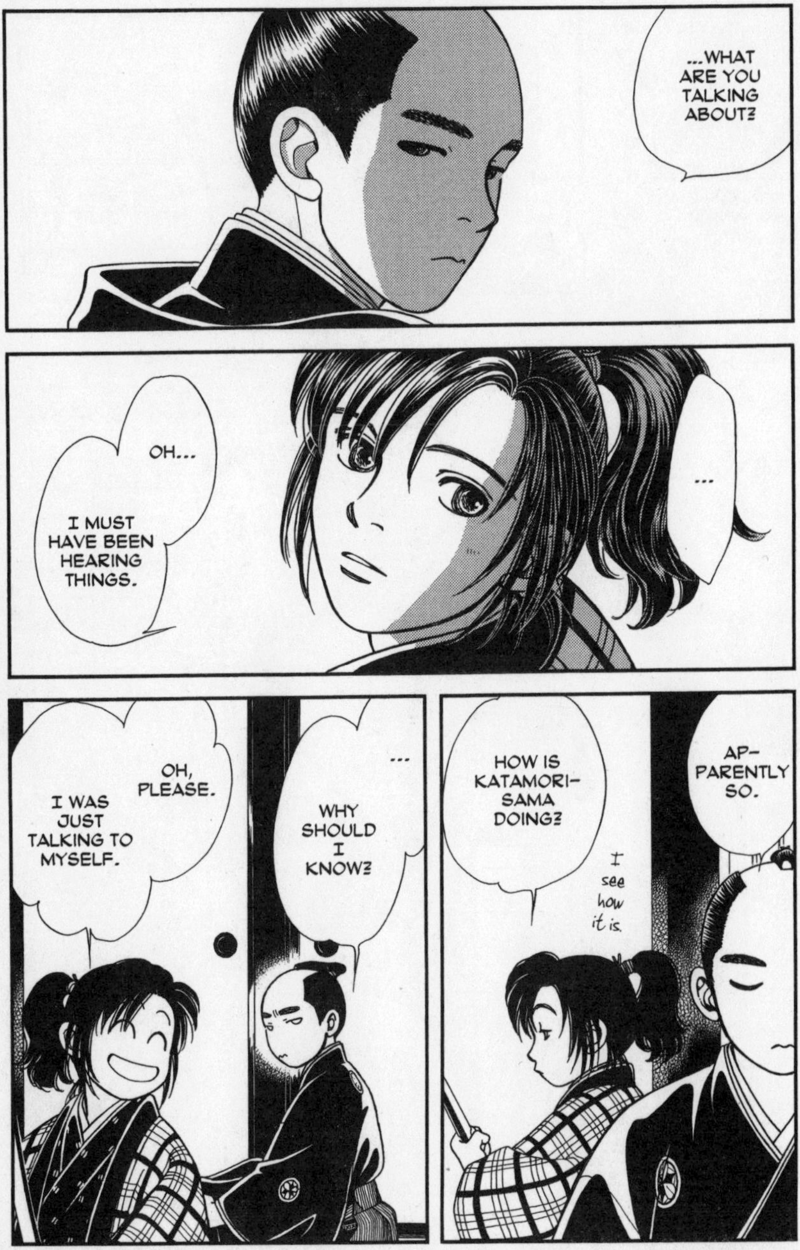
...WHAT ARE YOU TALKING ABOUT?
...
OH...
I MUST HAVE BEEN HEARING THINGS.
AP-PARENTLY SO.
HOW IS KATAMORI-SAMA DOING?
I see how it is.
...
WHY SHOULD I KNOW?
OH, PLEASE.
I WAS JUST TALKING TO MYSELF.

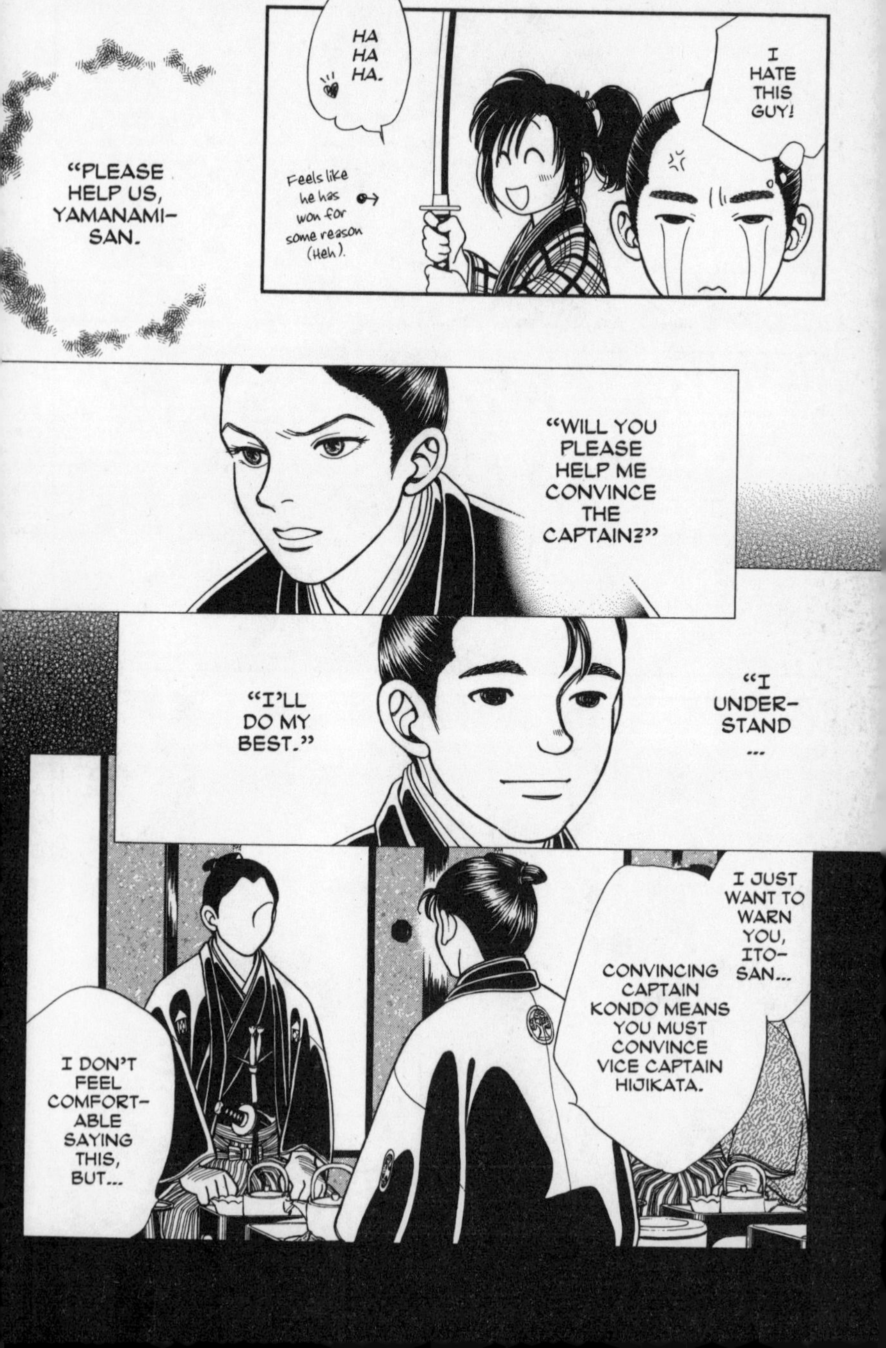
I HATE THIS GUY!
HA HA HA.
Feels like he has won for some reason (Heh).
"PLEASE HELP US, YAMANAMI-SAN.
"WILL YOU PLEASE HELP ME CONVINCE THE CAPTAIN?"
"I UNDER-STAND ...
"I'LL DO MY BEST."
I JUST WANT TO WARN YOU, ITO-SAN...
CONVINCING CAPTAIN KONDO MEANS YOU MUST CONVINCE VICE CAPTAIN HIJIKATA.
I DON'T FEEL COMFORT-ABLE SAYING THIS, BUT...

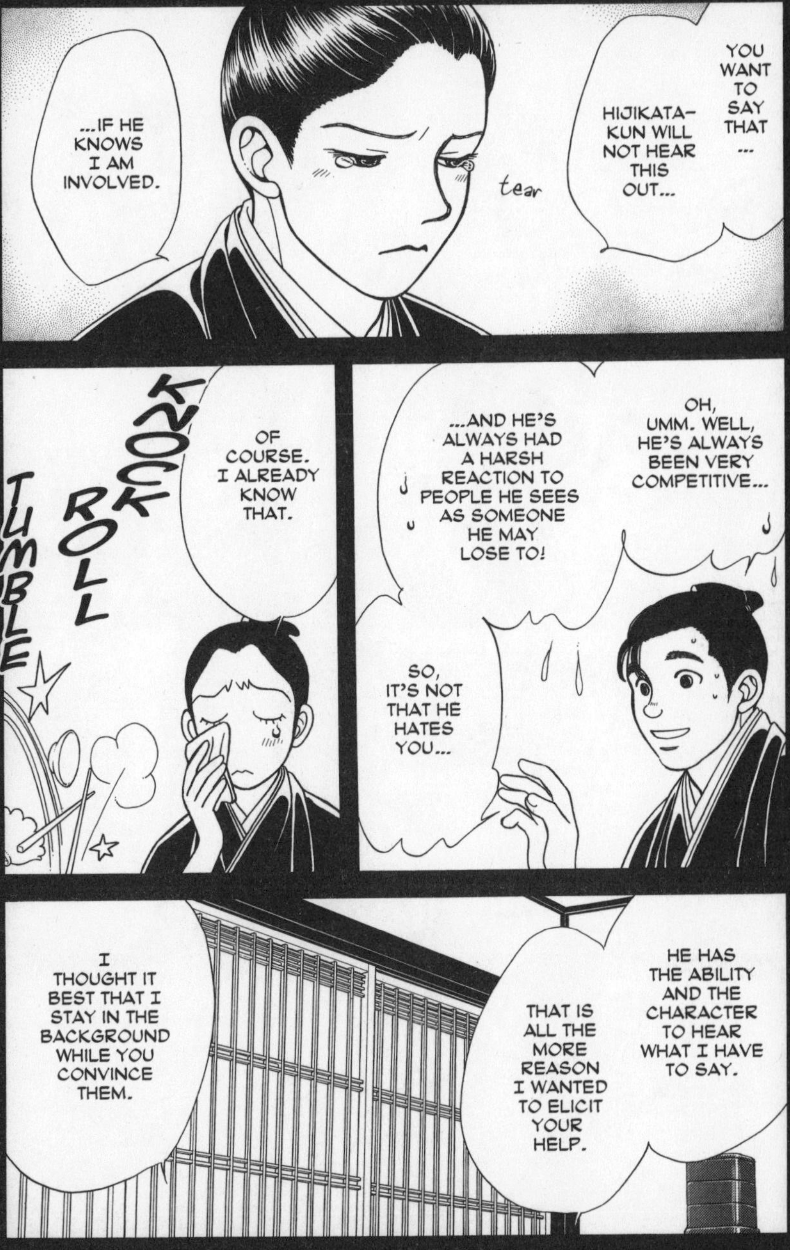
YOU WANT TO SAY THAT ---
HIJIKATA-KUN WILL NOT HEAR THIS OUT...
tear
...IF HE KNOWS I AM INVOLVED.
OH, UMM. WELL, HE'S ALWAYS BEEN VERY COMPETITIVE...
...AND HE'S ALWAYS HAD A HARSH REACTION TO PEOPLE HE SEES AS SOMEONE HE MAY LOSE TO!
SO, IT'S NOT THAT HE HATES YOU...
OF COURSE. I ALREADY KNOW THAT.
KNOCK
ROLL
TUMBLE
HE HAS THE ABILITY AND THE CHARACTER TO HEAR WHAT I HAVE TO SAY.
THAT IS ALL THE MORE REASON I WANTED TO ELICIT YOUR HELP.
I THOUGHT IT BEST THAT I STAY IN THE BACKGROUND WHILE YOU CONVINCE THEM.

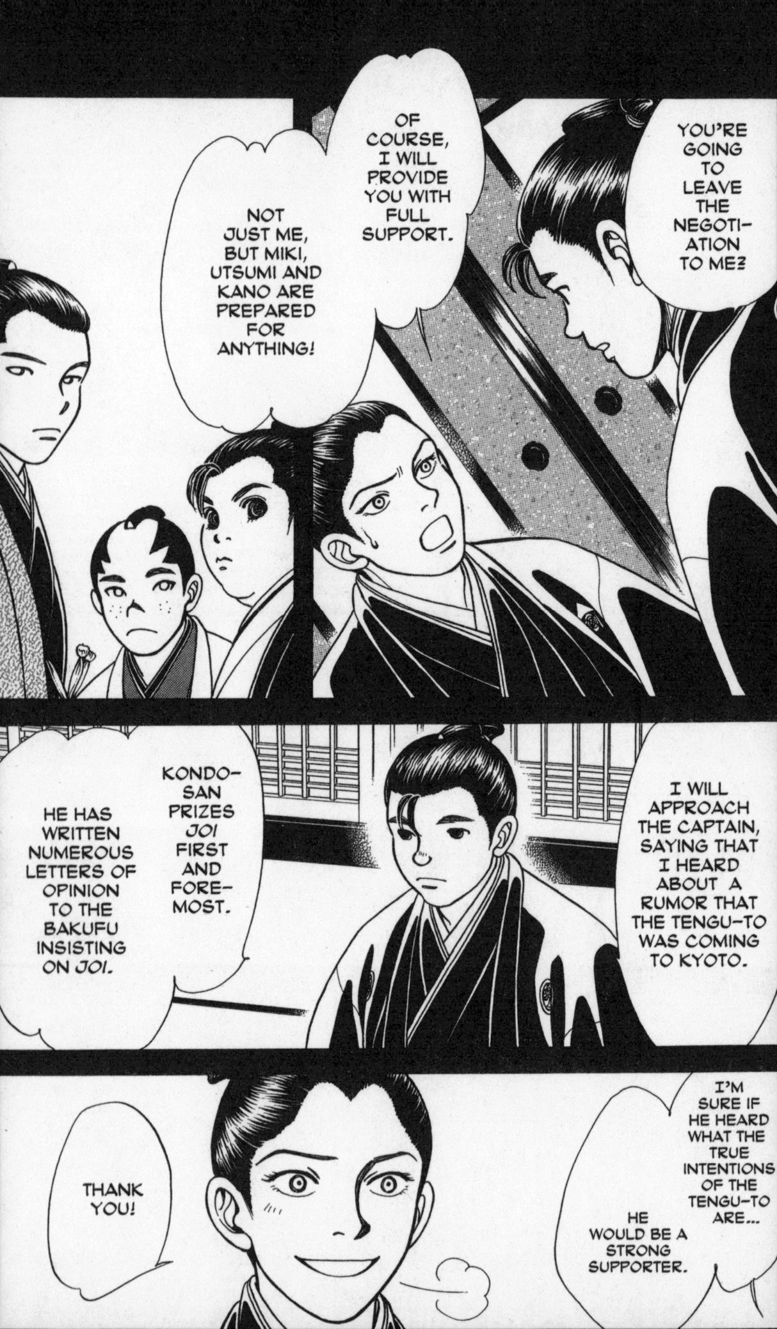
YOU'RE GOING TO LEAVE THE NEGOTI-ATION TO ME?
OF COURSE, I WILL PROVIDE YOU WITH FULL SUPPORT.
NOT JUST ME, BUT MIKI, UTSUMI AND KANO ARE PREPARED FOR ANYTHING!
I WILL APPROACH THE CAPTAIN, SAYING THAT I HEARD ABOUT A RUMOR THAT THE TENGU-TO WAS COMING TO KYOTO.
KONDO-SAN PRIZES *JOI* FIRST AND FORE-MOST.
HE HAS WRITTEN NUMEROUS LETTERS OF OPINION TO THE BAKUFU INSISTING ON *JOI*.
I'M SURE IF HE HEARD WHAT THE TRUE INTENTIONS OF THE TENGU-TO ARE...
HE WOULD BE A STRONG SUPPORTER.
THANK YOU!

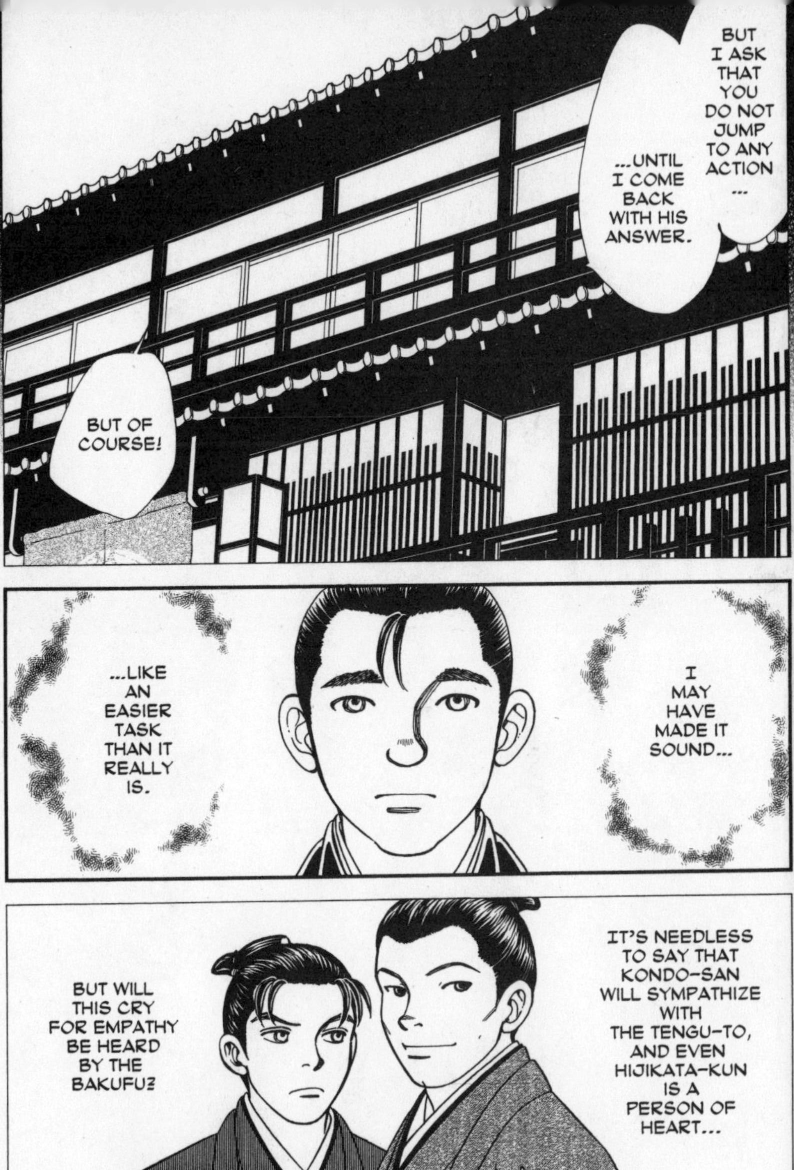
BUT I ASK THAT YOU DO NOT JUMP TO ANY ACTION...
...UNTIL I COME BACK WITH HIS ANSWER.
BUT OF COURSE!
I MAY HAVE MADE IT SOUND...
...LIKE AN EASIER TASK THAN IT REALLY IS.
IT'S NEEDLESS TO SAY THAT KONDO-SAN WILL SYMPATHIZE WITH THE TENGU-TO, AND EVEN HIJIKATA-KUN IS A PERSON OF HEART...
BUT WILL THIS CRY FOR EMPATHY BE HEARD BY THE BAKUFU?

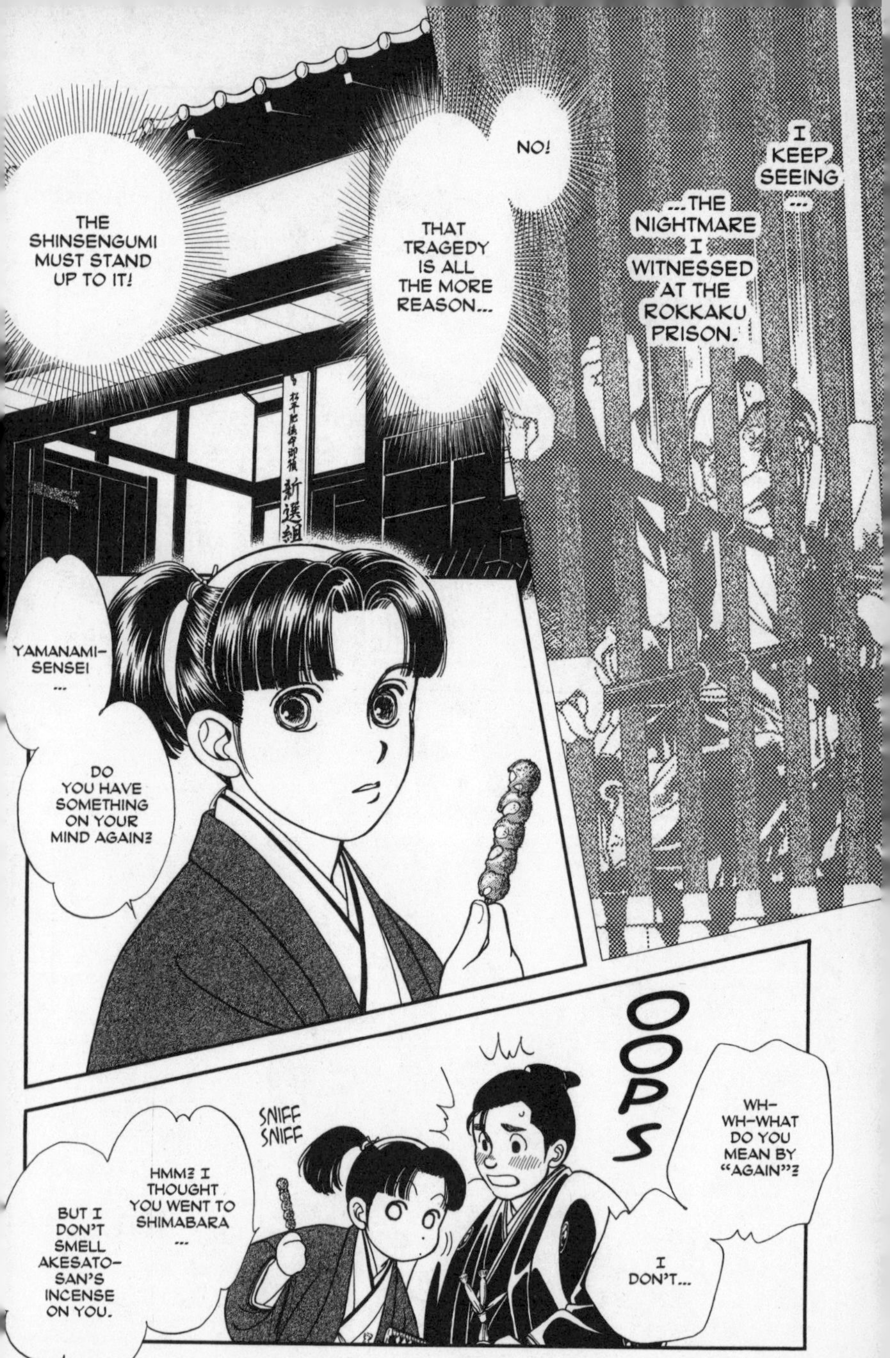

I KEEP SEEING...
...THE NIGHTMARE I WITNESSED AT THE ROKKAKU PRISON.
NO!
THAT TRAGEDY IS ALL THE MORE REASON...
THE SHINSENGUMI MUST STAND UP TO IT!
新選組
YAMANAMI-SENSEI...
DO YOU HAVE SOMETHING ON YOUR MIND AGAIN?
OOPS
WH-WH-WHAT DO YOU MEAN BY "AGAIN"?
I DON'T...
SNIFF SNIFF
HMM? I THOUGHT YOU WENT TO SHIMABARA...
BUT I DON'T SMELL AKESATO-SAN'S INCENSE ON YOU.

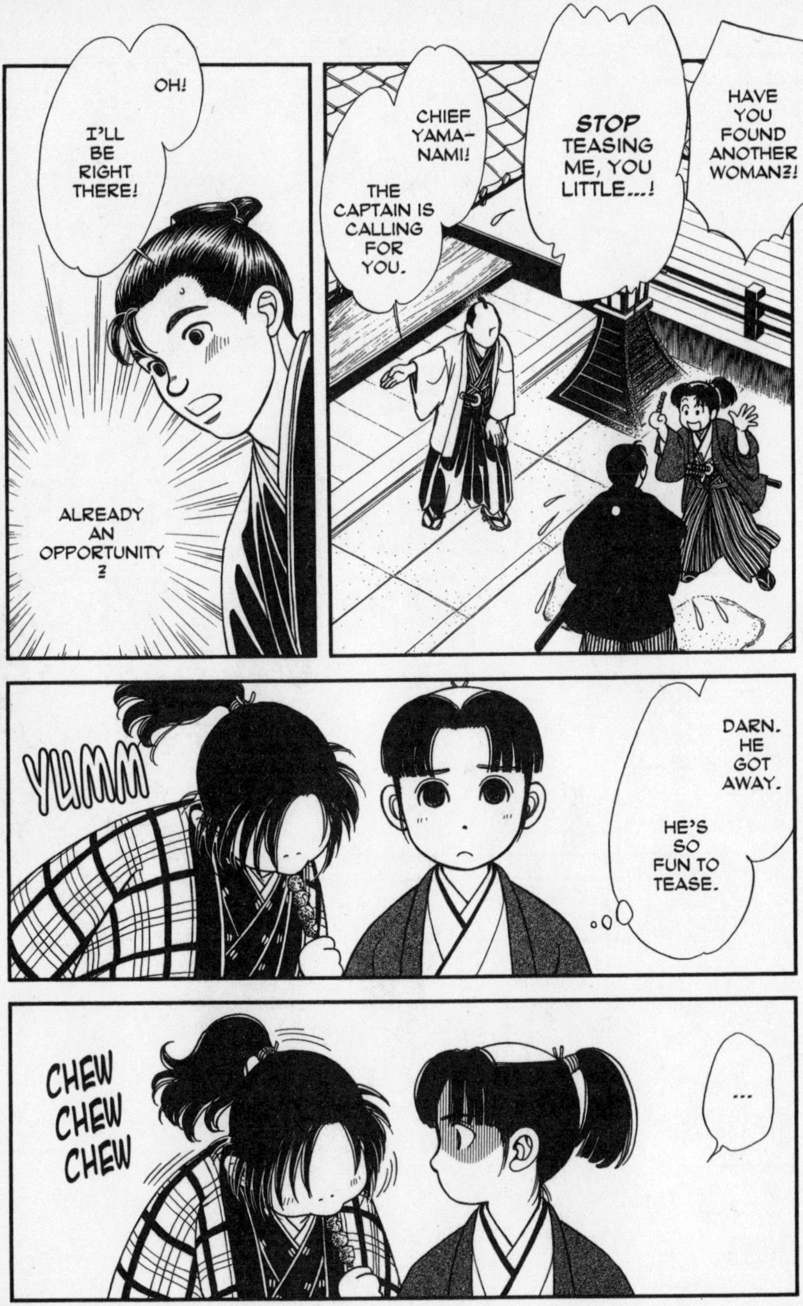
HAVE YOU FOUND ANOTHER WOMAN?!
STOP TEASING ME, YOU LITTLE...!
CHIEF YAMA-NAMI!
THE CAPTAIN IS CALLING FOR YOU.
OH!
I'LL BE RIGHT THERE!
ALREADY AN OPPORTUNITY?
DARN. HE GOT AWAY.
HE'S SO FUN TO TEASE.
YUMM
...
CHEW CHEW CHEW

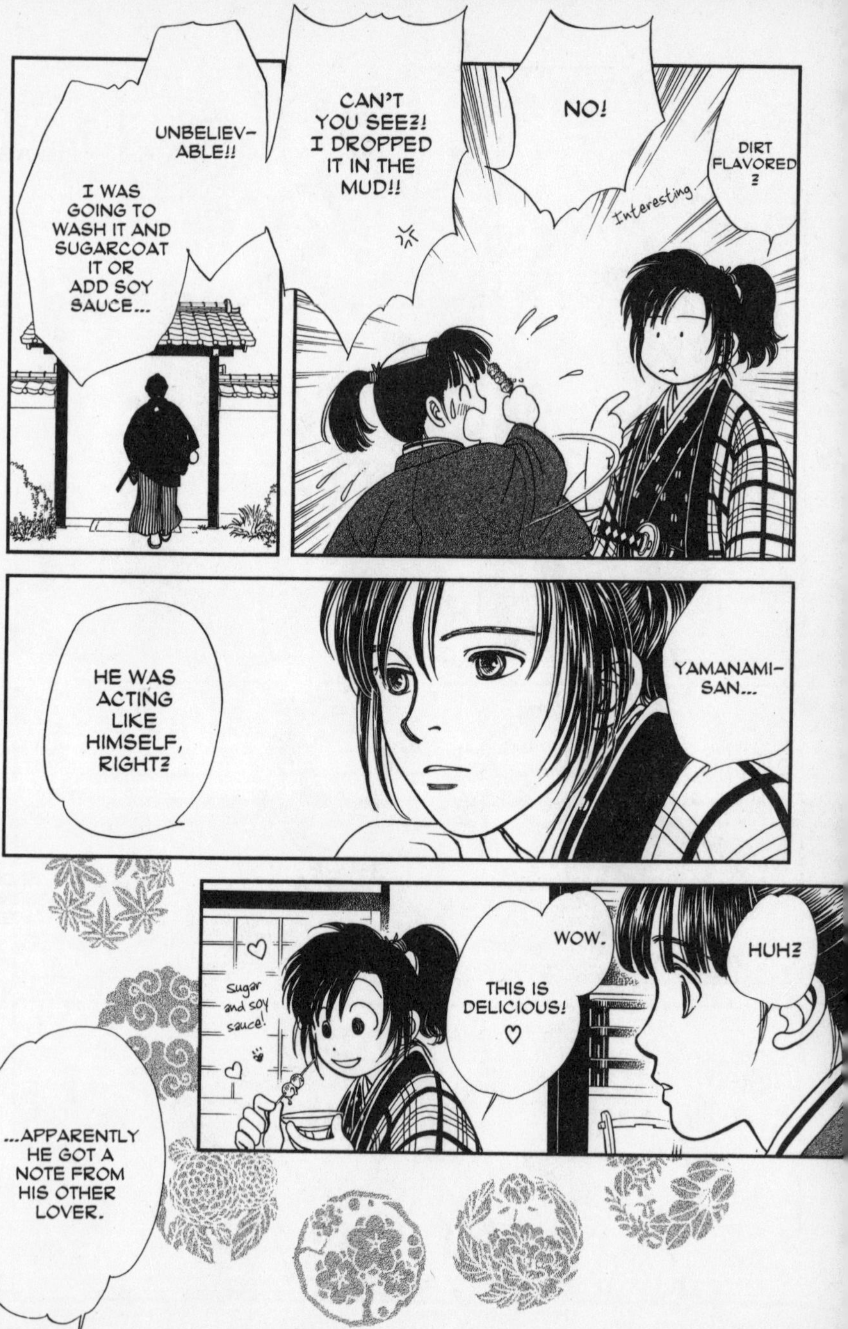
DIRT FLAVORED?
Interesting.
NO!
CAN'T YOU SEE?! I DROPPED IT IN THE MUD!!
UNBELIEV-ABLE!!
I WAS GOING TO WASH IT AND SUGARCOAT IT OR ADD SOY SAUCE...
YAMANAMI-SAN...
HE WAS ACTING LIKE HIMSELF, RIGHT?
HUH?
WOW.
THIS IS DELICIOUS! ♡
sugar and soy sauce!
...APPARENTLY HE GOT A NOTE FROM HIS OTHER LOVER.

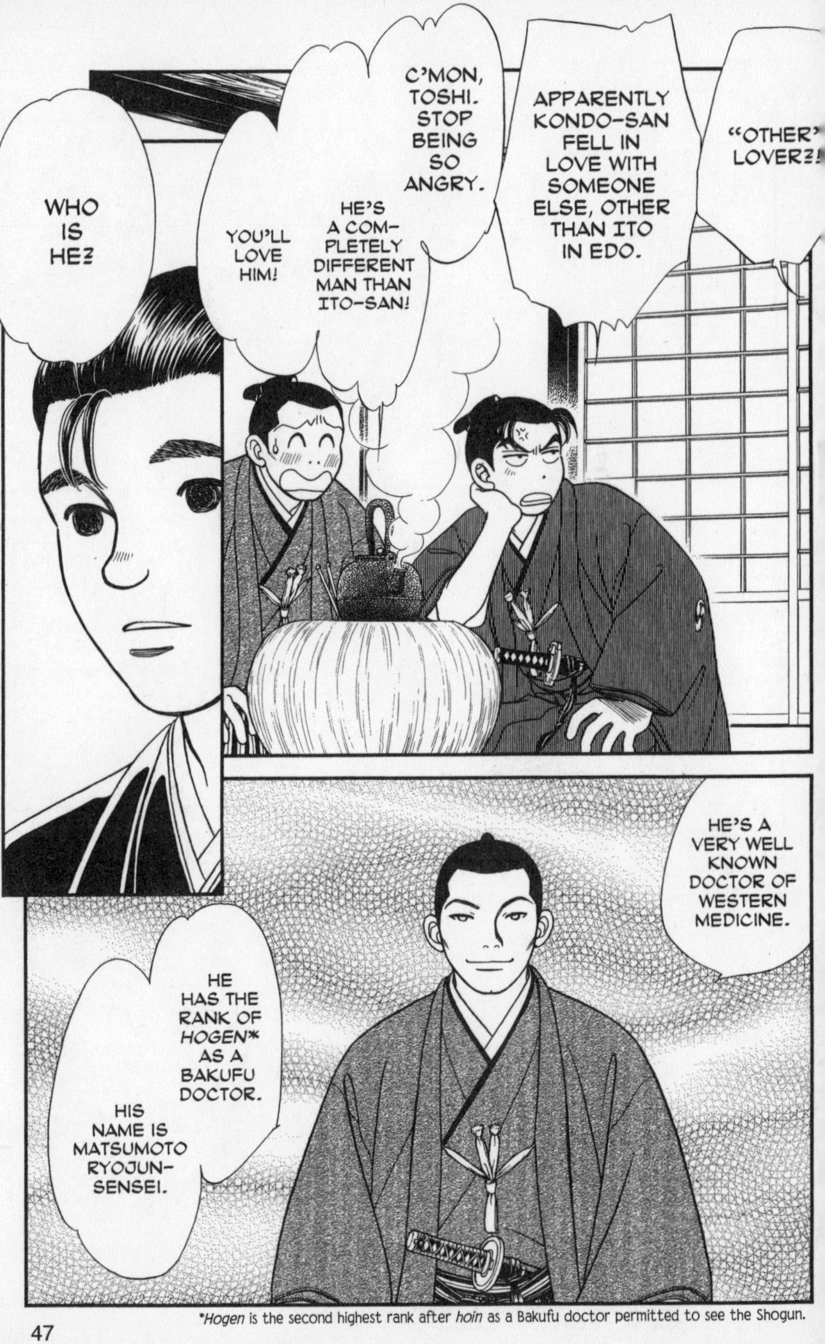
"OTHER" LOVER?!
APPARENTLY KONDO-SAN FELL IN LOVE WITH SOMEONE ELSE, OTHER THAN ITO IN EDO.
C'MON, TOSHI. STOP BEING SO ANGRY.
HE'S A COM-PLETELY DIFFERENT MAN THAN ITO-SAN!
YOU'LL LOVE HIM!
WHO IS HE?
HE'S A VERY WELL KNOWN DOCTOR OF WESTERN MEDICINE.
HE HAS THE RANK OF *HOGEN** AS A BAKUFU DOCTOR.
HIS NAME IS MATSUMOTO RYOJUN-SENSEI.

**Hogen* is the second highest rank after *hoin* as a Bakufu doctor permitted to see the Shogun.

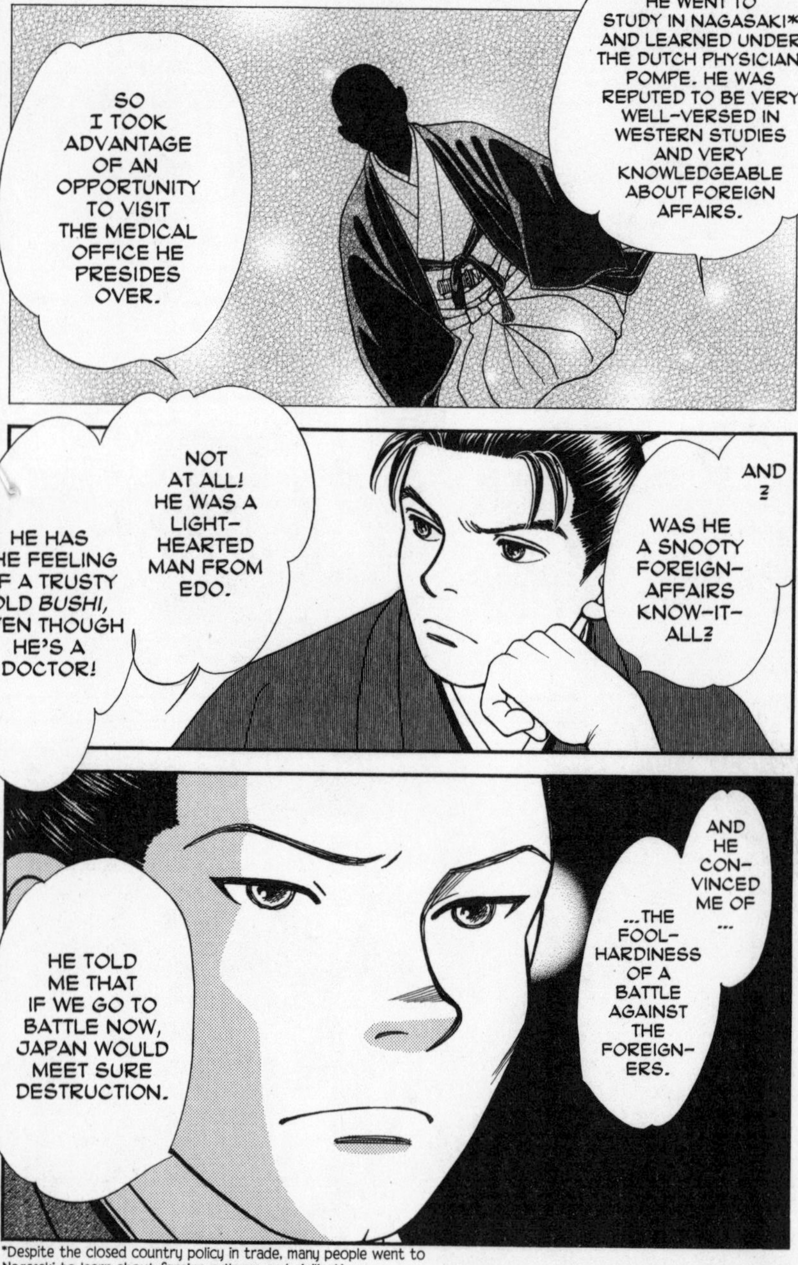
HE WENT TO STUDY IN NAGASAKI* AND LEARNED UNDER THE DUTCH PHYSICIAN, POMPE. HE WAS REPUTED TO BE VERY WELL-VERSED IN WESTERN STUDIES AND VERY KNOWLEDGEABLE ABOUT FOREIGN AFFAIRS.
SO I TOOK ADVANTAGE OF AN OPPORTUNITY TO VISIT THE MEDICAL OFFICE HE PRESIDES OVER.
AND?
WAS HE A SNOOTY FOREIGN-AFFAIRS KNOW-IT-ALL?
NOT AT ALL! HE WAS A LIGHT-HEARTED MAN FROM EDO.
HE HAS THE FEELING OF A TRUSTY OLD *BUSHI*, EVEN THOUGH HE'S A DOCTOR!
AND HE CONVINCED ME OF ...
...THE FOOLHARDINESS OF A BATTLE AGAINST THE FOREIGNERS.
HE TOLD ME THAT IF WE GO TO BATTLE NOW, JAPAN WOULD MEET SURE DESTRUCTION.

*Despite the closed country policy in trade, many people went to Nagasaki to learn about foreign cultures and civilizations.

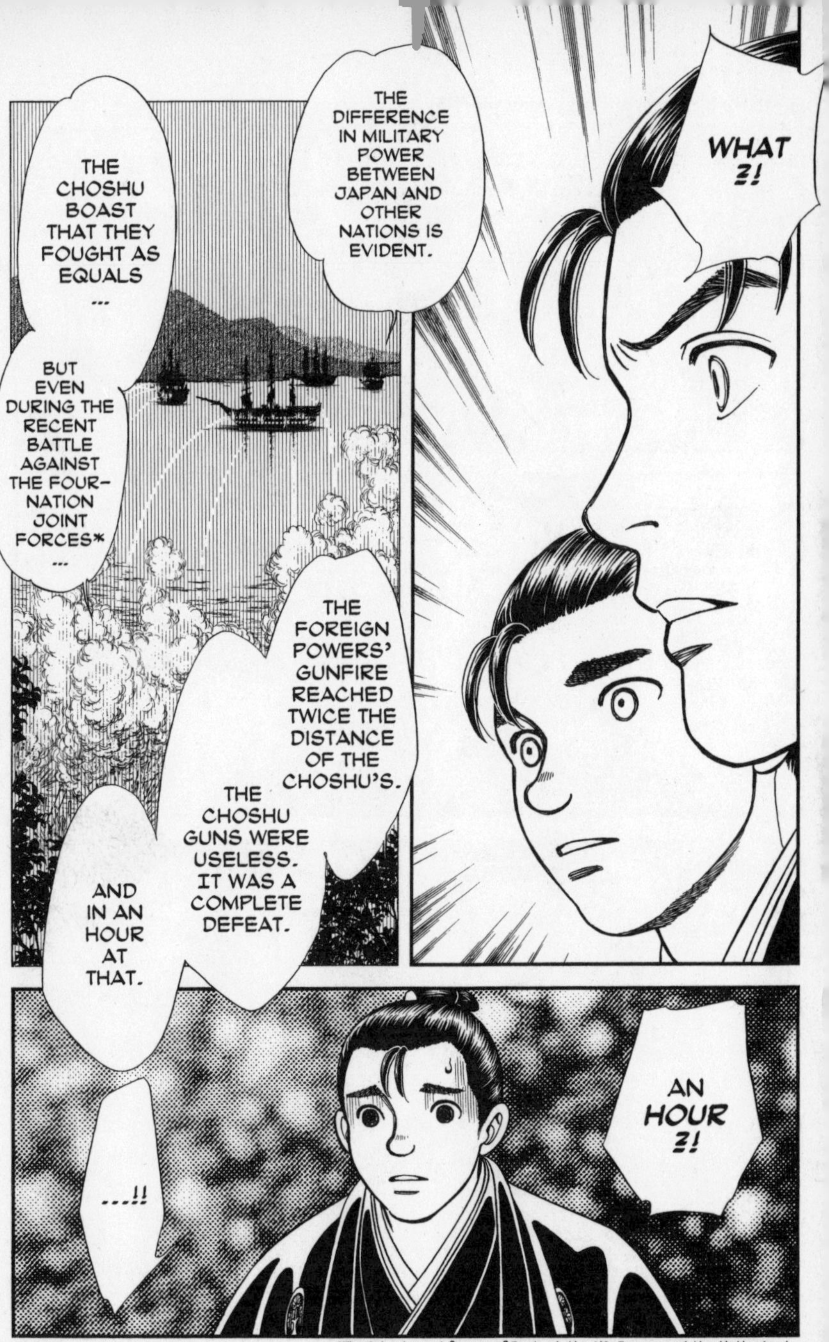
WHAT?!
THE DIFFERENCE IN MILITARY POWER BETWEEN JAPAN AND OTHER NATIONS IS EVIDENT.
THE CHOSHU BOAST THAT THEY FOUGHT AS EQUALS ...
BUT EVEN DURING THE RECENT BATTLE AGAINST THE FOUR-NATION JOINT FORCES* ...
THE FOREIGN POWERS' GUNFIRE REACHED TWICE THE DISTANCE OF THE CHOSHU'S.
THE CHOSHU GUNS WERE USELESS. IT WAS A COMPLETE DEFEAT.
AND IN AN HOUR AT THAT.
AN HOUR?!
...!!

*The joined naval forces of England, the US, France and the Netherlands.

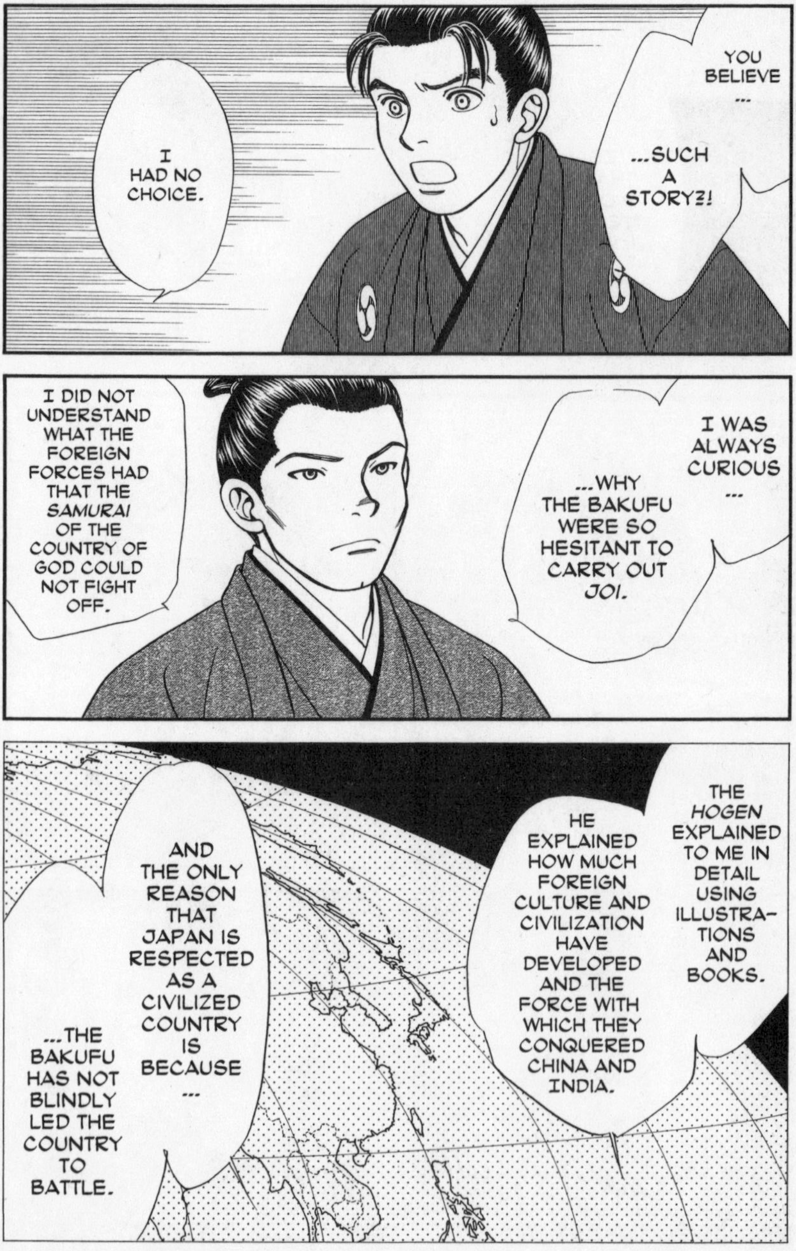
YOU BELIEVE ...
...SUCH A STORY?!
I HAD NO CHOICE.
I WAS ALWAYS CURIOUS ...
...WHY THE BAKUFU WERE SO HESITANT TO CARRY OUT *JOI*.
I DID NOT UNDERSTAND WHAT THE FOREIGN FORCES HAD THAT THE *SAMURAI* OF THE COUNTRY OF GOD COULD NOT FIGHT OFF.
THE *HOGEN* EXPLAINED TO ME IN DETAIL USING ILLUSTRATIONS AND BOOKS.
HE EXPLAINED HOW MUCH FOREIGN CULTURE AND CIVILIZATION HAVE DEVELOPED AND THE FORCE WITH WHICH THEY CONQUERED CHINA AND INDIA.
AND THE ONLY REASON THAT JAPAN IS RESPECTED AS A CIVILIZED COUNTRY IS BECAUSE ...
...THE BAKUFU HAS NOT BLINDLY LED THE COUNTRY TO BATTLE.

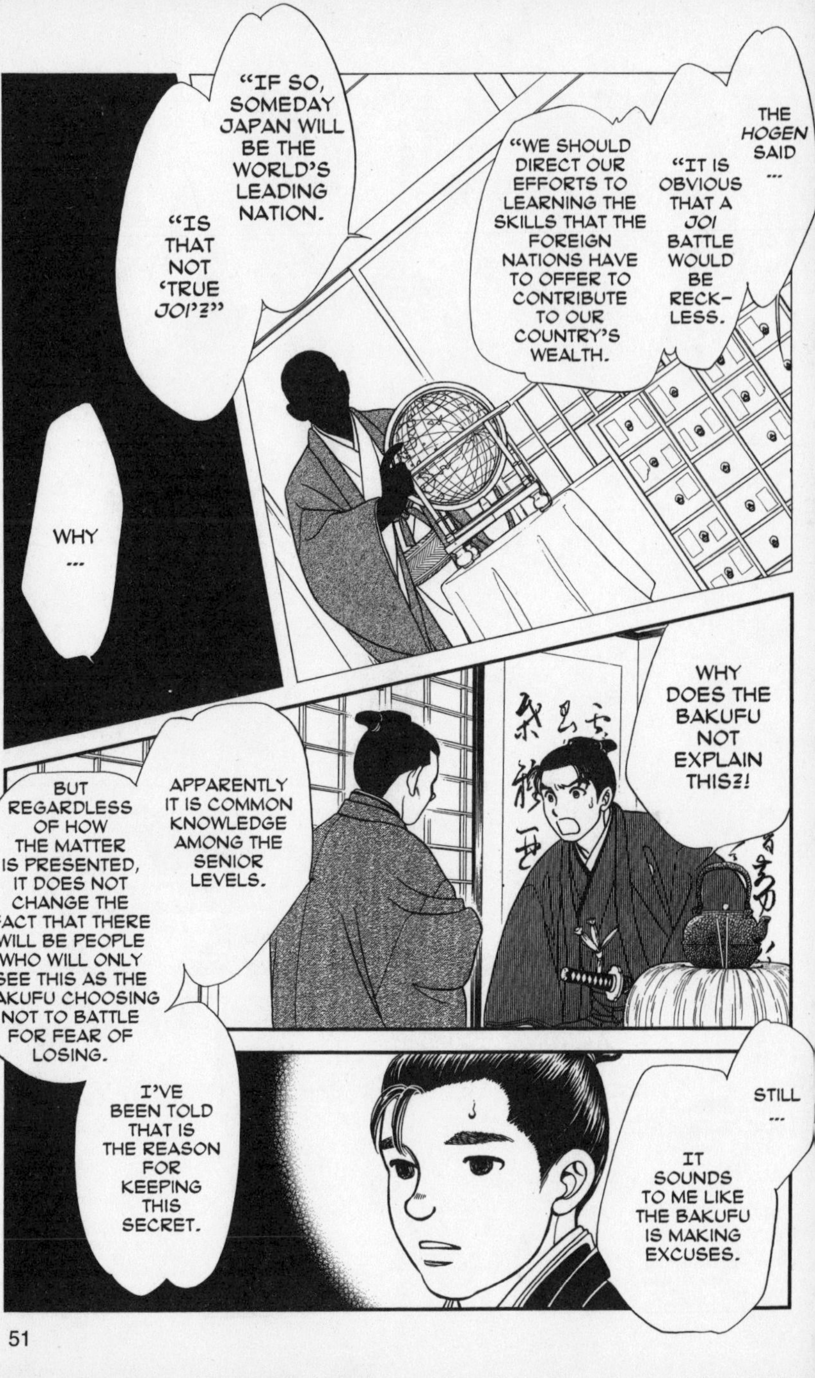
THE *HOGEN* SAID ...
"IT IS OBVIOUS THAT A *JOI* BATTLE WOULD BE RECK-LESS.
"WE SHOULD DIRECT OUR EFFORTS TO LEARNING THE SKILLS THAT THE FOREIGN NATIONS HAVE TO OFFER TO CONTRIBUTE TO OUR COUNTRY'S WEALTH.
"IF SO, SOMEDAY JAPAN WILL BE THE WORLD'S LEADING NATION.
"IS THAT NOT 'TRUE *JOI*'?"
WHY ...
WHY DOES THE BAKUFU NOT EXPLAIN THIS?!
APPARENTLY IT IS COMMON KNOWLEDGE AMONG THE SENIOR LEVELS.
BUT REGARDLESS OF HOW THE MATTER IS PRESENTED, IT DOES NOT CHANGE THE FACT THAT THERE WILL BE PEOPLE WHO WILL ONLY SEE THIS AS THE BAKUFU CHOOSING NOT TO BATTLE FOR FEAR OF LOSING.
STILL ...
IT SOUNDS TO ME LIKE THE BAKUFU IS MAKING EXCUSES.
I'VE BEEN TOLD THAT IS THE REASON FOR KEEPING THIS SECRET.

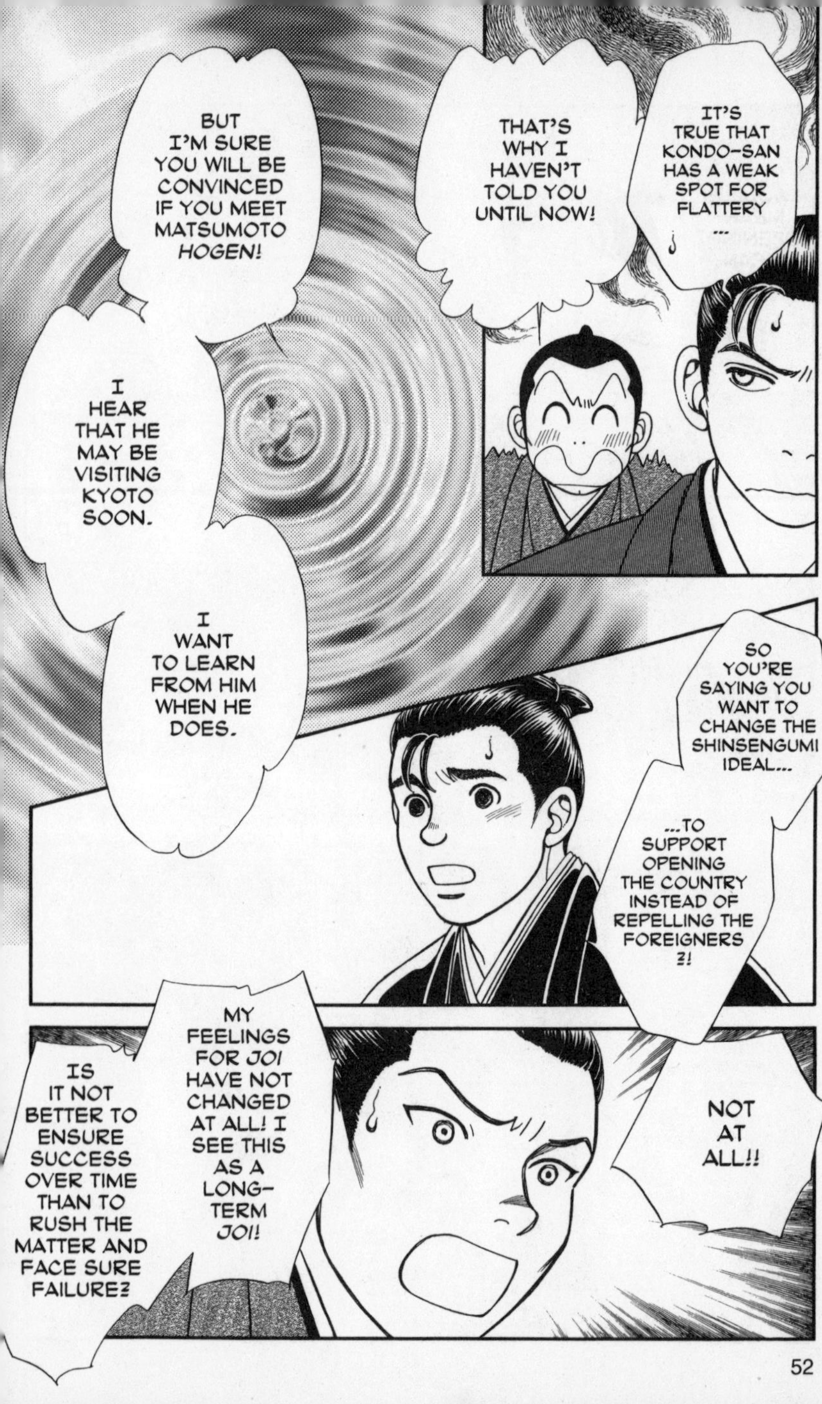
IT'S TRUE THAT KONDO-SAN HAS A WEAK SPOT FOR FLATTERY...
THAT'S WHY I HAVEN'T TOLD YOU UNTIL NOW!
BUT I'M SURE YOU WILL BE CONVINCED IF YOU MEET MATSUMOTO *HOGEN*!
I HEAR THAT HE MAY BE VISITING KYOTO SOON.
I WANT TO LEARN FROM HIM WHEN HE DOES.
SO YOU'RE SAYING YOU WANT TO CHANGE THE SHINSENGUMI IDEAL...
...TO SUPPORT OPENING THE COUNTRY INSTEAD OF REPELLING THE FOREIGNERS?!
NOT AT ALL!!
MY FEELINGS FOR *JOI* HAVE NOT CHANGED AT ALL! I SEE THIS AS A LONG-TERM *JOI*!
IS IT NOT BETTER TO ENSURE SUCCESS OVER TIME THAN TO RUSH THE MATTER AND FACE SURE FAILURE?

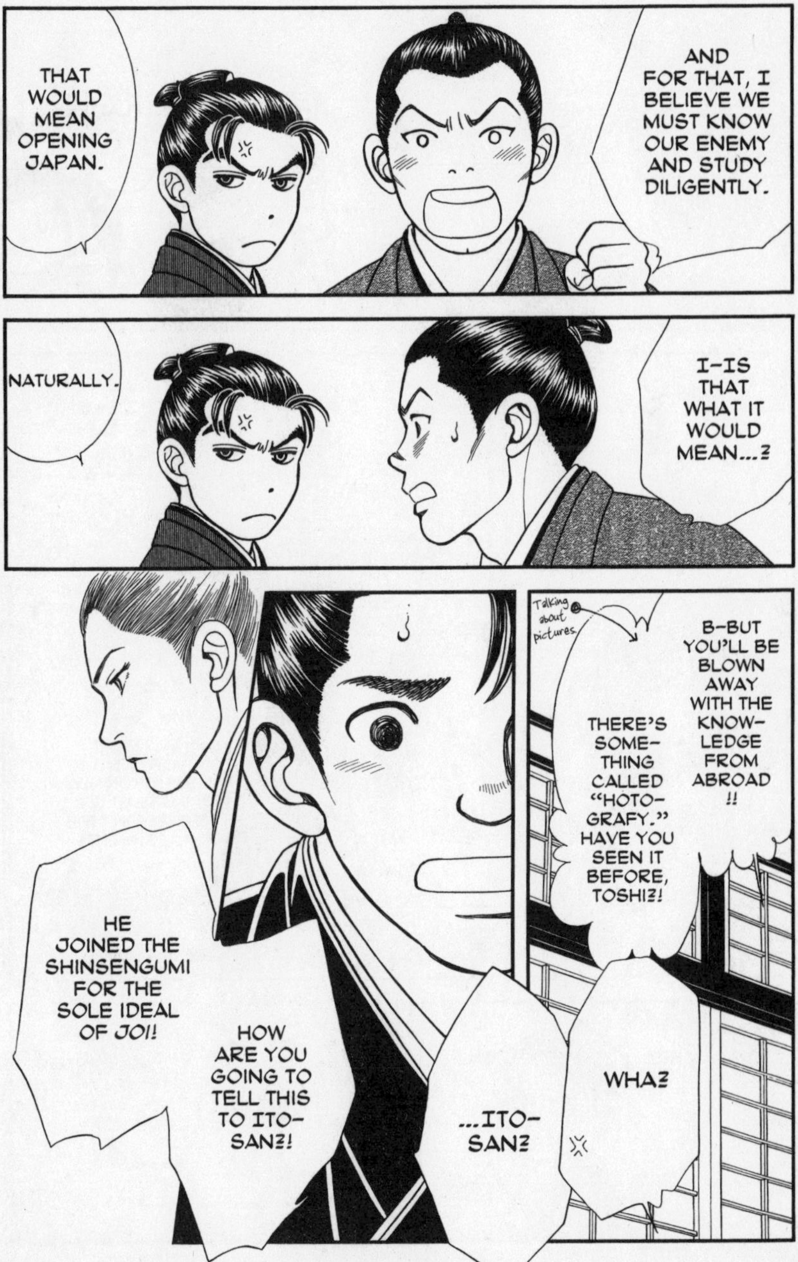
AND FOR THAT, I BELIEVE WE MUST KNOW OUR ENEMY AND STUDY DILIGENTLY.
THAT WOULD MEAN OPENING JAPAN.
I-IS THAT WHAT IT WOULD MEAN...?
NATURALLY.
B-BUT YOU'LL BE BLOWN AWAY WITH THE KNOW-LEDGE FROM ABROAD!!
Talking about pictures.
THERE'S SOME-THING CALLED "HOTO-GRAFY." HAVE YOU SEEN IT BEFORE, TOSHI?!
WHA?
HE JOINED THE SHINSENGUMI FOR THE SOLE IDEAL OF *JOI*!
HOW ARE YOU GOING TO TELL THIS TO ITO-SAN?!
...ITO-SAN?

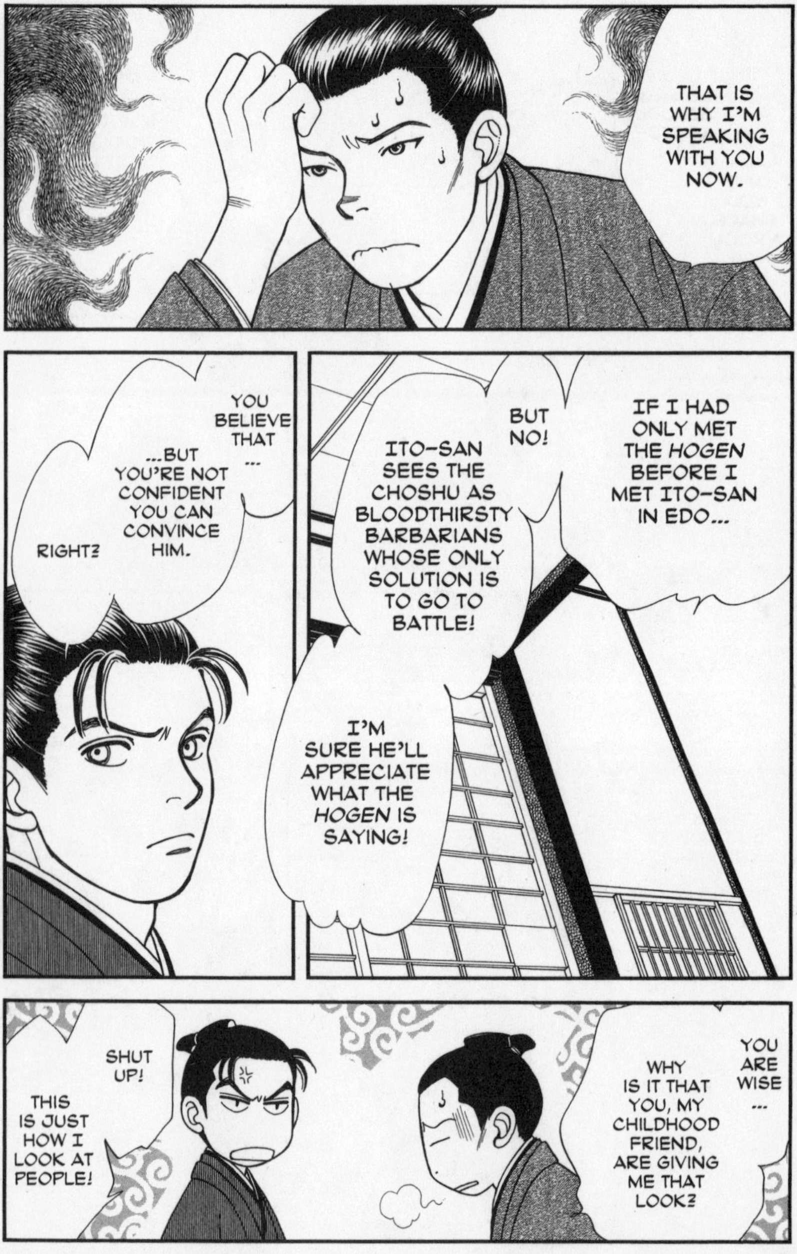
THAT IS WHY I'M SPEAKING WITH YOU NOW.
IF I HAD ONLY MET THE *HOGEN* BEFORE I MET ITO-SAN IN EDO...
BUT NO!
ITO-SAN SEES THE CHOSHU AS BLOODTHIRSTY BARBARIANS WHOSE ONLY SOLUTION IS TO GO TO BATTLE!
I'M SURE HE'LL APPRECIATE WHAT THE *HOGEN* IS SAYING!
YOU BELIEVE THAT ...
...BUT YOU'RE NOT CONFIDENT YOU CAN CONVINCE HIM.
RIGHT?
YOU ARE WISE ...
WHY IS IT THAT YOU, MY CHILDHOOD FRIEND, ARE GIVING ME THAT LOOK?
SHUT UP!
THIS IS JUST HOW I LOOK AT PEOPLE!

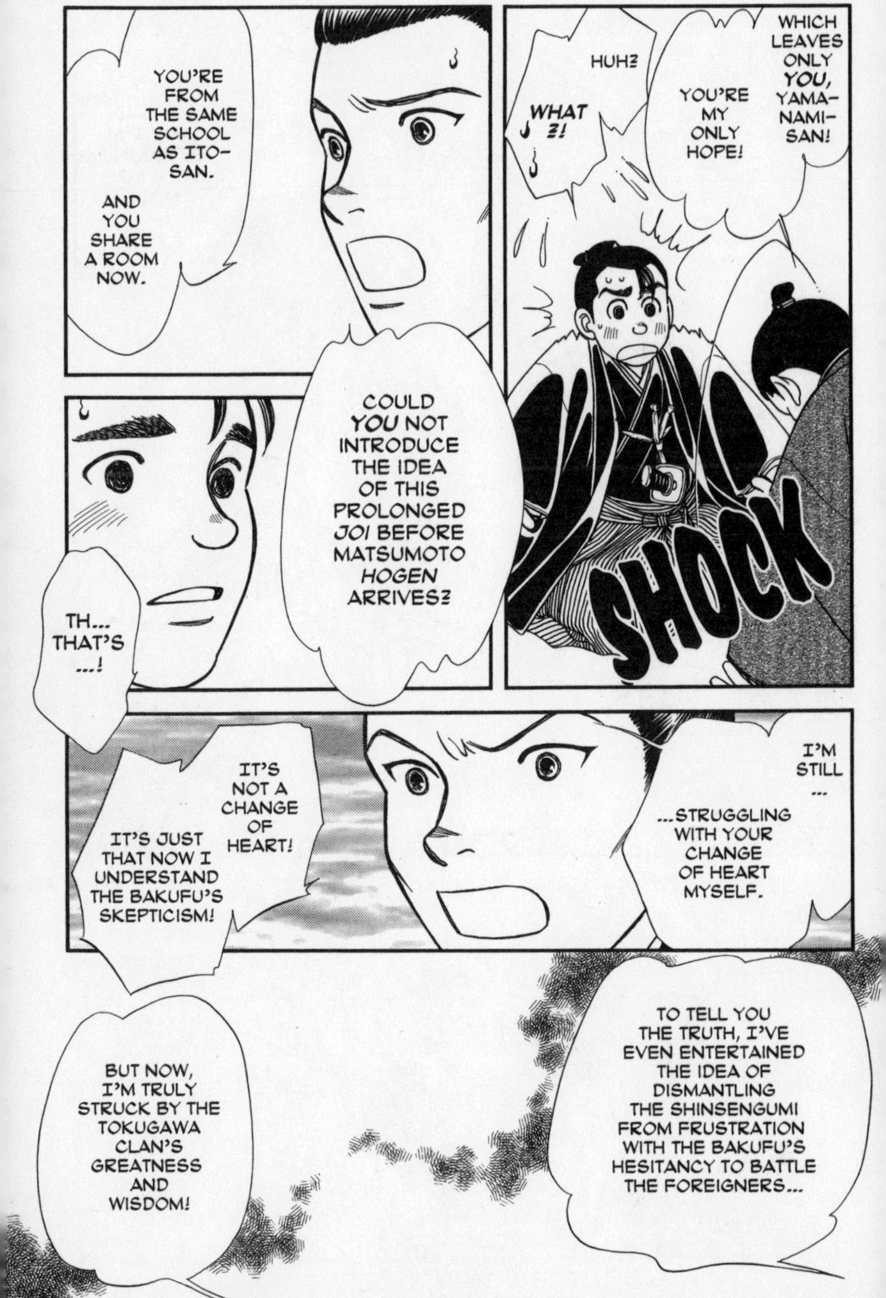
WHICH LEAVES ONLY YOU, YAMANAMI-SAN!
YOU'RE MY ONLY HOPE!
HUH?
WHAT?!
SHOCK
YOU'RE FROM THE SAME SCHOOL AS ITO-SAN.
AND YOU SHARE A ROOM NOW.
COULD YOU NOT INTRODUCE THE IDEA OF THIS PROLONGED JOI BEFORE MATSUMOTO HOGEN ARRIVES?
TH... THAT'S ...!
I'M STILL ...
...STRUGGLING WITH YOUR CHANGE OF HEART MYSELF.
IT'S NOT A CHANGE OF HEART!
IT'S JUST THAT NOW I UNDERSTAND THE BAKUFU'S SKEPTICISM!
TO TELL YOU THE TRUTH, I'VE EVEN ENTERTAINED THE IDEA OF DISMANTLING THE SHINSENGUMI FROM FRUSTRATION WITH THE BAKUFU'S HESITANCY TO BATTLE THE FOREIGNERS...
BUT NOW, I'M TRULY STRUCK BY THE TOKUGAWA CLAN'S GREATNESS AND WISDOM!

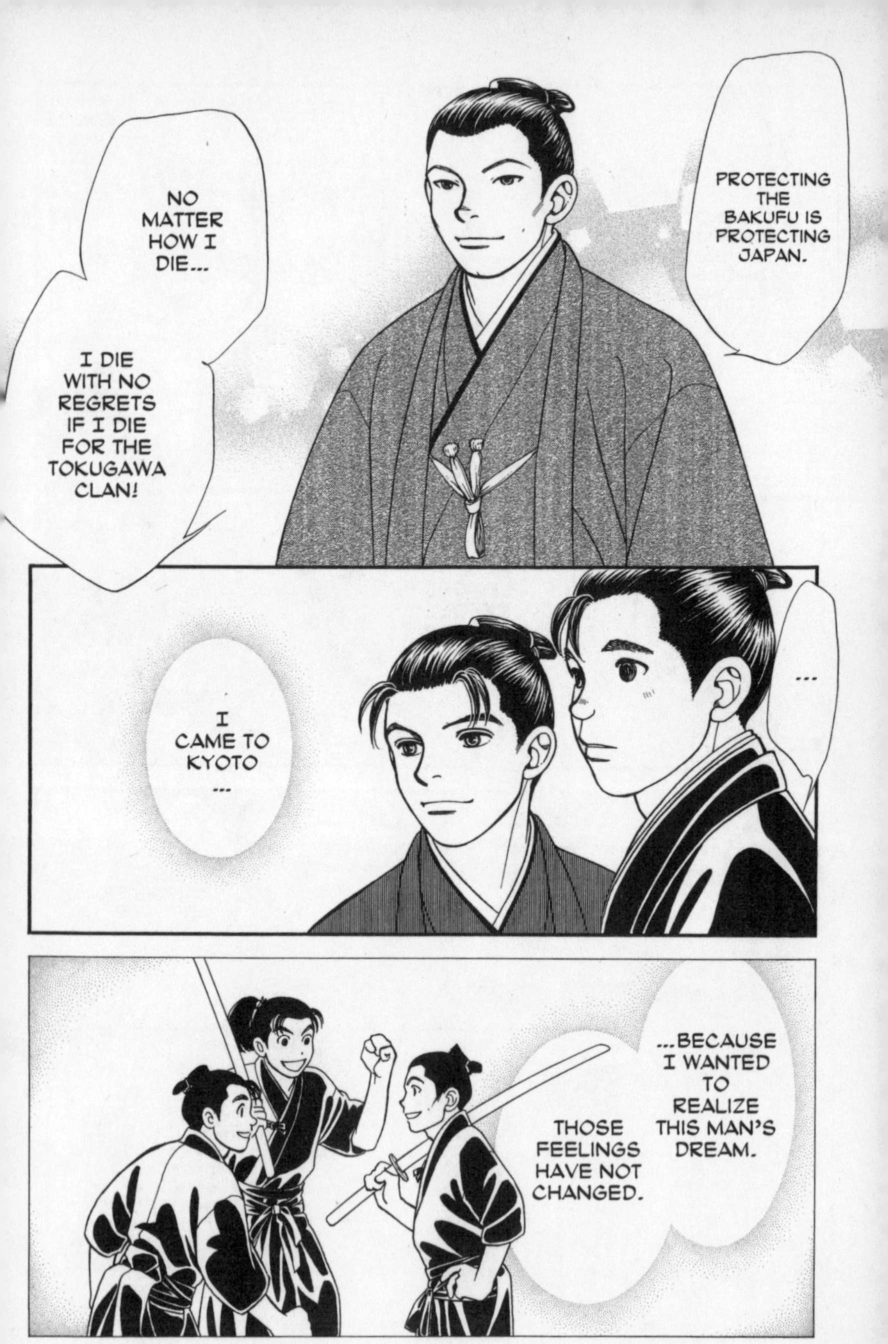
PROTECTING THE BAKUFU IS PROTECTING JAPAN.
NO MATTER HOW I DIE...
I DIE WITH NO REGRETS IF I DIE FOR THE TOKUGAWA CLAN!
...
I CAME TO KYOTO ...
...BECAUSE I WANTED TO REALIZE THIS MAN'S DREAM.
THOSE FEELINGS HAVE NOT CHANGED.

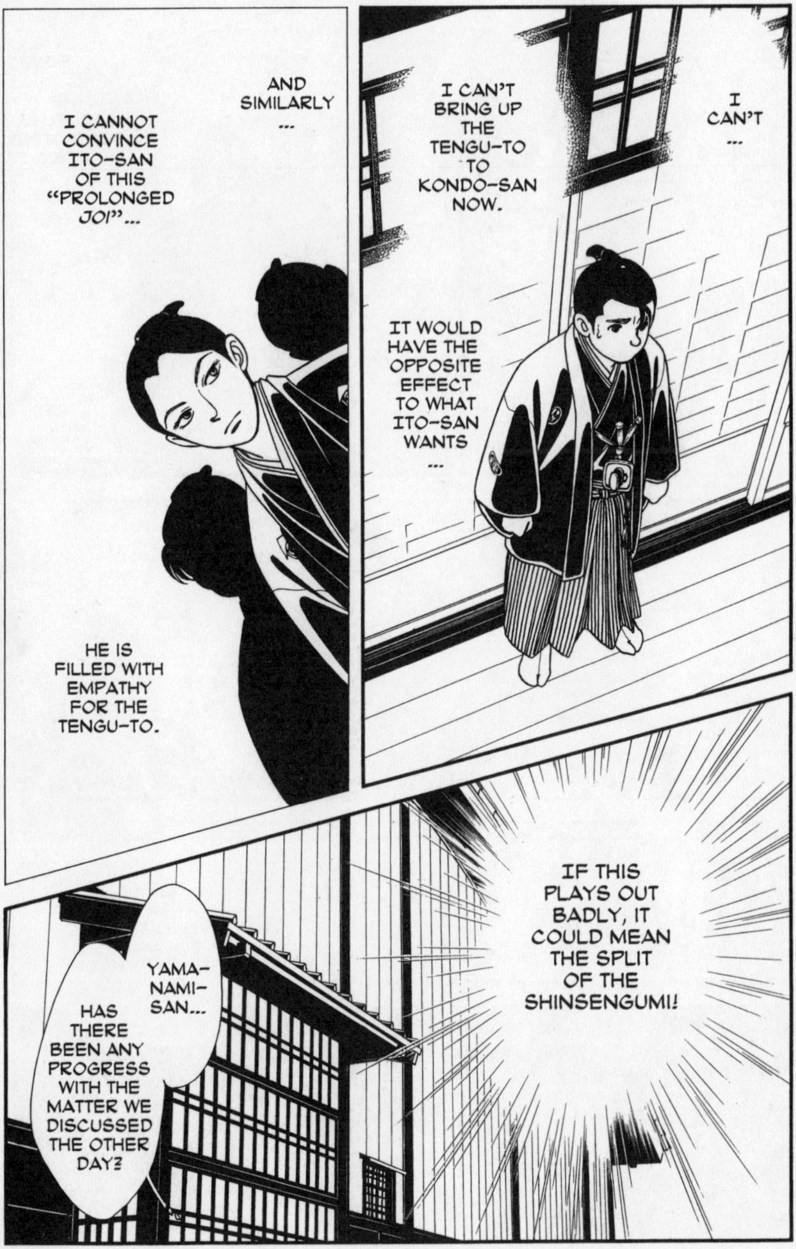
I CAN'T ...
I CAN'T BRING UP THE TENGU-TO TO KONDO-SAN NOW.
IT WOULD HAVE THE OPPOSITE EFFECT TO WHAT ITO-SAN WANTS ...
AND SIMILARLY ...
I CANNOT CONVINCE ITO-SAN OF THIS "PROLONGED JOI"...
HE IS FILLED WITH EMPATHY FOR THE TENGU-TO.
IF THIS PLAYS OUT BADLY, IT COULD MEAN THE SPLIT OF THE SHINSENGUMI!
YAMA-NAMI-SAN... HAS THERE BEEN ANY PROGRESS WITH THE MATTER WE DISCUSSED THE OTHER DAY?

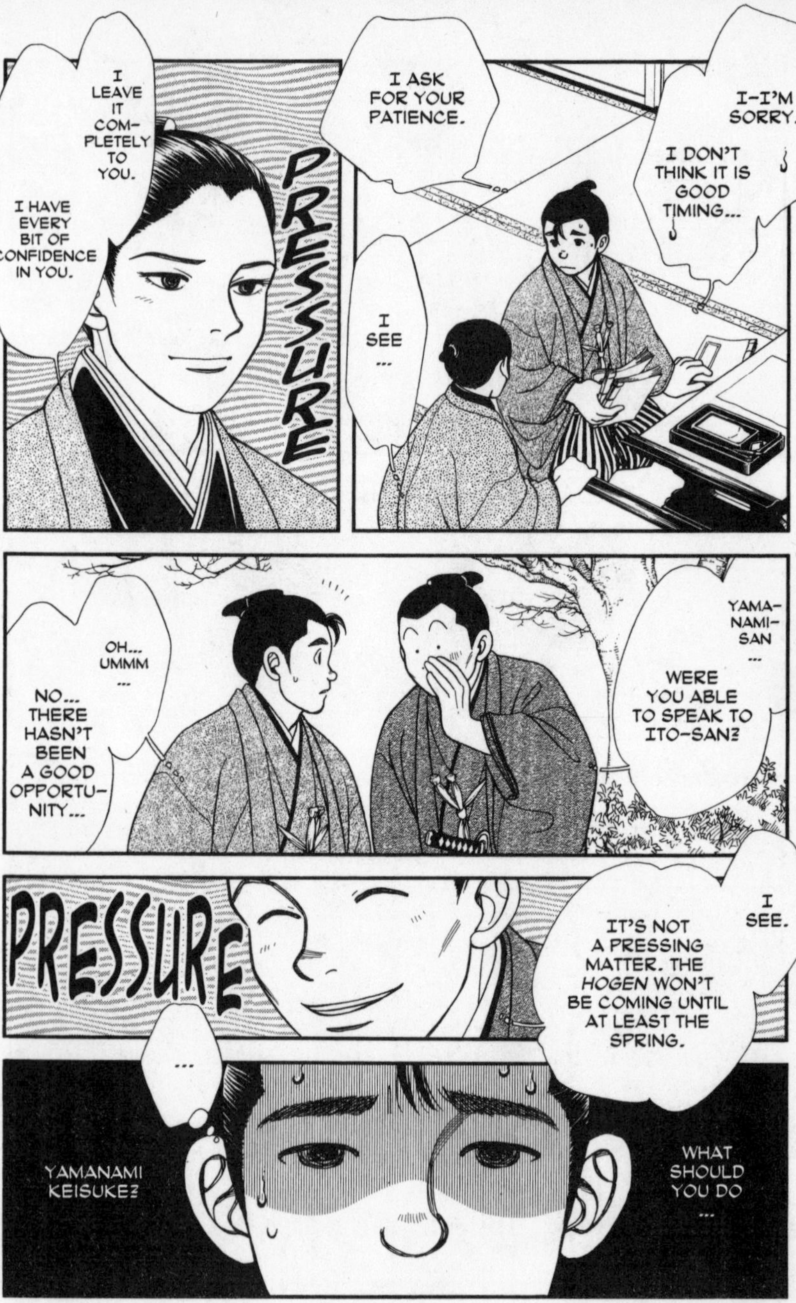
I-I'M SORRY.
I DON'T THINK IT IS GOOD TIMING...
I ASK FOR YOUR PATIENCE.
I SEE...
I LEAVE IT COMPLETELY TO YOU.
I HAVE EVERY BIT OF CONFIDENCE IN YOU.
PRESSURE
YAMANAMI-SAN...
WERE YOU ABLE TO SPEAK TO ITO-SAN?
OH... UMMM...
NO... THERE HASN'T BEEN A GOOD OPPORTUNITY...
I SEE.
IT'S NOT A PRESSING MATTER. THE *HOGEN* WON'T BE COMING UNTIL AT LEAST THE SPRING.
PRESSURE
...
WHAT SHOULD YOU DO...
YAMANAMI KEISUKE?

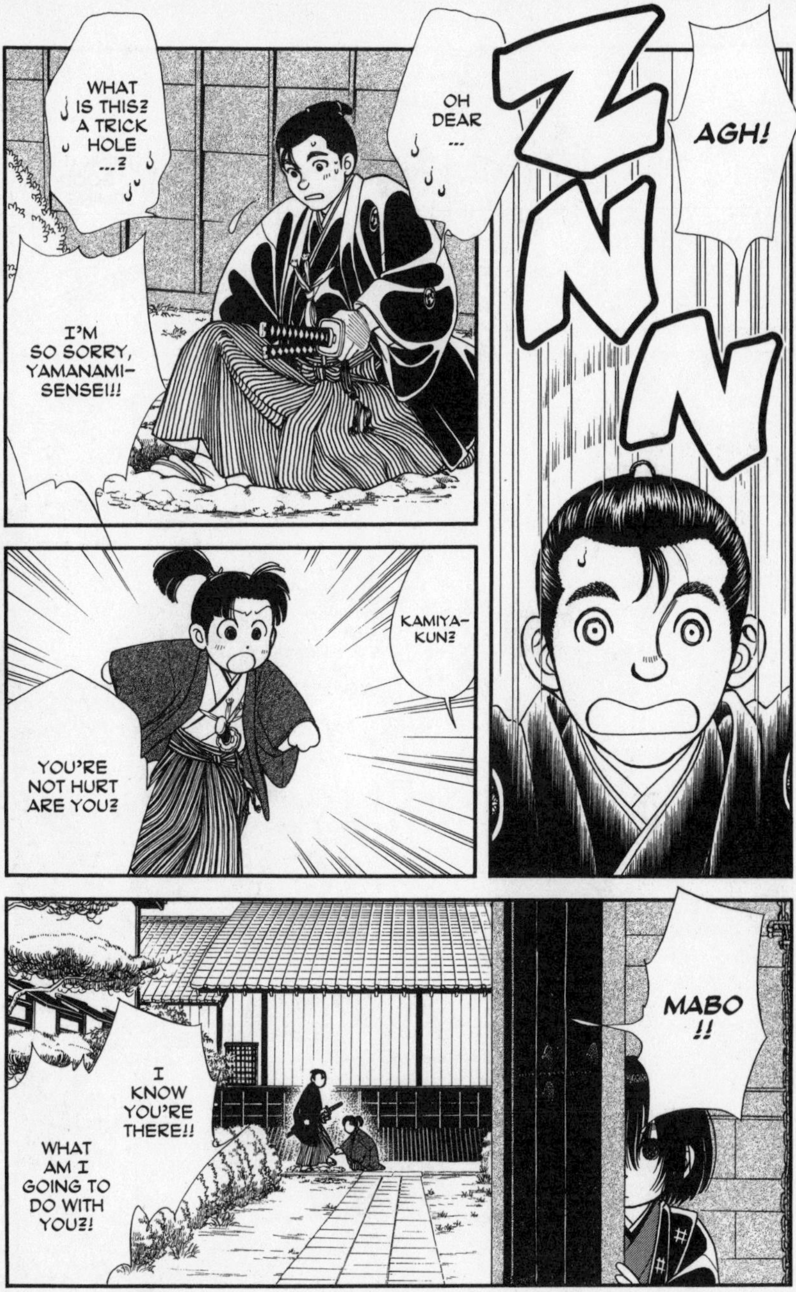
AGH!
ZNNN
OH DEAR ...
WHAT IS THIS? A TRICK HOLE ...?
I'M SO SORRY, YAMANAMI-SENSEI!!
KAMIYA-KUN?
YOU'RE NOT HURT ARE YOU?
MABO !!
I KNOW YOU'RE THERE!!
WHAT AM I GOING TO DO WITH YOU?!

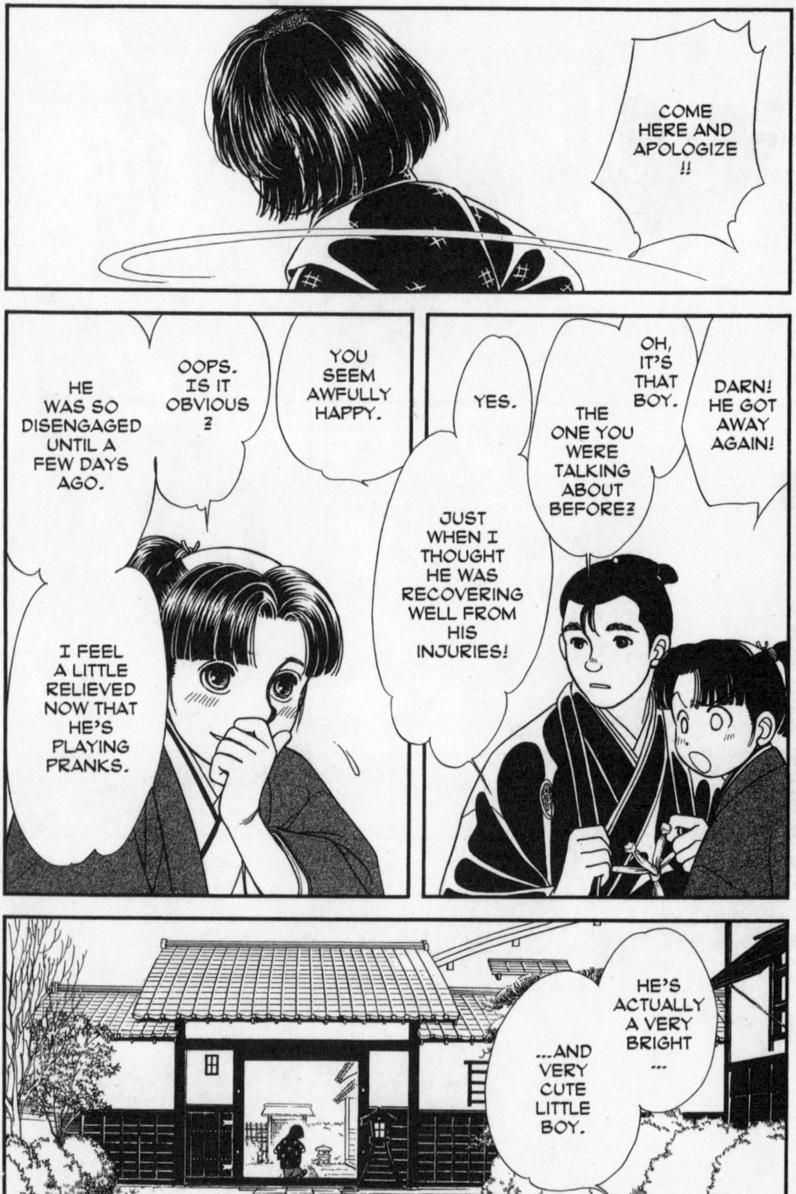
COME HERE AND APOLOGIZE !!
DARN! HE GOT AWAY AGAIN!
OH, IT'S THAT BOY.
THE ONE YOU WERE TALKING ABOUT BEFORE?
YES.
JUST WHEN I THOUGHT HE WAS RECOVERING WELL FROM HIS INJURIES!
YOU SEEM AWFULLY HAPPY.
OOPS. IS IT OBVIOUS?
HE WAS SO DISENGAGED UNTIL A FEW DAYS AGO.
I FEEL A LITTLE RELIEVED NOW THAT HE'S PLAYING PRANKS.
HE'S ACTUALLY A VERY BRIGHT ...
...AND VERY CUTE LITTLE BOY.

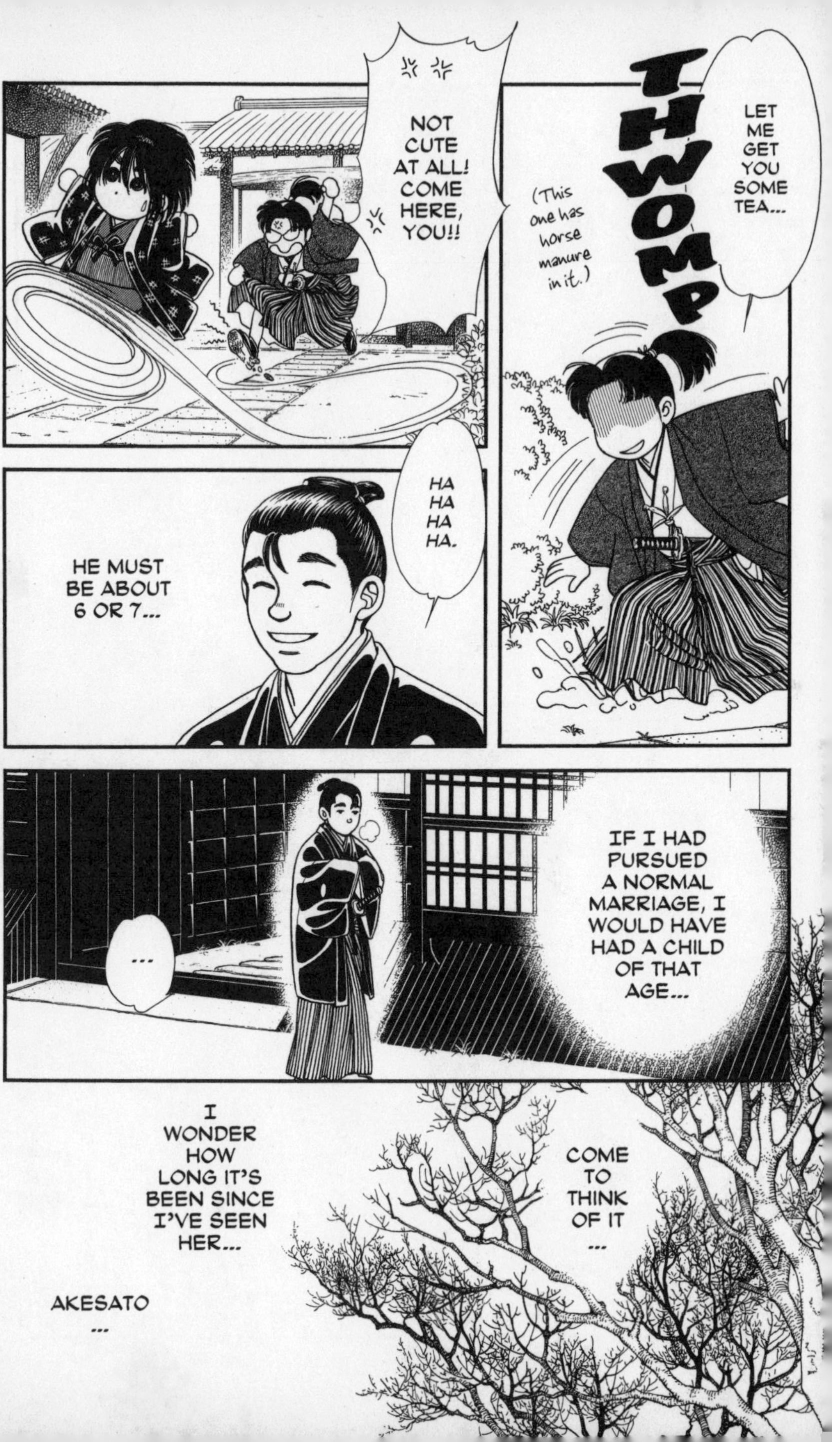
LET ME GET YOU SOME TEA...
THWOMP
(This one has horse manure in it.)
NOT CUTE AT ALL! COME HERE, YOU!!
HA HA HA HA.
HE MUST BE ABOUT 6 OR 7...
IF I HAD PURSUED A NORMAL MARRIAGE, I WOULD HAVE HAD A CHILD OF THAT AGE...
...
COME TO THINK OF IT ...
I WONDER HOW LONG IT'S BEEN SINCE I'VE SEEN HER...
AKESATO ...

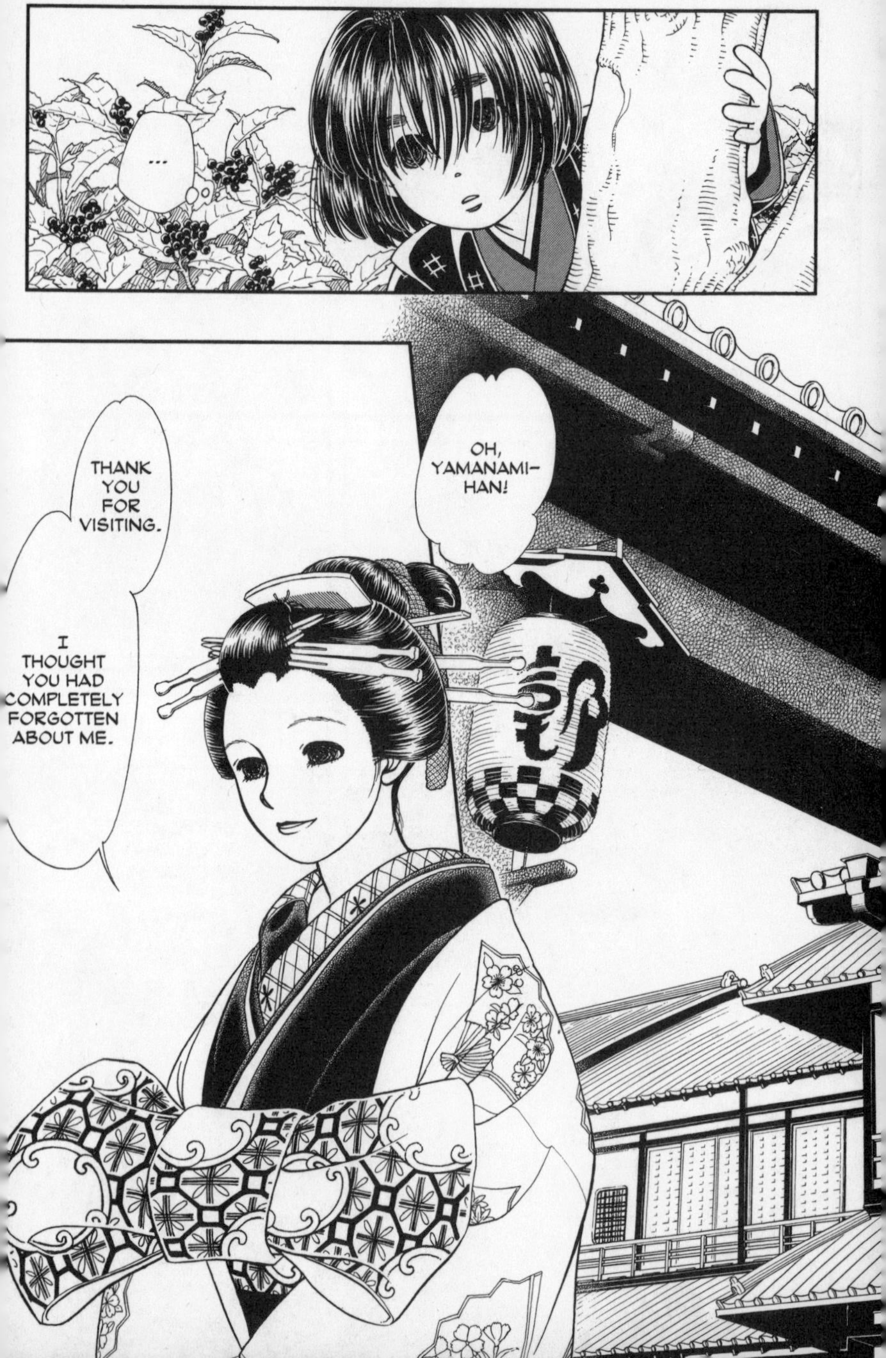
...
OH, YAMANAMI-HAN!
THANK YOU FOR VISITING.
I THOUGHT YOU HAD COMPLETELY FORGOTTEN ABOUT ME.

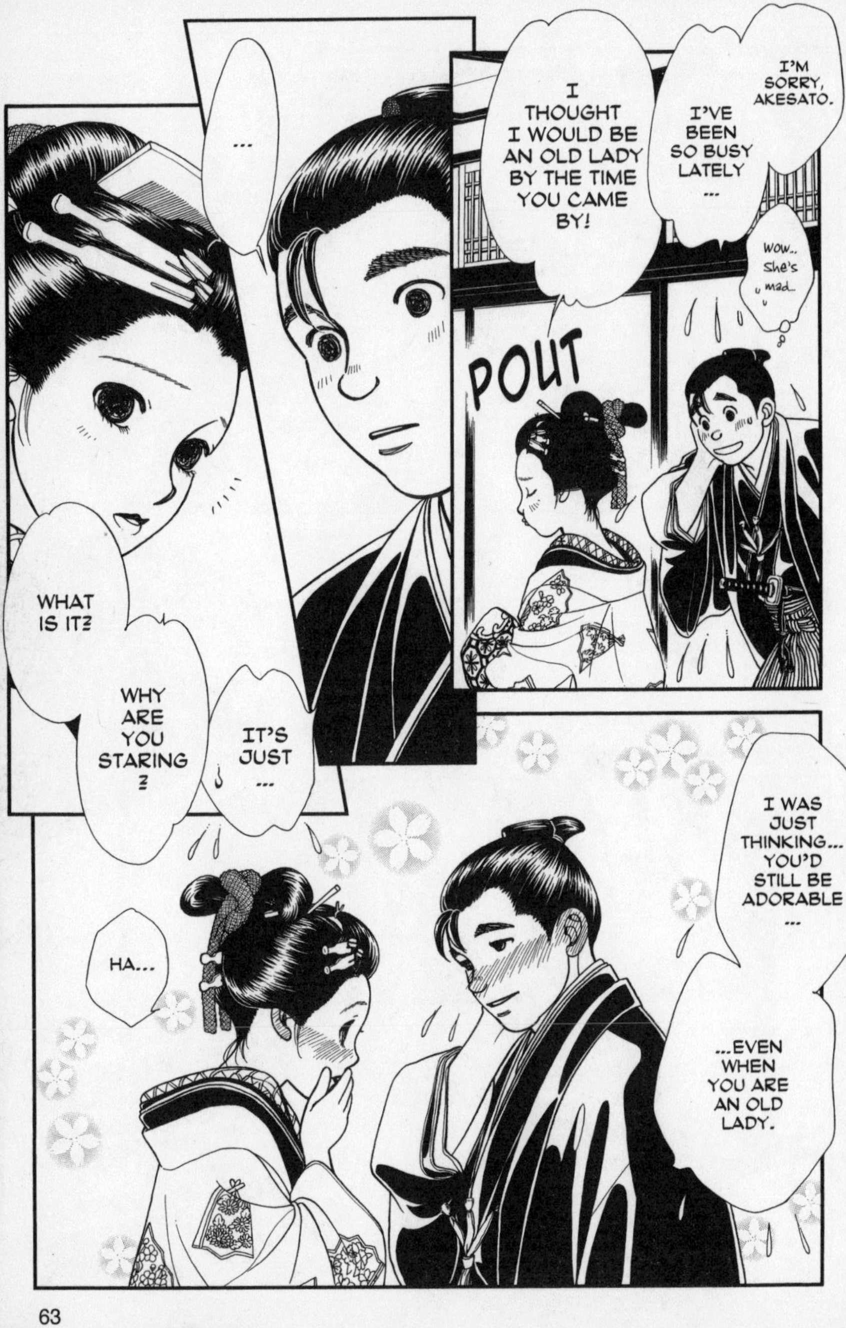
I'M SORRY, AKESATO.
I'VE BEEN SO BUSY LATELY ...
I THOUGHT I WOULD BE AN OLD LADY BY THE TIME YOU CAME BY!
Wow.. She's mad..
POUT
...
WHAT IS IT?
WHY ARE YOU STARING?
IT'S JUST ...
I WAS JUST THINKING... YOU'D STILL BE ADORABLE ...
...EVEN WHEN YOU ARE AN OLD LADY.
HA...

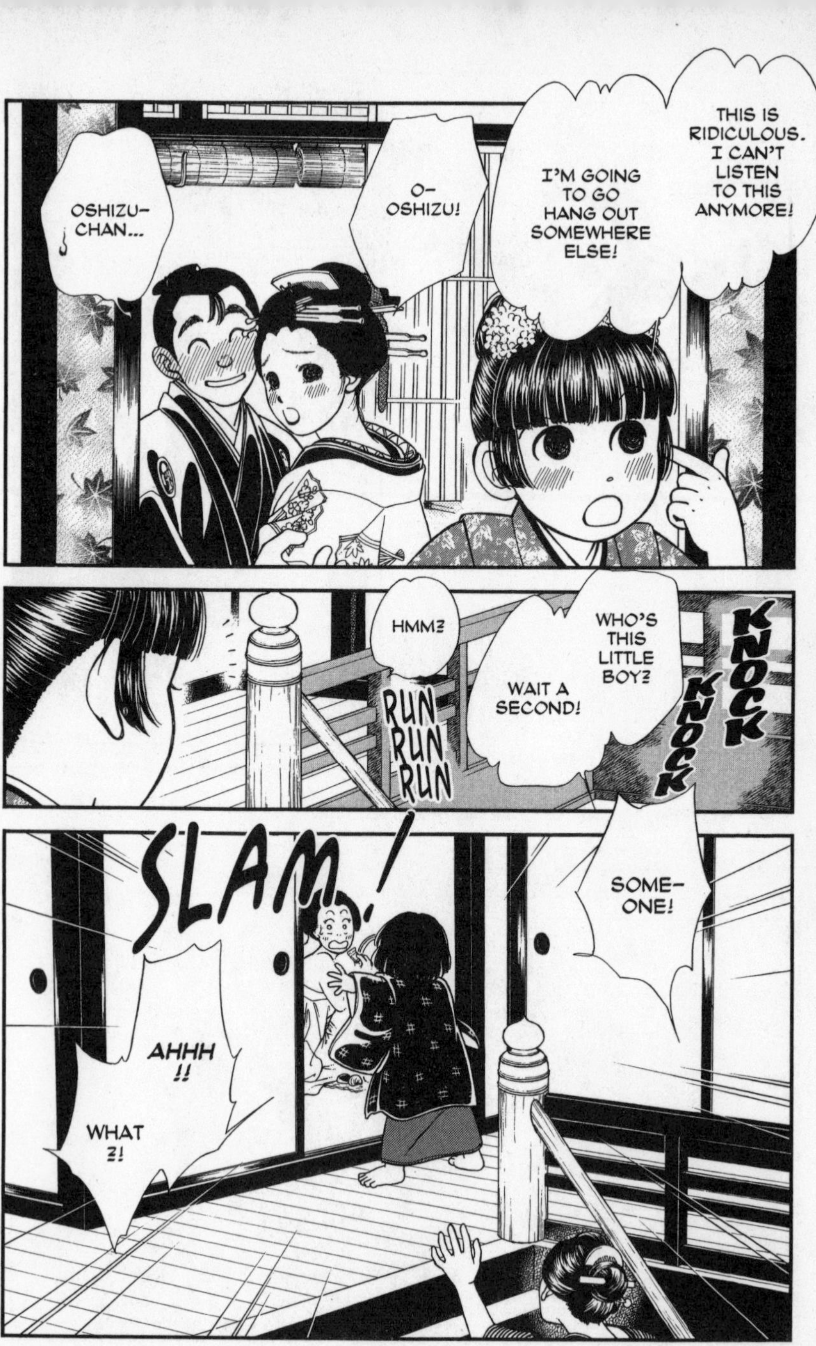
THIS IS RIDICULOUS. I CAN'T LISTEN TO THIS ANYMORE!
I'M GOING TO GO HANG OUT SOMEWHERE ELSE!
O- OSHIZU!
OSHIZU-CHAN...
KNOCK KNOCK
WHO'S THIS LITTLE BOY?
WAIT A SECOND!
HMM?
RUN RUN RUN
SOME-ONE!
SLAM!
AHHH!!
WHAT?!

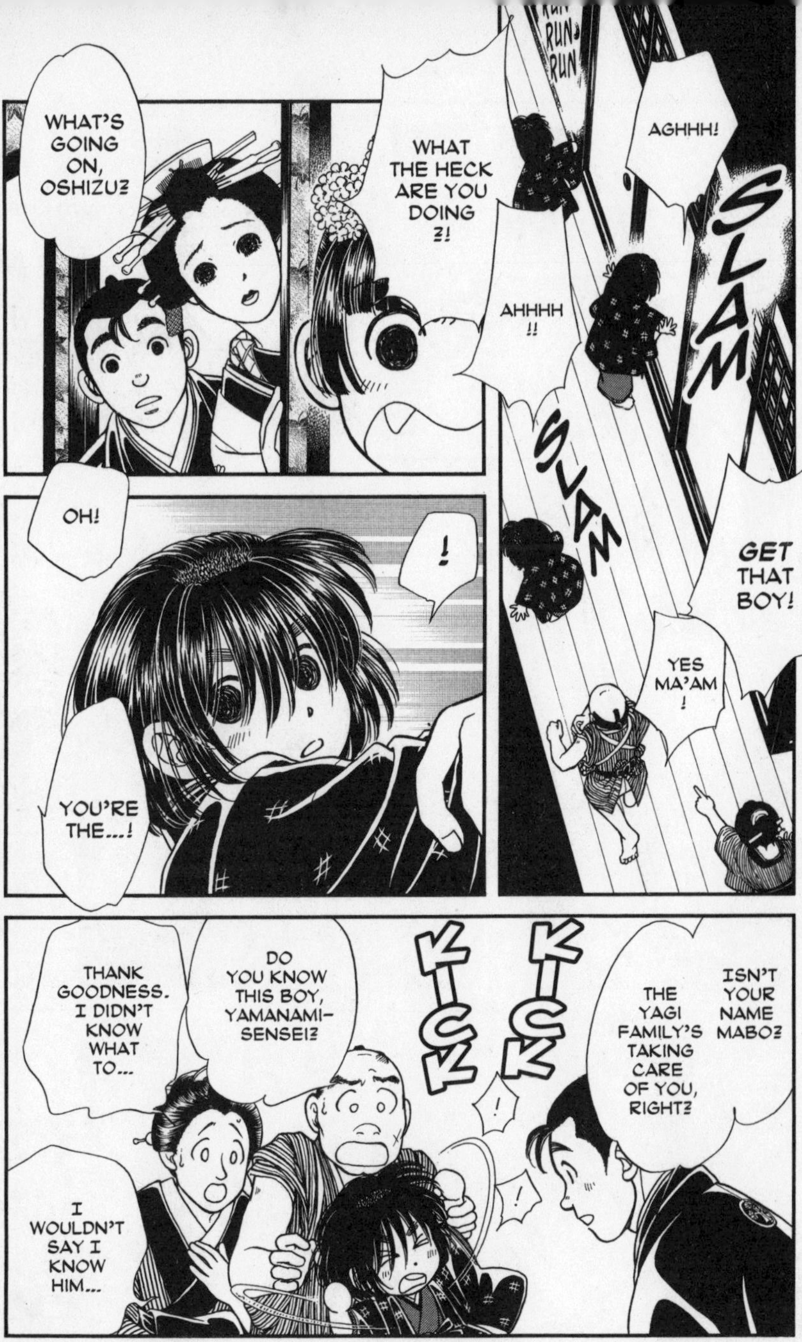
RUN RUN RUN
AGHHH!
SLAM
AHHHH!!
SLAM
GET THAT BOY!
YES MA'AM!
WHAT THE HECK ARE YOU DOING?!
WHAT'S GOING ON, OSHIZU?
!
OH!
YOU'RE THE...!
KICK
KICK
ISN'T YOUR NAME MABO?
THE YAGI FAMILY'S TAKING CARE OF YOU, RIGHT?
!
!
DO YOU KNOW THIS BOY, YAMANAMI-SENSEI?
THANK GOODNESS. I DIDN'T KNOW WHAT TO...
I WOULDN'T SAY I KNOW HIM...

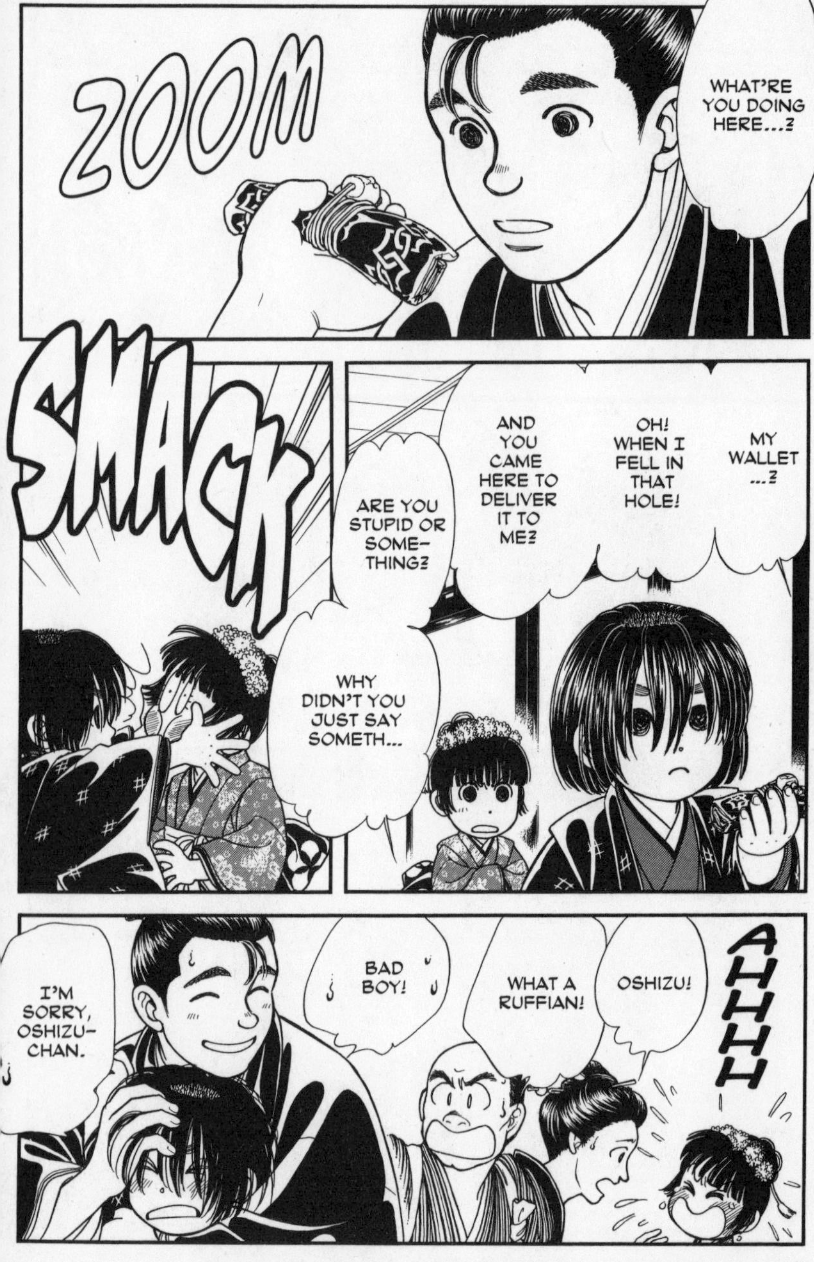
WHAT'RE YOU DOING HERE...?
ZOOM
MY WALLET ...?
OH! WHEN I FELL IN THAT HOLE!
AND YOU CAME HERE TO DELIVER IT TO ME?
ARE YOU STUPID OR SOME-THING?
WHY DIDN'T YOU JUST SAY SOMETH...
SMACK
AHHHH
OSHIZU!
WHAT A RUFFIAN!
BAD BOY!
I'M SORRY, OSHIZU-CHAN.

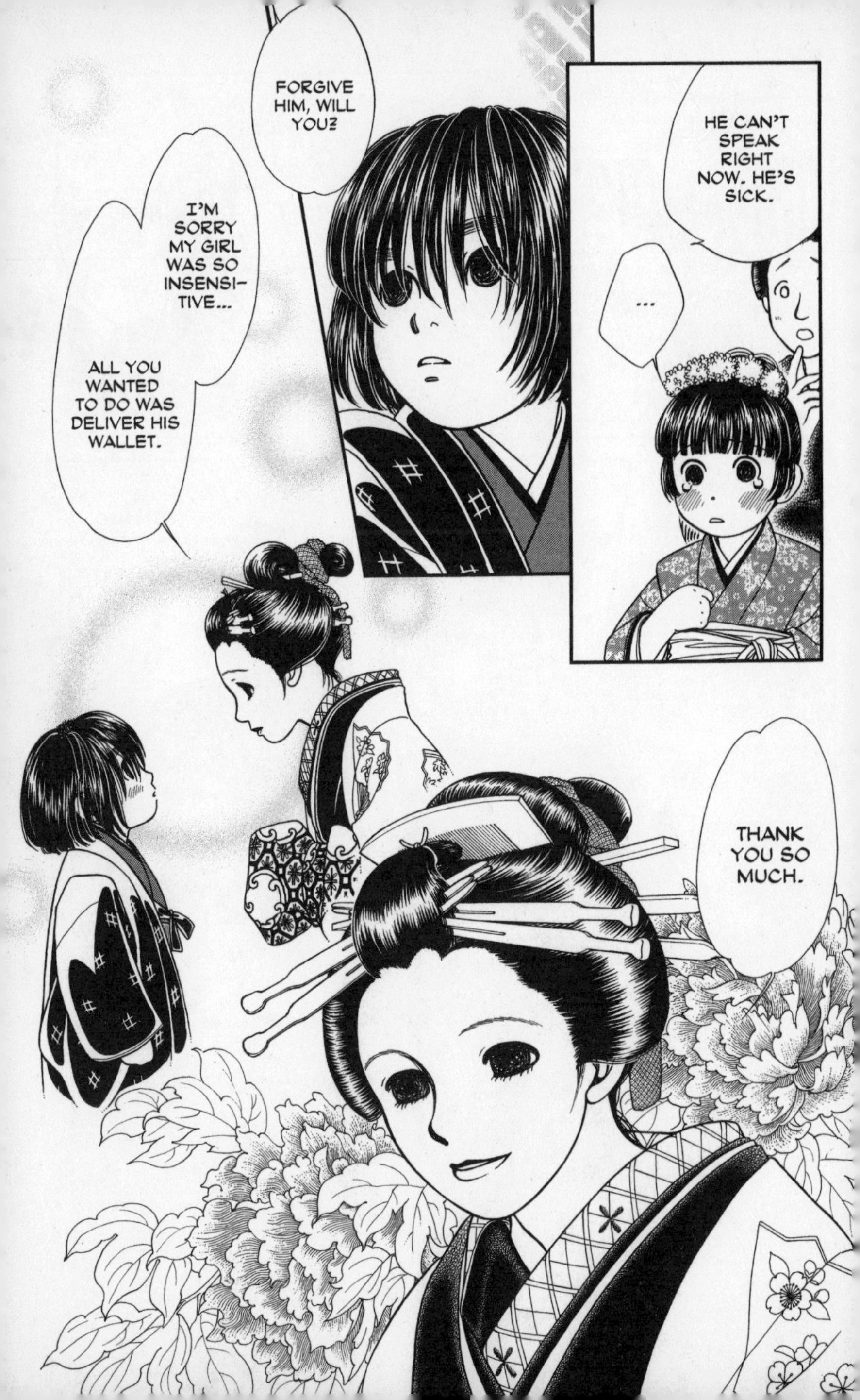
HE CAN'T SPEAK RIGHT NOW. HE'S SICK.
...
FORGIVE HIM, WILL YOU?
I'M SORRY MY GIRL WAS SO INSENSI-TIVE...
ALL YOU WANTED TO DO WAS DELIVER HIS WALLET.
THANK YOU SO MUCH.

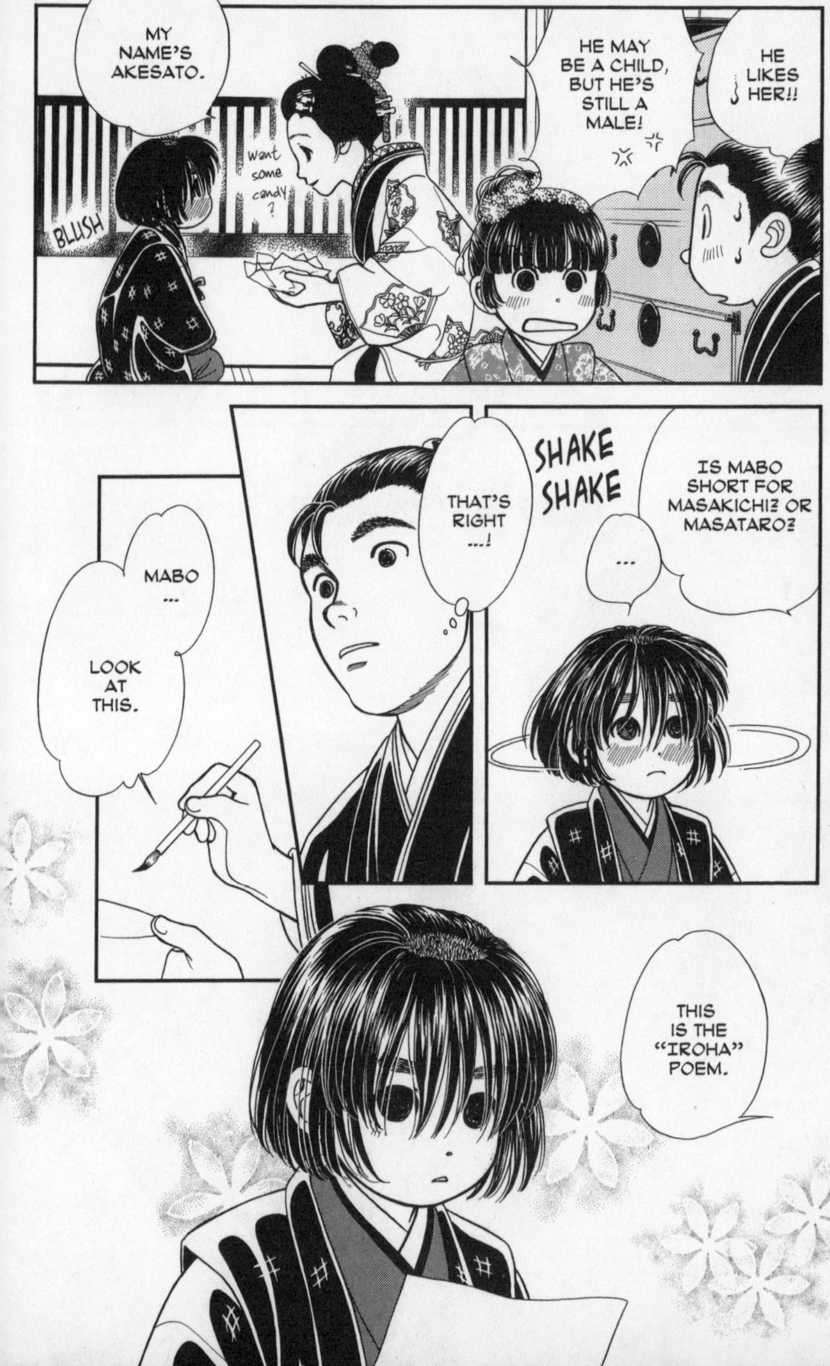
HE LIKES HER!!
HE MAY BE A CHILD, BUT HE'S STILL A MALE!
want some candy?
BLUSH
MY NAME'S AKESATO.
IS MABO SHORT FOR MASAKICHI? OR MASATARO?
...
SHAKE SHAKE
THAT'S RIGHT ...!
MABO ...
LOOK AT THIS.
THIS IS THE "IROHA" POEM.

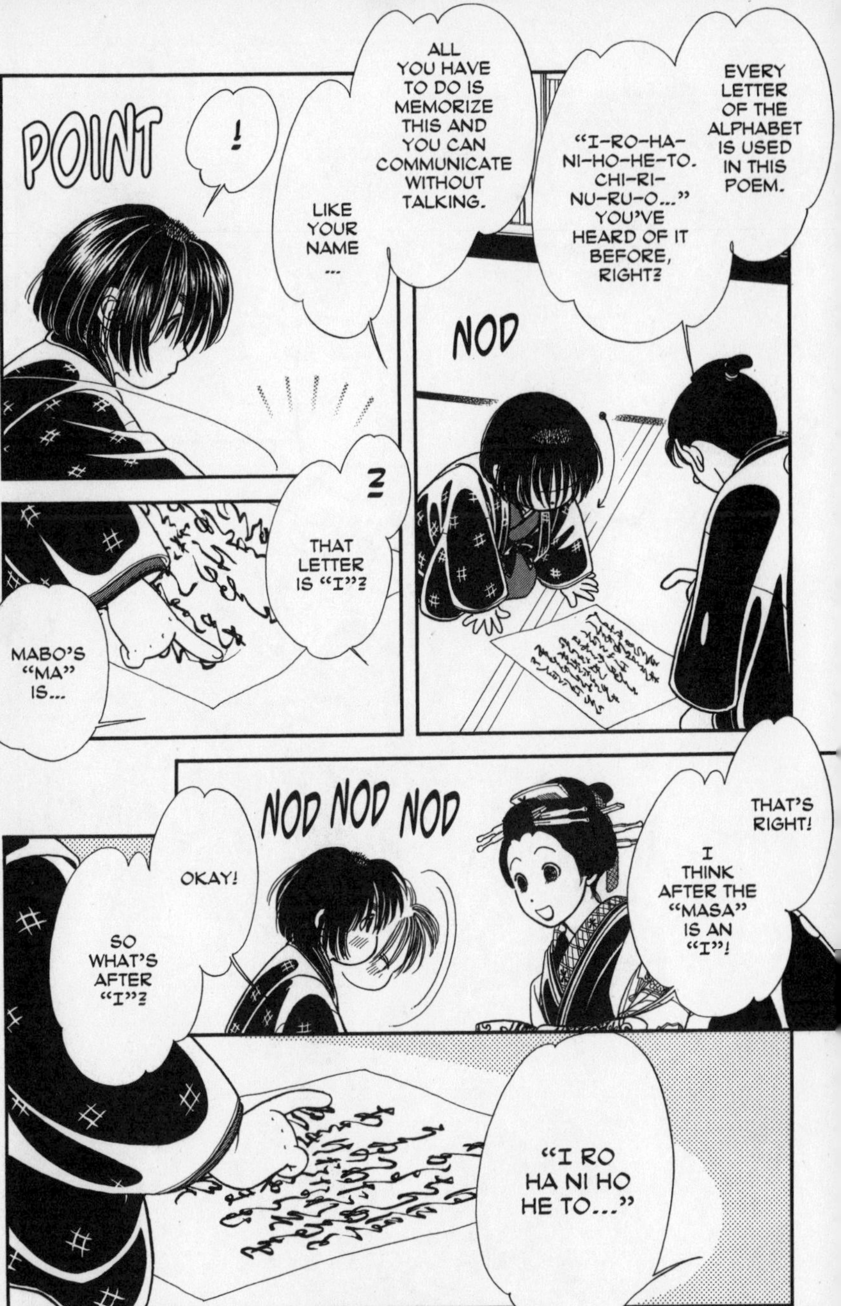
EVERY LETTER OF THE ALPHABET IS USED IN THIS POEM.
"I-RO-HA-NI-HO-HE-TO. CHI-RI-NU-RU-O..." YOU'VE HEARD OF IT BEFORE, RIGHT?
ALL YOU HAVE TO DO IS MEMORIZE THIS AND YOU CAN COMMUNICATE WITHOUT TALKING.
POINT
!
LIKE YOUR NAME ...
NOD
?
THAT LETTER IS "I"?
MABO'S "MA" IS...
THAT'S RIGHT!
I THINK AFTER THE "MASA" IS AN "I"!
NOD NOD NOD
OKAY!
SO WHAT'S AFTER "I"?
"I RO HA NI HO HE TO..."

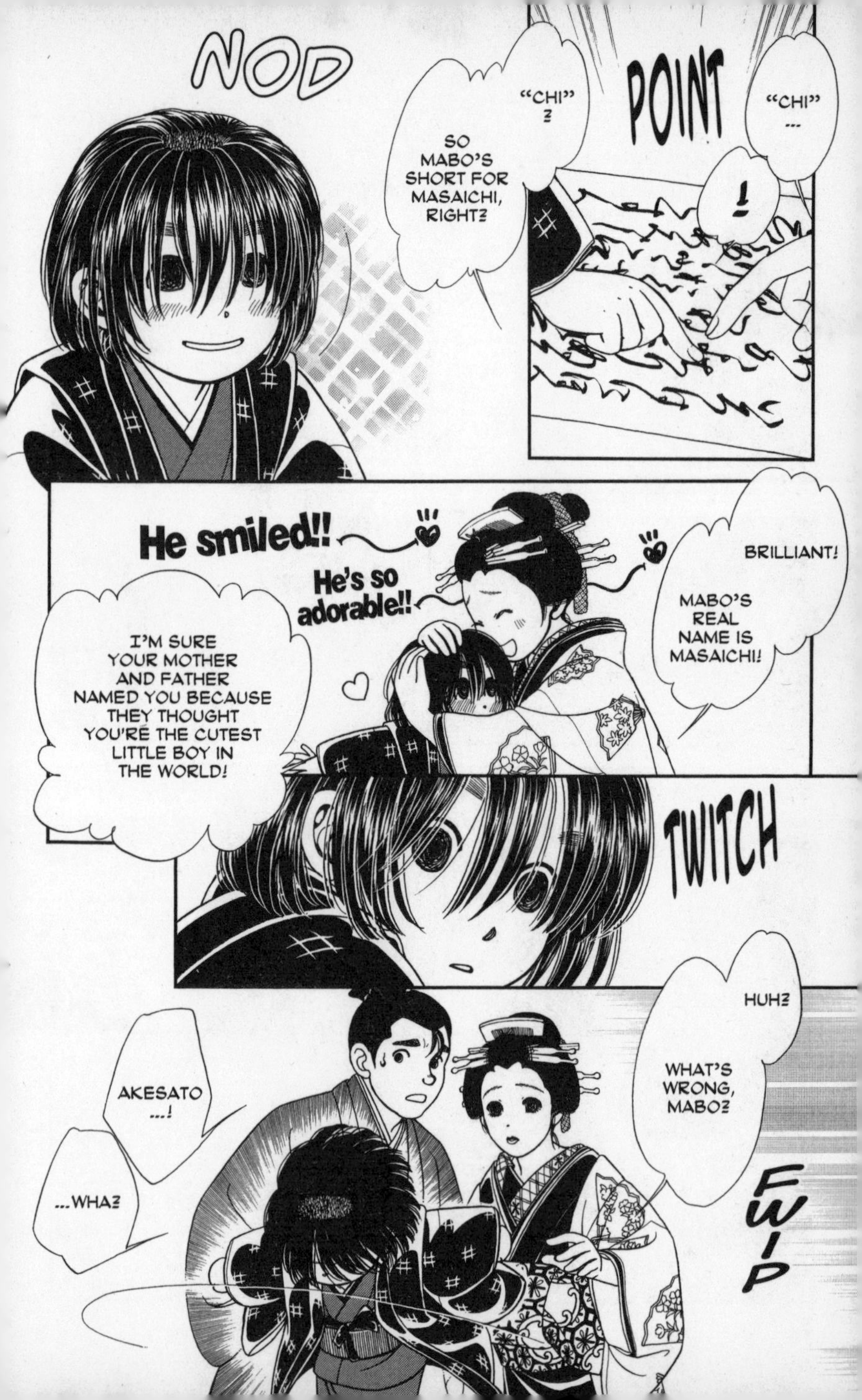
POINT
"CHI" ...
!
"CHI"?
SO MABO'S SHORT FOR MASAICHI, RIGHT?
NOD
BRILLIANT!
MABO'S REAL NAME IS MASAICHI!
He smiled!!
He's so adorable!!
I'M SURE YOUR MOTHER AND FATHER NAMED YOU BECAUSE THEY THOUGHT YOU'RE THE CUTEST LITTLE BOY IN THE WORLD!
TWITCH
HUH?
WHAT'S WRONG, MABO?
FWIP
AKESATO ...!
...WHA?

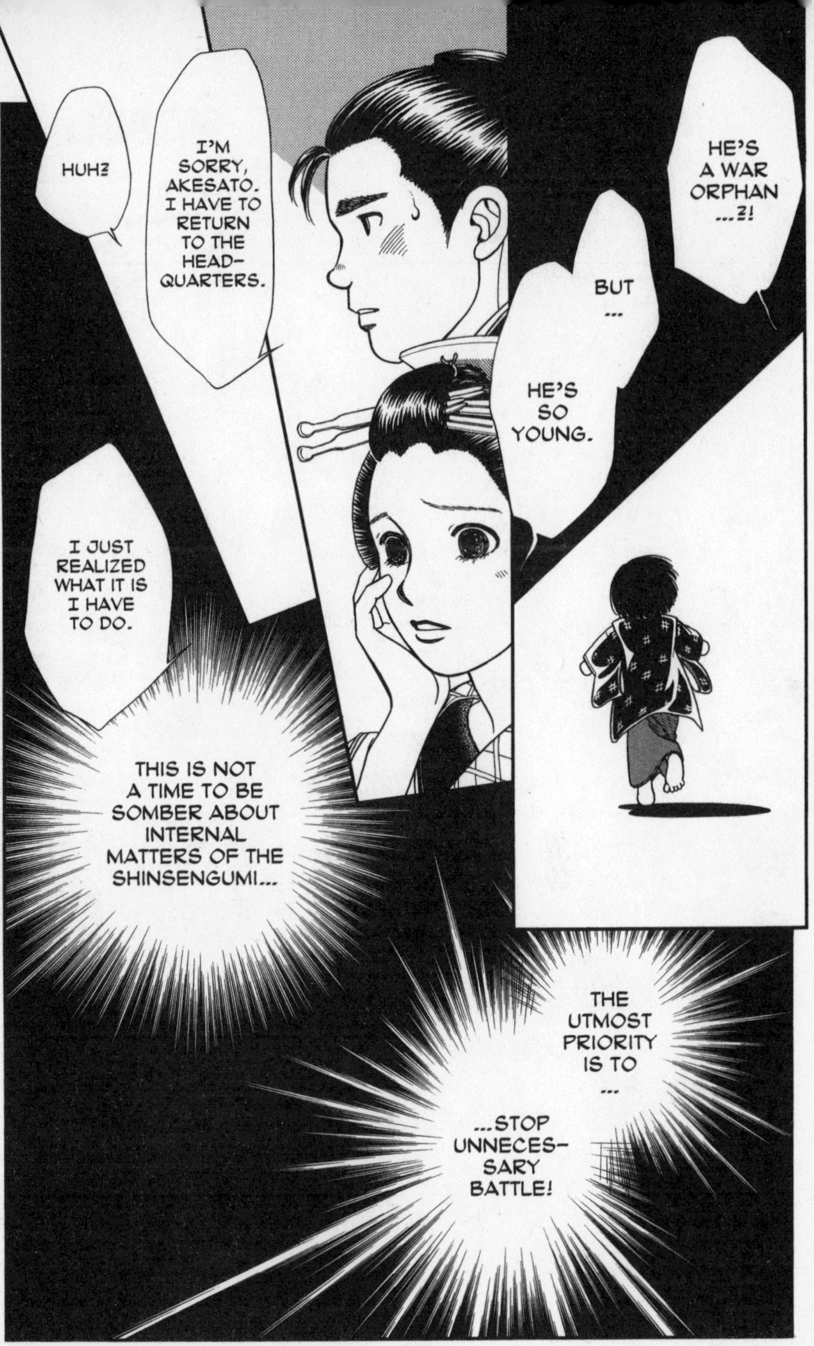
HE'S A WAR ORPHAN ...?!
BUT ...
HE'S SO YOUNG.
I'M SORRY, AKESATO. I HAVE TO RETURN TO THE HEAD-QUARTERS.
HUH?
I JUST REALIZED WHAT IT IS I HAVE TO DO.
THIS IS NOT A TIME TO BE SOMBER ABOUT INTERNAL MATTERS OF THE SHINSENGUMI...
THE UTMOST PRIORITY IS TO ...
...STOP UNNECES-SARY BATTLE!

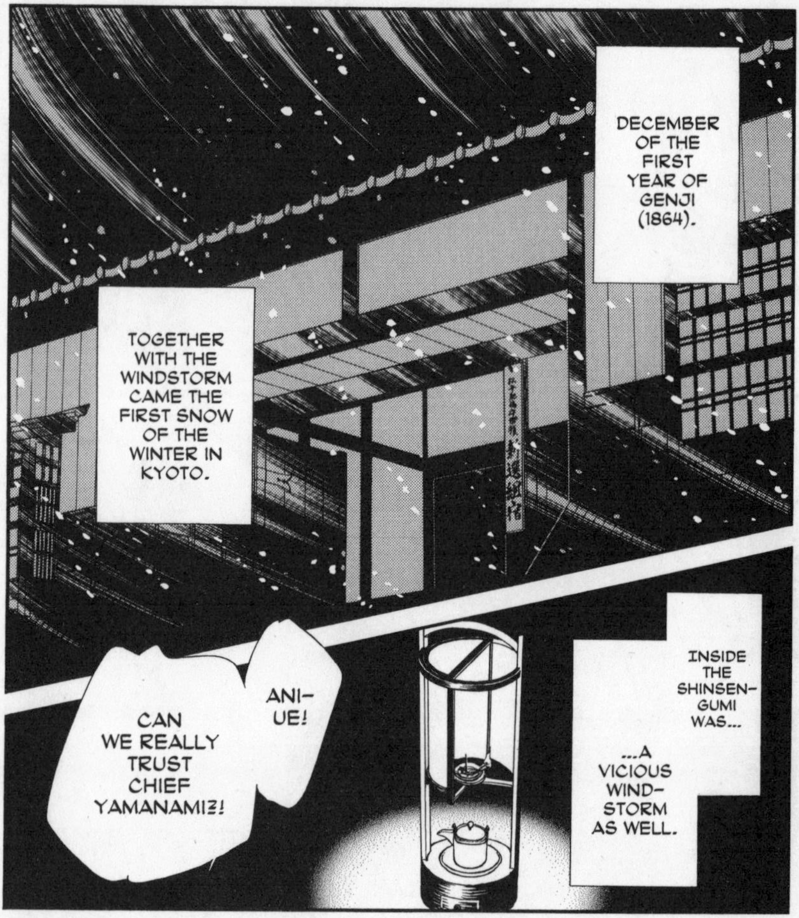
DECEMBER OF THE FIRST YEAR OF GENJI (1864).
TOGETHER WITH THE WINDSTORM CAME THE FIRST SNOW OF THE WINTER IN KYOTO.
INSIDE THE SHINSEN-GUMI WAS...
...A VICIOUS WIND-STORM AS WELL.
ANI-UE!
CAN WE REALLY TRUST CHIEF YAMANAMI?!

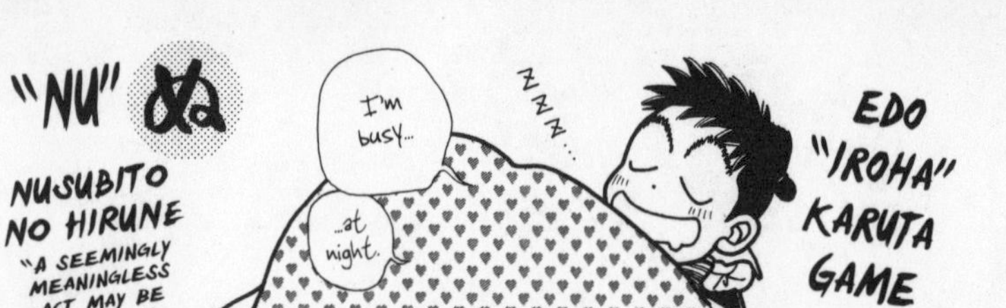
EDO "IROHA" KARUTA GAME
ZZZ...
I'm busy...
...at night.
"NU" ぬ
NUSUBITO NO HIRUNE
"A SEEMINGLY MEANINGLESS ACT MAY BE FRUITFUL"
(lit. A thief's catnap)

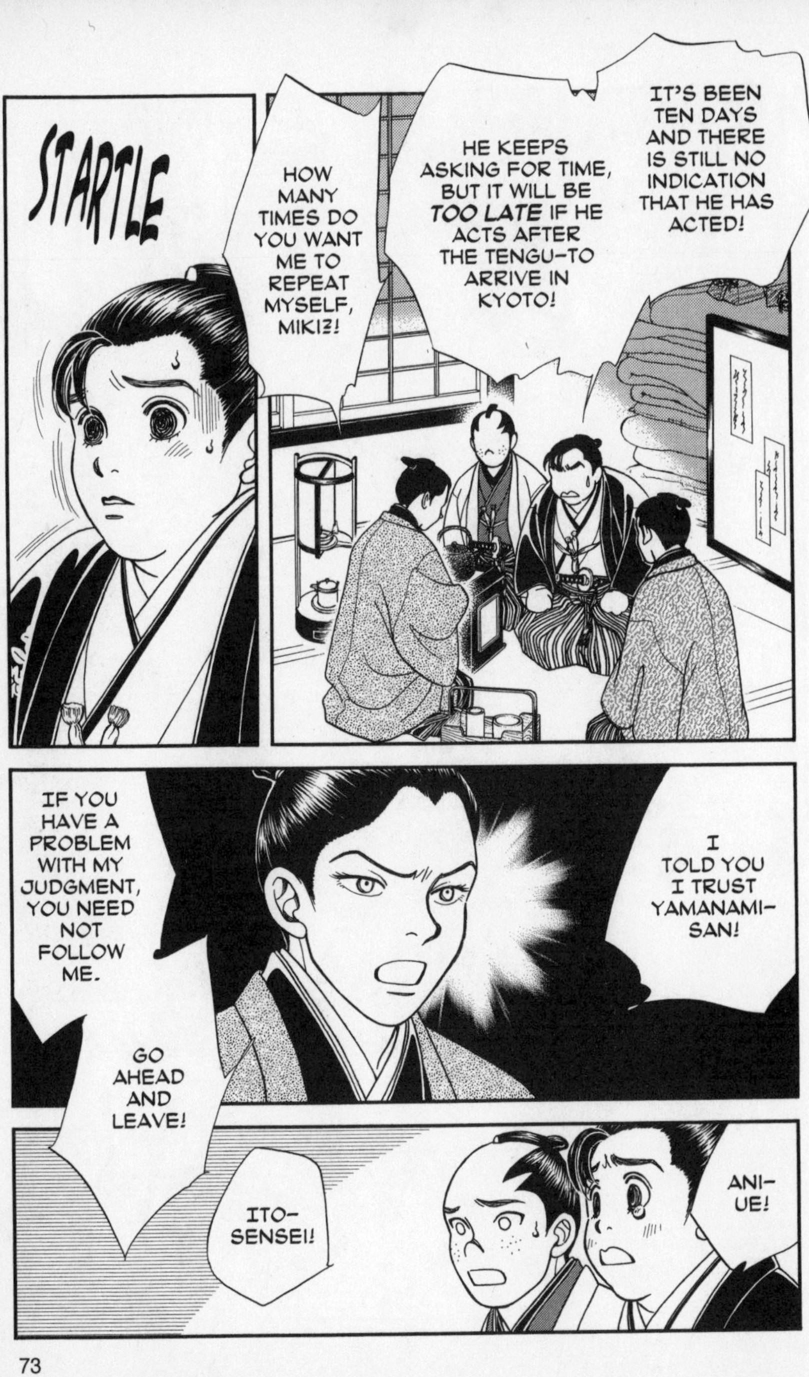
IT'S BEEN TEN DAYS AND THERE IS STILL NO INDICATION THAT HE HAS ACTED!
HE KEEPS ASKING FOR TIME, BUT IT WILL BE TOO LATE IF HE ACTS AFTER THE TENGU-TO ARRIVE IN KYOTO!
HOW MANY TIMES DO YOU WANT ME TO REPEAT MYSELF, MIKI?!
STARTLE
I TOLD YOU I TRUST YAMANAMI-SAN!
IF YOU HAVE A PROBLEM WITH MY JUDGMENT, YOU NEED NOT FOLLOW ME.
GO AHEAD AND LEAVE!
ANI-UE!
ITO-SENSEI!

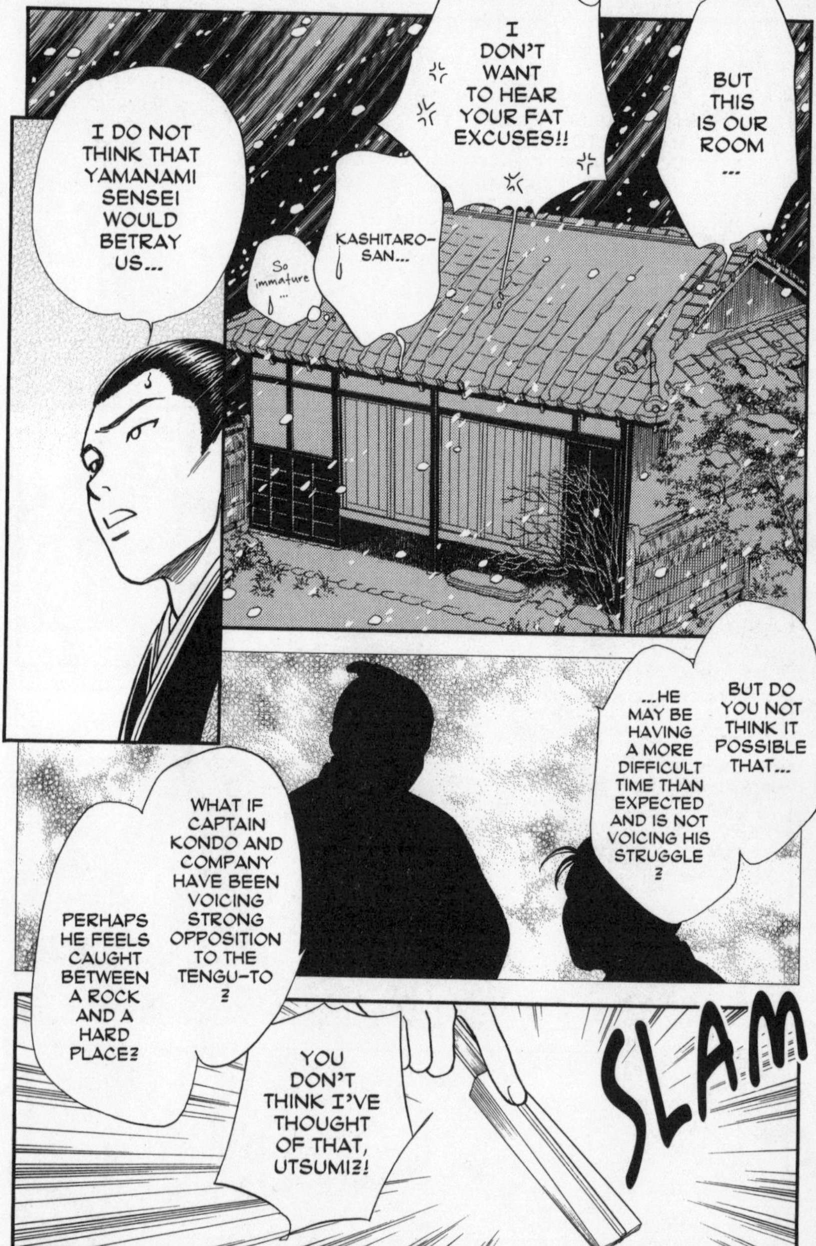
BUT THIS IS OUR ROOM ...
I DON'T WANT TO HEAR YOUR FAT EXCUSES!!
KASHITARO-SAN...
So immature ...
I DO NOT THINK THAT YAMANAMI SENSEI WOULD BETRAY US...
BUT DO YOU NOT THINK IT POSSIBLE THAT...
...HE MAY BE HAVING A MORE DIFFICULT TIME THAN EXPECTED AND IS NOT VOICING HIS STRUGGLE?
WHAT IF CAPTAIN KONDO AND COMPANY HAVE BEEN VOICING STRONG OPPOSITION TO THE TENGU-TO?
PERHAPS HE FEELS CAUGHT BETWEEN A ROCK AND A HARD PLACE?
SLAM
YOU DON'T THINK I'VE THOUGHT OF THAT, UTSUMI?!

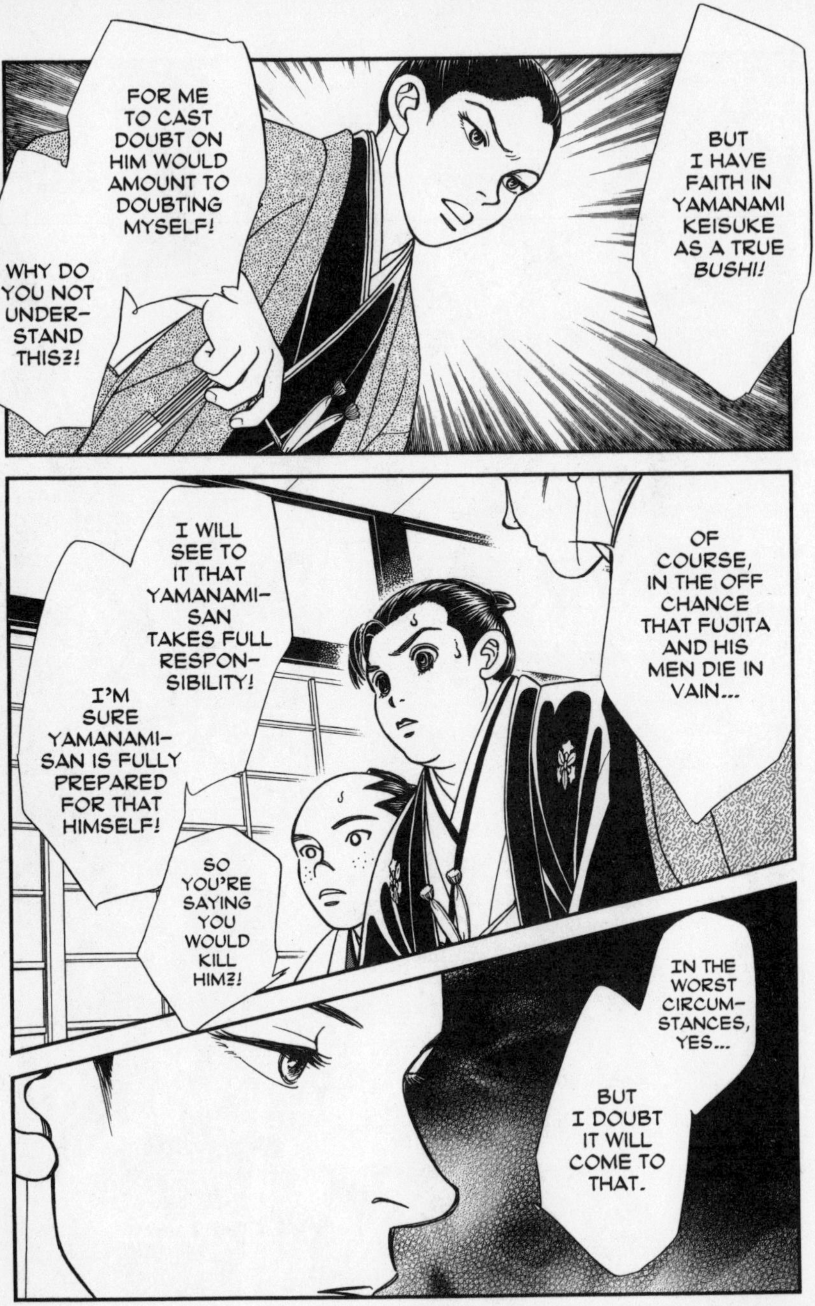
BUT I HAVE FAITH IN YAMANAMI KEISUKE AS A TRUE *BUSHI!*
FOR ME TO CAST DOUBT ON HIM WOULD AMOUNT TO DOUBTING MYSELF!
WHY DO YOU NOT UNDER-STAND THIS?!
OF COURSE, IN THE OFF CHANCE THAT FUJITA AND HIS MEN DIE IN VAIN...
I WILL SEE TO IT THAT YAMANAMI-SAN TAKES FULL RESPON-SIBILITY!
I'M SURE YAMANAMI-SAN IS FULLY PREPARED FOR THAT HIMSELF!
SO YOU'RE SAYING YOU WOULD KILL HIM?!
IN THE WORST CIRCUM-STANCES, YES...
BUT I DOUBT IT WILL COME TO THAT.

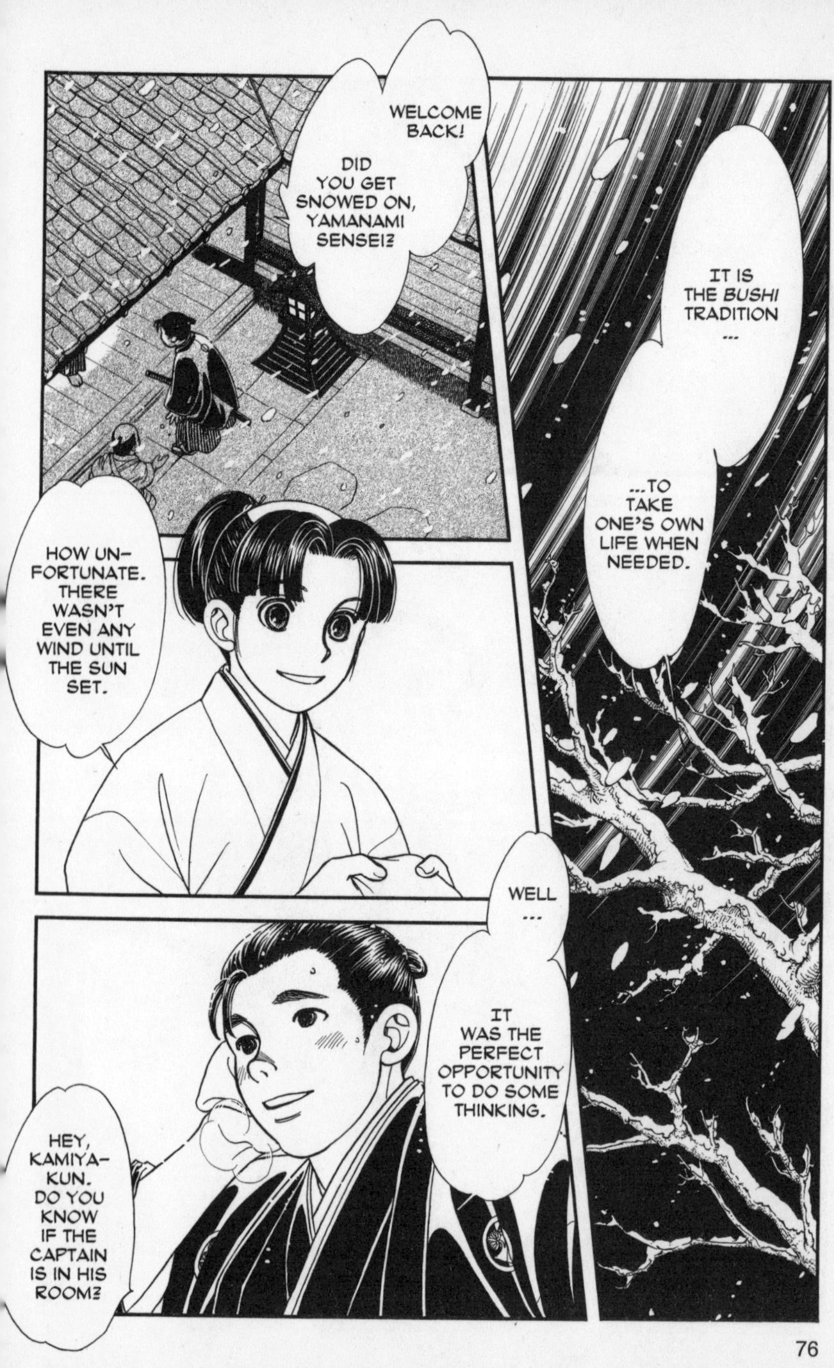
IT IS THE *BUSHI* TRADITION ...
...TO TAKE ONE'S OWN LIFE WHEN NEEDED.
WELCOME BACK!
DID YOU GET SNOWED ON, YAMANAMI SENSEI?
HOW UN-FORTUNATE. THERE WASN'T EVEN ANY WIND UNTIL THE SUN SET.
WELL ...
IT WAS THE PERFECT OPPORTUNITY TO DO SOME THINKING.
HEY, KAMIYA-KUN. DO YOU KNOW IF THE CAPTAIN IS IN HIS ROOM?

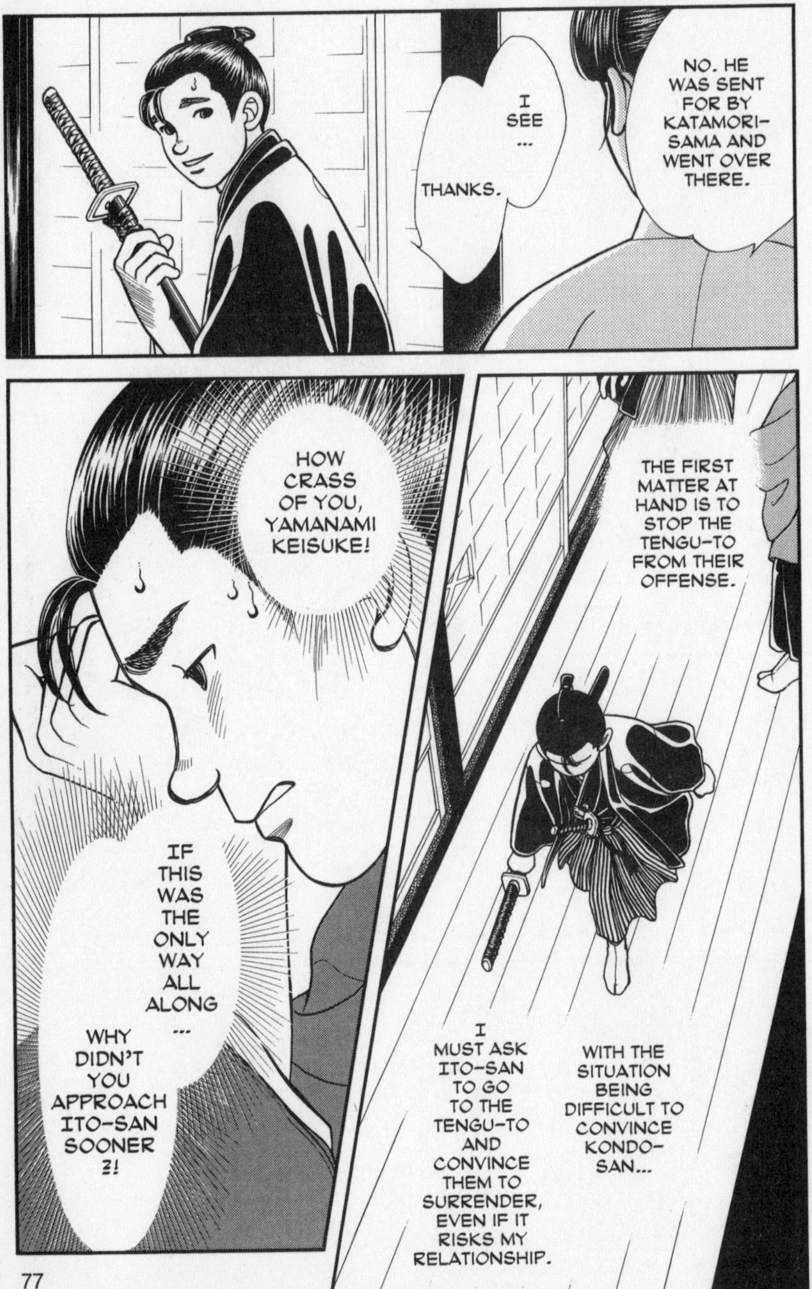
NO. HE WAS SENT FOR BY KATAMORI-SAMA AND WENT OVER THERE.
I SEE... THANKS.
THE FIRST MATTER AT HAND IS TO STOP THE TENGU-TO FROM THEIR OFFENSE.
WITH THE SITUATION BEING DIFFICULT TO CONVINCE KONDO-SAN...
I MUST ASK ITO-SAN TO GO TO THE TENGU-TO AND CONVINCE THEM TO SURRENDER, EVEN IF IT RISKS MY RELATIONSHIP.
HOW CRASS OF YOU, YAMANAMI KEISUKE!
IF THIS WAS THE ONLY WAY ALL ALONG...
WHY DIDN'T YOU APPROACH ITO-SAN SOONER?!

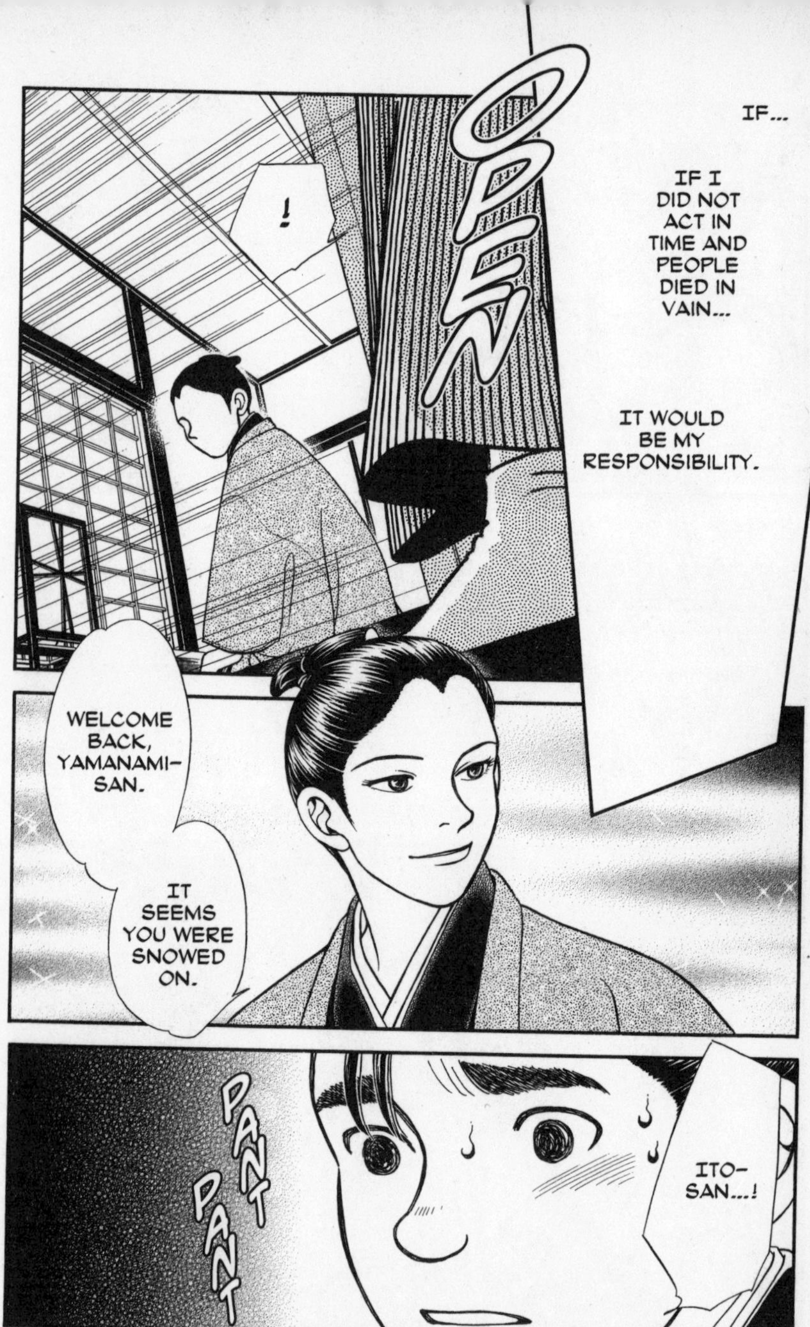
IF...
IF I DID NOT ACT IN TIME AND PEOPLE DIED IN VAIN...
IT WOULD BE MY RESPONSIBILITY.
OPEN
!
WELCOME BACK, YAMANAMI-SAN.
IT SEEMS YOU WERE SNOWED ON.
ITO-SAN...!
PANT PANT

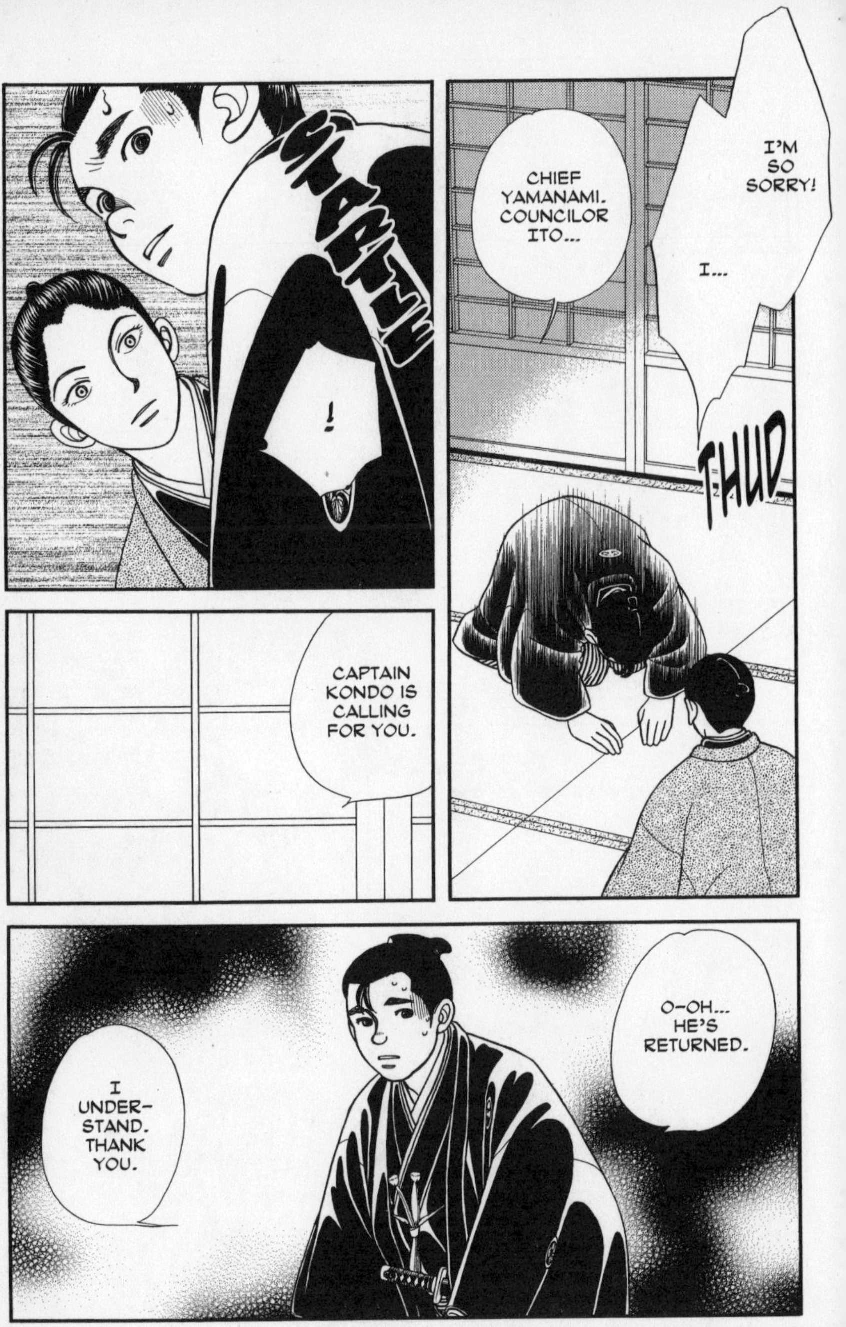
I'M SO SORRY!
I...
CHIEF YAMANAMI. COUNCILOR ITO...
THUD
SLAM
!
CAPTAIN KONDO IS CALLING FOR YOU.
O-OH... HE'S RETURNED.
I UNDERSTAND. THANK YOU.

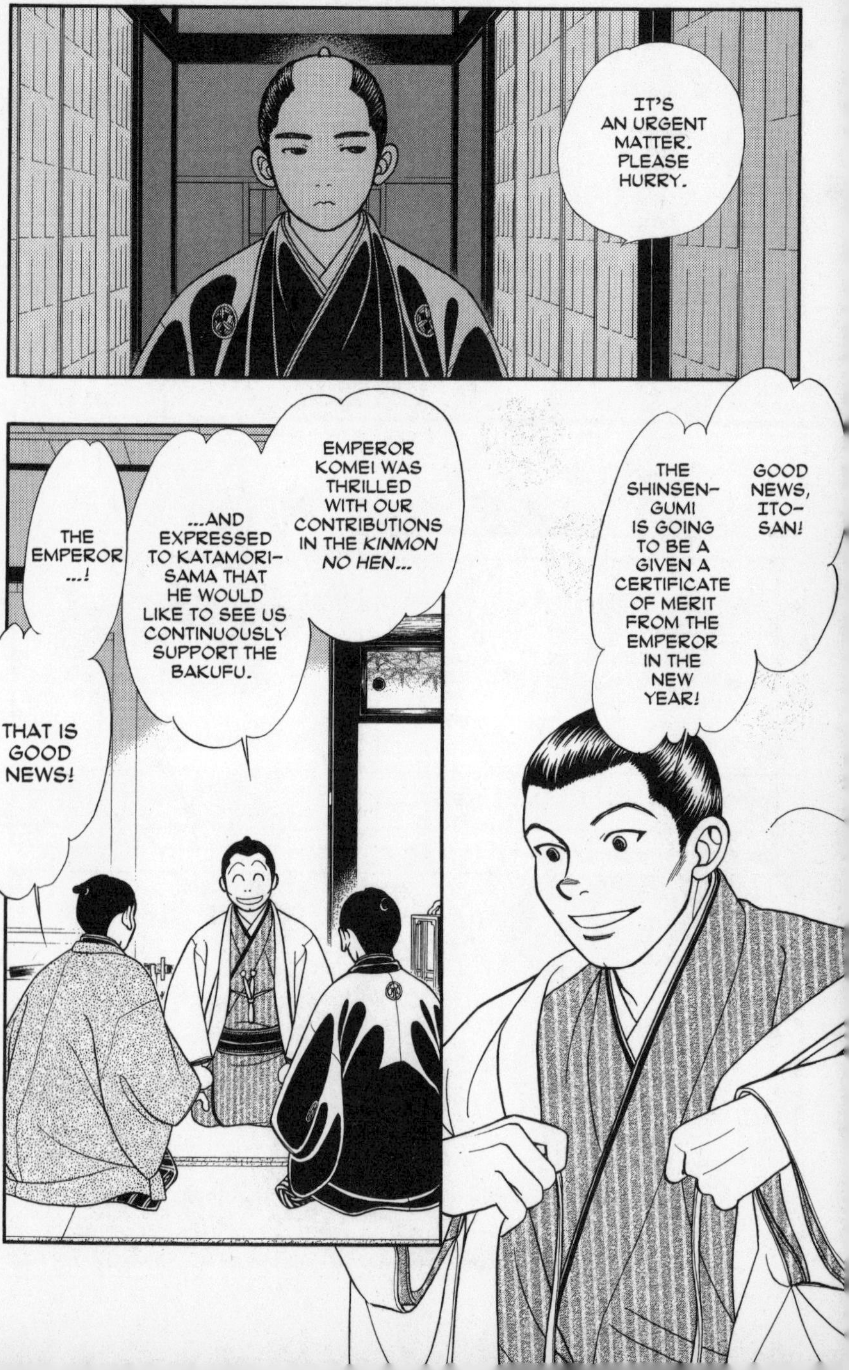
IT'S AN URGENT MATTER. PLEASE HURRY.
GOOD NEWS, ITO-SAN!
THE SHINSEN-GUMI IS GOING TO BE A GIVEN A CERTIFICATE OF MERIT FROM THE EMPEROR IN THE NEW YEAR!
EMPEROR KOMEI WAS THRILLED WITH OUR CONTRIBUTIONS IN THE *KINMON NO HEN*...
...AND EXPRESSED TO KATAMORI-SAMA THAT HE WOULD LIKE TO SEE US CONTINUOUSLY SUPPORT THE BAKUFU.
THE EMPEROR ...!
THAT IS GOOD NEWS!

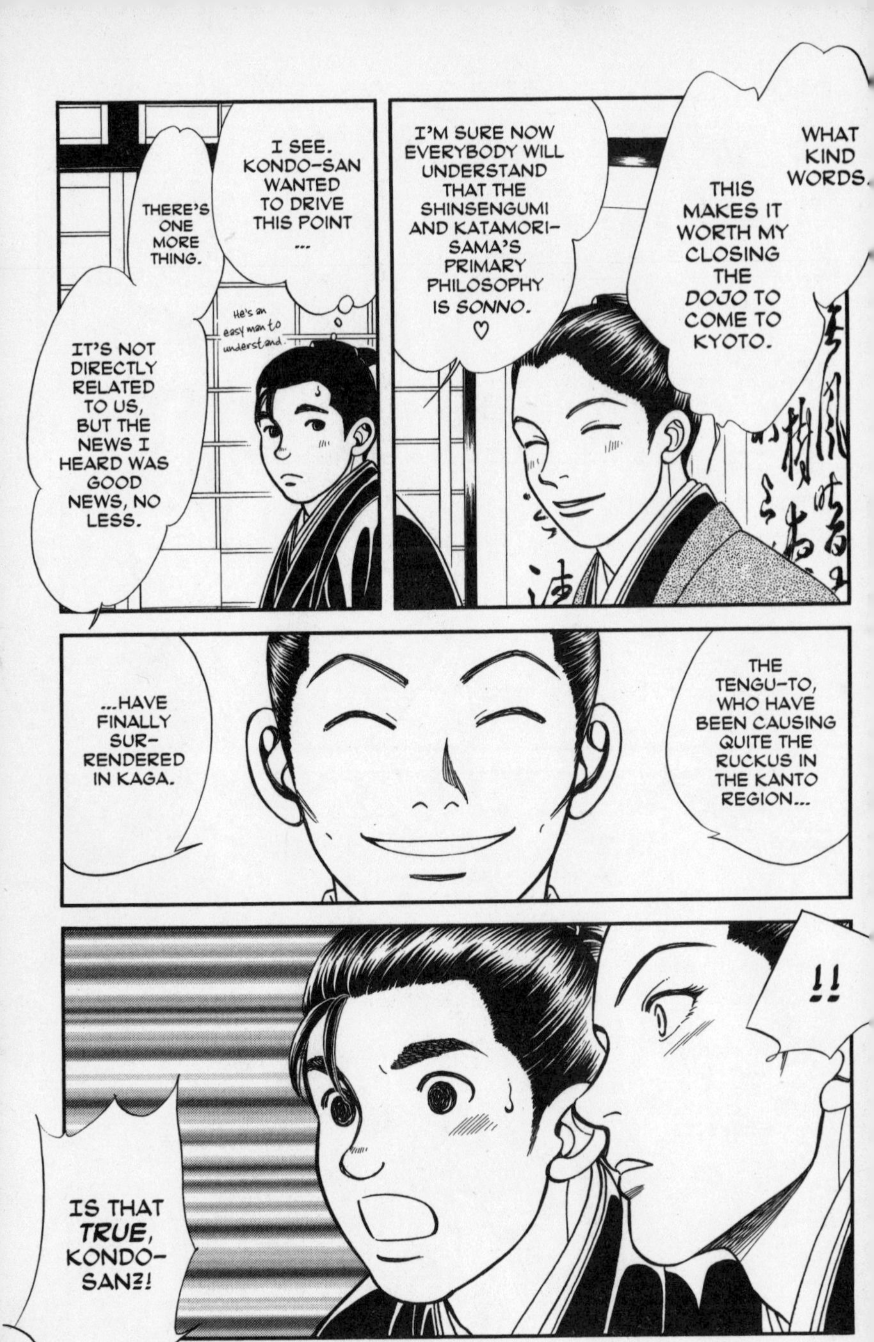

WHAT KIND WORDS.
THIS MAKES IT WORTH MY CLOSING THE *DOJO* TO COME TO KYOTO.
I'M SURE NOW EVERYBODY WILL UNDERSTAND THAT THE SHINSENGUMI AND KATAMORI-SAMA'S PRIMARY PHILOSOPHY IS *SONNO*. ♡
I SEE. KONDO-SAN WANTED TO DRIVE THIS POINT ...
He's an easy man to understand.
THERE'S ONE MORE THING.
IT'S NOT DIRECTLY RELATED TO US, BUT THE NEWS I HEARD WAS GOOD NEWS, NO LESS.
THE TENGU-TO, WHO HAVE BEEN CAUSING QUITE THE RUCKUS IN THE KANTO REGION...
...HAVE FINALLY SUR-RENDERED IN KAGA.
!!
IS THAT ***TRUE***, KONDO-SAN?!

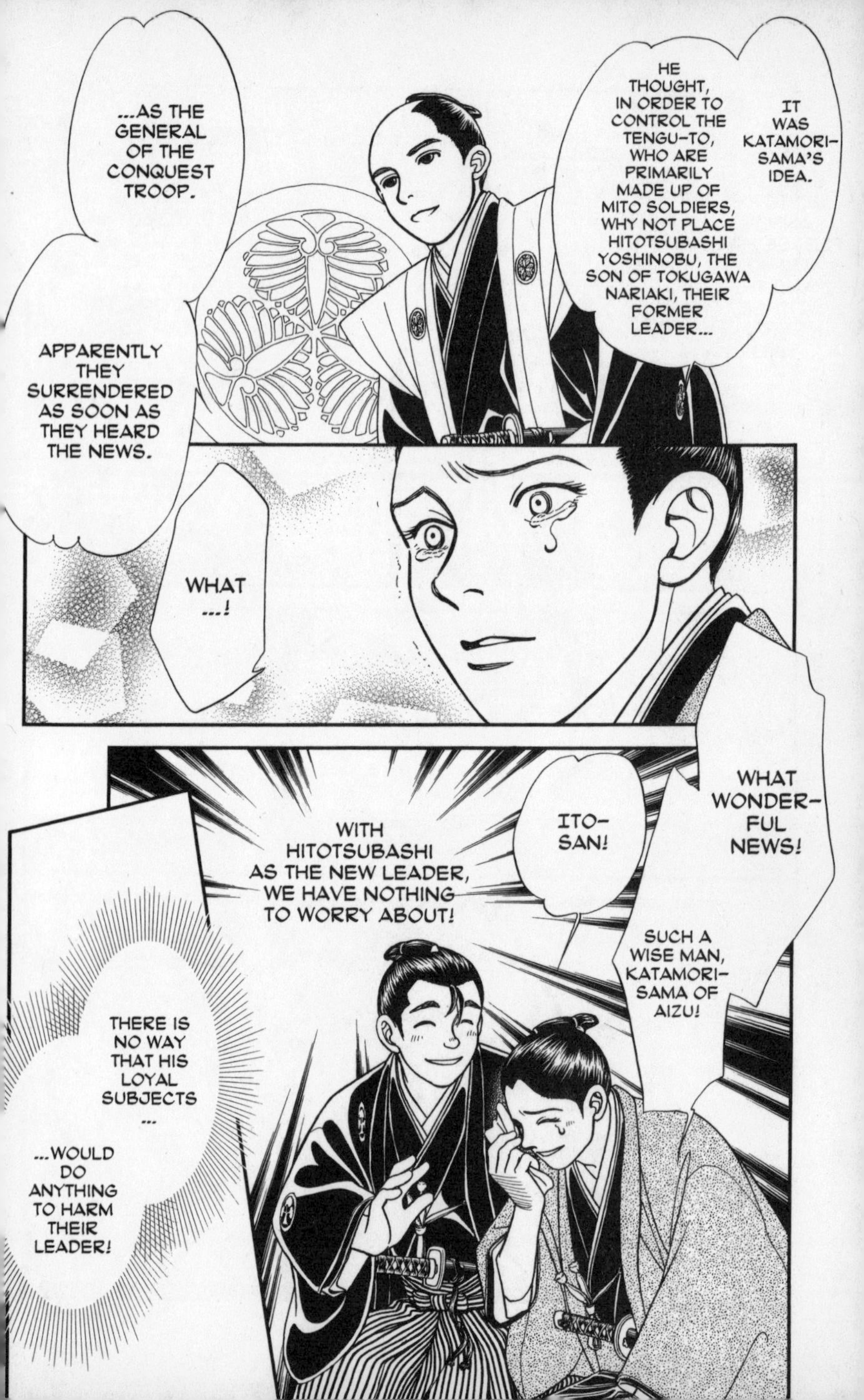
IT WAS KATAMORI-SAMA'S IDEA.
HE THOUGHT, IN ORDER TO CONTROL THE TENGU-TO, WHO ARE PRIMARILY MADE UP OF MITO SOLDIERS, WHY NOT PLACE HITOTSUBASHI YOSHINOBU, THE SON OF TOKUGAWA NARIAKI, THEIR FORMER LEADER...
...AS THE GENERAL OF THE CONQUEST TROOP.
APPARENTLY THEY SURRENDERED AS SOON AS THEY HEARD THE NEWS.
WHAT ...!
WHAT WONDER-FUL NEWS!
ITO-SAN!
WITH HITOTSUBASHI AS THE NEW LEADER, WE HAVE NOTHING TO WORRY ABOUT!
SUCH A WISE MAN, KATAMORI-SAMA OF AIZU!
THERE IS NO WAY THAT HIS LOYAL SUBJECTS ...
...WOULD DO ANYTHING TO HARM THEIR LEADER!

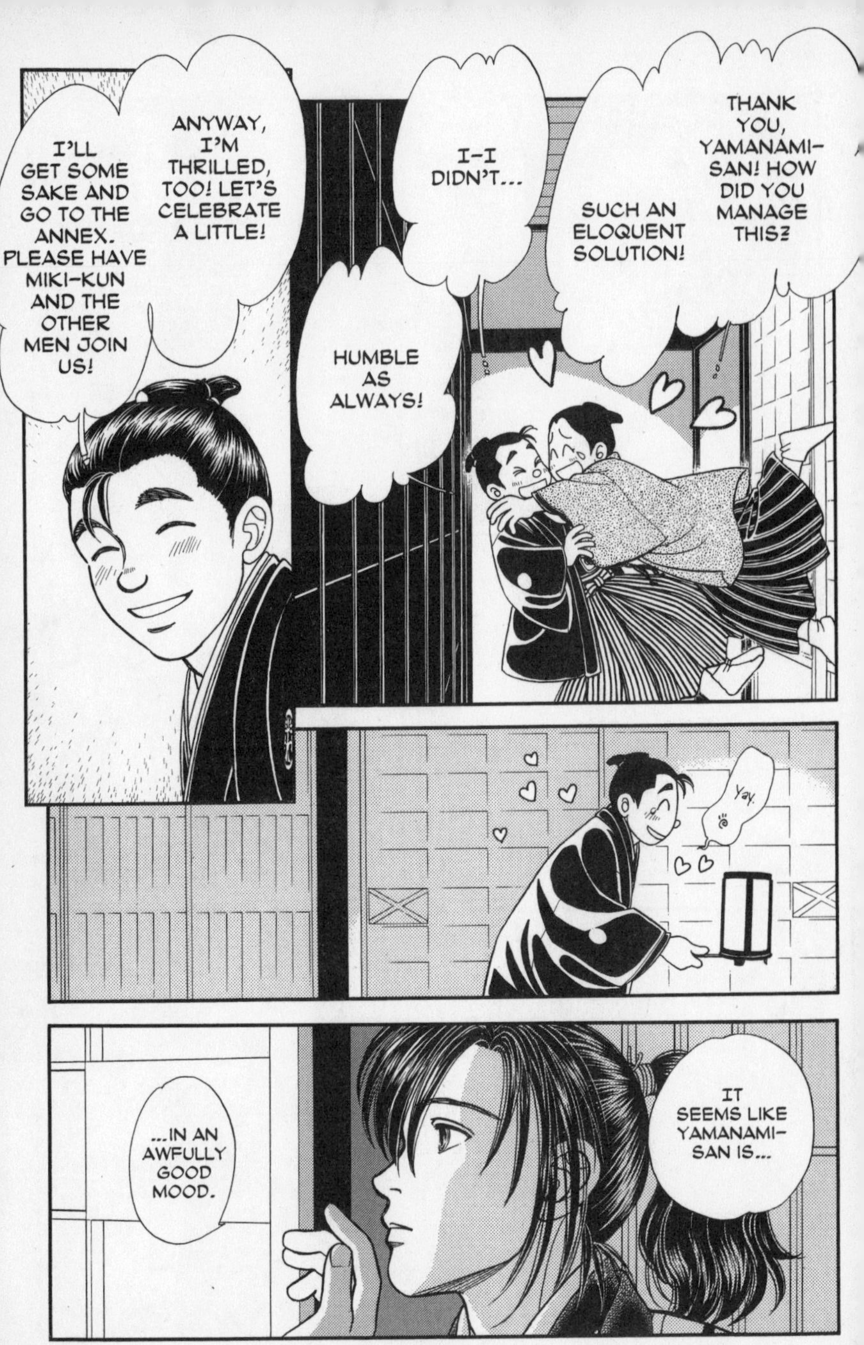
THANK YOU, YAMANAMI-SAN! HOW DID YOU MANAGE THIS?
SUCH AN ELOQUENT SOLUTION!
I-I DIDN'T...
HUMBLE AS ALWAYS!
ANYWAY, I'M THRILLED, TOO! LET'S CELEBRATE A LITTLE!
I'LL GET SOME SAKE AND GO TO THE ANNEX. PLEASE HAVE MIKI-KUN AND THE OTHER MEN JOIN US!
Yay.
IT SEEMS LIKE YAMANAMI-SAN IS...
...IN AN AWFULLY GOOD MOOD.

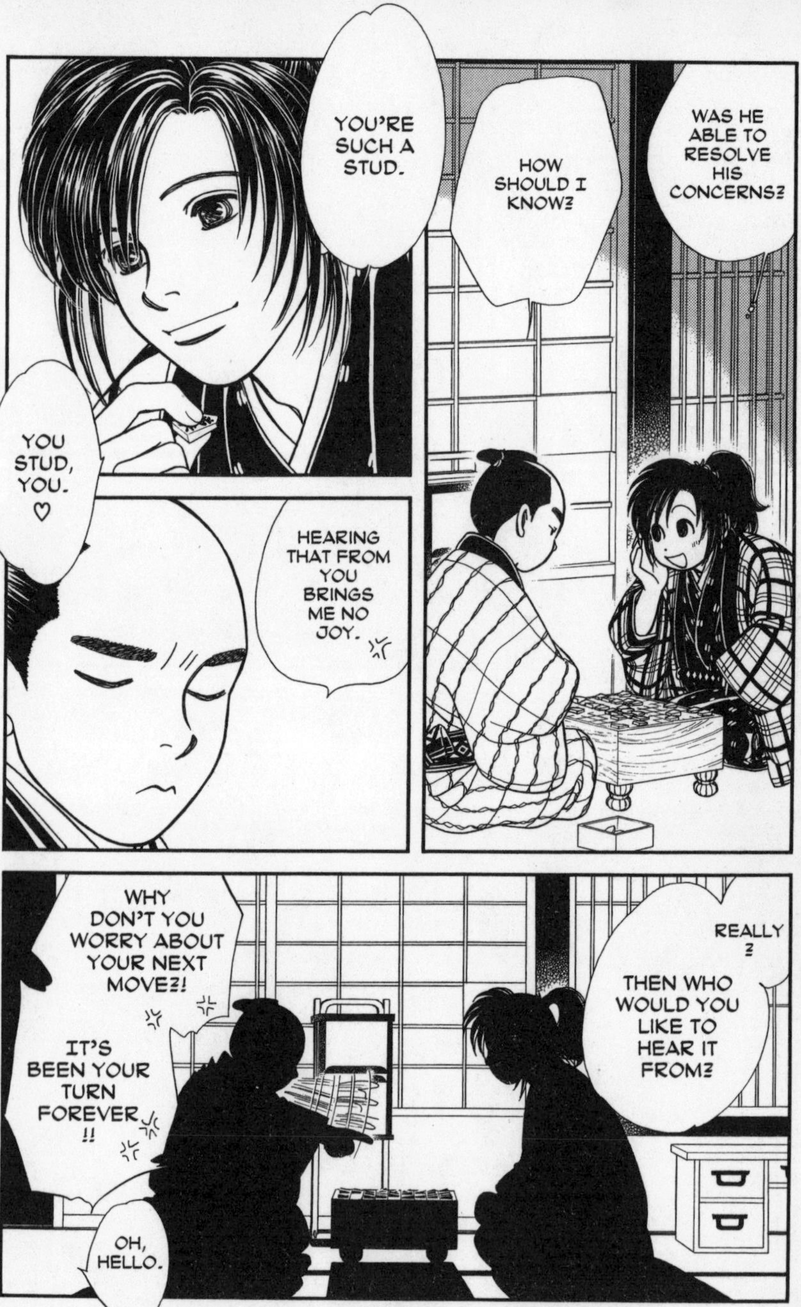
WAS HE ABLE TO RESOLVE HIS CONCERNS?
HOW SHOULD I KNOW?
YOU'RE SUCH A STUD.
YOU STUD, YOU. ♡
HEARING THAT FROM YOU BRINGS ME NO JOY.
REALLY?
THEN WHO WOULD YOU LIKE TO HEAR IT FROM?
WHY DON'T YOU WORRY ABOUT YOUR NEXT MOVE?!
IT'S BEEN YOUR TURN FOREVER!!
OH, HELLO.

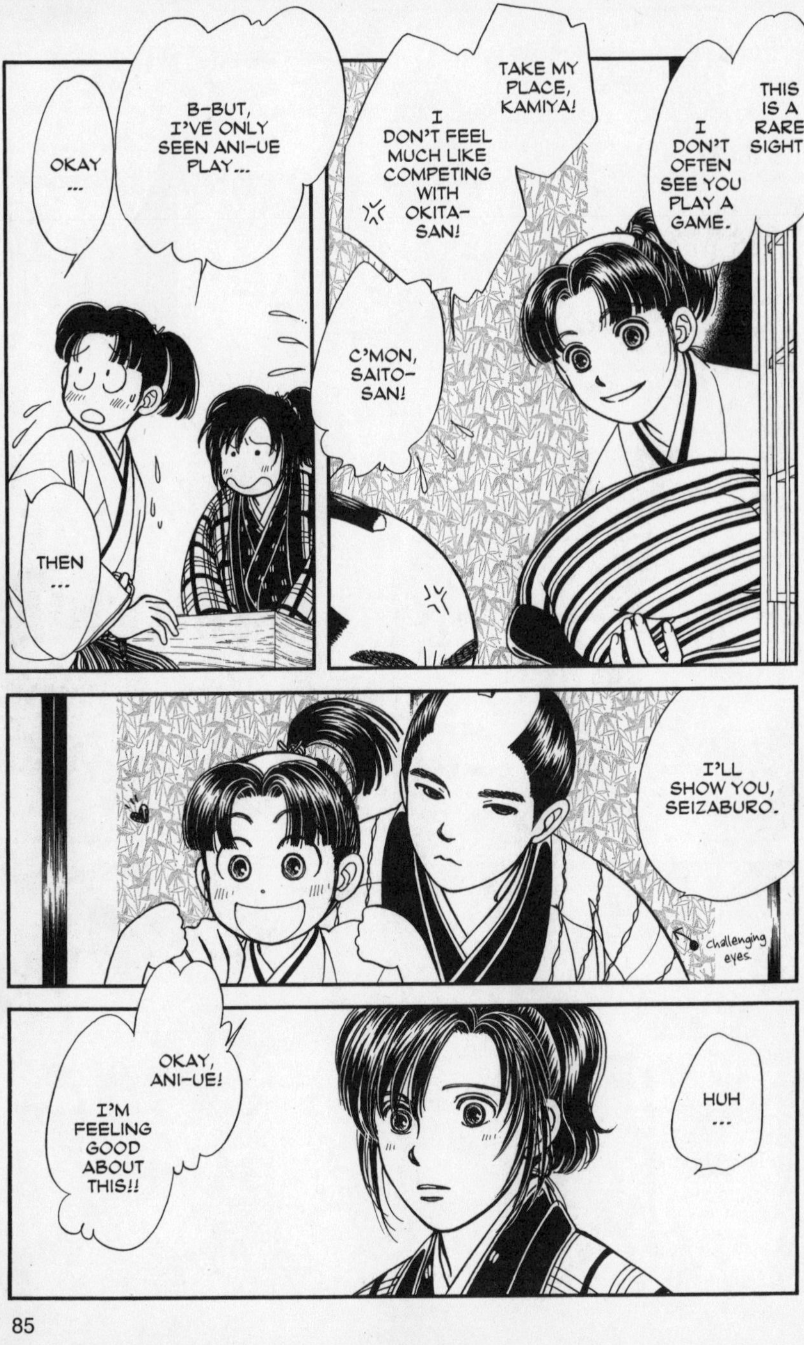
THIS IS A RARE SIGHT.
I DON'T OFTEN SEE YOU PLAY A GAME.
TAKE MY PLACE, KAMIYA!
I DON'T FEEL MUCH LIKE COMPETING WITH OKITA-SAN!
C'MON, SAITO-SAN!
B-BUT, I'VE ONLY SEEN ANI-UE PLAY...
OKAY ...
THEN ...
I'LL SHOW YOU, SEIZABURO.
challenging eyes.
HUH ...
OKAY, ANI-UE!
I'M FEELING GOOD ABOUT THIS!!

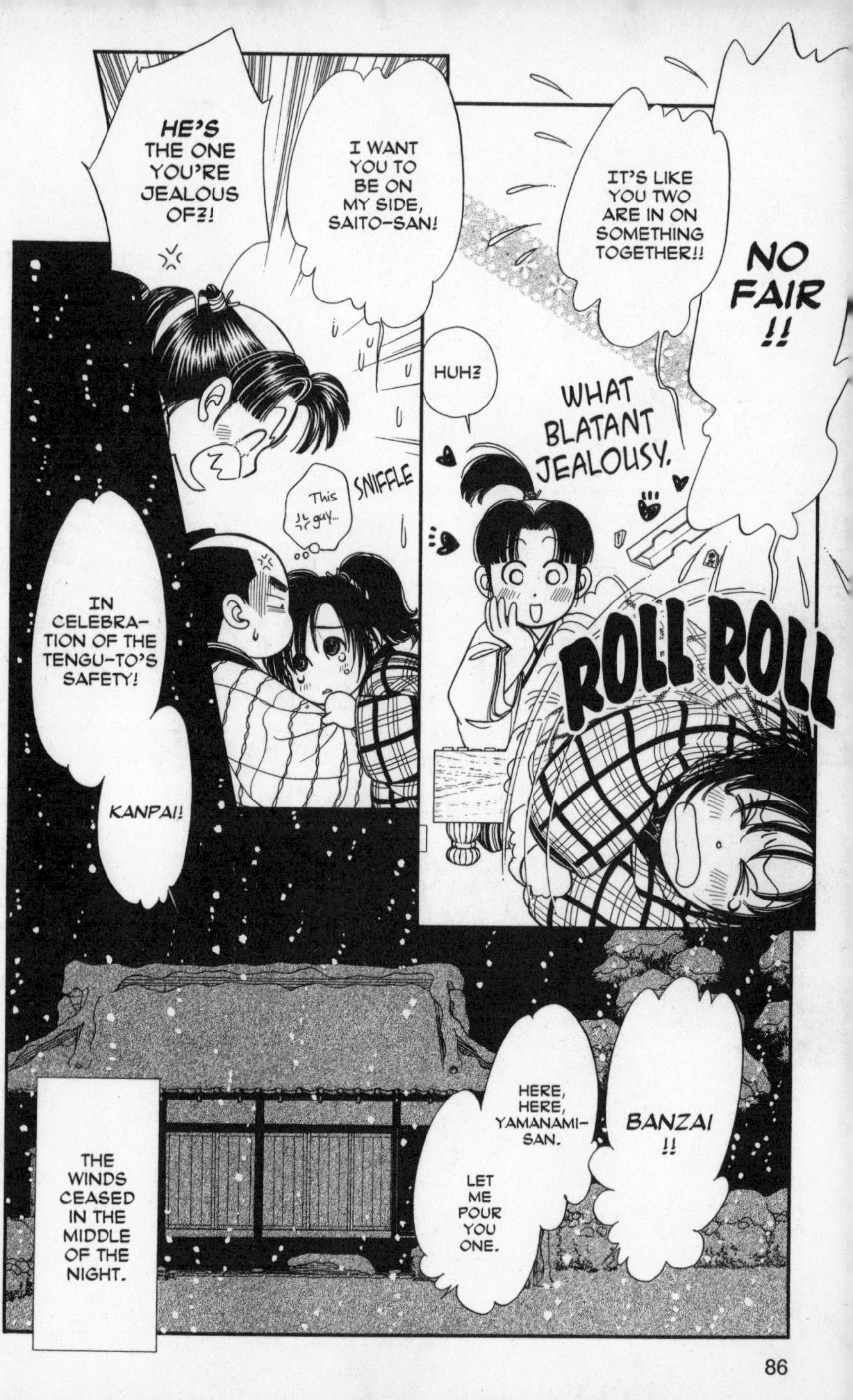
NO FAIR !!
IT'S LIKE YOU TWO ARE IN ON SOMETHING TOGETHER!!
HUH?
WHAT BLATANT JEALOUSY.
ROLL ROLL
I WANT YOU TO BE ON MY SIDE, SAITO-SAN!
HE'S THE ONE YOU'RE JEALOUS OF?!
SNIFFLE
This guy...
IN CELEBRATION OF THE TENGU-TO'S SAFETY!
KANPAI!
BANZAI !!
HERE, HERE, YAMANAMI-SAN.
LET ME POUR YOU ONE.
THE WINDS CEASED IN THE MIDDLE OF THE NIGHT.

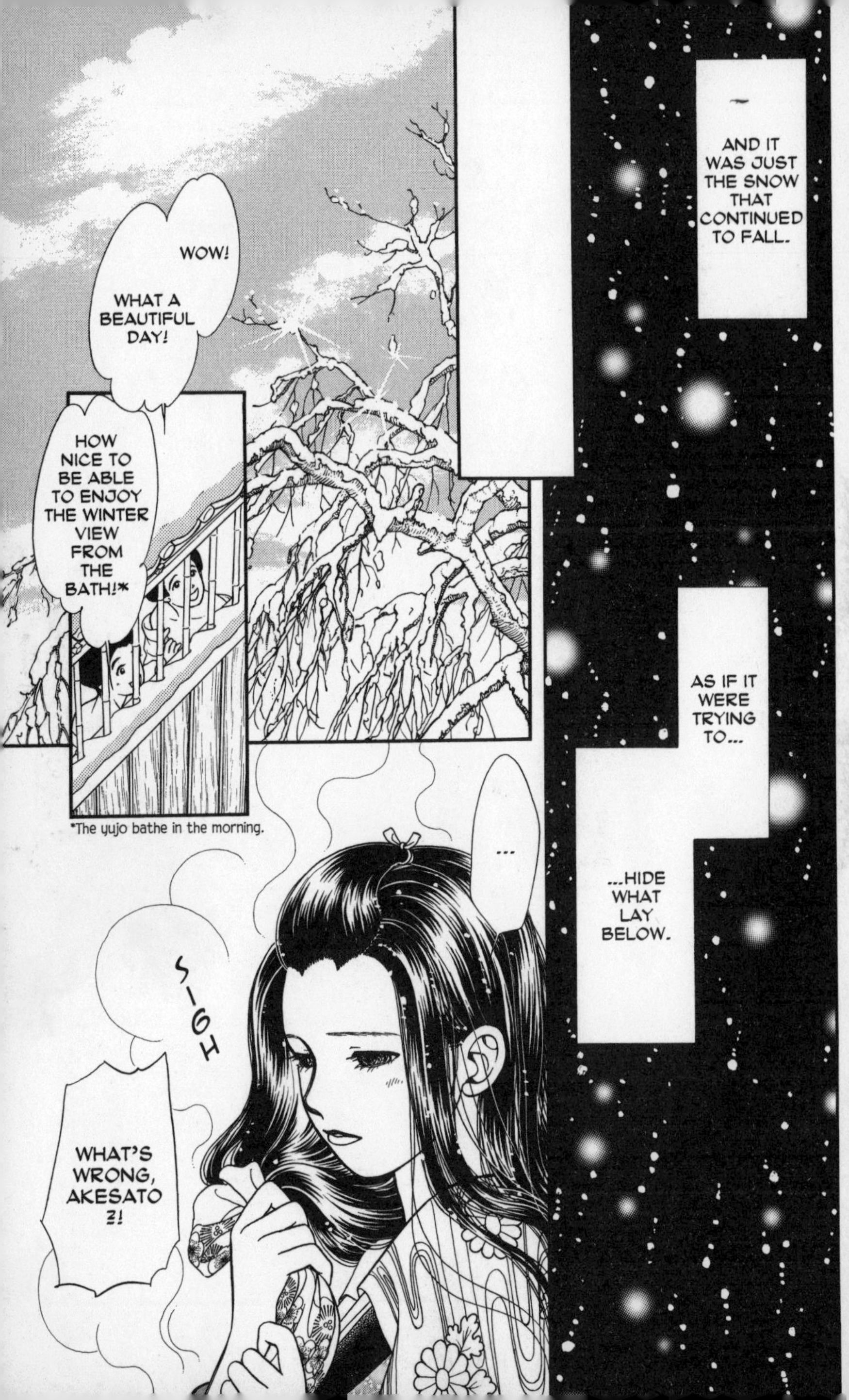
AND IT WAS JUST THE SNOW THAT CONTINUED TO FALL.
AS IF IT WERE TRYING TO...
...HIDE WHAT LAY BELOW.
WOW!
WHAT A BEAUTIFUL DAY!
HOW NICE TO BE ABLE TO ENJOY THE WINTER VIEW FROM THE BATH!*
...
SIGH
WHAT'S WRONG, AKESATO?!
*The yujo bathe in the morning.

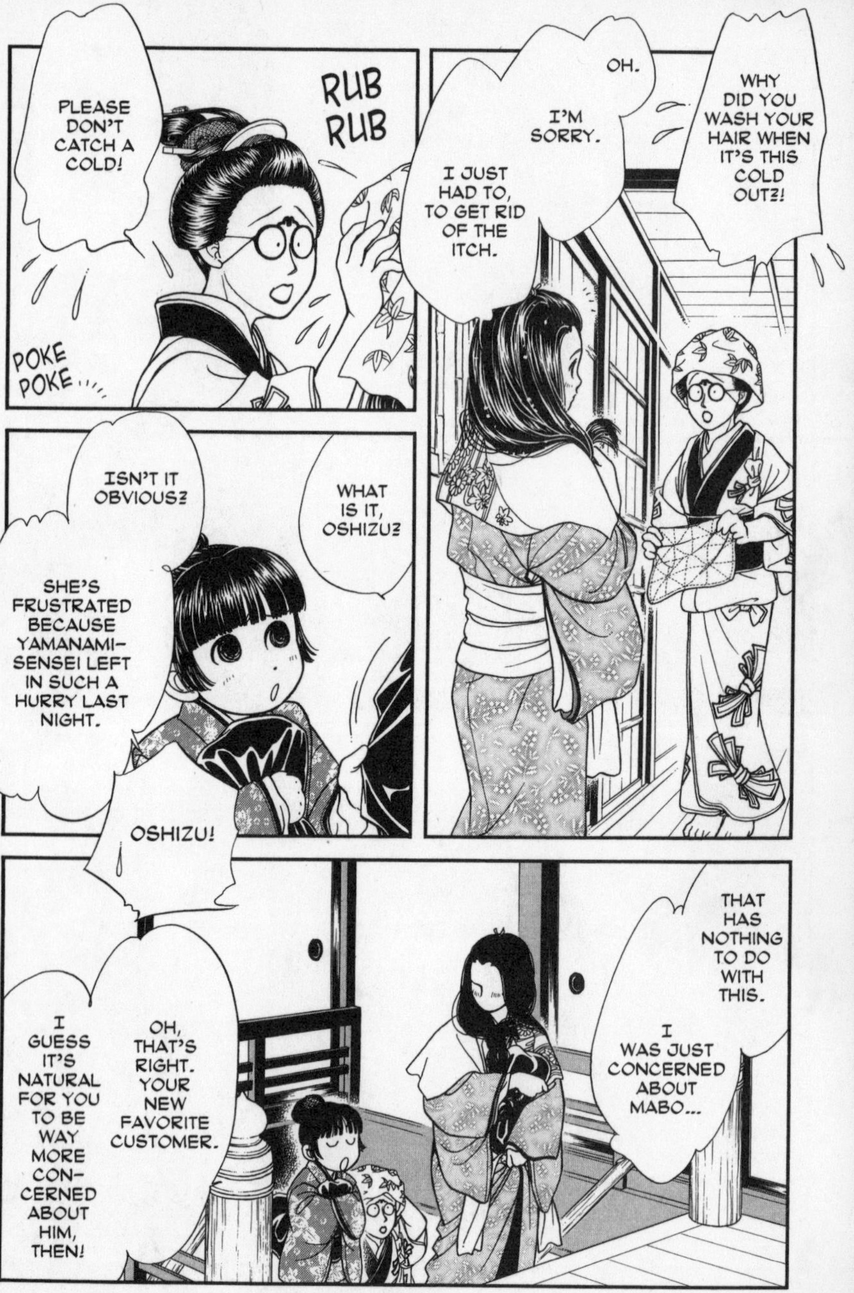
WHY DID YOU WASH YOUR HAIR WHEN IT'S THIS COLD OUT?!
OH.
I'M SORRY.
I JUST HAD TO, TO GET RID OF THE ITCH.
RUB RUB
PLEASE DON'T CATCH A COLD!
POKE POKE...
WHAT IS IT, OSHIZU?
ISN'T IT OBVIOUS?
SHE'S FRUSTRATED BECAUSE YAMANAMI-SENSEI LEFT IN SUCH A HURRY LAST NIGHT.
OSHIZU!
THAT HAS NOTHING TO DO WITH THIS.
I WAS JUST CONCERNED ABOUT MABO...
OH, THAT'S RIGHT. YOUR NEW FAVORITE CUSTOMER.
I GUESS IT'S NATURAL FOR YOU TO BE WAY MORE CON-CERNED ABOUT HIM, THEN!

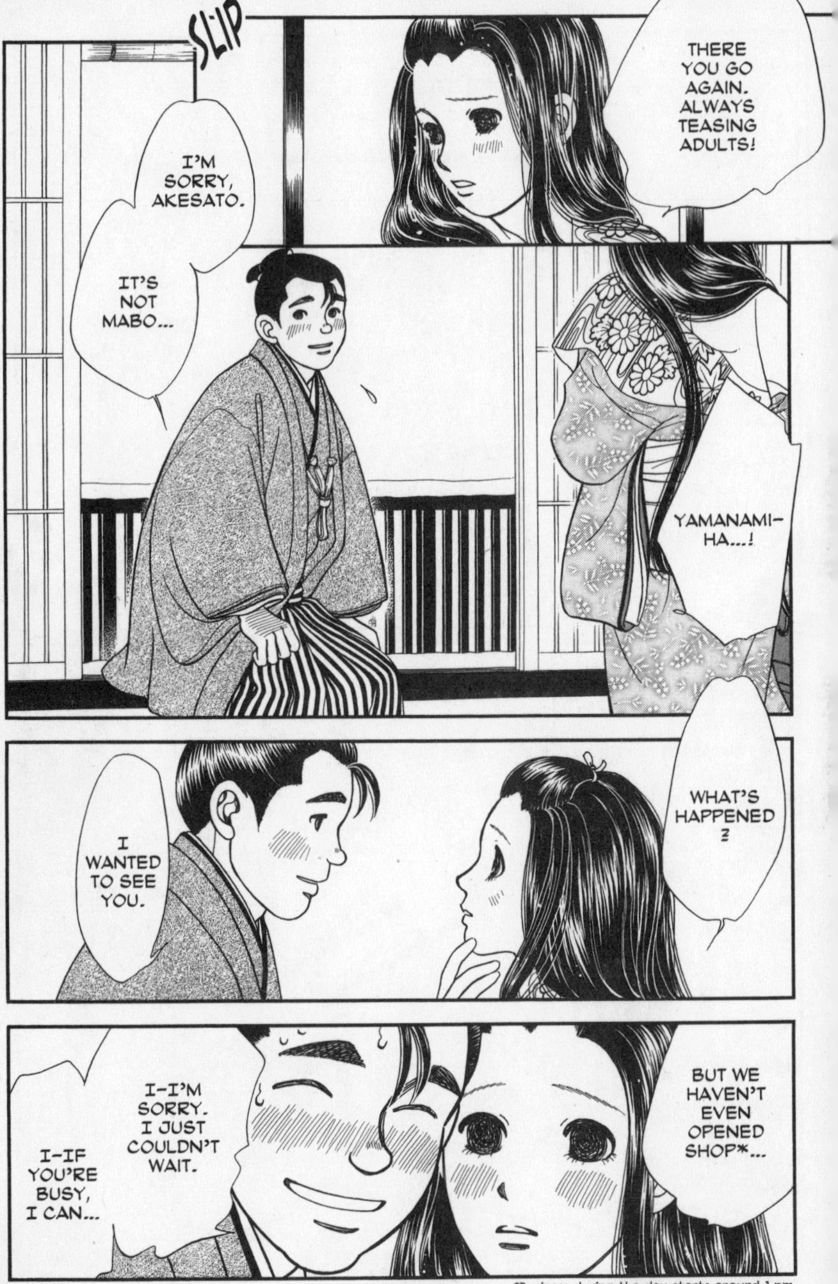
SLIP
THERE YOU GO AGAIN. ALWAYS TEASING ADULTS!
I'M SORRY, AKESATO.
IT'S NOT MABO...
YAMANAMI-HA...!
WHAT'S HAPPENED?
I WANTED TO SEE YOU.
BUT WE HAVEN'T EVEN OPENED SHOP*...
I-I'M SORRY. I JUST COULDN'T WAIT.
I-IF YOU'RE BUSY, I CAN...

*Business during the day starts around 1 pm.

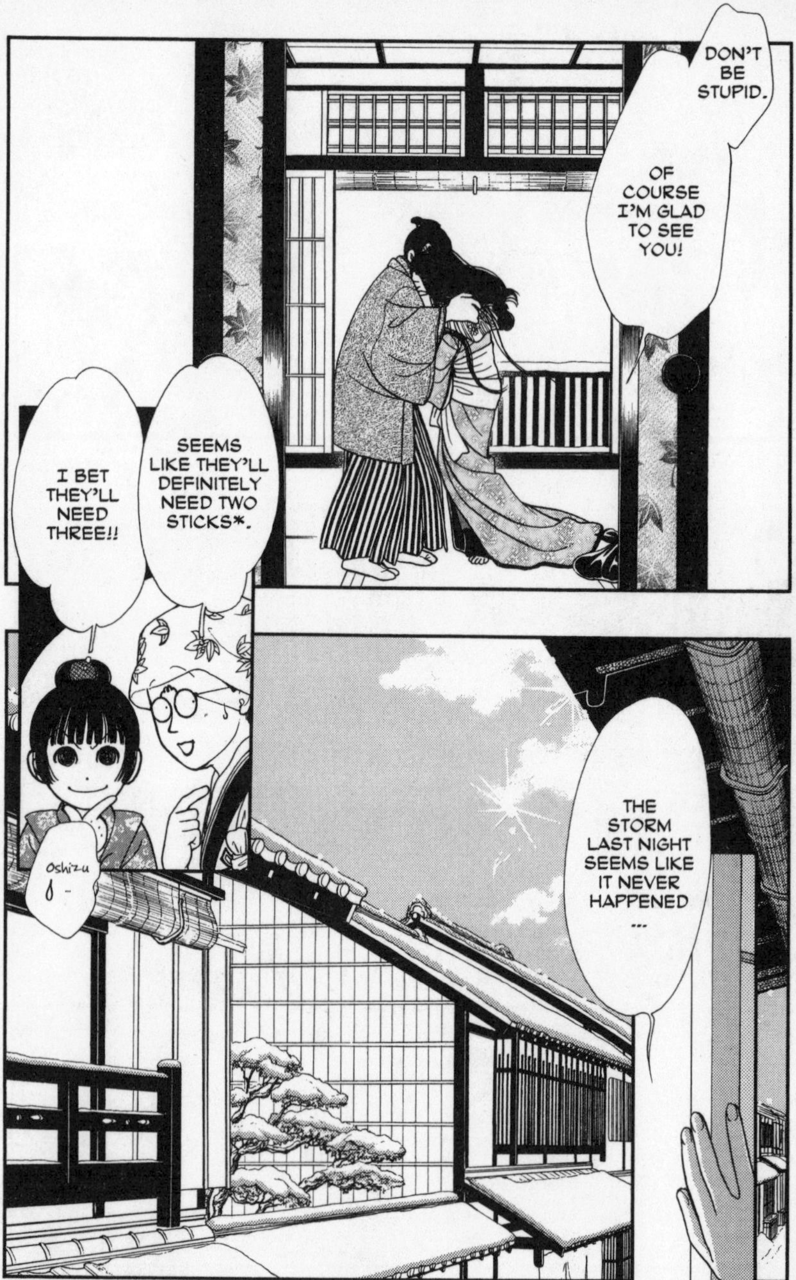
DON'T BE STUPID.
OF COURSE I'M GLAD TO SEE YOU!
SEEMS LIKE THEY'LL DEFINITELY NEED TWO STICKS*.
I BET THEY'LL NEED THREE!!
Oshizu ...
THE STORM LAST NIGHT SEEMS LIKE IT NEVER HAPPENED ...

*Used as a unit of measure for time spent with customers.
One incense stick usually lasts for about 45 minutes.

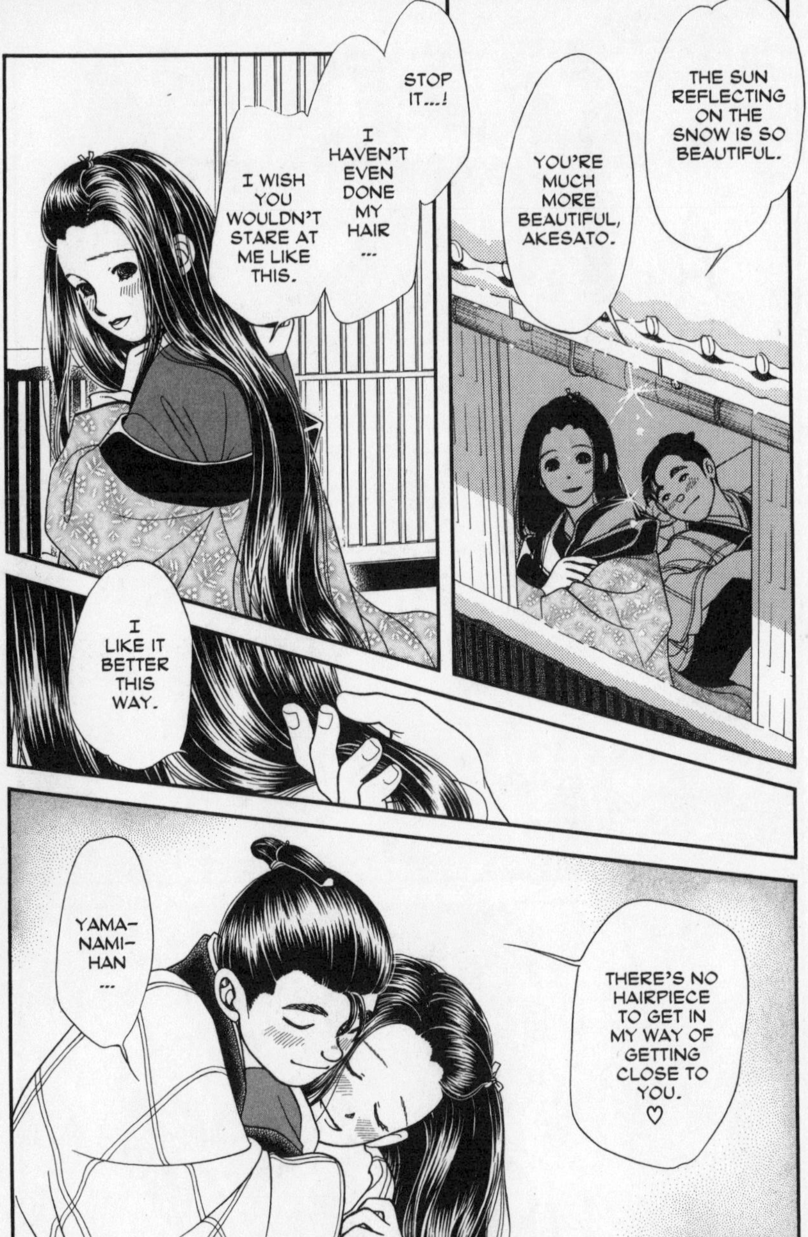
THE SUN REFLECTING ON THE SNOW IS SO BEAUTIFUL.
YOU'RE MUCH MORE BEAUTIFUL, AKESATO.
STOP IT...!
I HAVEN'T EVEN DONE MY HAIR ...
I WISH YOU WOULDN'T STARE AT ME LIKE THIS.
I LIKE IT BETTER THIS WAY.
THERE'S NO HAIRPIECE TO GET IN MY WAY OF GETTING CLOSE TO YOU. ♡
YAMA-NAMI-HAN ...

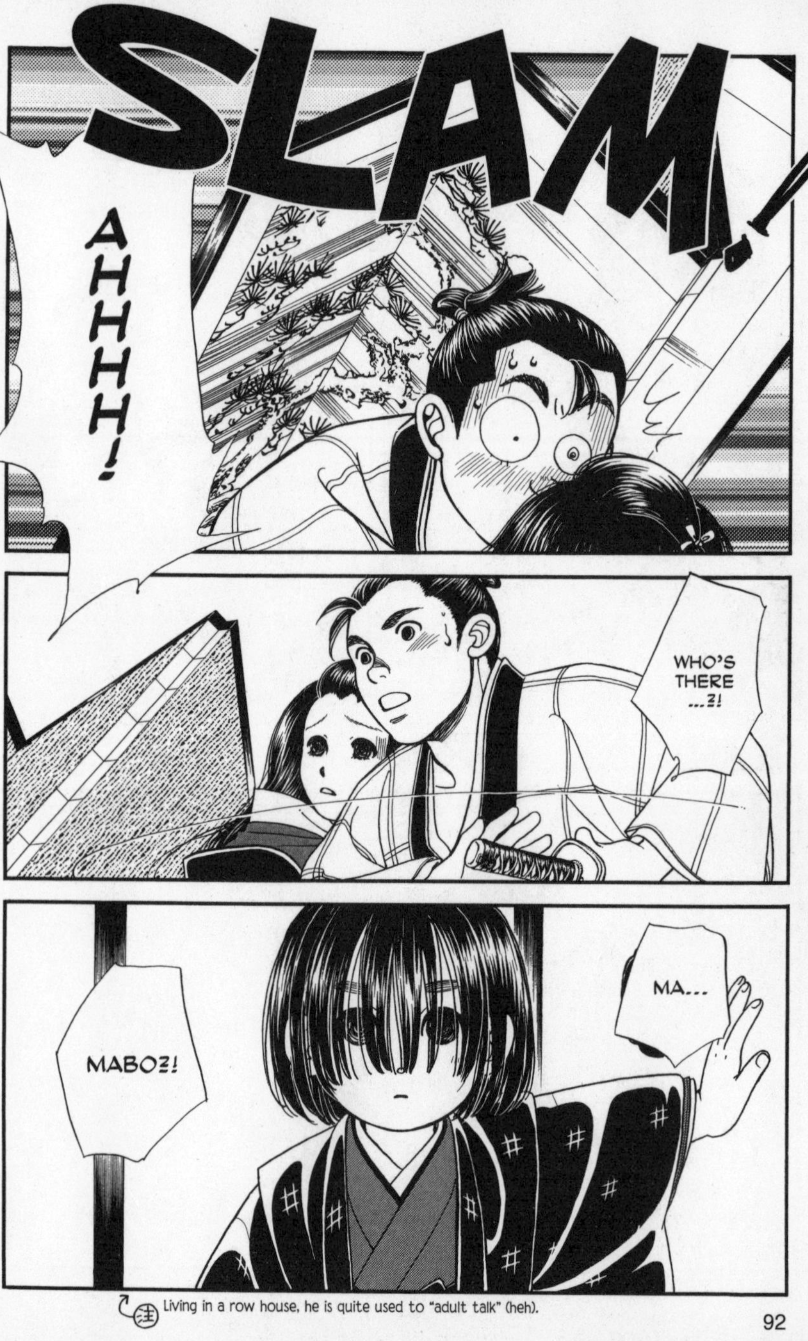
SLAM!
AHHHH!
WHO'S THERE ...?!
MA...
MABO?!

注 Living in a row house, he is quite used to "adult talk" (heh).

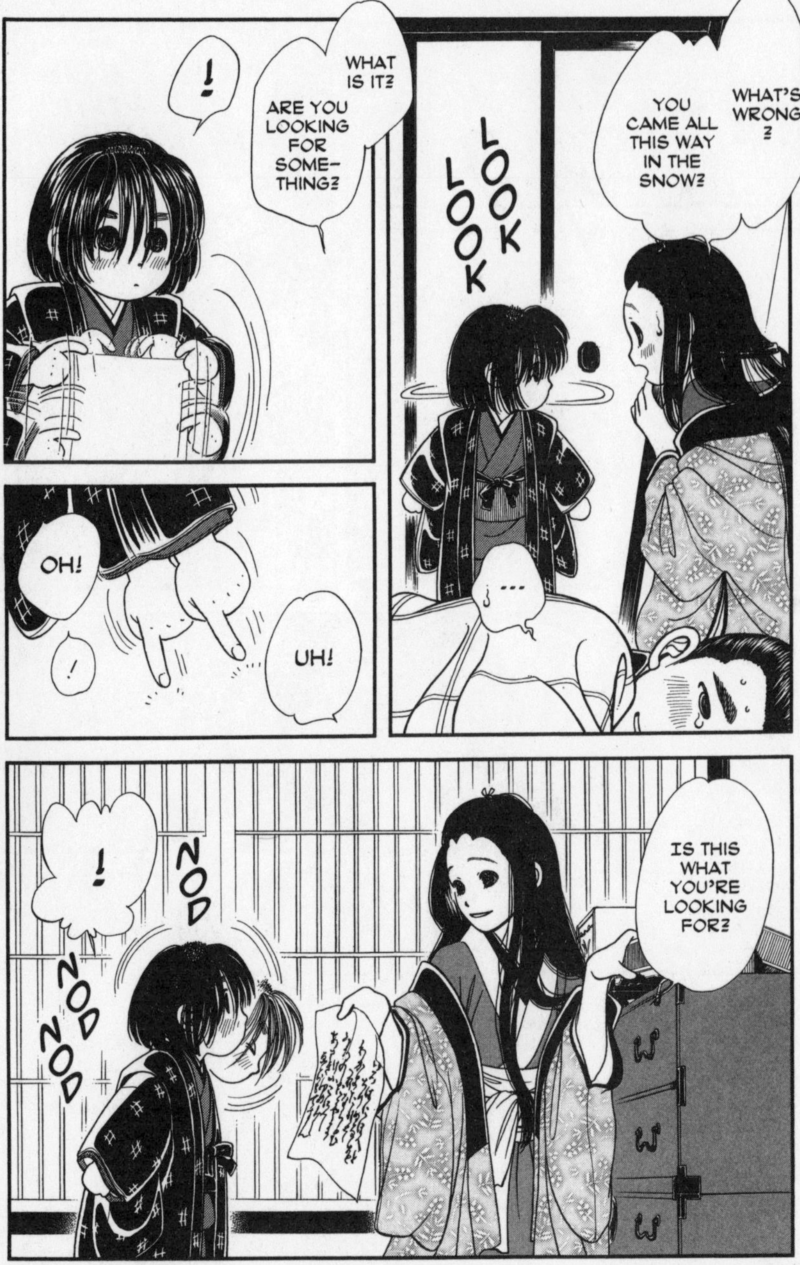
WHAT'S WRONG?
YOU CAME ALL THIS WAY IN THE SNOW?
LOOK LOOK
...
WHAT IS IT?
ARE YOU LOOKING FOR SOMETHING?
!
UH!
OH!
!
IS THIS WHAT YOU'RE LOOKING FOR?
NOD
NOD NOD
!

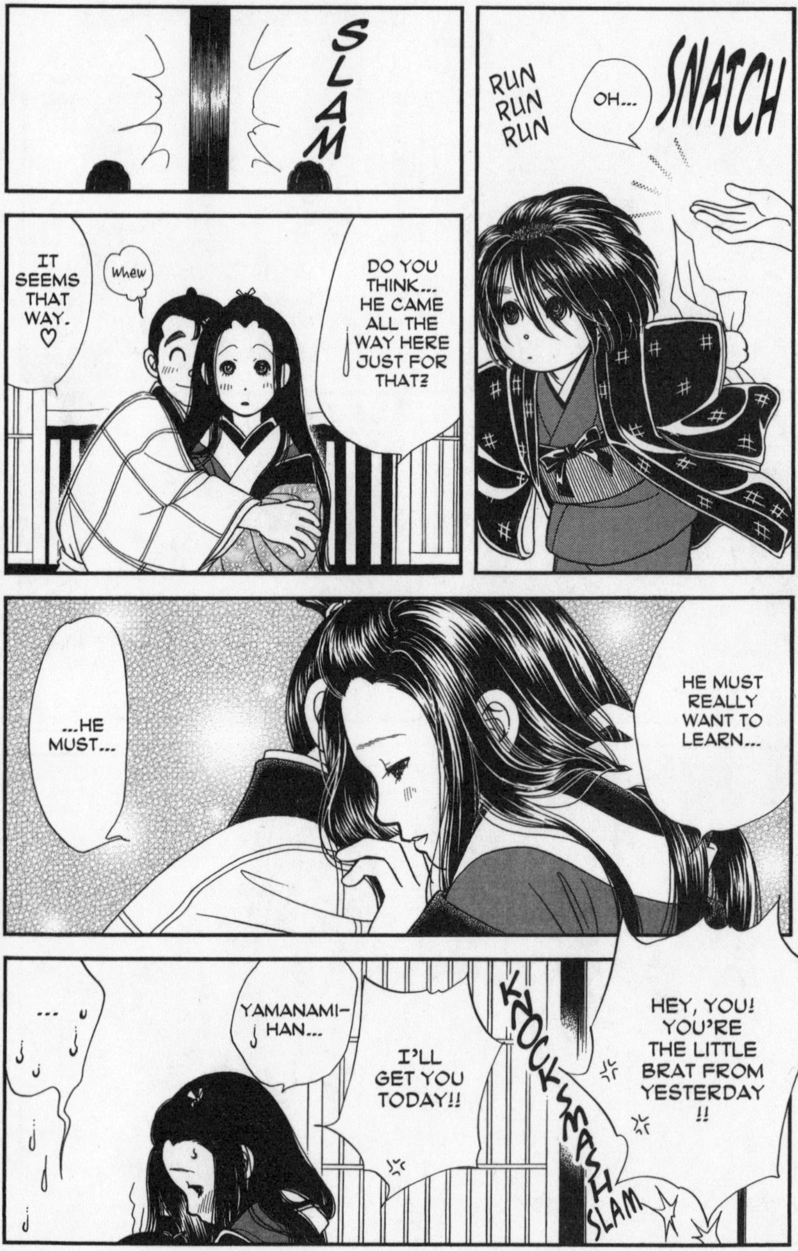
SNATCH
OH...
RUN RUN RUN
SLAM
DO YOU THINK... HE CAME ALL THE WAY HERE JUST FOR THAT?
Whew
IT SEEMS THAT WAY. ♡
HE MUST REALLY WANT TO LEARN...
...HE MUST...
HEY, YOU! YOU'RE THE LITTLE BRAT FROM YESTERDAY!!
KNOCK SMASH
SLAM
I'LL GET YOU TODAY!!
YAMANAMI-HAN...
...

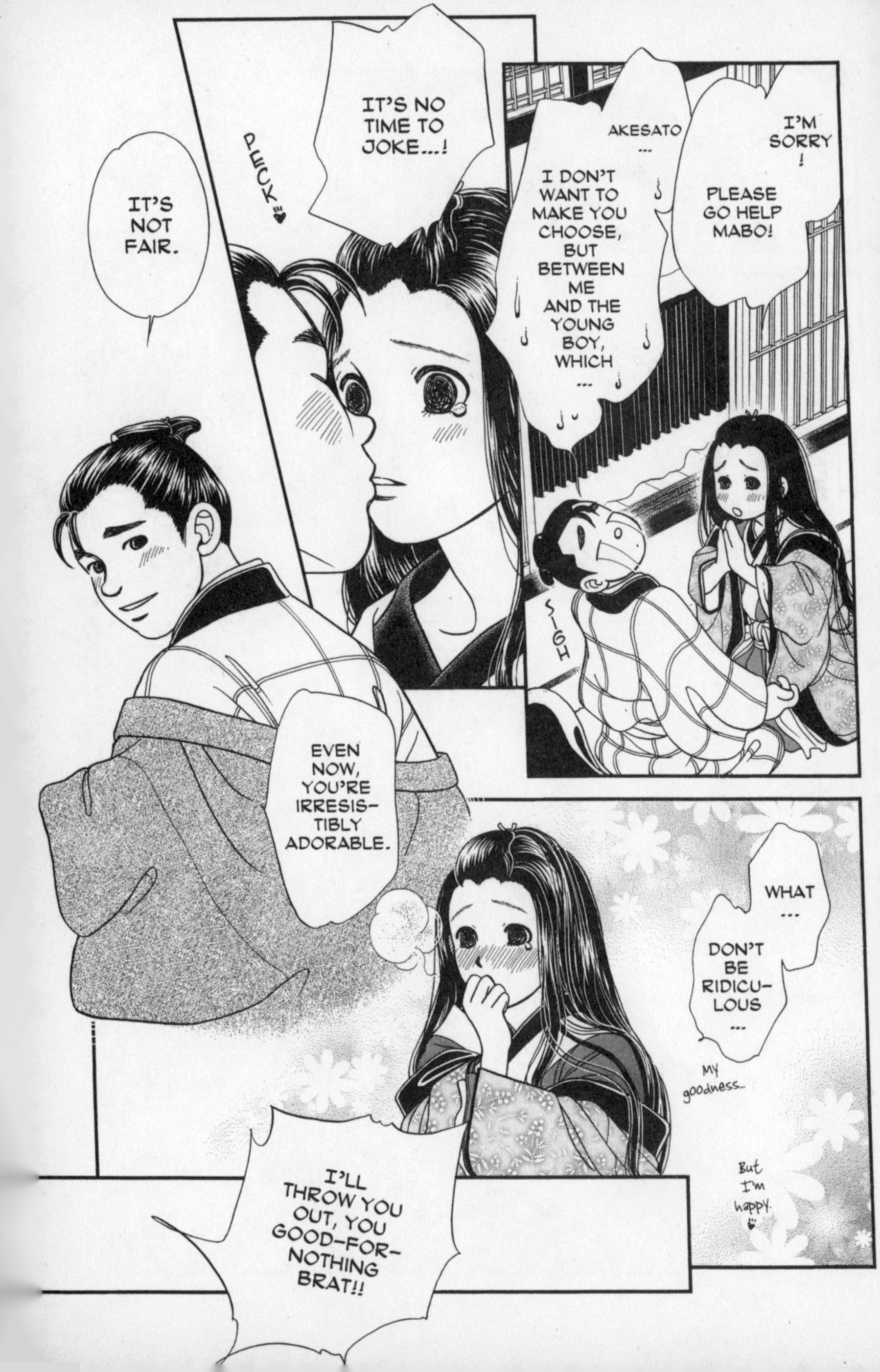
I'M SORRY! PLEASE GO HELP MABO!
AKESATO... I DON'T WANT TO MAKE YOU CHOOSE, BUT BETWEEN ME AND THE YOUNG BOY, WHICH...
SIGH
IT'S NO TIME TO JOKE...!
PECK
IT'S NOT FAIR.
EVEN NOW, YOU'RE IRRESISTIBLY ADORABLE.
WHAT... DON'T BE RIDICULOUS...
MY goodness...
But I'm happy.
I'LL THROW YOU OUT, YOU GOOD-FOR-NOTHING BRAT!!

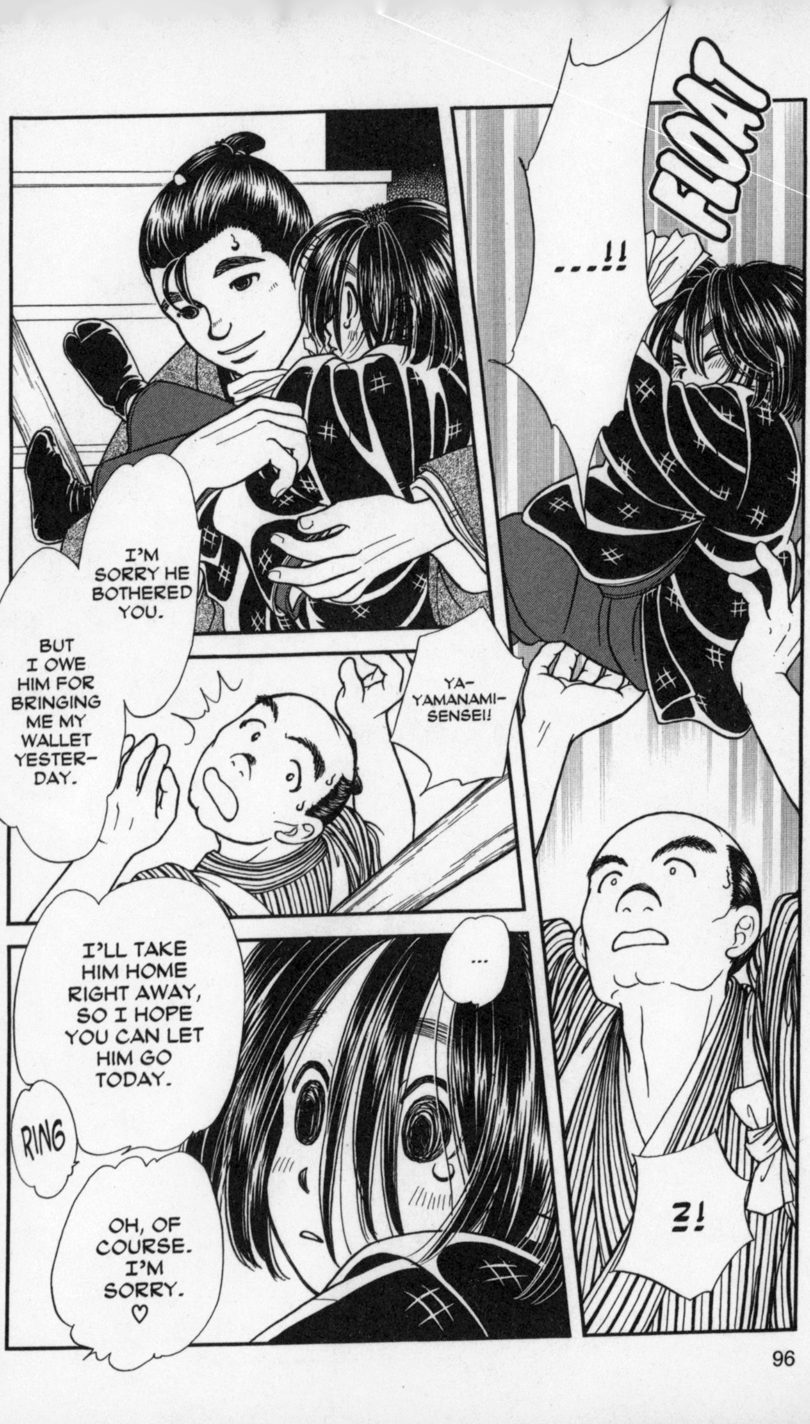
FLOAT
...!!
?!
I'M SORRY HE BOTHERED YOU.
BUT I OWE HIM FOR BRINGING ME MY WALLET YESTER-DAY.
YA-YAMANAMI-SENSEI!
...
I'LL TAKE HIM HOME RIGHT AWAY, SO I HOPE YOU CAN LET HIM GO TODAY.
RING
OH, OF COURSE. I'M SORRY. ♡

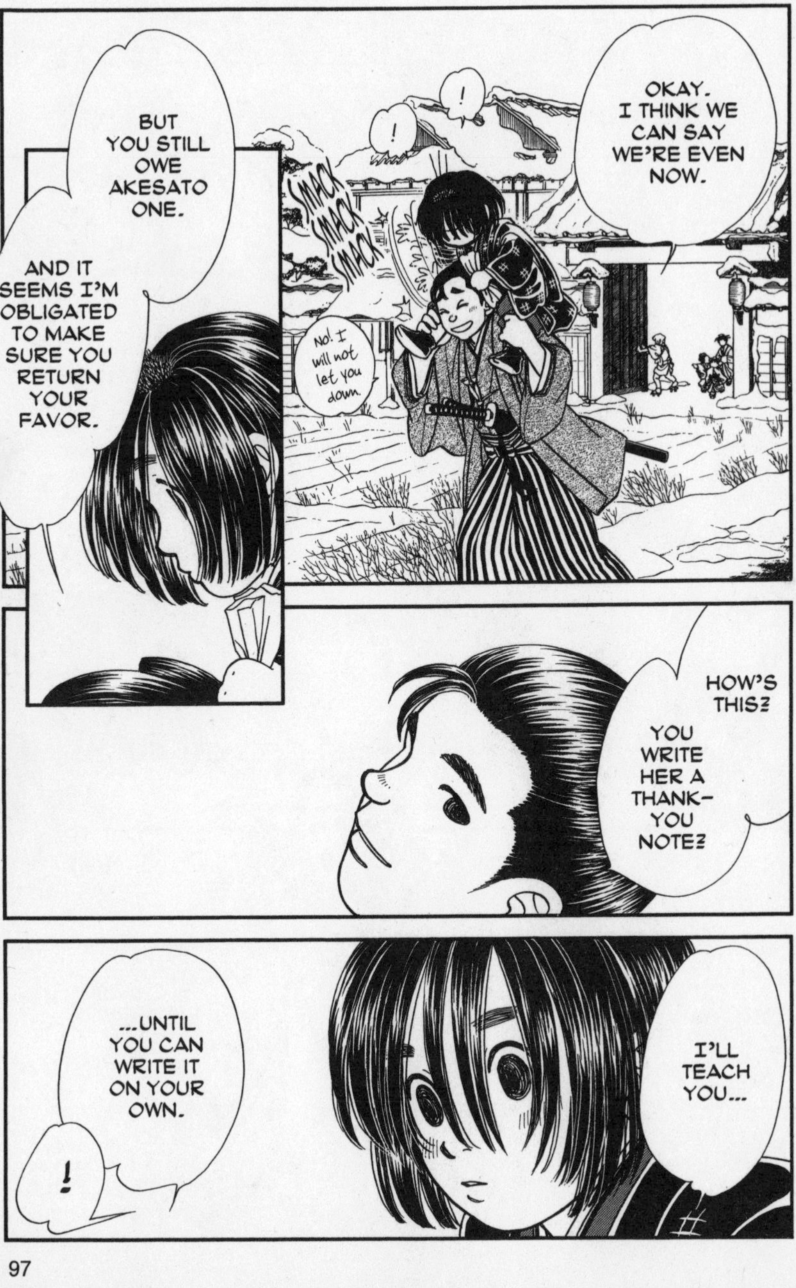
OKAY. I THINK WE CAN SAY WE'RE EVEN NOW.
!
!
SMACK SMACK SMACK
No! I will not let you down.
BUT YOU STILL OWE AKESATO ONE.
AND IT SEEMS I'M OBLIGATED TO MAKE SURE YOU RETURN YOUR FAVOR.
HOW'S THIS?
YOU WRITE HER A THANK-YOU NOTE?
I'LL TEACH YOU...
...UNTIL YOU CAN WRITE IT ON YOUR OWN.
!

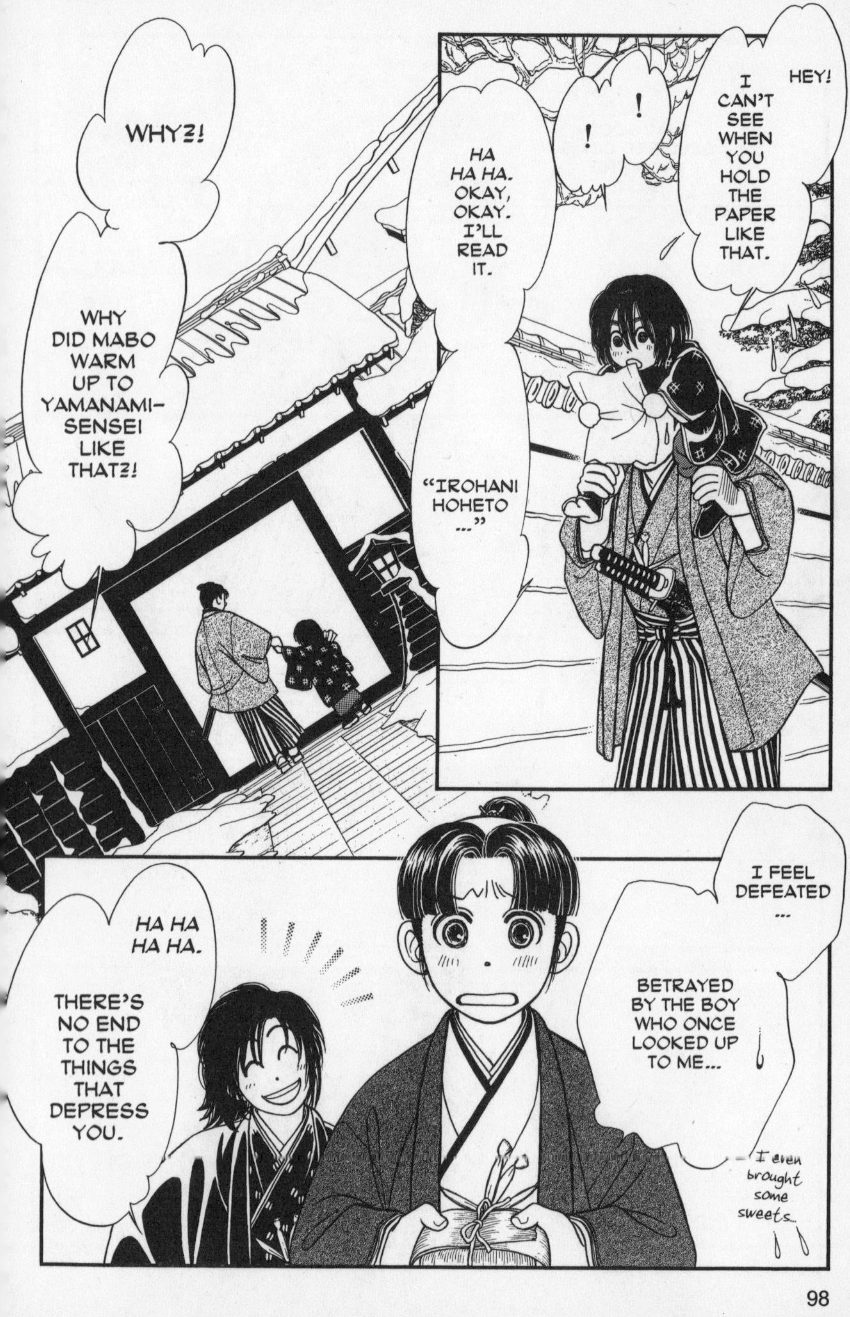
HEY!
I CAN'T SEE WHEN YOU HOLD THE PAPER LIKE THAT.
! !
HA HA HA. OKAY, OKAY. I'LL READ IT.
"IROHANI HOHETO..."
WHY?!
WHY DID MABO WARM UP TO YAMANAMI-SENSEI LIKE THAT?!
I FEEL DEFEATED...
BETRAYED BY THE BOY WHO ONCE LOOKED UP TO ME...
I even brought some sweets...
HA HA HA HA.
THERE'S NO END TO THE THINGS THAT DEPRESS YOU.

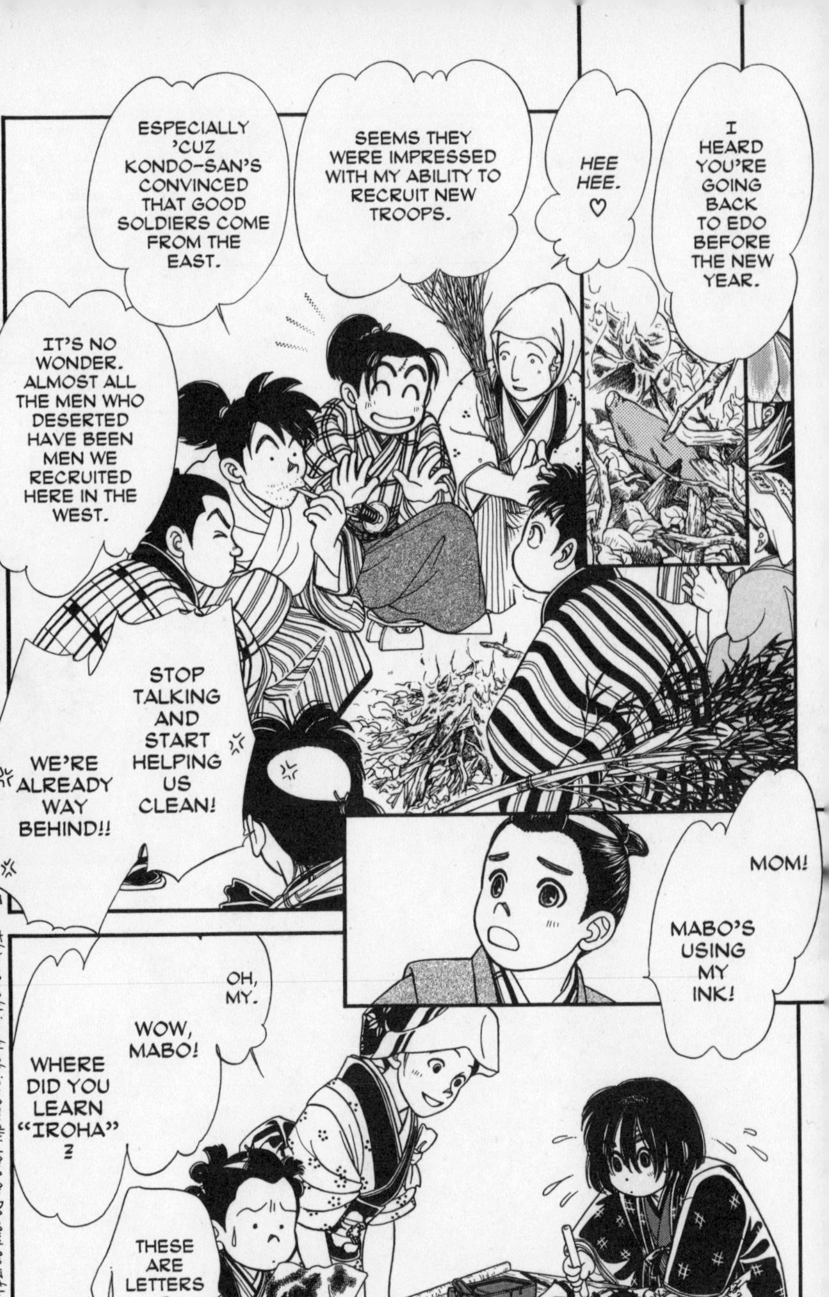
I HEARD YOU'RE GOING BACK TO EDO BEFORE THE NEW YEAR.
HEE HEE. ♡
SEEMS THEY WERE IMPRESSED WITH MY ABILITY TO RECRUIT NEW TROOPS.
ESPECIALLY 'CUZ KONDO-SAN'S CONVINCED THAT GOOD SOLDIERS COME FROM THE EAST.
IT'S NO WONDER. ALMOST ALL THE MEN WHO DESERTED HAVE BEEN MEN WE RECRUITED HERE IN THE WEST.
STOP TALKING AND START HELPING US CLEAN!
WE'RE ALREADY WAY BEHIND!!
MOM!
MABO'S USING MY INK!
OH, MY.
WOW, MABO!
WHERE DID YOU LEARN "IROHA"?
THESE ARE LETTERS?

It's something that is normally done on December 13th

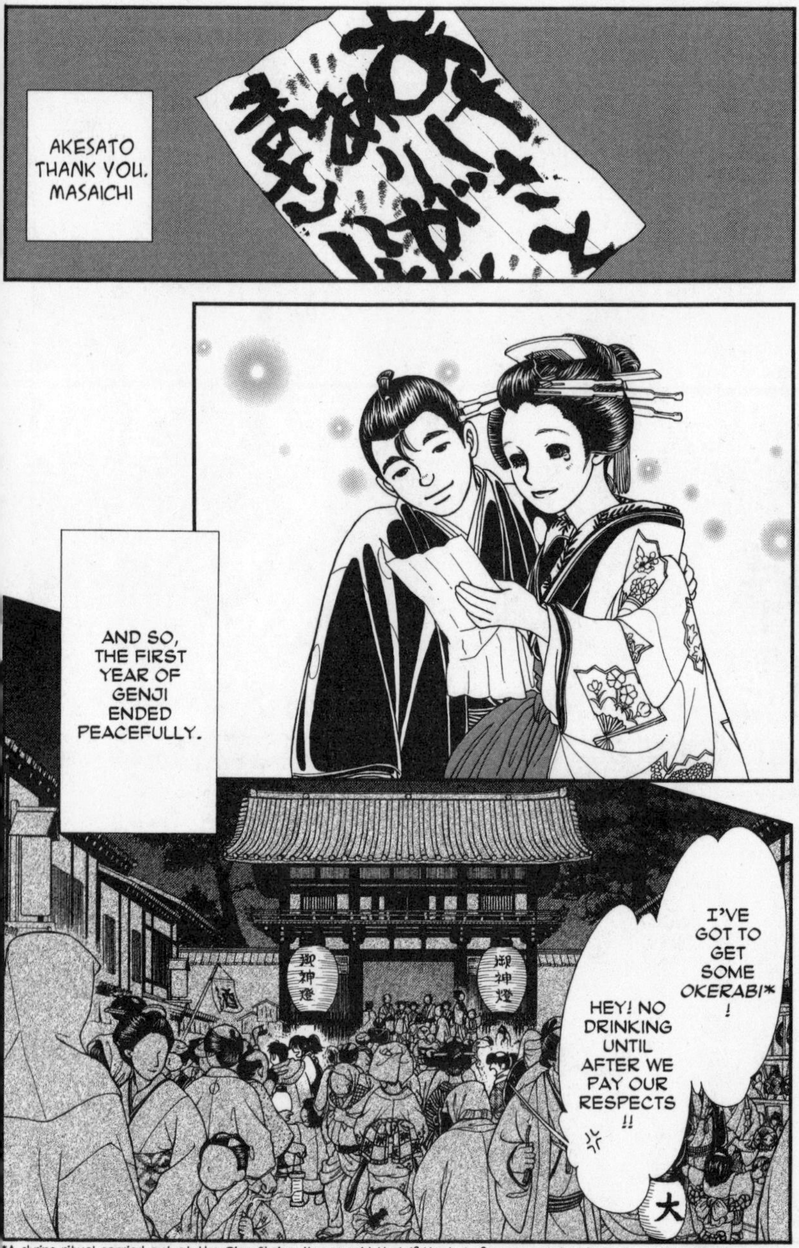
AKESATO
THANK YOU.
MASAICHI
AND SO, THE FIRST YEAR OF GENJI ENDED PEACEFULLY.
I'VE GOT TO GET SOME OKERABI*!
HEY! NO DRINKING UNTIL AFTER WE PAY OUR RESPECTS!!

*A shrine ritual carried out at the Gion Shrine. It was said that if the holy flame was taken home in an "auspicious bond" and used when making rice cake soup, one would be immune to disease and disasters for the year.

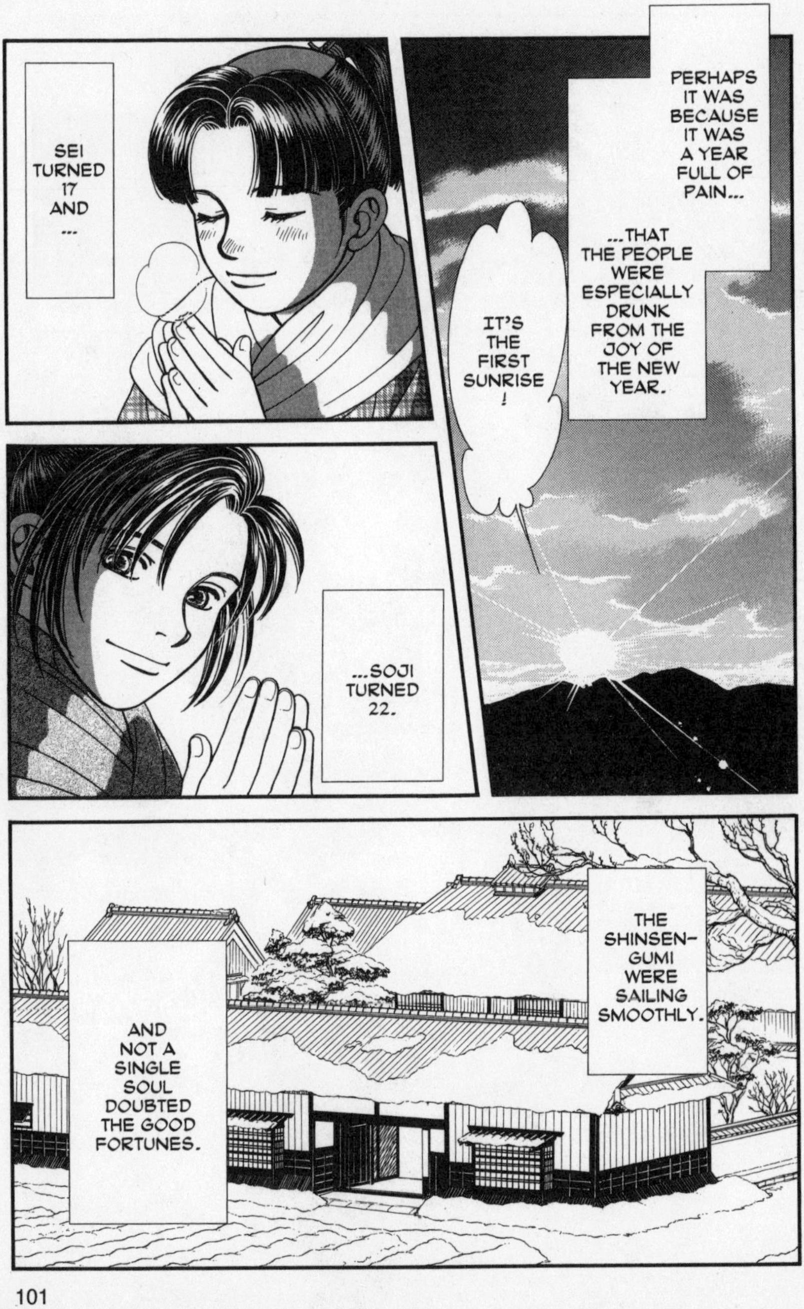
PERHAPS IT WAS BECAUSE IT WAS A YEAR FULL OF PAIN...
...THAT THE PEOPLE WERE ESPECIALLY DRUNK FROM THE JOY OF THE NEW YEAR.
IT'S THE FIRST SUNRISE!
SEI TURNED 17 AND ...
...SOJI TURNED 22.
THE SHINSEN-GUMI WERE SAILING SMOOTHLY.
AND NOT A SINGLE SOUL DOUBTED THE GOOD FORTUNES.

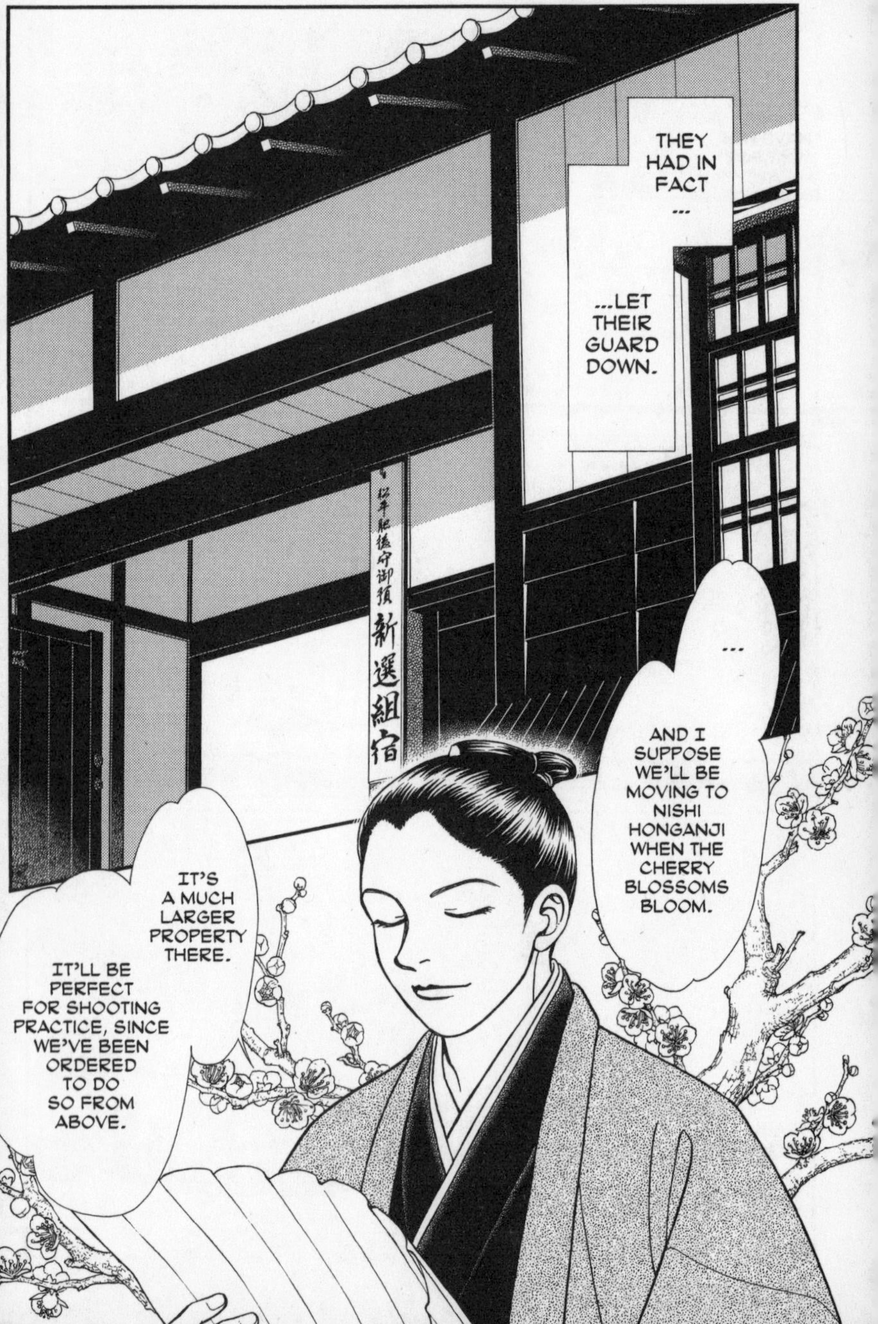
THEY HAD IN FACT ...
...LET THEIR GUARD DOWN.
松平肥後守御預
新選組宿
...
AND I SUPPOSE WE'LL BE MOVING TO NISHI HONGANJI WHEN THE CHERRY BLOSSOMS BLOOM.
IT'S A MUCH LARGER PROPERTY THERE.
IT'LL BE PERFECT FOR SHOOTING PRACTICE, SINCE WE'VE BEEN ORDERED TO DO SO FROM ABOVE.

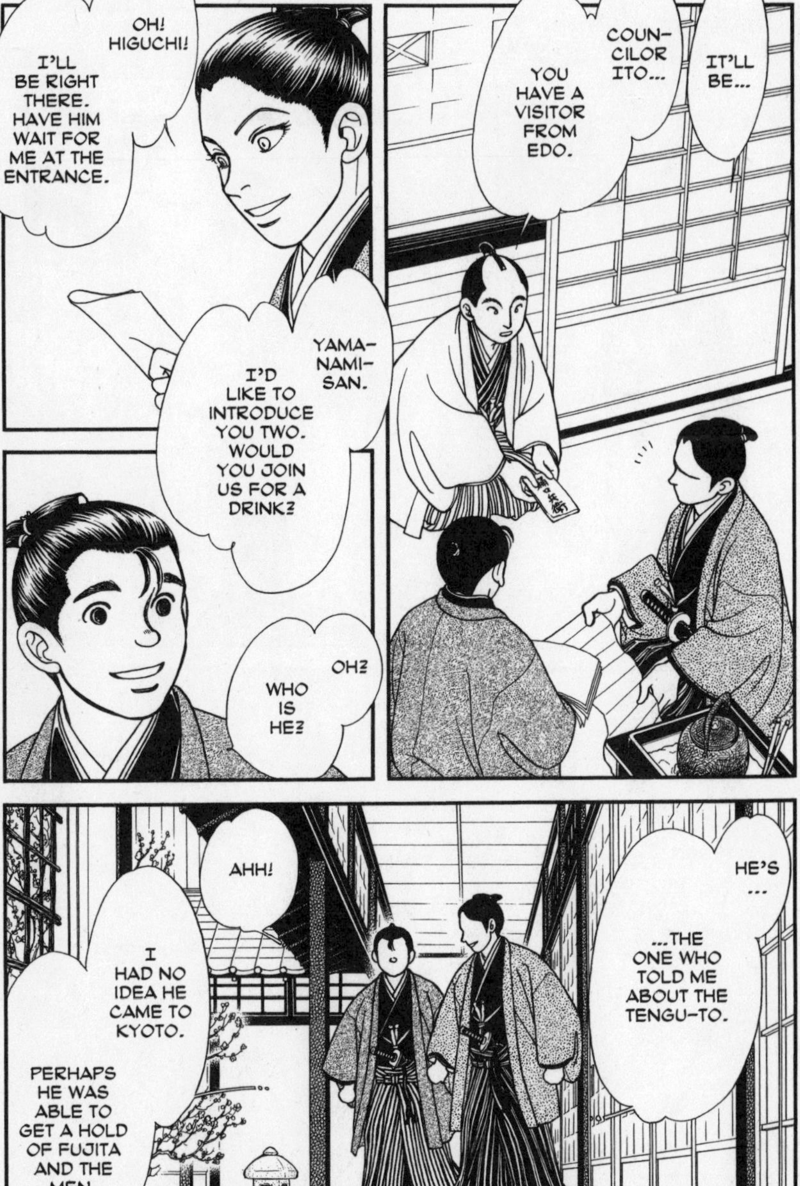
IT'LL BE...
COUNCILOR ITO...
YOU HAVE A VISITOR FROM EDO.
OH! HIGUCHI!
I'LL BE RIGHT THERE. HAVE HIM WAIT FOR ME AT THE ENTRANCE.
YAMANAMI-SAN.
I'D LIKE TO INTRODUCE YOU TWO. WOULD YOU JOIN US FOR A DRINK?
OH? WHO IS HE?
HE'S...
...THE ONE WHO TOLD ME ABOUT THE TENGU-TO.
AHH!
I HAD NO IDEA HE CAME TO KYOTO.
PERHAPS HE WAS ABLE TO GET A HOLD OF FUJITA AND THE MEN.

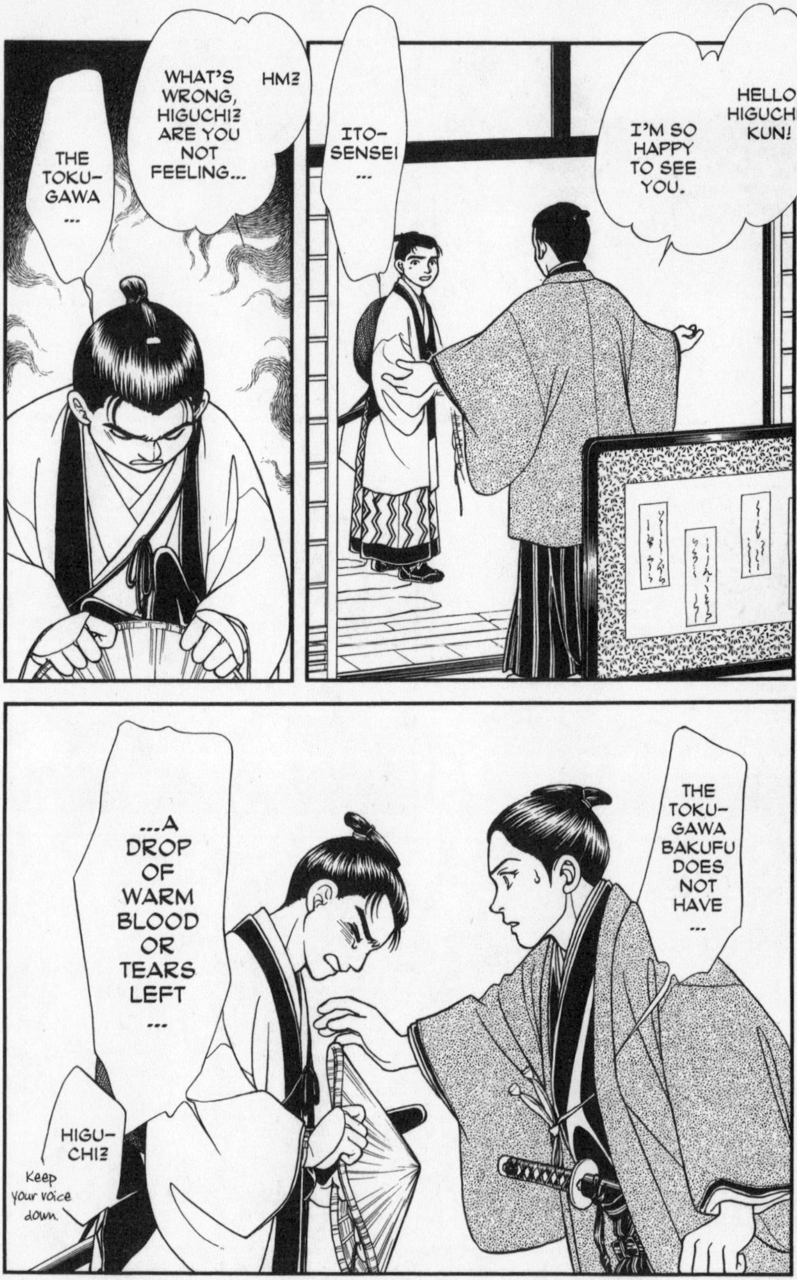
HELLO, HIGUCHI-KUN!
I'M SO HAPPY TO SEE YOU.
ITO-SENSEI...
HM?
WHAT'S WRONG, HIGUCHI? ARE YOU NOT FEELING...
THE TOKUGAWA...
THE TOKUGAWA BAKUFU DOES NOT HAVE...
...A DROP OF WARM BLOOD OR TEARS LEFT...
HIGUCHI?
Keep your voice down.

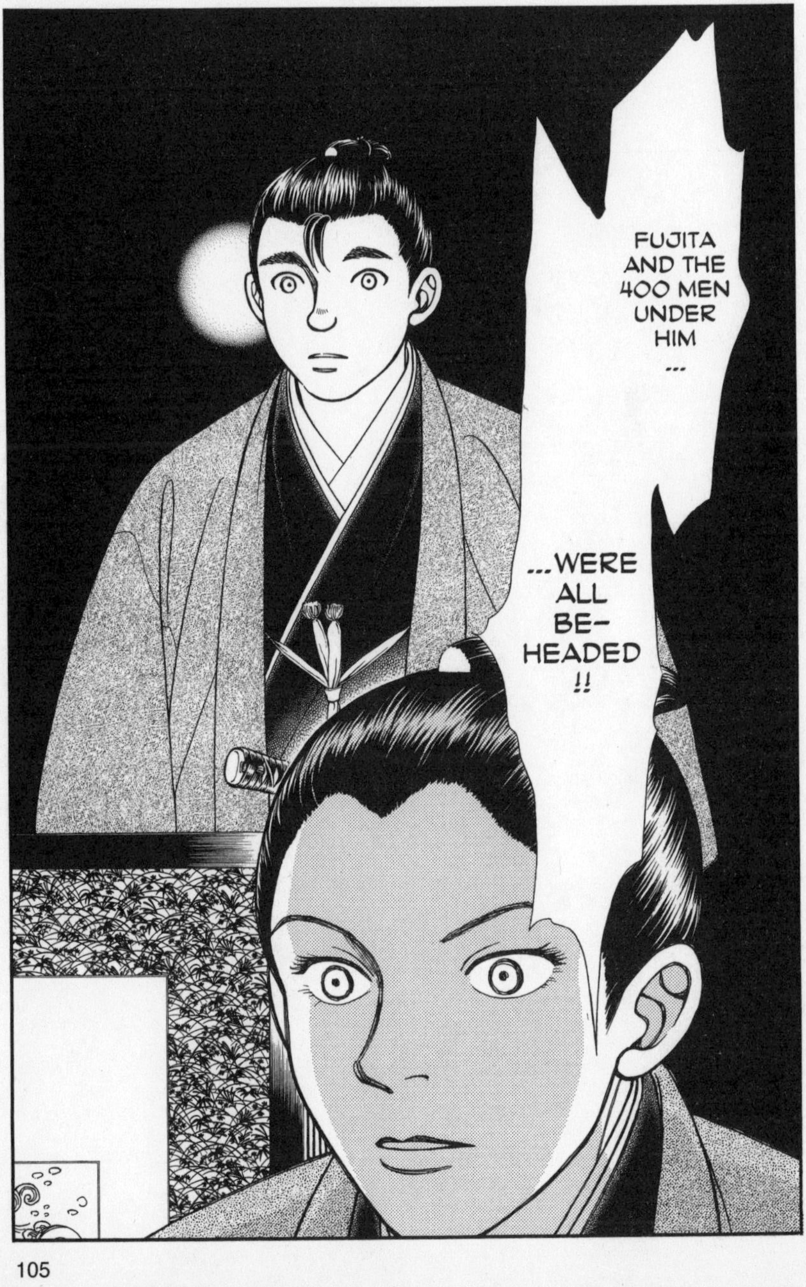
FUJITA AND THE 400 MEN UNDER HIM
...
...WERE ALL BE-HEADED !!

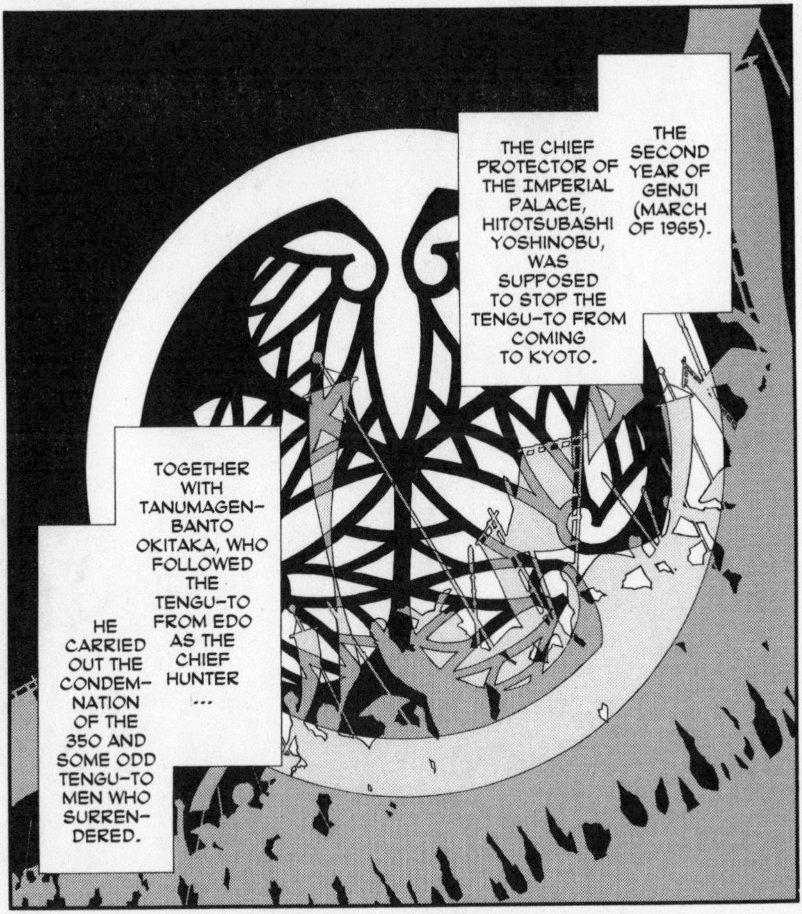
THE SECOND YEAR OF GENJI (MARCH OF 1965).
THE CHIEF PROTECTOR OF THE IMPERIAL PALACE, HITOTSUBASHI YOSHINOBU, WAS SUPPOSED TO STOP THE TENGU-TO FROM COMING TO KYOTO.
TOGETHER WITH TANUMAGEN-BANTO OKITAKA, WHO FOLLOWED THE TENGU-TO FROM EDO AS THE CHIEF HUNTER...
HE CARRIED OUT THE CONDEMNATION OF THE 350 AND SOME ODD TENGU-TO MEN WHO SURRENDERED.

EDO "IROHA" KARUTA GAME

"RU" る

RURI MO HARI MO TERASEBA HIKARU
"LAPIS AND GLASS WILL BOTH SHINE WHEN ILLUMINATED"
(Jewels must be polished before they shine)

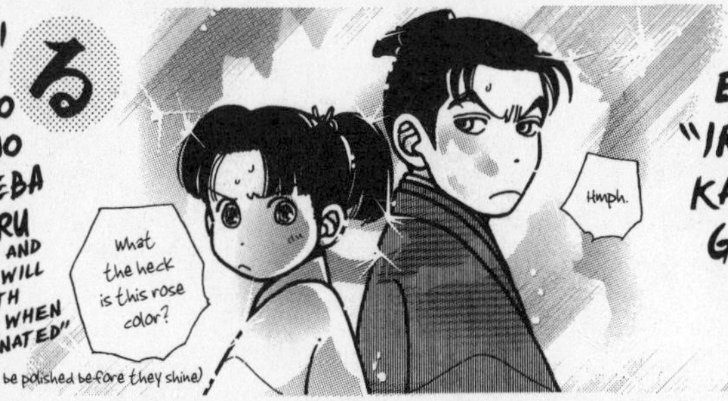
Hmph.
What the heck is this rose color?

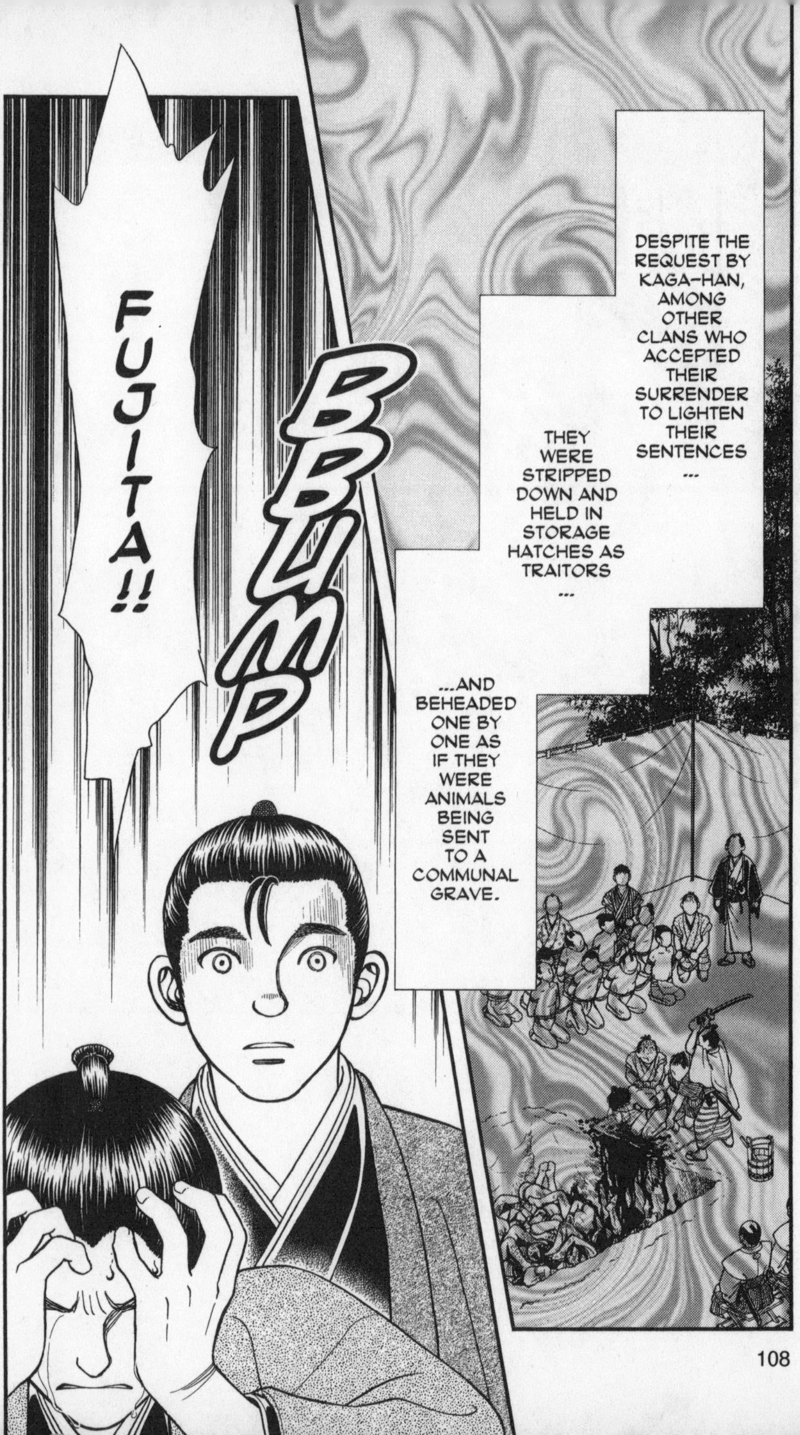
DESPITE THE REQUEST BY KAGA-HAN, AMONG OTHER CLANS WHO ACCEPTED THEIR SURRENDER TO LIGHTEN THEIR SENTENCES ...
THEY WERE STRIPPED DOWN AND HELD IN STORAGE HATCHES AS TRAITORS ...
...AND BEHEADED ONE BY ONE AS IF THEY WERE ANIMALS BEING SENT TO A COMMUNAL GRAVE.
BBUMP
FUJITA!!

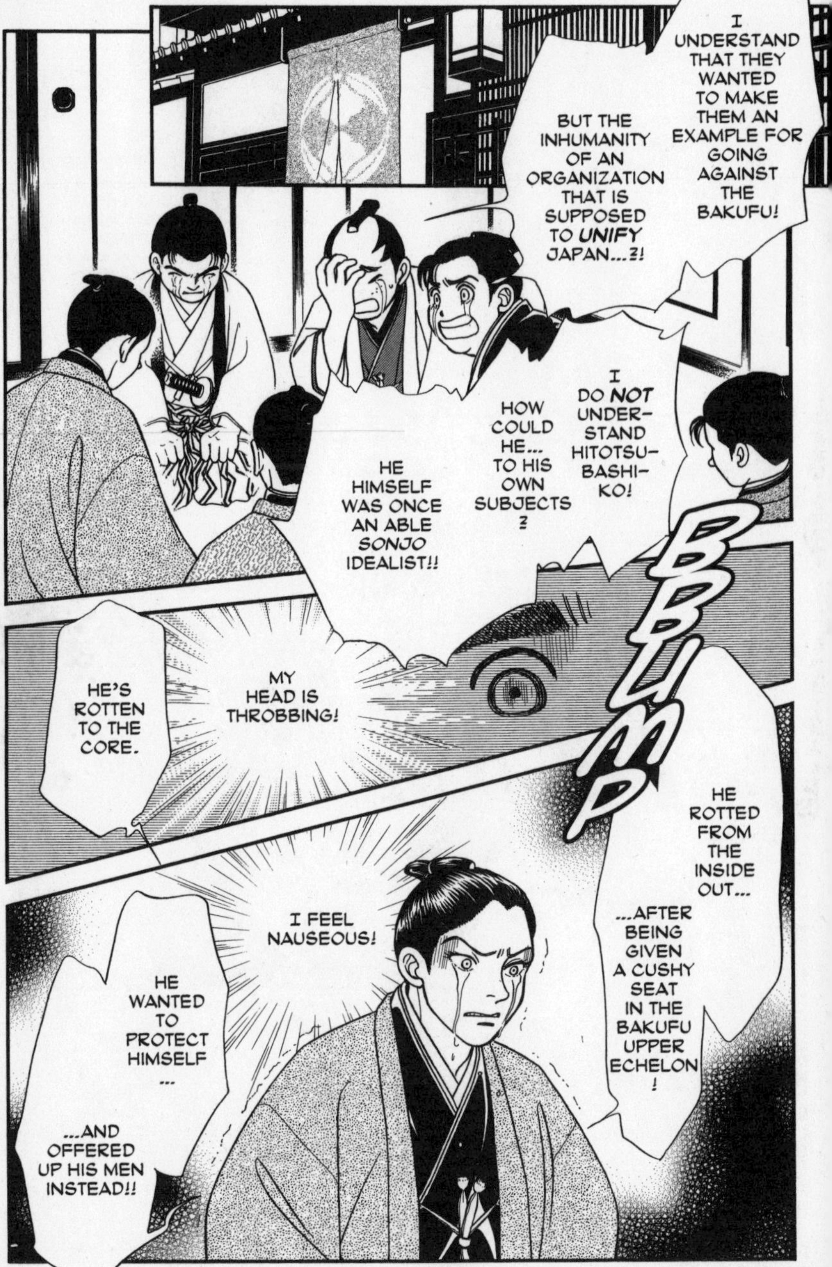
I UNDERSTAND THAT THEY WANTED TO MAKE THEM AN EXAMPLE FOR GOING AGAINST THE BAKUFU!
BUT THE INHUMANITY OF AN ORGANIZATION THAT IS SUPPOSED TO *UNIFY* JAPAN...?!
I DO **NOT** UNDERSTAND HITOTSU-BASHI-KO!
HOW COULD HE... TO HIS OWN SUBJECTS?
HE HIMSELF WAS ONCE AN ABLE *SONJO* IDEALIST!!
BBUMP
MY HEAD IS THROBBING!
HE'S ROTTEN TO THE CORE.
HE ROTTED FROM THE INSIDE OUT...
...AFTER BEING GIVEN A CUSHY SEAT IN THE BAKUFU UPPER ECHELON!
I FEEL NAUSEOUS!
HE WANTED TO PROTECT HIMSELF...
...AND OFFERED UP HIS MEN INSTEAD!!

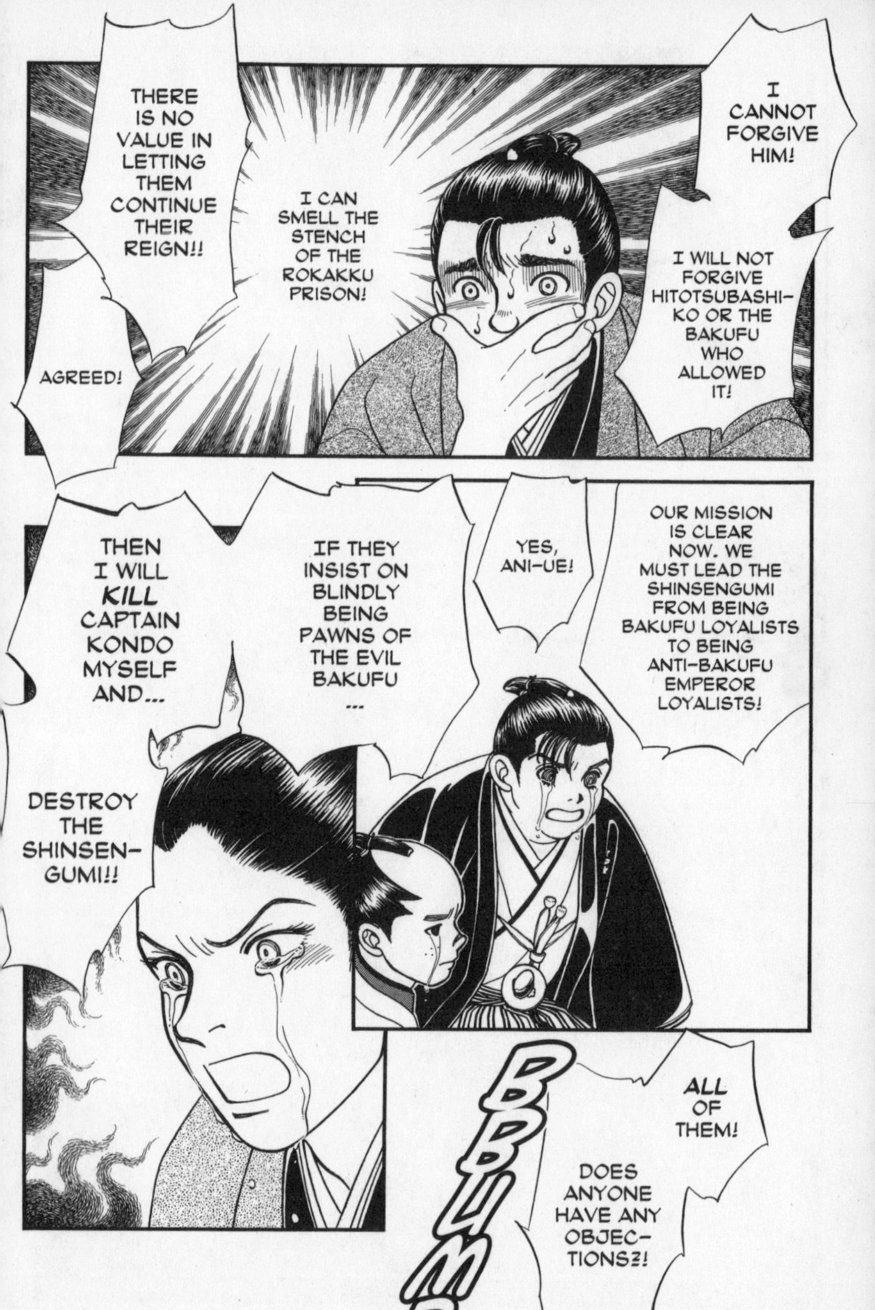
I CANNOT FORGIVE HIM!
I WILL NOT FORGIVE HITOTSUBASHI-KO OR THE BAKUFU WHO ALLOWED IT!
I CAN SMELL THE STENCH OF THE ROKAKKU PRISON!
THERE IS NO VALUE IN LETTING THEM CONTINUE THEIR REIGN!!
AGREED!
OUR MISSION IS CLEAR NOW. WE MUST LEAD THE SHINSENGUMI FROM BEING BAKUFU LOYALISTS TO BEING ANTI-BAKUFU EMPEROR LOYALISTS!
YES, ANI-UE!
IF THEY INSIST ON BLINDLY BEING PAWNS OF THE EVIL BAKUFU ...
THEN I WILL *KILL* CAPTAIN KONDO MYSELF AND...
DESTROY THE SHINSEN-GUMI!!
ALL OF THEM!
DOES ANYONE HAVE ANY OBJECTIONS?!
BBUMP

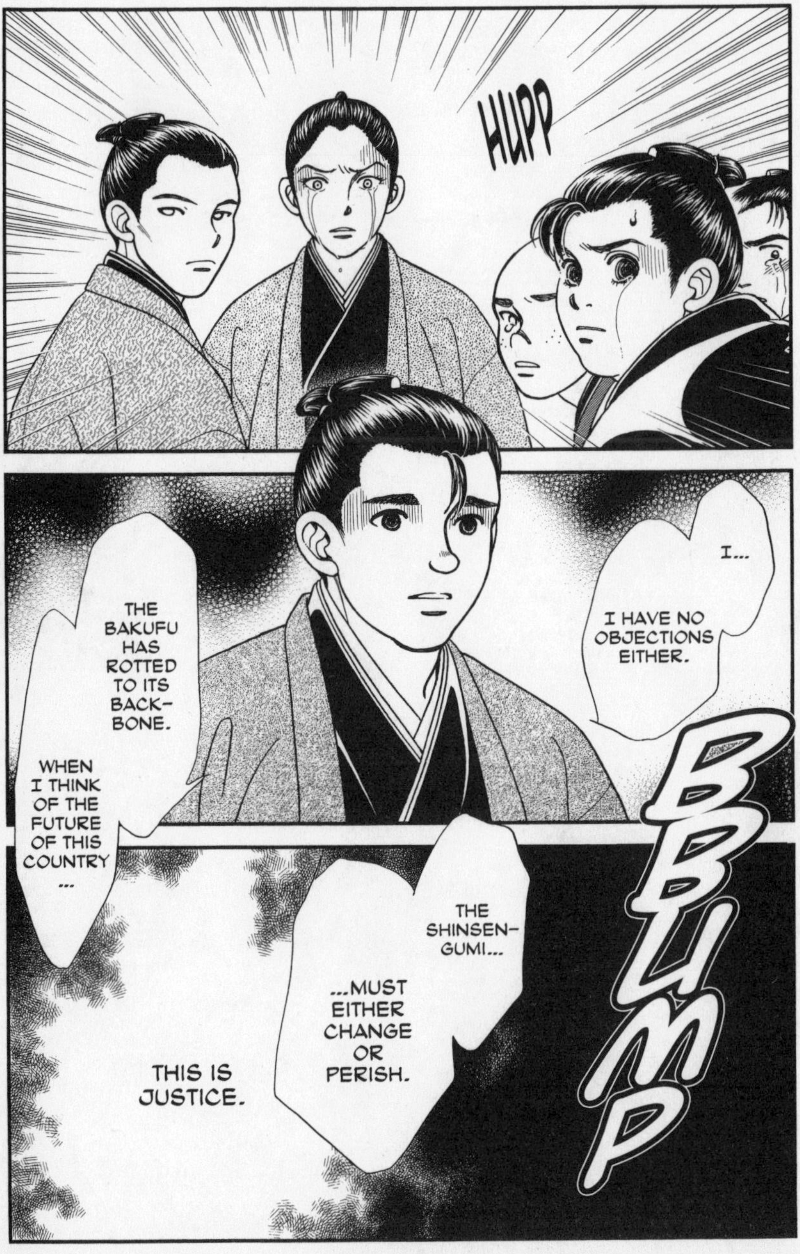
HUPP
I... I HAVE NO OBJECTIONS EITHER.
BBUMP
THE BAKUFU HAS ROTTED TO ITS BACKBONE.
WHEN I THINK OF THE FUTURE OF THIS COUNTRY...
THE SHINSEN-GUMI...
...MUST EITHER CHANGE OR PERISH.
THIS IS JUSTICE.

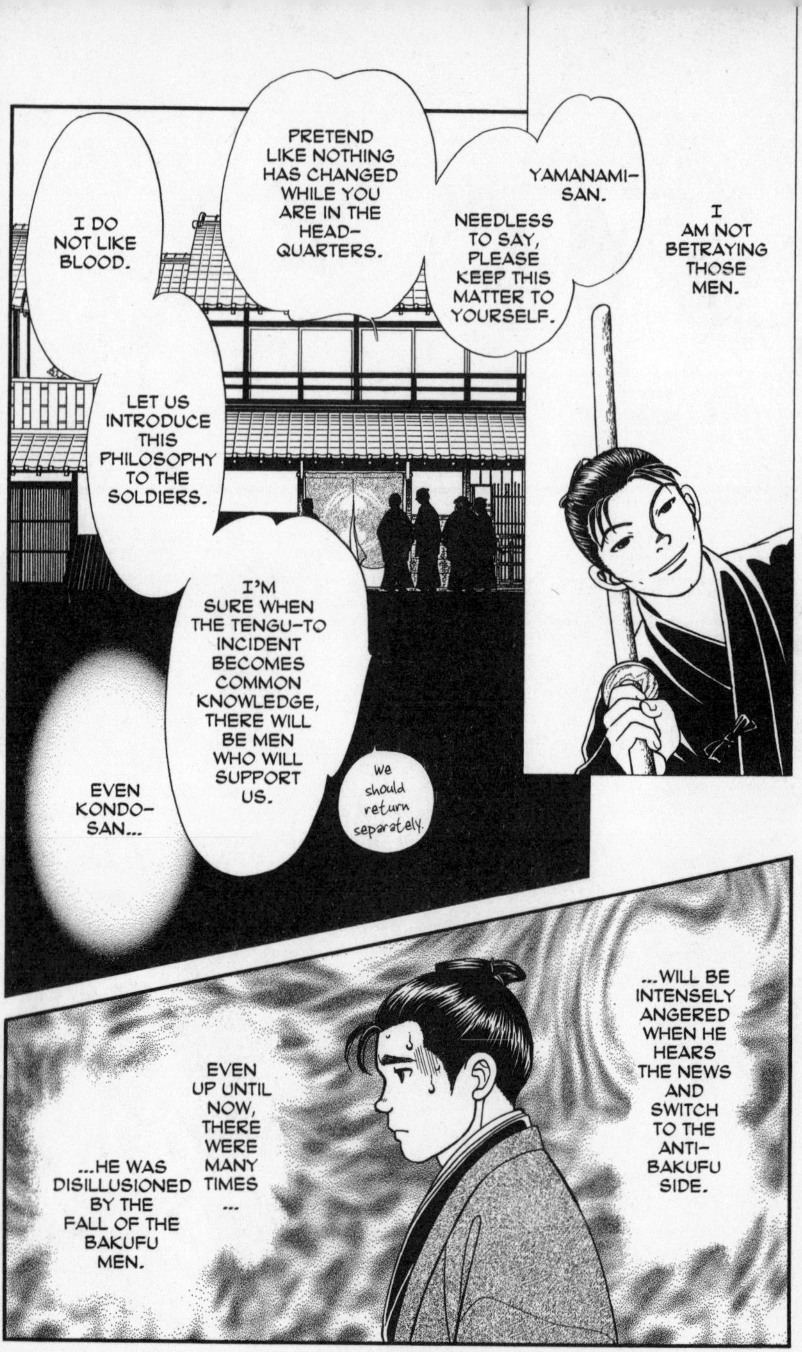
I AM NOT BETRAYING THOSE MEN.
YAMANAMI-SAN.
NEEDLESS TO SAY, PLEASE KEEP THIS MATTER TO YOURSELF.
PRETEND LIKE NOTHING HAS CHANGED WHILE YOU ARE IN THE HEAD-QUARTERS.
I DO NOT LIKE BLOOD.
LET US INTRODUCE THIS PHILOSOPHY TO THE SOLDIERS.
I'M SURE WHEN THE TENGU-TO INCIDENT BECOMES COMMON KNOWLEDGE, THERE WILL BE MEN WHO WILL SUPPORT US.
We should return separately.
EVEN KONDO-SAN...
...WILL BE INTENSELY ANGERED WHEN HE HEARS THE NEWS AND SWITCH TO THE ANTI-BAKUFU SIDE.
EVEN UP UNTIL NOW, THERE WERE MANY TIMES...
...HE WAS DISILLUSIONED BY THE FALL OF THE BAKUFU MEN.

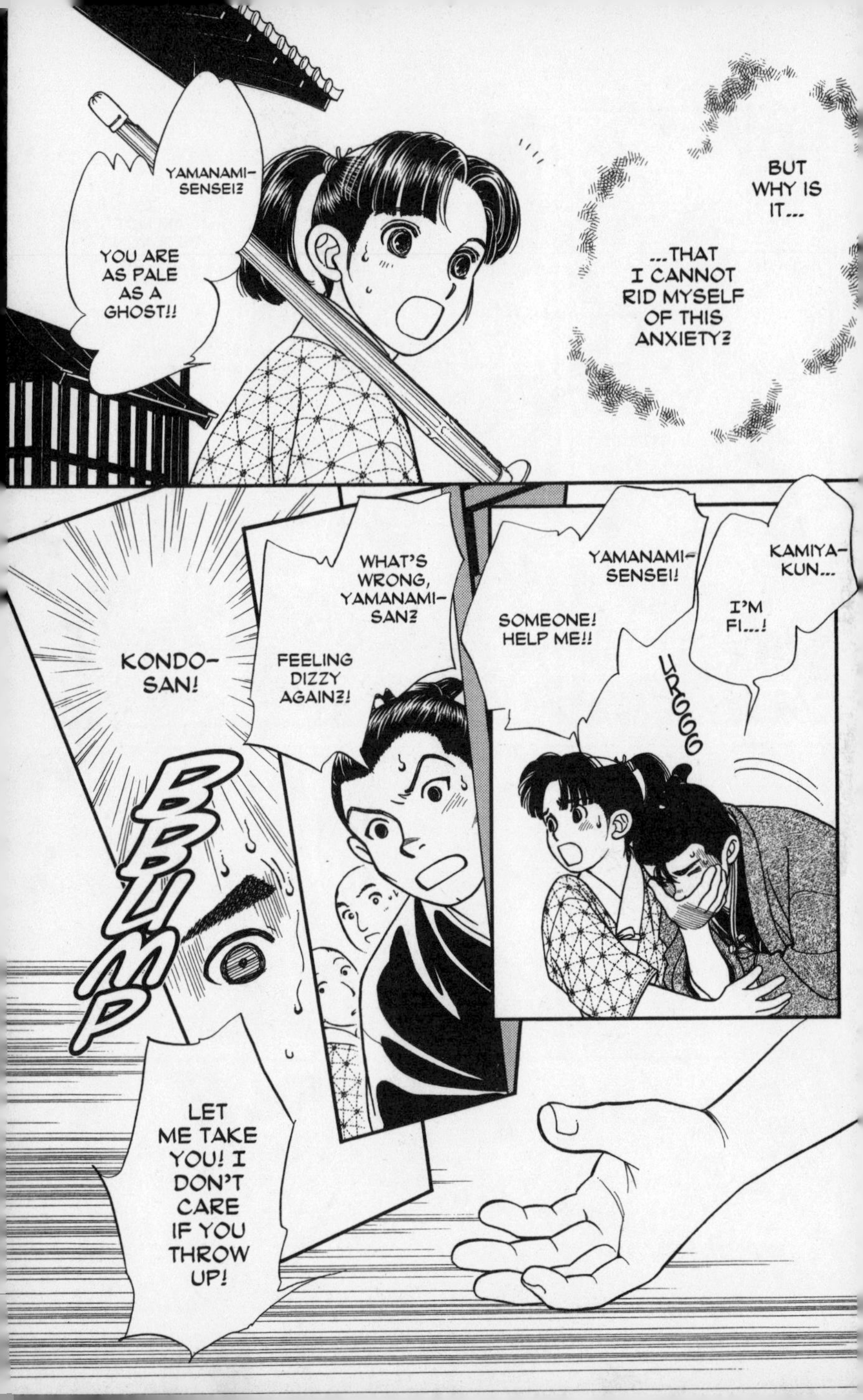
BUT WHY IS IT...
...THAT I CANNOT RID MYSELF OF THIS ANXIETY?
YAMANAMI-SENSEI?
YOU ARE AS PALE AS A GHOST!!
KAMIYA-KUN...
I'M FI...!
UROGGG
YAMANAMI-SENSEI!
SOMEONE! HELP ME!!
WHAT'S WRONG, YAMANAMI-SAN?
FEELING DIZZY AGAIN?!
KONDO-SAN!
BBUMP
LET ME TAKE YOU! I DON'T CARE IF YOU THROW UP!

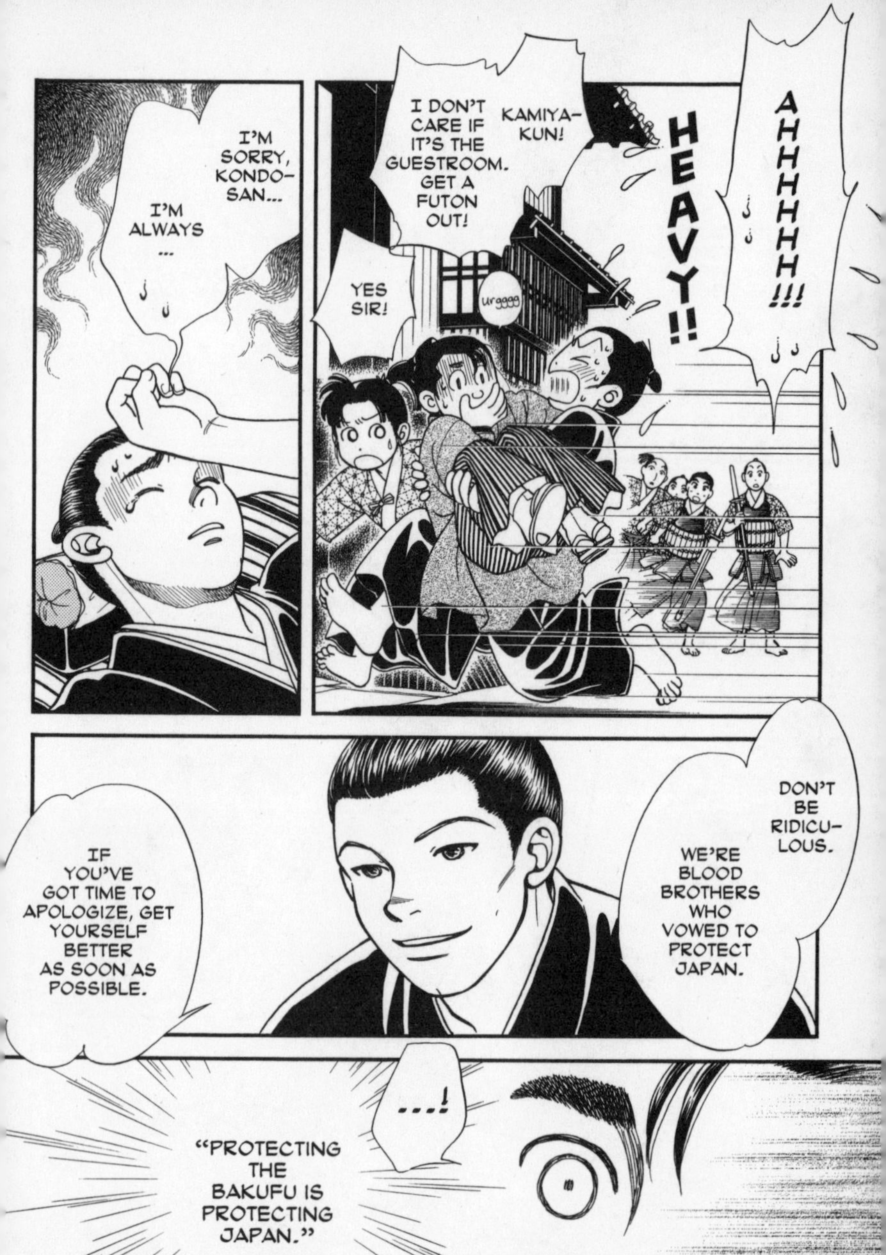
AHHHHHH!!!
HEAVY!!
KAMIYA-KUN!
I DON'T CARE IF IT'S THE GUESTROOM. GET A FUTON OUT!
Urgggg
YES SIR!
I'M SORRY, KONDO-SAN...
I'M ALWAYS ...
DON'T BE RIDICULOUS.
WE'RE BLOOD BROTHERS WHO VOWED TO PROTECT JAPAN.
IF YOU'VE GOT TIME TO APOLOGIZE, GET YOURSELF BETTER AS SOON AS POSSIBLE.
...!
"PROTECTING THE BAKUFU IS PROTECTING JAPAN."

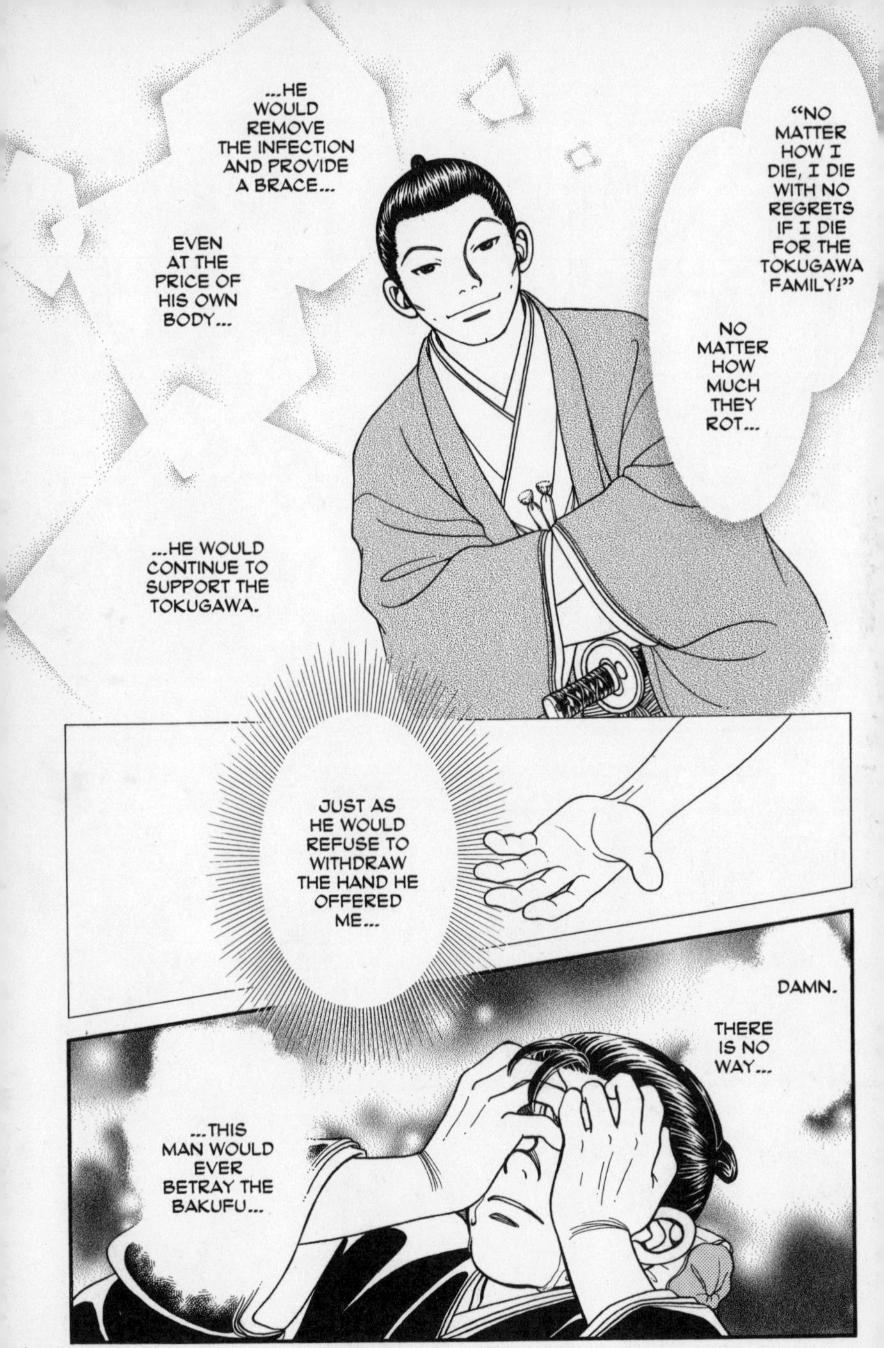
"NO MATTER HOW I DIE, I DIE WITH NO REGRETS IF I DIE FOR THE TOKUGAWA FAMILY!"
NO MATTER HOW MUCH THEY ROT...
...HE WOULD REMOVE THE INFECTION AND PROVIDE A BRACE...
EVEN AT THE PRICE OF HIS OWN BODY...
...HE WOULD CONTINUE TO SUPPORT THE TOKUGAWA.
JUST AS HE WOULD REFUSE TO WITHDRAW THE HAND HE OFFERED ME...
DAMN.
THERE IS NO WAY...
...THIS MAN WOULD EVER BETRAY THE BAKUFU...

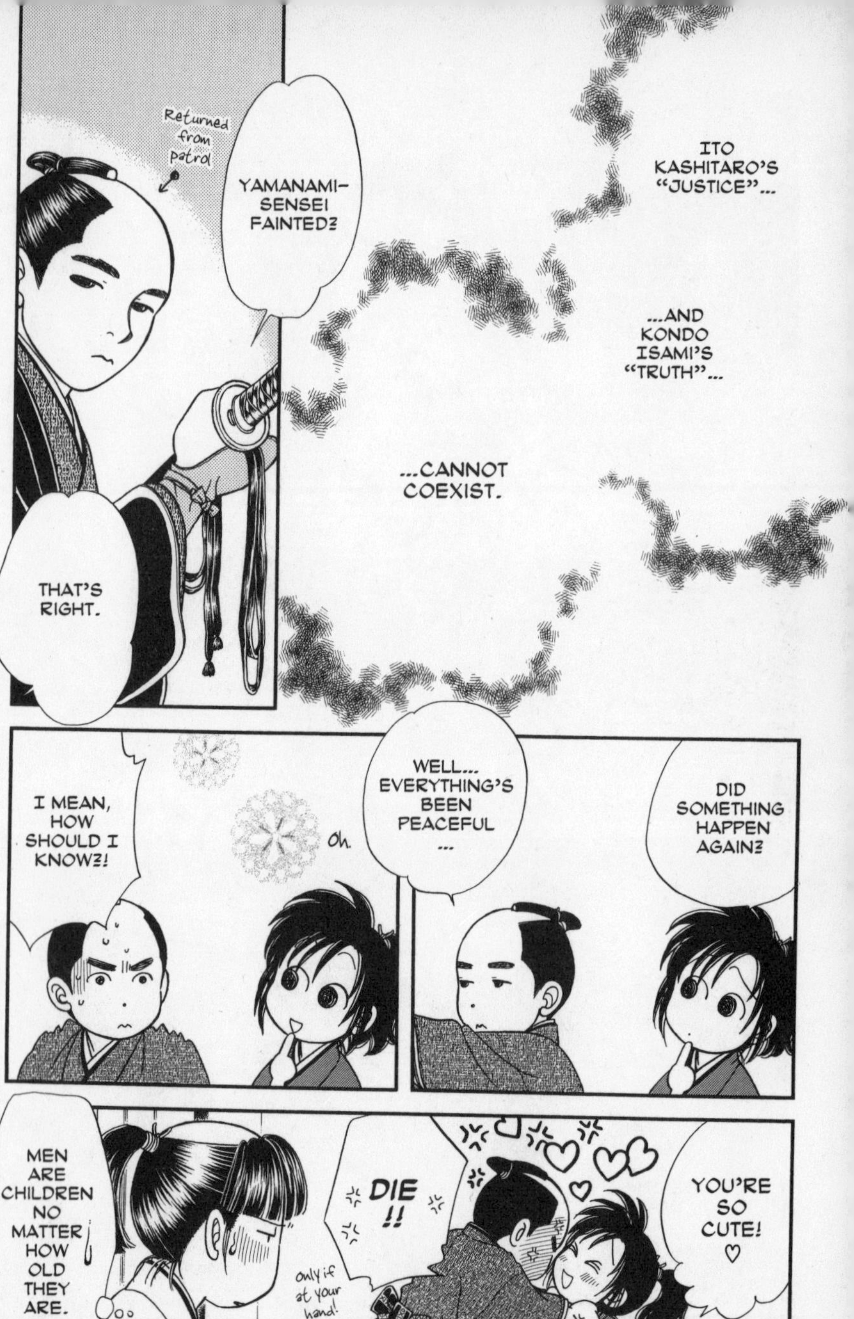
ITO KASHITARO'S "JUSTICE"...
...AND KONDO ISAMI'S "TRUTH"...
...CANNOT COEXIST.
Returned from patrol
YAMANAMI-SENSEI FAINTED?
THAT'S RIGHT.
DID SOMETHING HAPPEN AGAIN?
WELL... EVERYTHING'S BEEN PEACEFUL...
Oh.
I MEAN, HOW SHOULD I KNOW?!
YOU'RE SO CUTE! ♡
DIE!!
only if at your hand! ♥
MEN ARE CHILDREN NO MATTER HOW OLD THEY ARE.

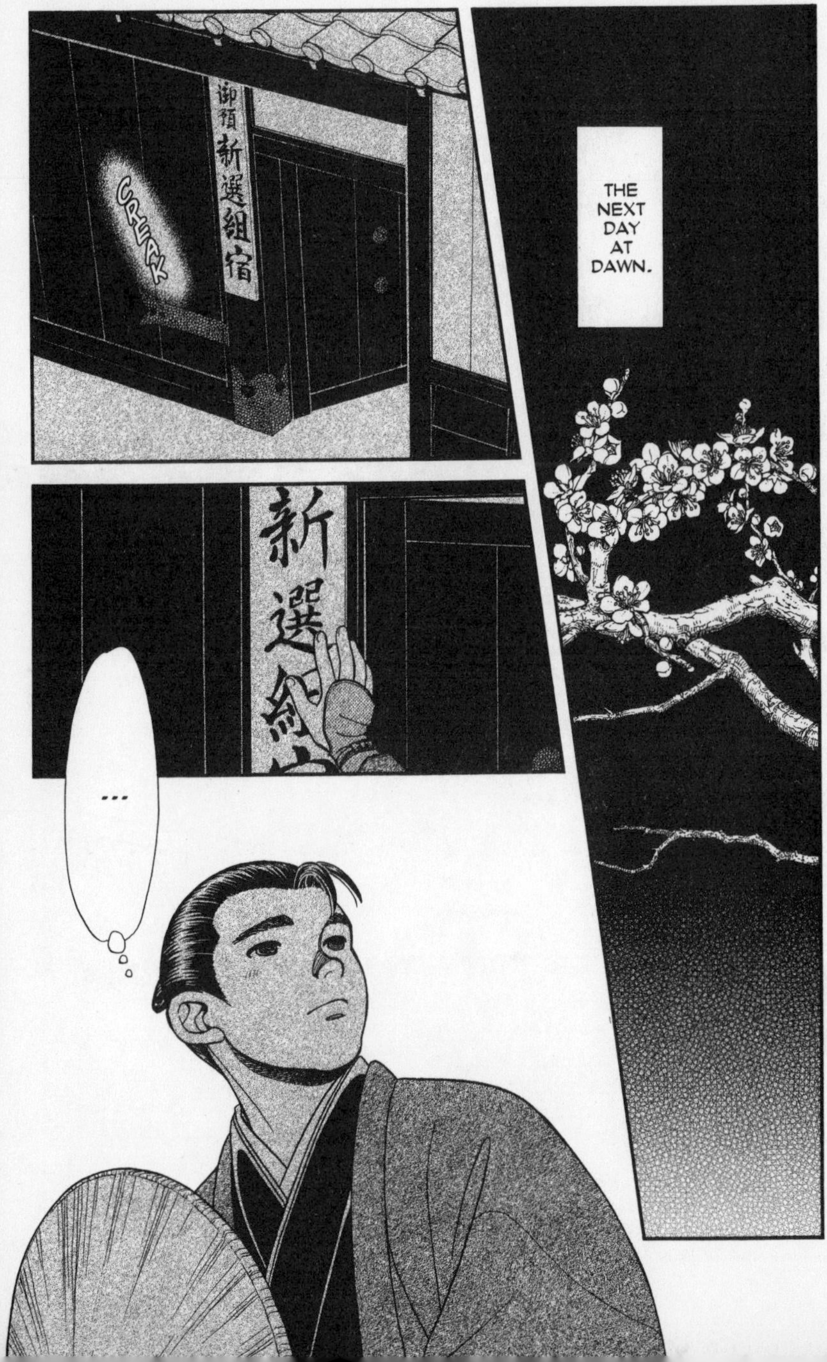
THE NEXT DAY AT DAWN.
御預 新選組宿
CREAK
...

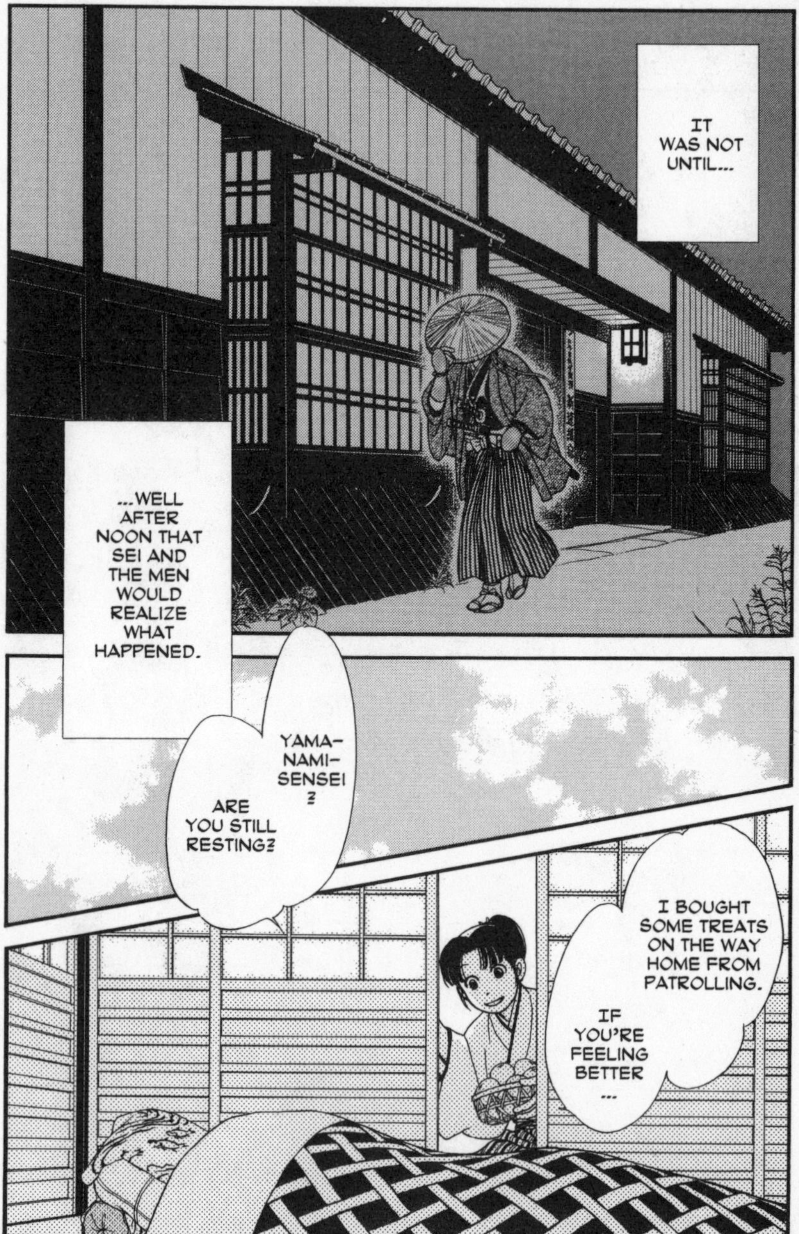
IT WAS NOT UNTIL...
...WELL AFTER NOON THAT SEI AND THE MEN WOULD REALIZE WHAT HAPPENED.
YAMA-NAMI-SENSEI?
ARE YOU STILL RESTING?
I BOUGHT SOME TREATS ON THE WAY HOME FROM PATROLLING.
IF YOU'RE FEELING BETTER ...

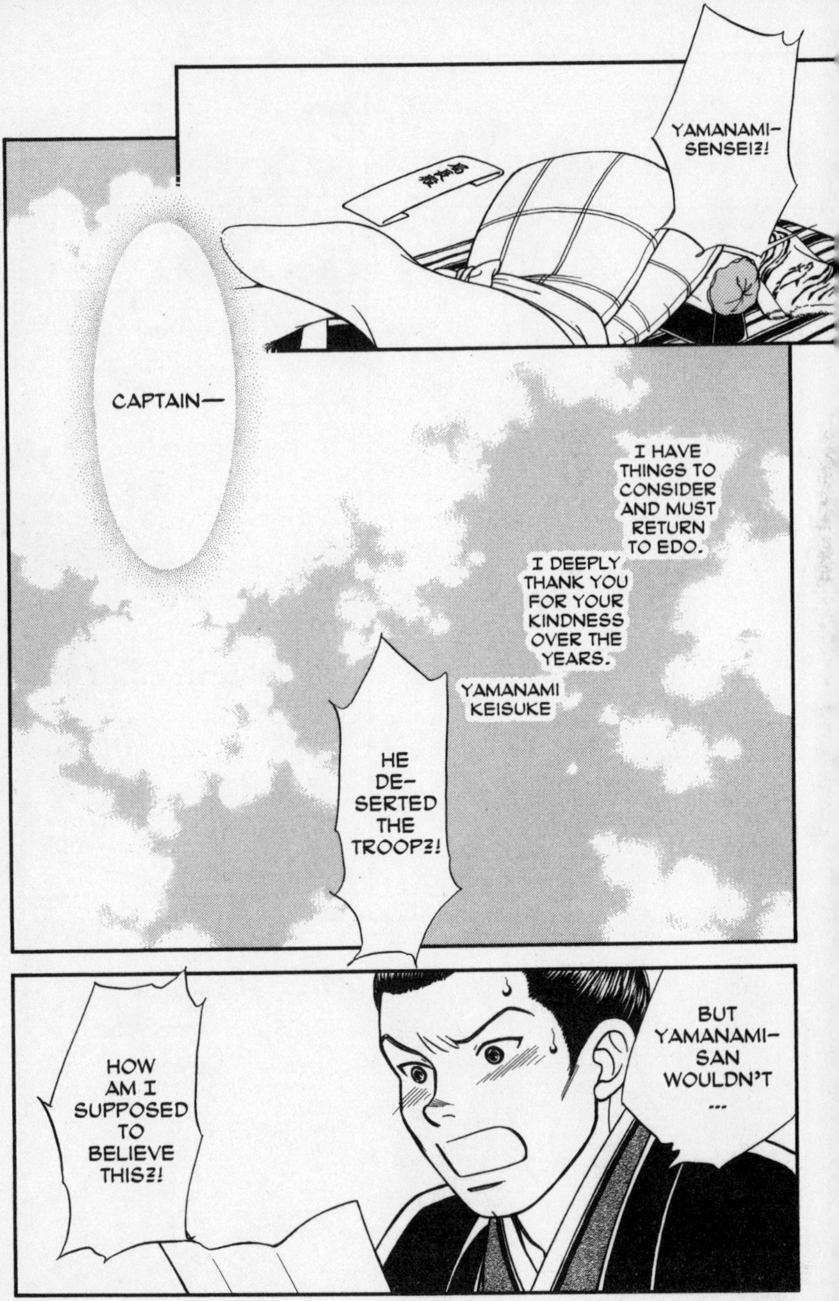
YAMANAMI-SENSEI?!
CAPTAIN—
I HAVE THINGS TO CONSIDER AND MUST RETURN TO EDO.
I DEEPLY THANK YOU FOR YOUR KINDNESS OVER THE YEARS.
YAMANAMI KEISUKE
HE DE-SERTED THE TROOP?!
BUT YAMANAMI-SAN WOULDN'T ...
HOW AM I SUPPOSED TO BELIEVE THIS?!

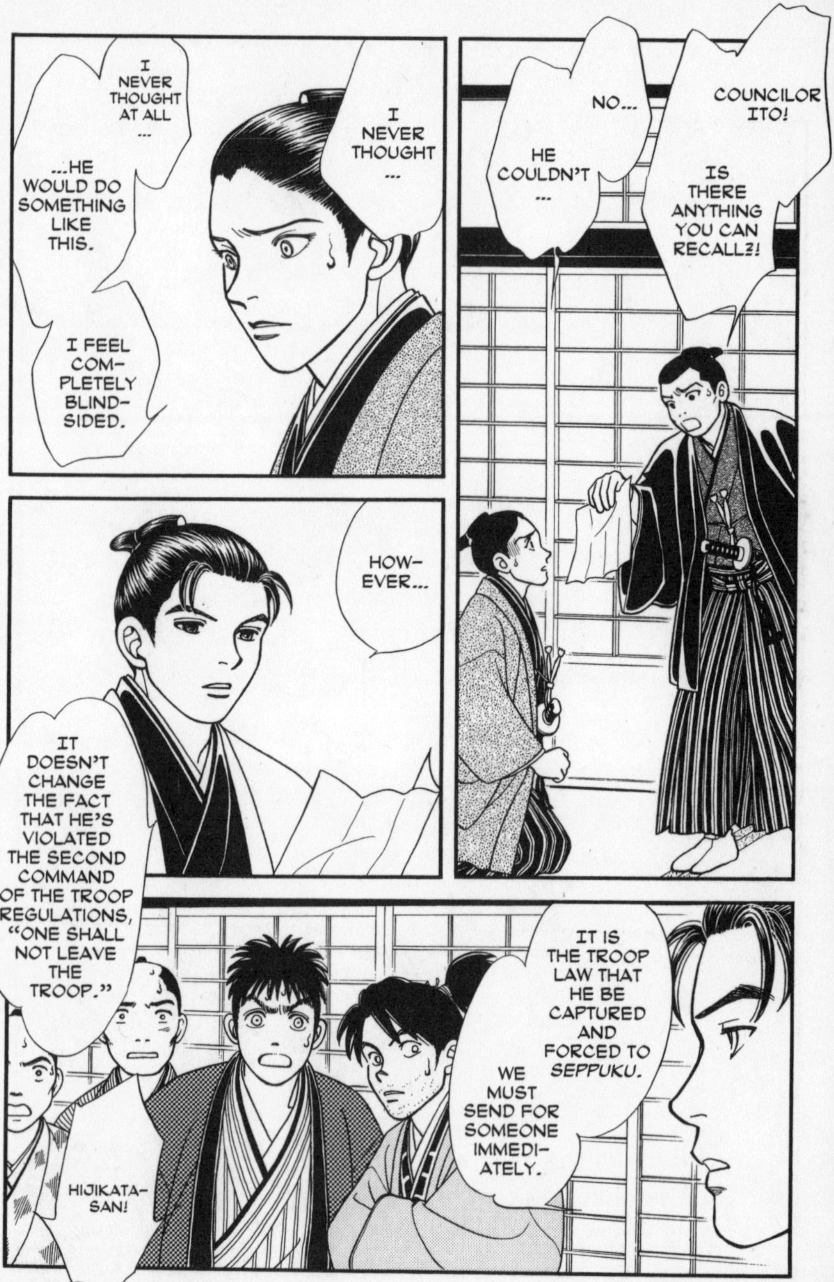
COUNCILOR ITO!
IS THERE ANYTHING YOU CAN RECALL?!
NO...
HE COULDN'T ...
I NEVER THOUGHT ...
I NEVER THOUGHT AT ALL ...
...HE WOULD DO SOMETHING LIKE THIS.
I FEEL COMPLETELY BLINDSIDED.
HOWEVER...
IT DOESN'T CHANGE THE FACT THAT HE'S VIOLATED THE SECOND COMMAND OF THE TROOP REGULATIONS, "ONE SHALL NOT LEAVE THE TROOP."
IT IS THE TROOP LAW THAT HE BE CAPTURED AND FORCED TO *SEPPUKU*.
WE MUST SEND FOR SOMEONE IMMEDIATELY.
HIJIKATA-SAN!

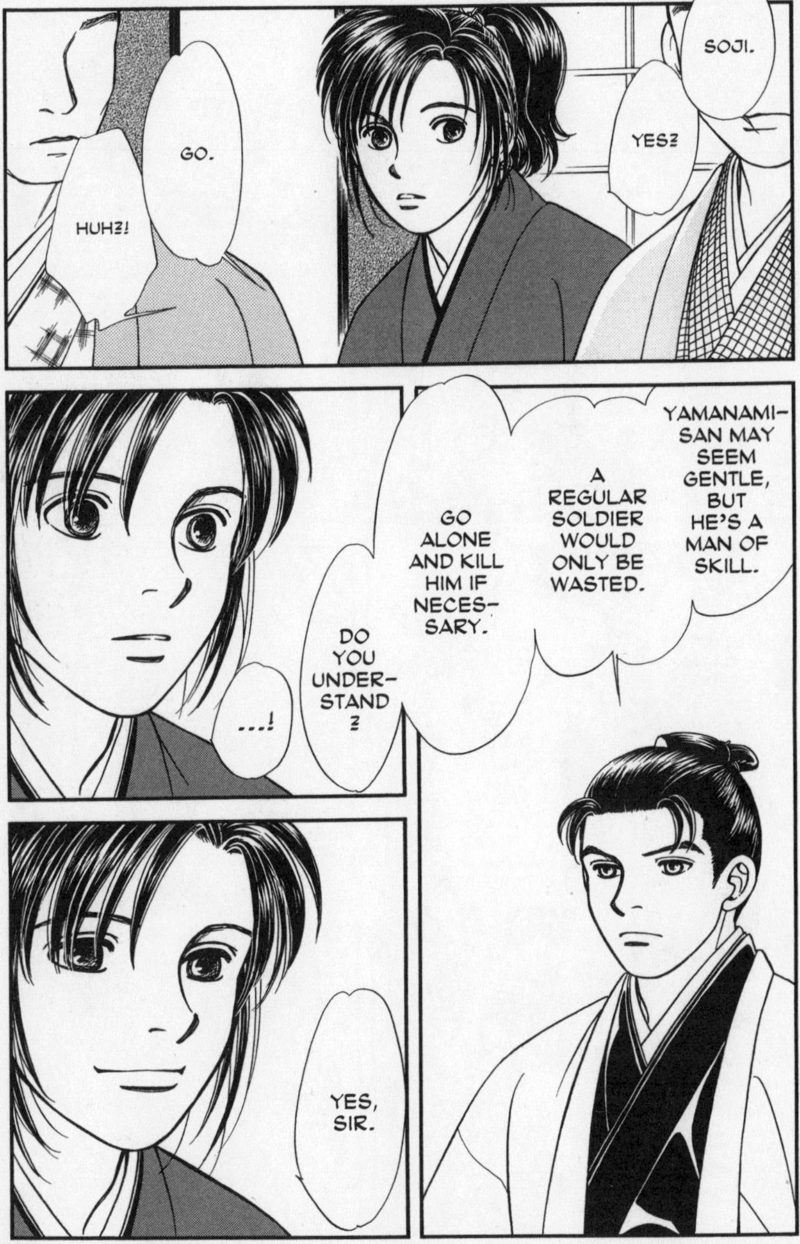
SOJI.
YES?
GO.
HUH?!
YAMANAMI-SAN MAY SEEM GENTLE, BUT HE'S A MAN OF SKILL.
A REGULAR SOLDIER WOULD ONLY BE WASTED.
GO ALONE AND KILL HIM IF NECESSARY.
DO YOU UNDERSTAND?
...!
YES, SIR.

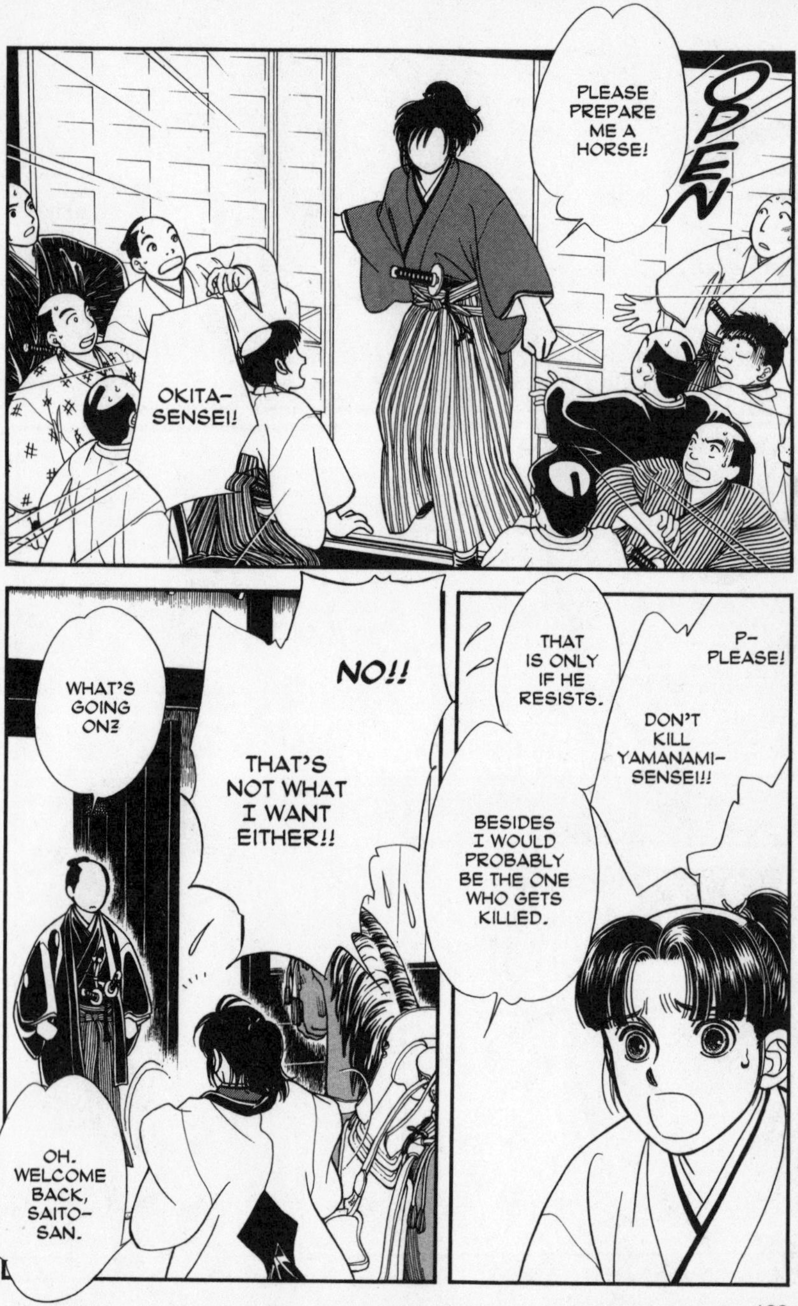
OPEN
PLEASE PREPARE ME A HORSE!
OKITA-SENSEI!
P-PLEASE!
DON'T KILL YAMANAMI-SENSEI!!
THAT IS ONLY IF HE RESISTS.
BESIDES I WOULD PROBABLY BE THE ONE WHO GETS KILLED.
NO!!
THAT'S NOT WHAT I WANT EITHER!!
WHAT'S GOING ON?
OH. WELCOME BACK, SAITO-SAN.

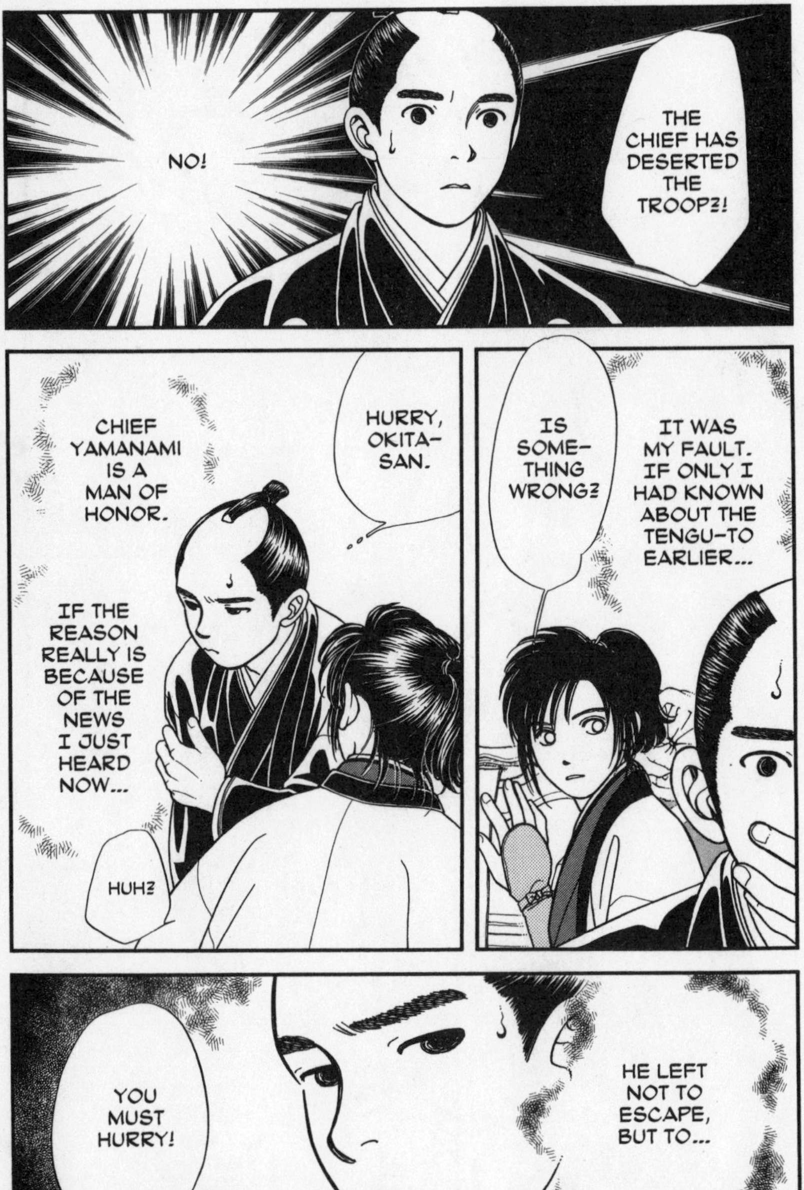
THE CHIEF HAS DESERTED THE TROOP?!
NO!
IT WAS MY FAULT. IF ONLY I HAD KNOWN ABOUT THE TENGU-TO EARLIER...
IS SOME-THING WRONG?
HURRY, OKITA-SAN.
CHIEF YAMANAMI IS A MAN OF HONOR.
IF THE REASON REALLY IS BECAUSE OF THE NEWS I JUST HEARD NOW...
HUH?
HE LEFT NOT TO ESCAPE, BUT TO...
YOU MUST HURRY!

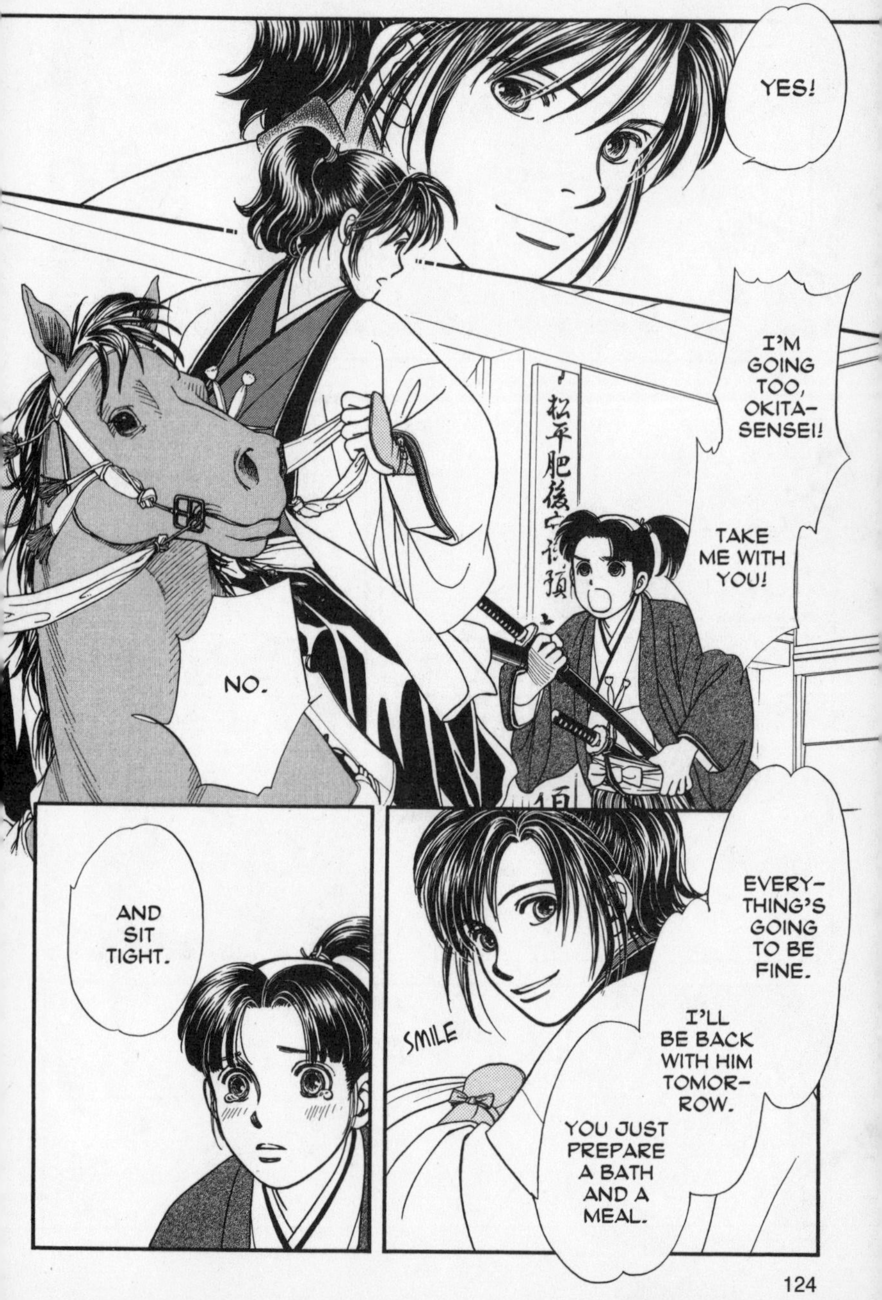
YES!
I'M GOING TOO, OKITA-SENSEI!
TAKE ME WITH YOU!
NO.
EVERY-THING'S GOING TO BE FINE.
I'LL BE BACK WITH HIM TOMOR-ROW.
YOU JUST PREPARE A BATH AND A MEAL.
SMILE
AND SIT TIGHT.

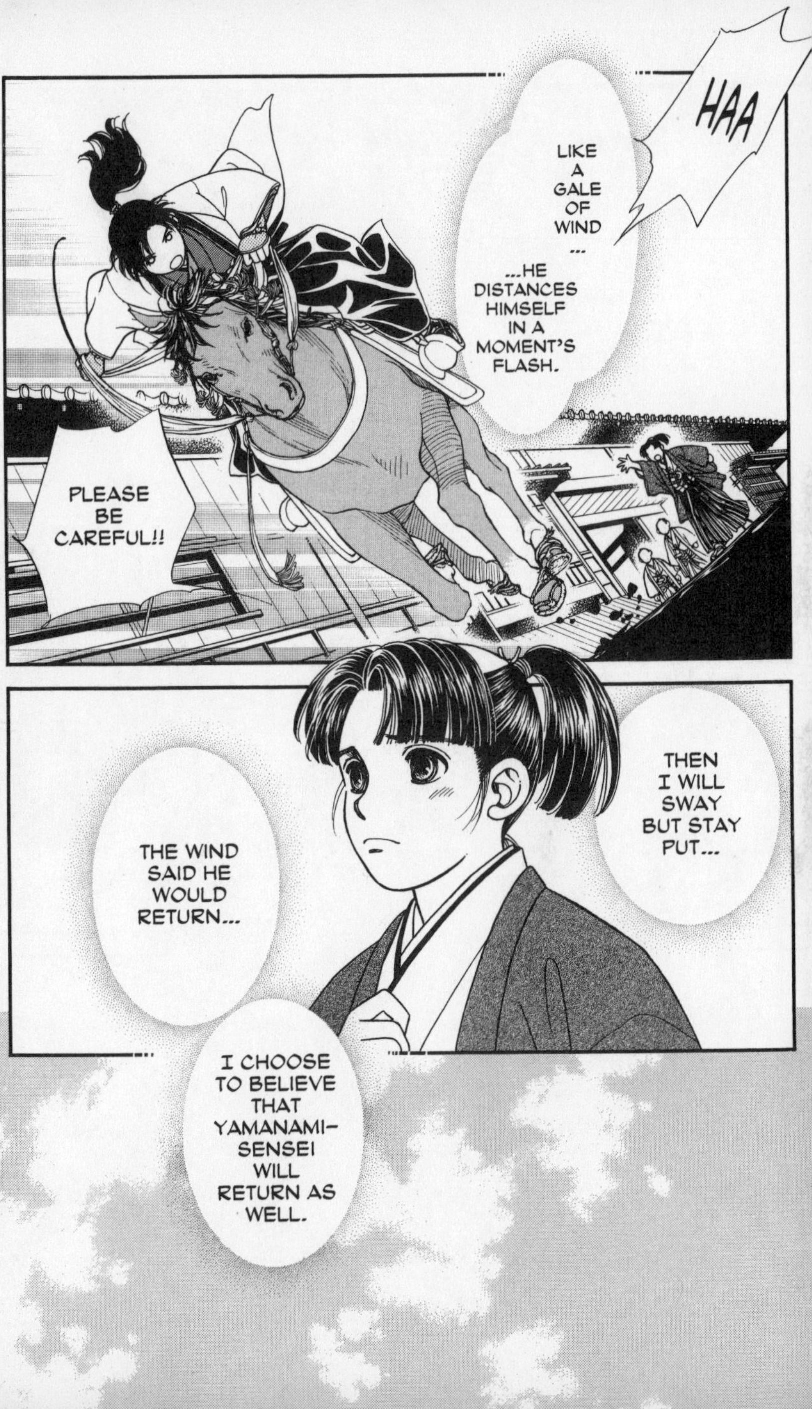
HAA
LIKE A GALE OF WIND ...
...HE DISTANCES HIMSELF IN A MOMENT'S FLASH.
PLEASE BE CAREFUL!!
THEN I WILL SWAY BUT STAY PUT...
THE WIND SAID HE WOULD RETURN...
I CHOOSE TO BELIEVE THAT YAMANAMI-SENSEI WILL RETURN AS WELL.

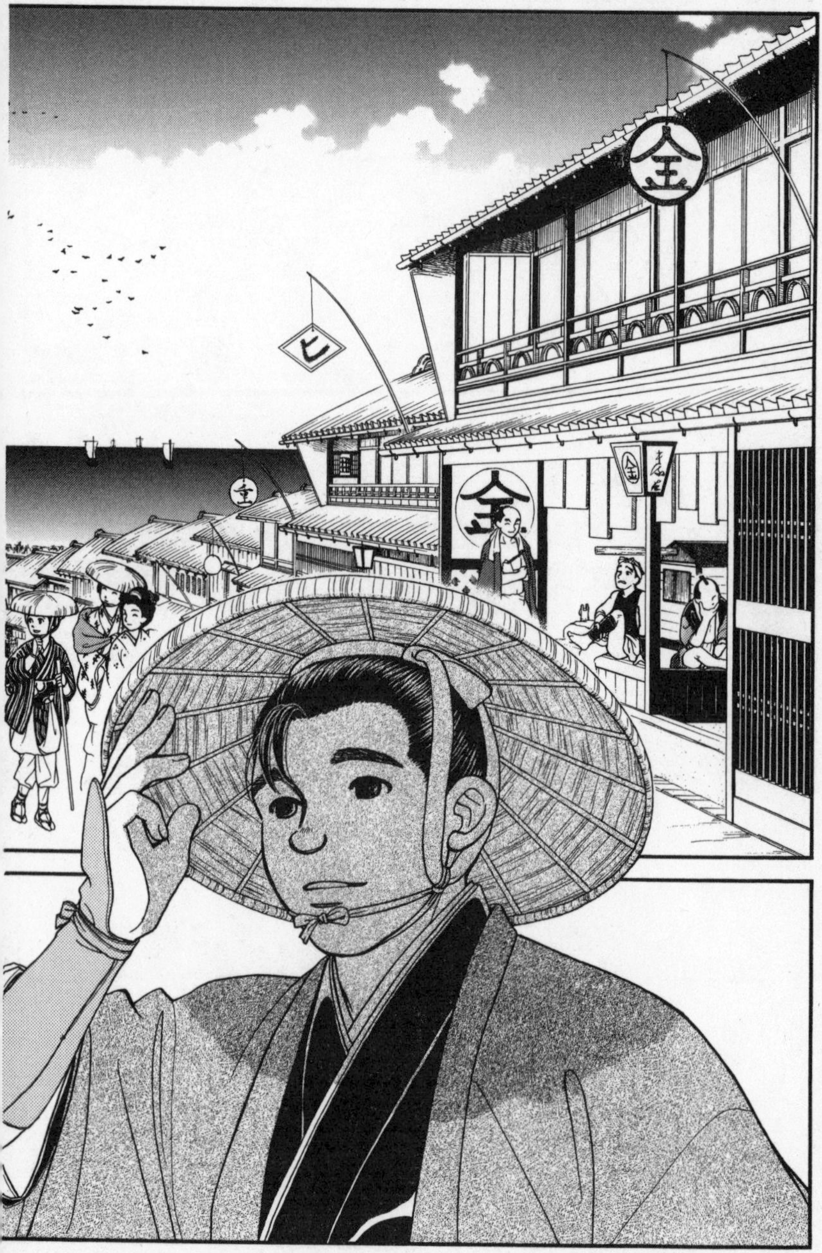

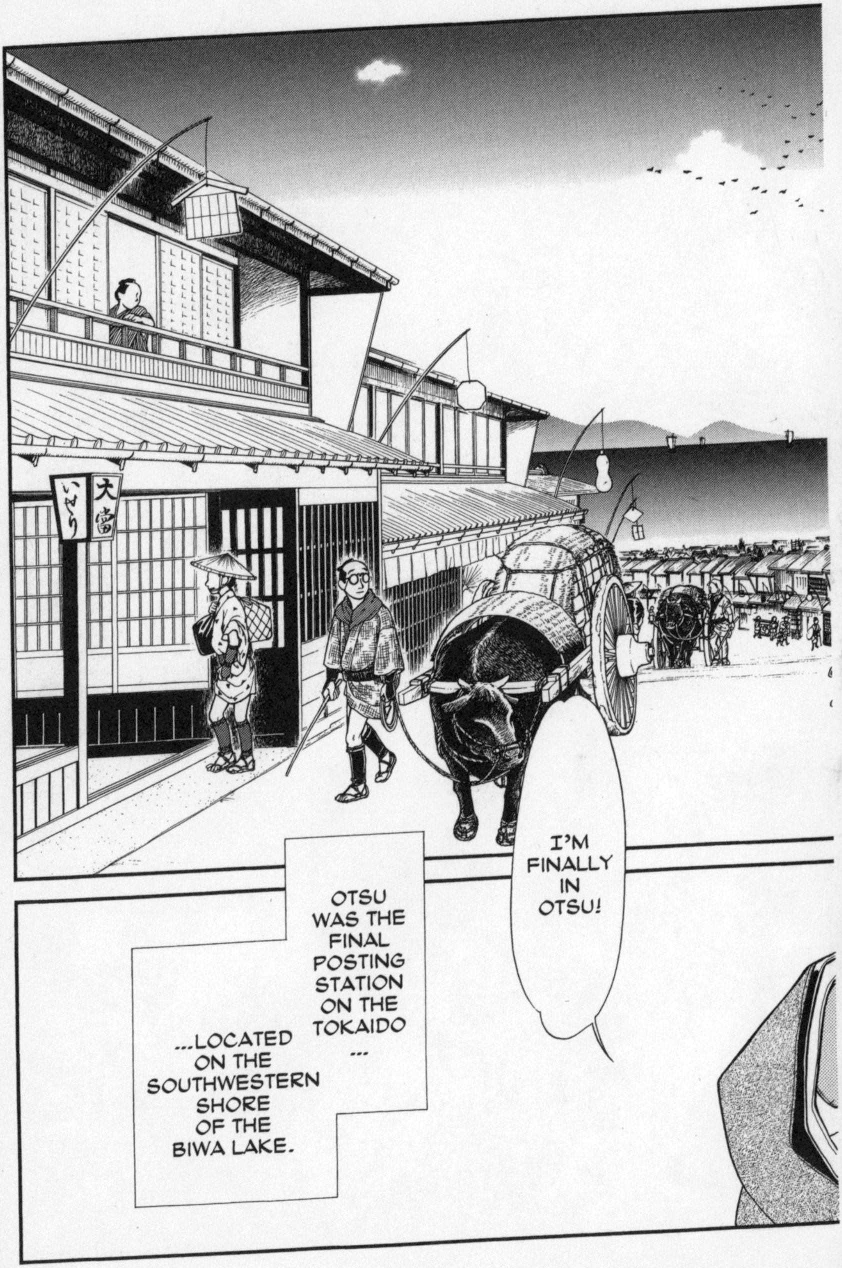
I'M FINALLY IN OTSU!
OTSU WAS THE FINAL POSTING STATION ON THE TOKAIDO ...
...LOCATED ON THE SOUTHWESTERN SHORE OF THE BIWA LAKE.

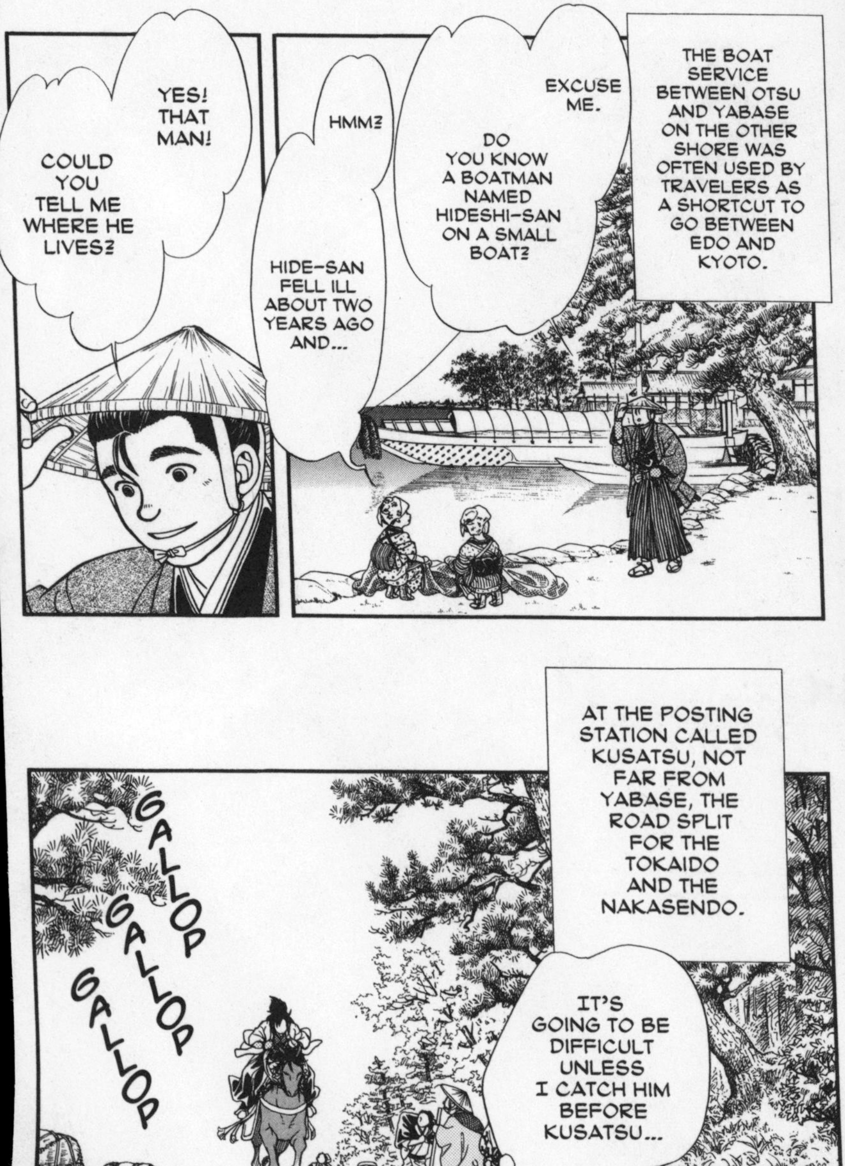
THE BOAT SERVICE BETWEEN OTSU AND YABASE ON THE OTHER SHORE WAS OFTEN USED BY TRAVELERS AS A SHORTCUT TO GO BETWEEN EDO AND KYOTO.
EXCUSE ME.
DO YOU KNOW A BOATMAN NAMED HIDESHI-SAN ON A SMALL BOAT?
HMM?
HIDE-SAN FELL ILL ABOUT TWO YEARS AGO AND...
YES! THAT MAN!
COULD YOU TELL ME WHERE HE LIVES?
AT THE POSTING STATION CALLED KUSATSU, NOT FAR FROM YABASE, THE ROAD SPLIT FOR THE TOKAIDO AND THE NAKASENDO.
GALLOP GALLOP GALLOP
IT'S GOING TO BE DIFFICULT UNLESS I CATCH HIM BEFORE KUSATSU...

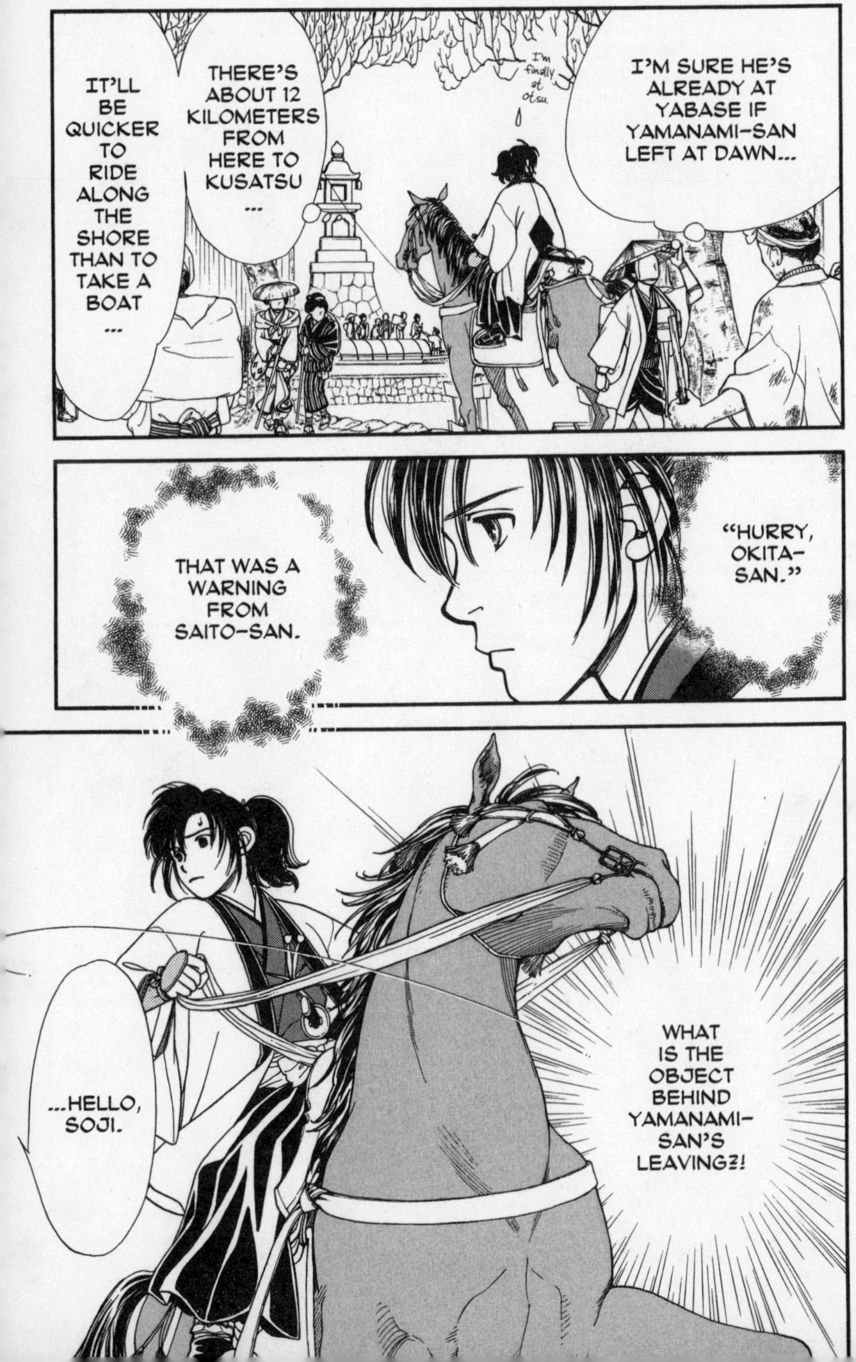
I'M SURE HE'S ALREADY AT YABASE IF YAMANAMI-SAN LEFT AT DAWN...
I'm finally at Otsu
THERE'S ABOUT 12 KILOMETERS FROM HERE TO KUSATSU...
IT'LL BE QUICKER TO RIDE ALONG THE SHORE THAN TO TAKE A BOAT...
"HURRY, OKITA-SAN."
THAT WAS A WARNING FROM SAITO-SAN.
WHAT IS THE OBJECT BEHIND YAMANAMI-SAN'S LEAVING?!
...HELLO, SOJI.

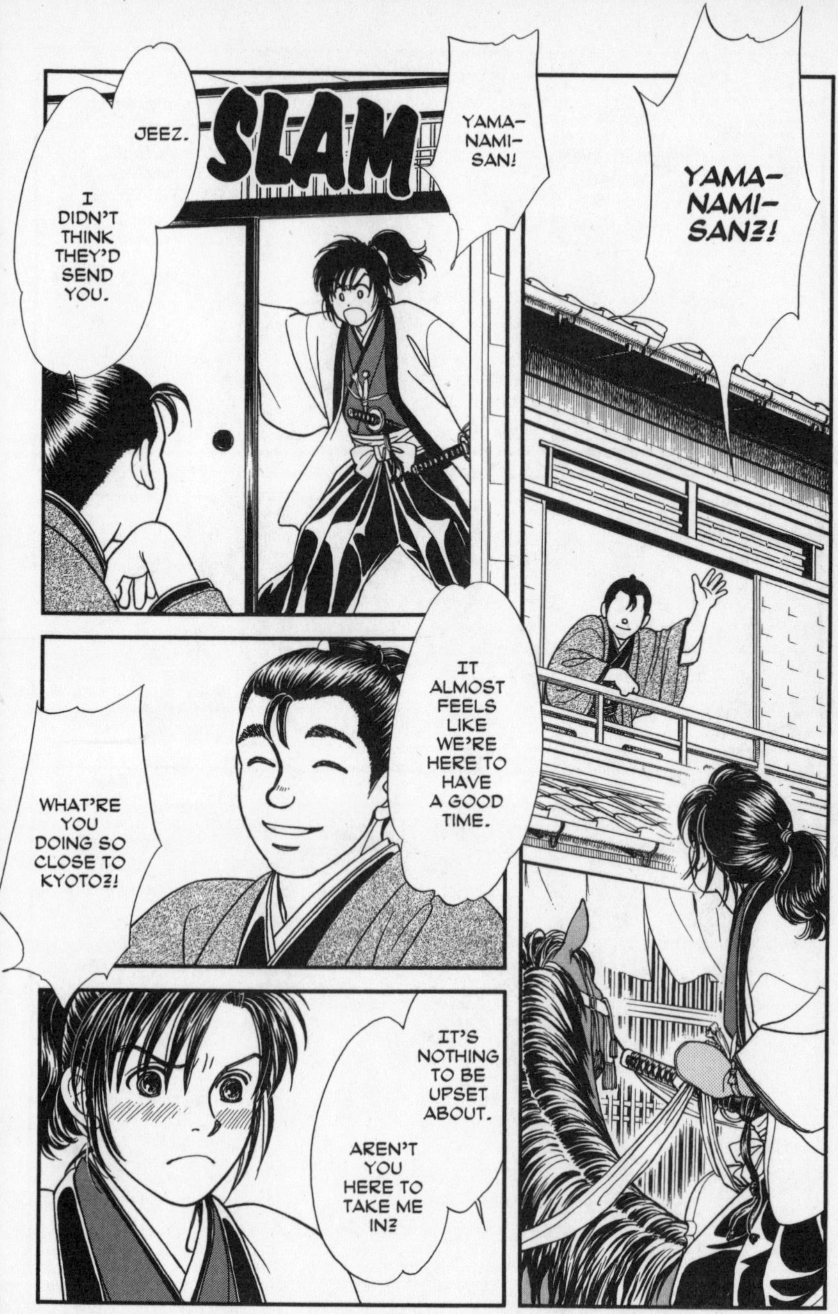
YAMA-NAMI-SAN?!
YAMA-NAMI-SAN!
SLAM
JEEZ.
I DIDN'T THINK THEY'D SEND YOU.
IT ALMOST FEELS LIKE WE'RE HERE TO HAVE A GOOD TIME.
WHAT'RE YOU DOING SO CLOSE TO KYOTO?!
IT'S NOTHING TO BE UPSET ABOUT.
AREN'T YOU HERE TO TAKE ME IN?

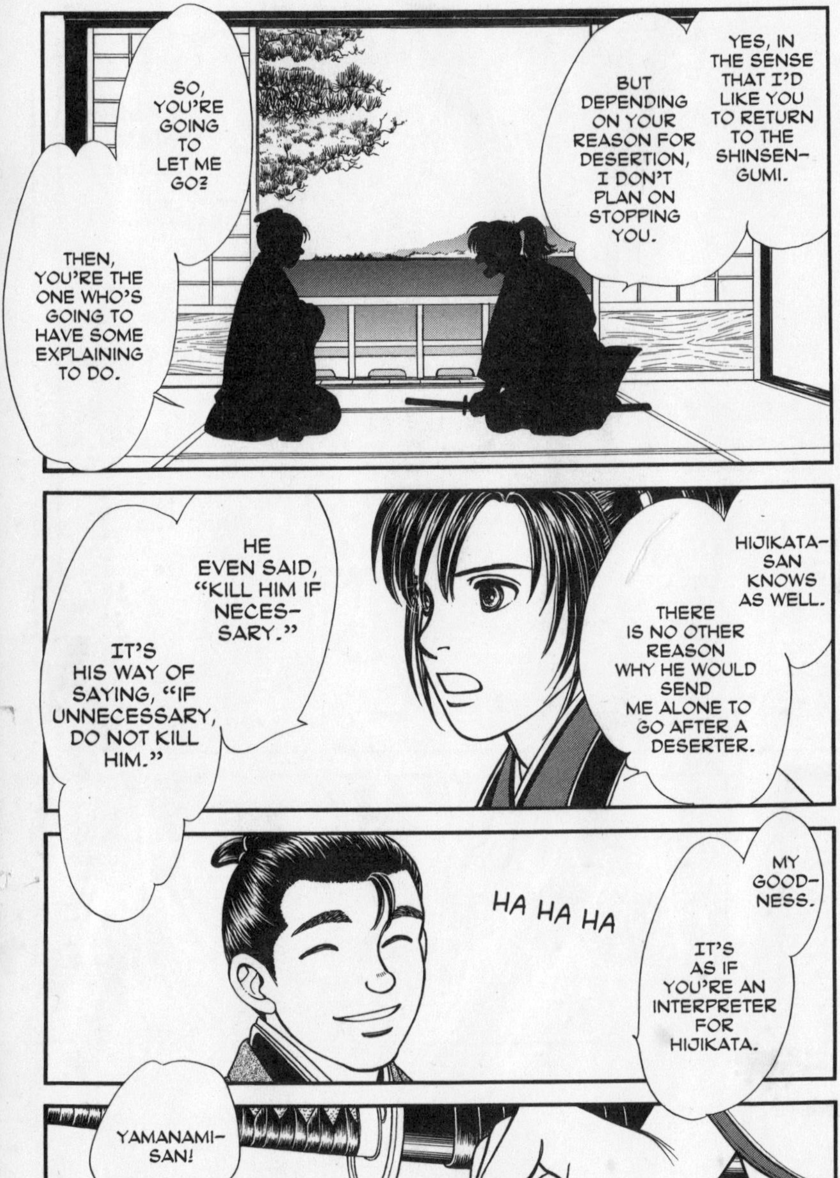
YES, IN THE SENSE THAT I'D LIKE YOU TO RETURN TO THE SHINSEN-GUMI.
BUT DEPENDING ON YOUR REASON FOR DESERTION, I DON'T PLAN ON STOPPING YOU.
SO, YOU'RE GOING TO LET ME GO?
THEN, YOU'RE THE ONE WHO'S GOING TO HAVE SOME EXPLAINING TO DO.
HIJIKATA-SAN KNOWS AS WELL.
THERE IS NO OTHER REASON WHY HE WOULD SEND ME ALONE TO GO AFTER A DESERTER.
HE EVEN SAID, "KILL HIM IF NECES-SARY."
IT'S HIS WAY OF SAYING, "IF UNNECESSARY, DO NOT KILL HIM."
MY GOODNESS.
IT'S AS IF YOU'RE AN INTERPRETER FOR HIJIKATA.
HA HA HA
YAMANAMI-SAN!

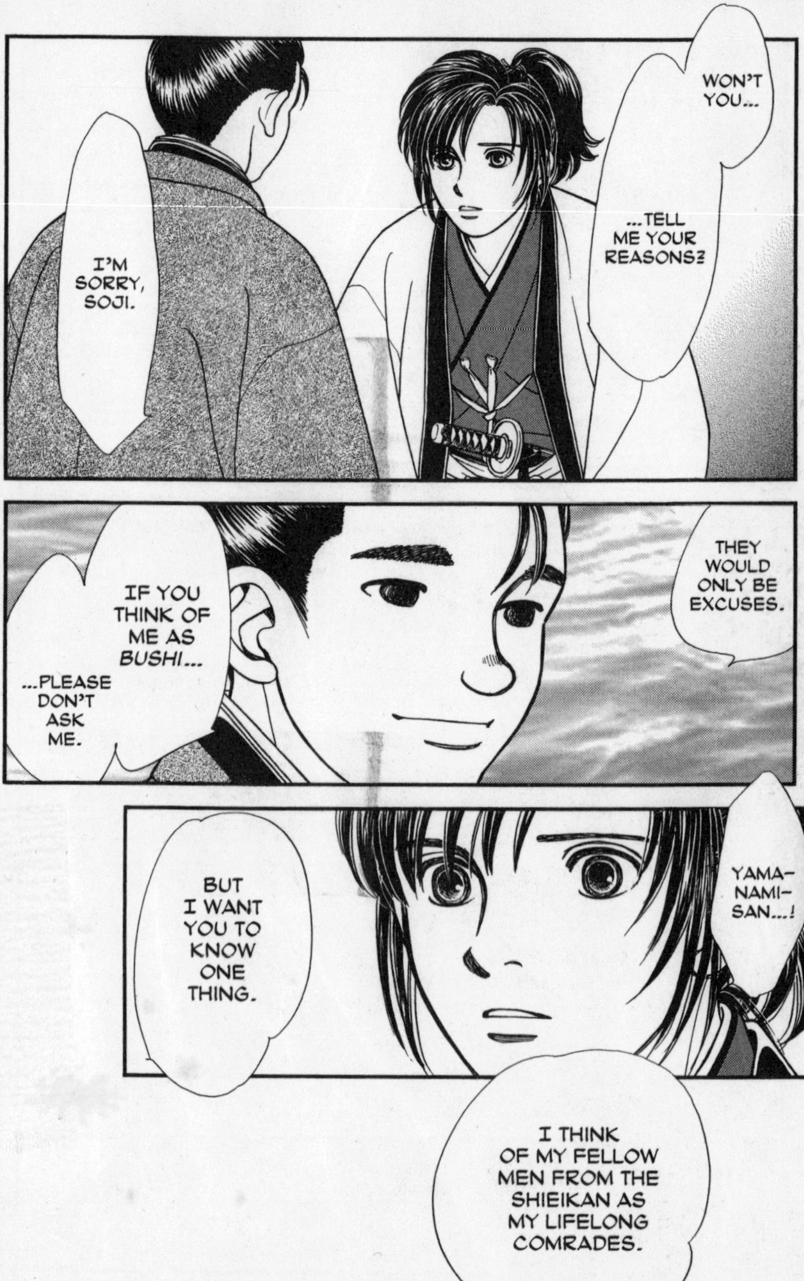
WON'T YOU...
...TELL ME YOUR REASONS?
I'M SORRY, SOJI.
THEY WOULD ONLY BE EXCUSES.
IF YOU THINK OF ME AS *BUSHI*...
...PLEASE DON'T ASK ME.
YAMA-NAMI-SAN...!
BUT I WANT YOU TO KNOW ONE THING.
I THINK OF MY FELLOW MEN FROM THE SHIEIKAN AS MY LIFELONG COMRADES.

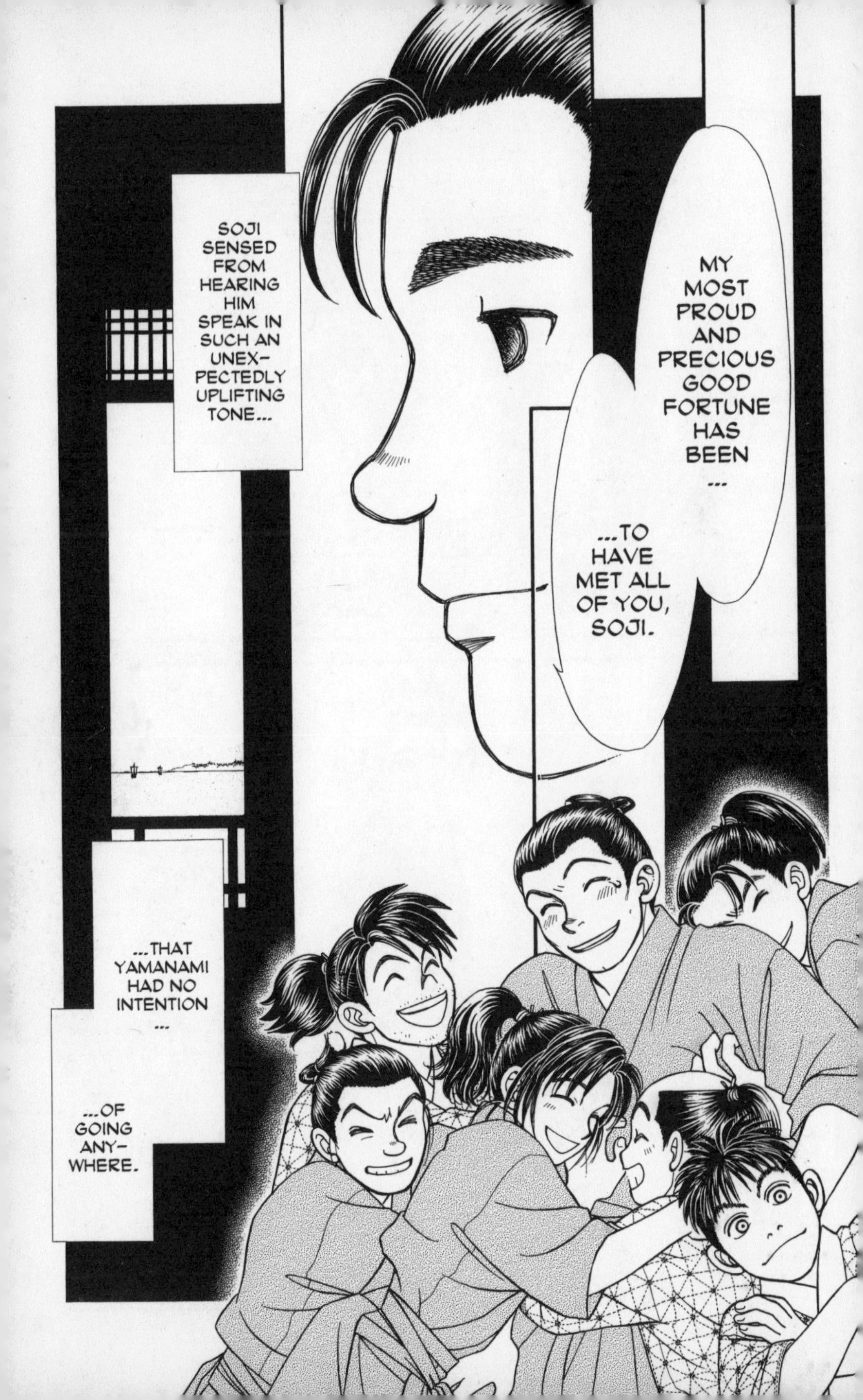
MY MOST PROUD AND PRECIOUS GOOD FORTUNE HAS BEEN ...
...TO HAVE MET ALL OF YOU, SOJI.
SOJI SENSED FROM HEARING HIM SPEAK IN SUCH AN UNEX-PECTEDLY UPLIFTING TONE...
...THAT YAMANAMI HAD NO INTENTION ...
...OF GOING ANY-WHERE.

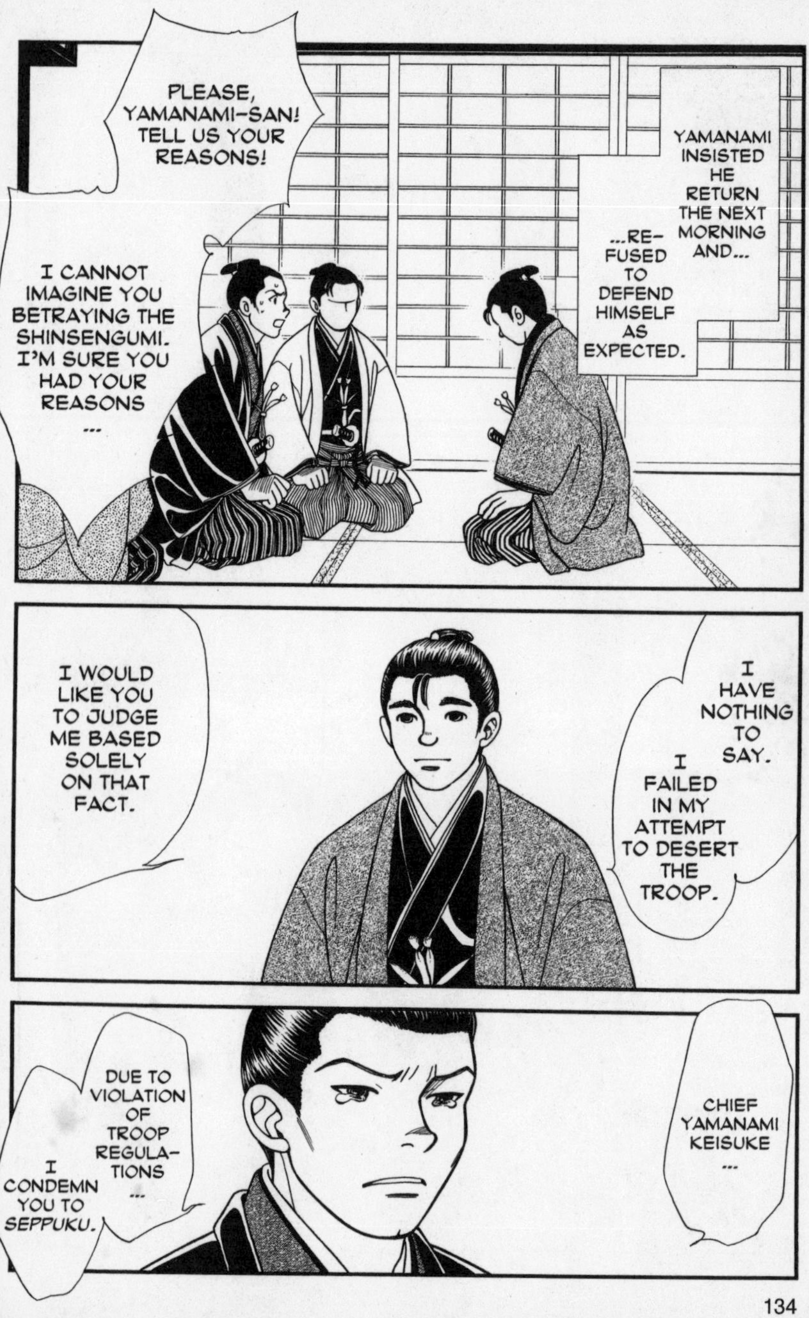
YAMANAMI INSISTED HE RETURN THE NEXT MORNING AND...
...RE-FUSED TO DEFEND HIMSELF AS EXPECTED.
PLEASE, YAMANAMI-SAN! TELL US YOUR REASONS!
I CANNOT IMAGINE YOU BETRAYING THE SHINSENGUMI. I'M SURE YOU HAD YOUR REASONS ...
I HAVE NOTHING TO SAY.
I FAILED IN MY ATTEMPT TO DESERT THE TROOP.
I WOULD LIKE YOU TO JUDGE ME BASED SOLELY ON THAT FACT.
CHIEF YAMANAMI KEISUKE ...
DUE TO VIOLATION OF TROOP REGULA-TIONS ...
I CONDEMN YOU TO SEPPUKU.

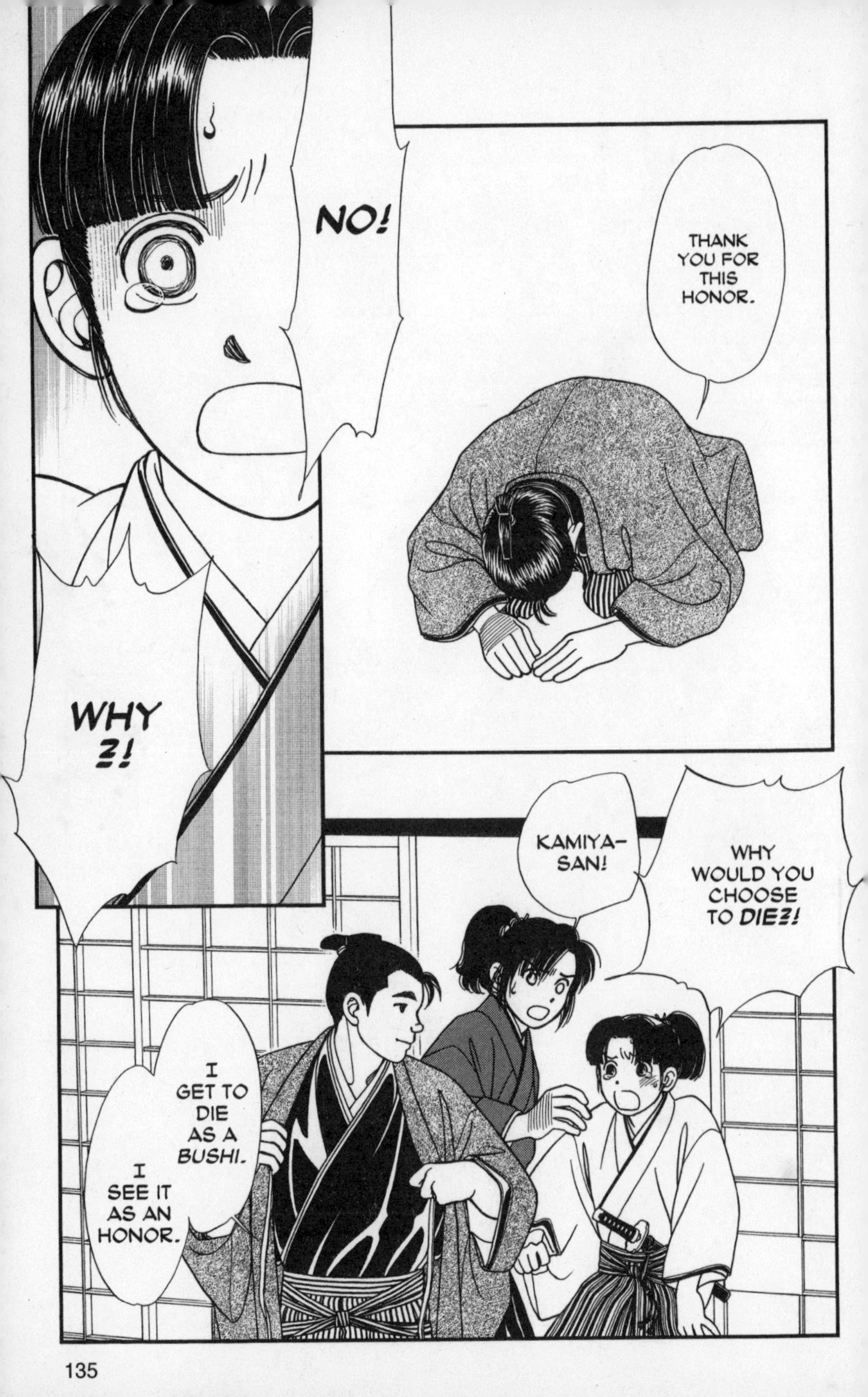
THANK YOU FOR THIS HONOR.
NO!
WHY?!
WHY WOULD YOU CHOOSE TO DIE?!
KAMIYA-SAN!
I GET TO DIE AS A BUSHI.
I SEE IT AS AN HONOR.

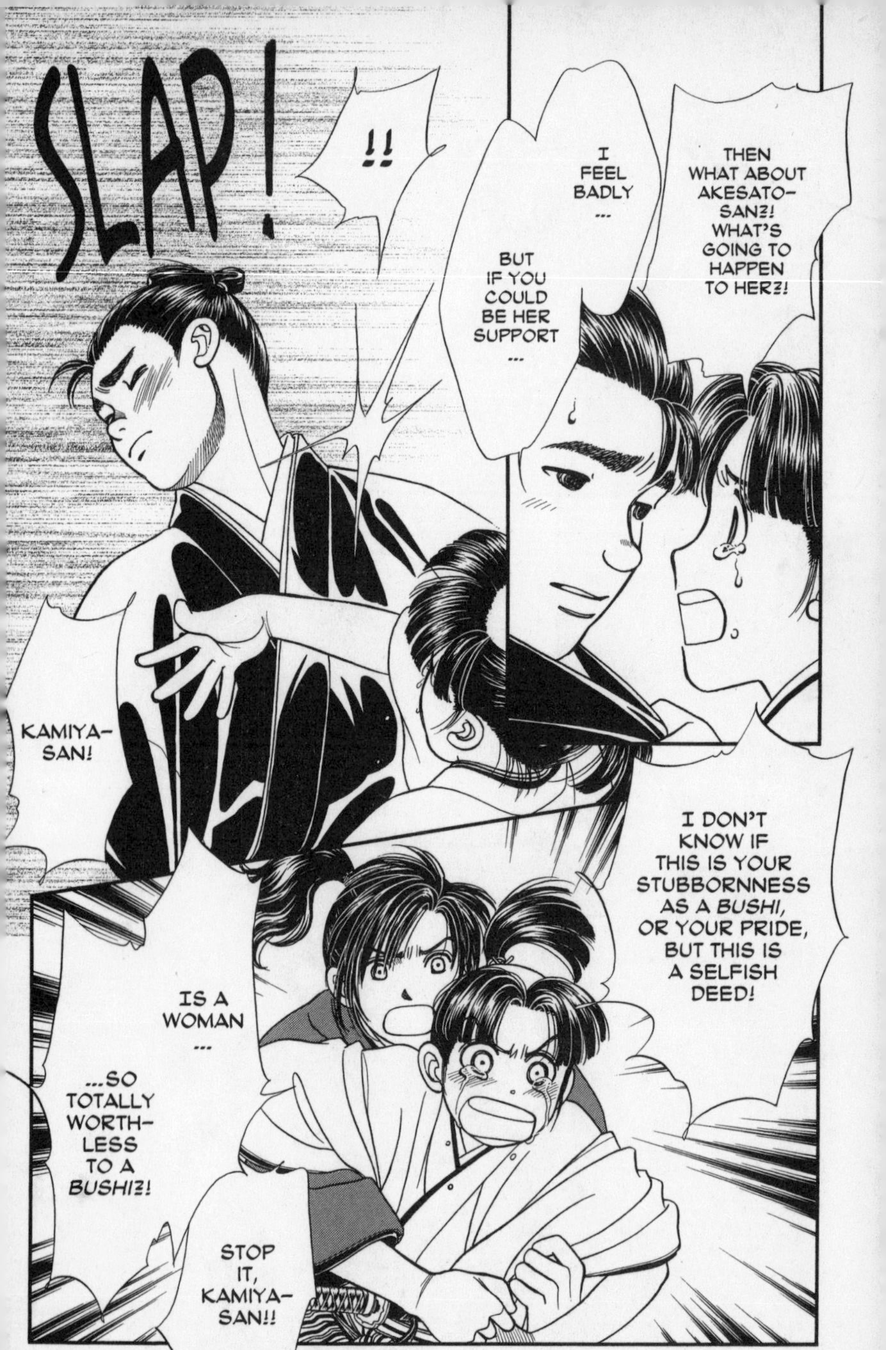

THEN WHAT ABOUT AKESATO-SAN?! WHAT'S GOING TO HAPPEN TO HER?!
I FEEL BADLY...
BUT IF YOU COULD BE HER SUPPORT...
I DON'T KNOW IF THIS IS YOUR STUBBORNNESS AS A *BUSHI*, OR YOUR PRIDE, BUT THIS IS A SELFISH DEED!
IS A WOMAN...
...SO TOTALLY WORTHLESS TO A *BUSHI*?!
STOP IT, KAMIYA-SAN!!
SLAP!
!!
KAMIYA-SAN!

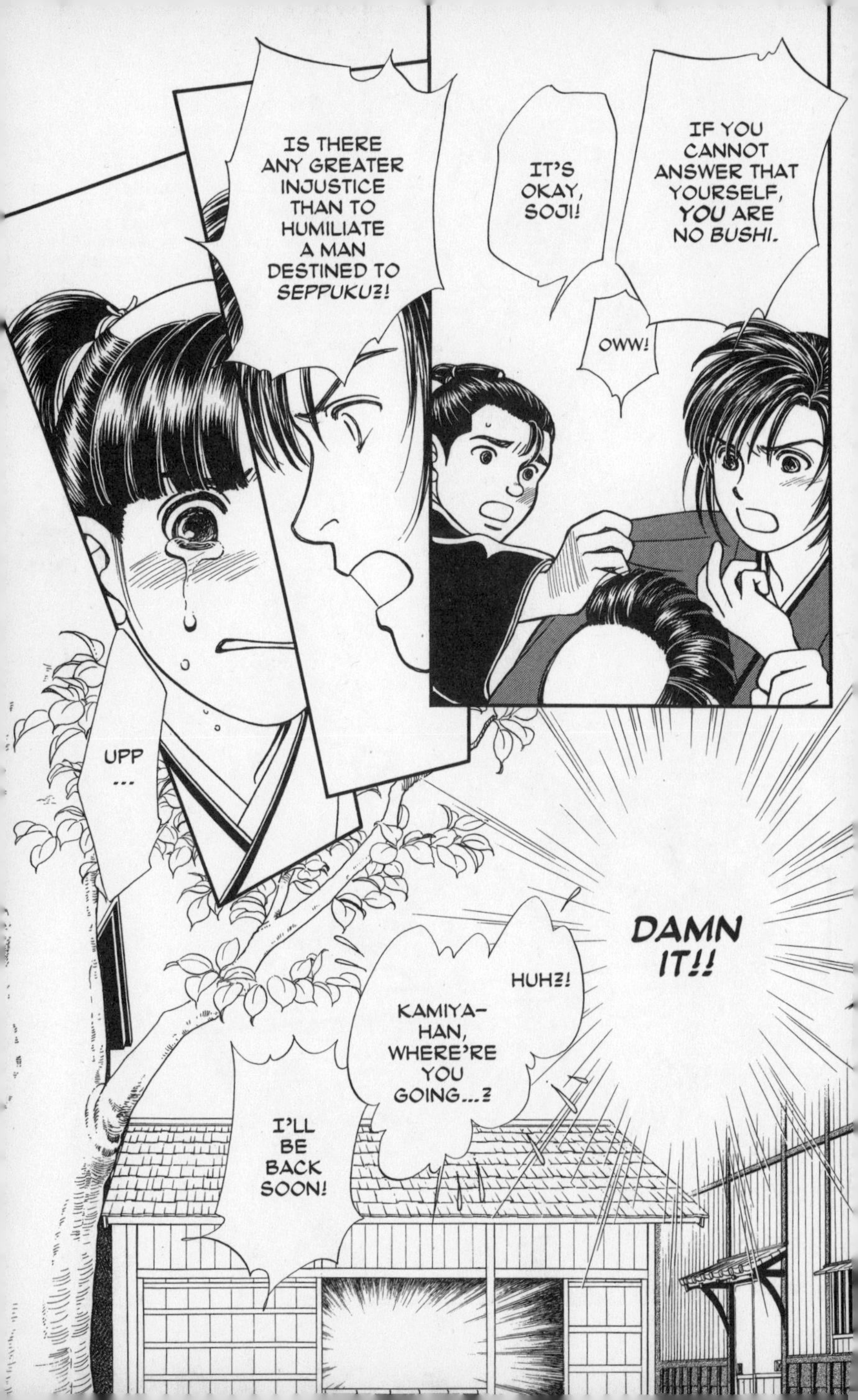

IF YOU CANNOT ANSWER THAT YOURSELF, *YOU* ARE NO *BUSHI*.
IT'S OKAY, SOJI!
OWW!
IS THERE ANY GREATER INJUSTICE THAN TO HUMILIATE A MAN DESTINED TO *SEPPUKU*?!
UPP ...
DAMN IT!!
HUH?!
KAMIYA-HAN, WHERE'RE YOU GOING...?
I'LL BE BACK SOON!

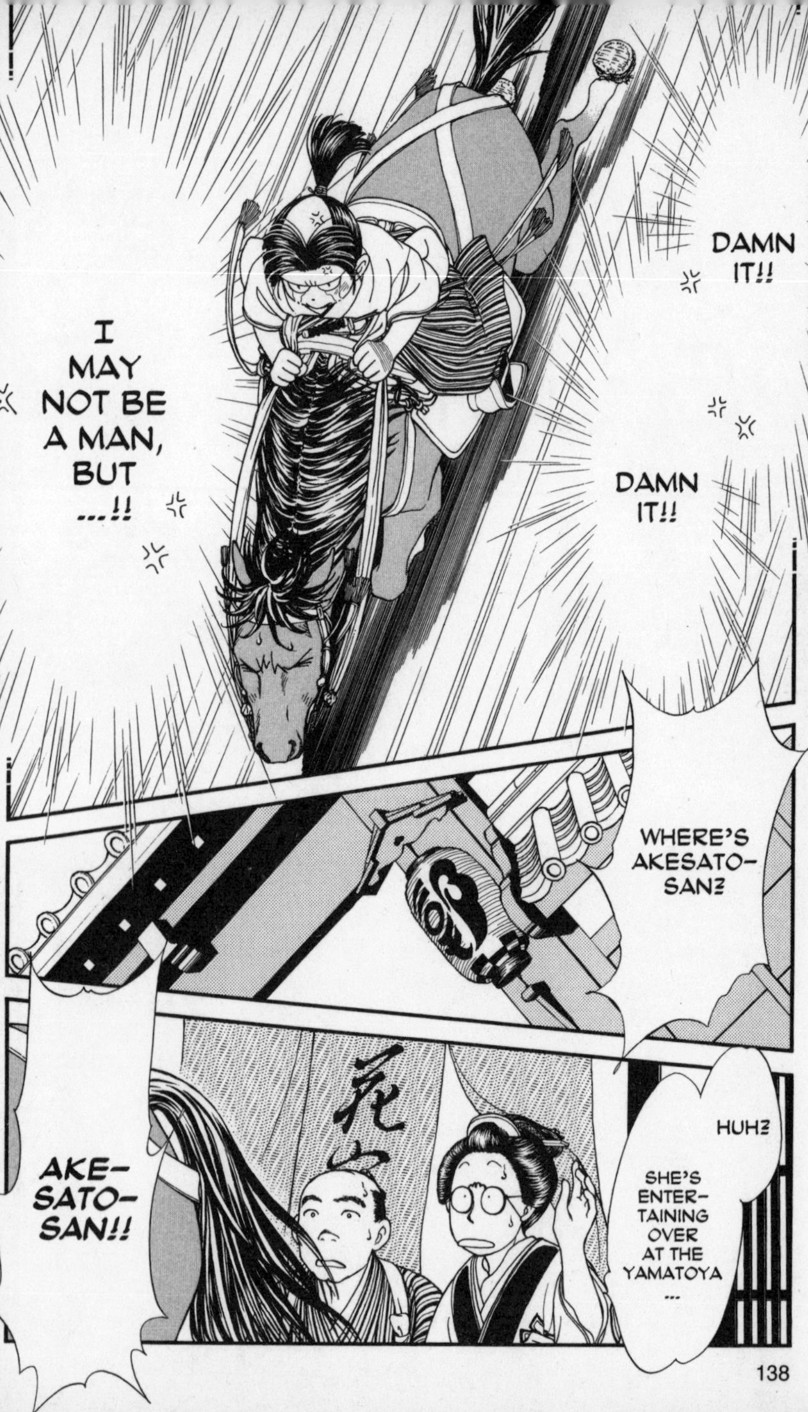
DAMN IT!!
DAMN IT!!
I MAY NOT BE A MAN, BUT ...!!
WHERE'S AKESATO-SAN?
HUH?
SHE'S ENTERTAINING OVER AT THE YAMATOYA ...
AKE-SATO-SAN!!

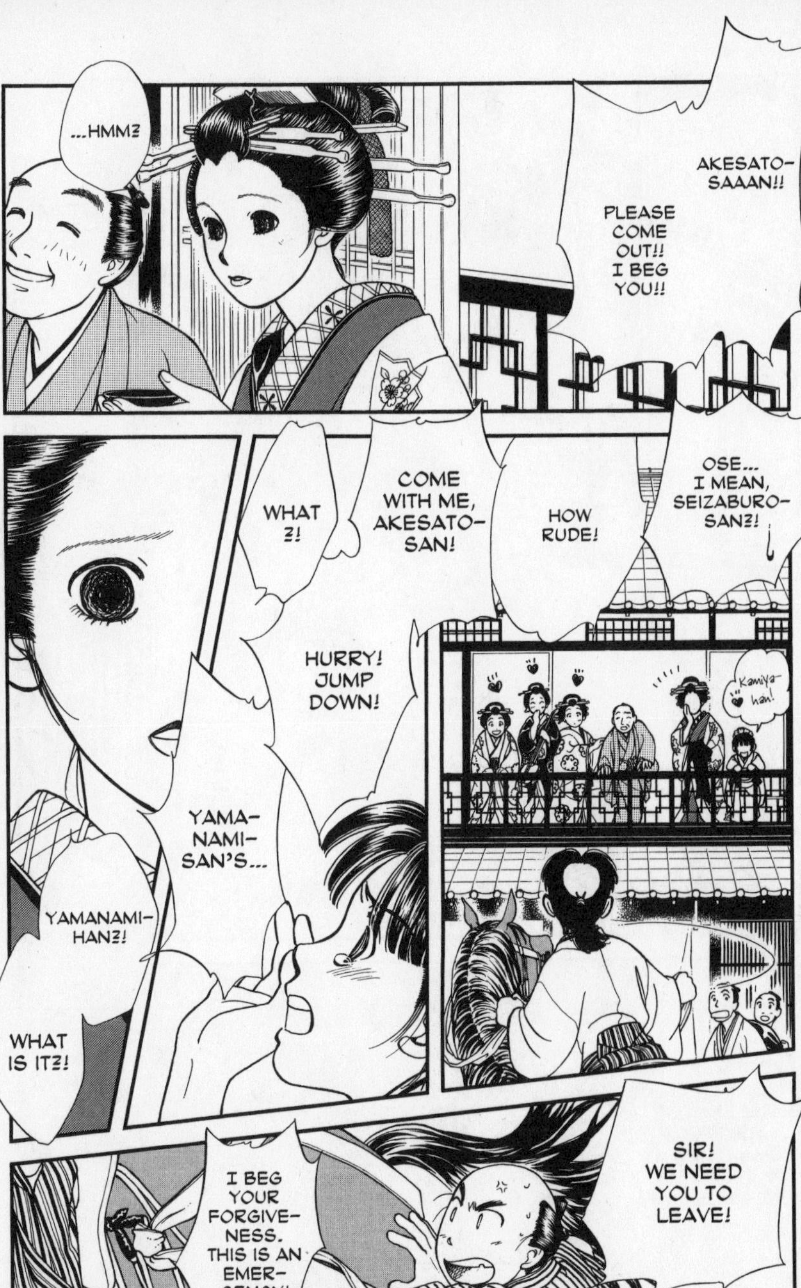
AKESATO-SAAAN!!
PLEASE COME OUT!! I BEG YOU!!
...HMM?
OSE... I MEAN, SEIZABURO-SAN?!
HOW RUDE!
Kamiya-han!
COME WITH ME, AKESATO-SAN!
WHAT?!
HURRY! JUMP DOWN!
YAMANAMI-SAN'S...
YAMANAMI-HAN?!
WHAT IS IT?!
SIR! WE NEED YOU TO LEAVE!
I BEG YOUR FORGIVENESS. THIS IS AN EMERGENCY!

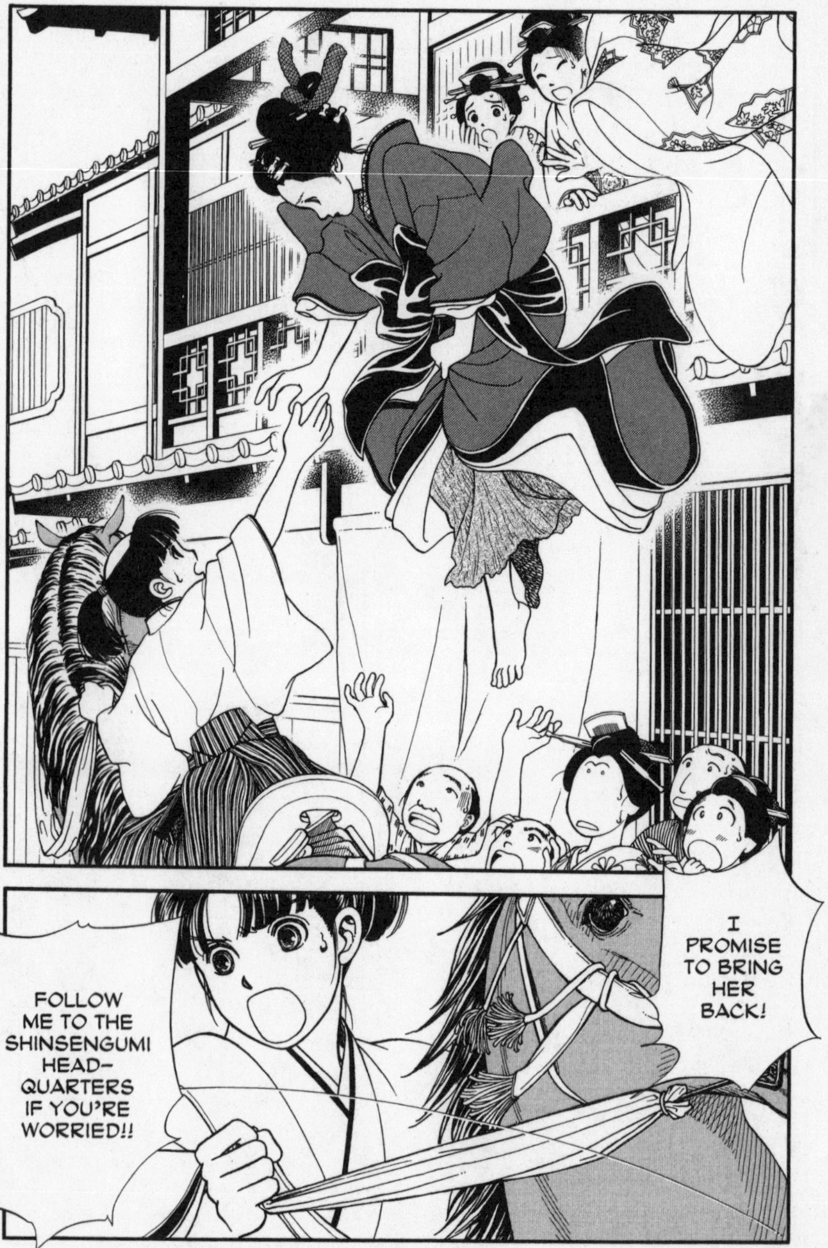
I PROMISE TO BRING HER BACK!
FOLLOW ME TO THE SHINSENGUMI HEAD-QUARTERS IF YOU'RE WORRIED!!

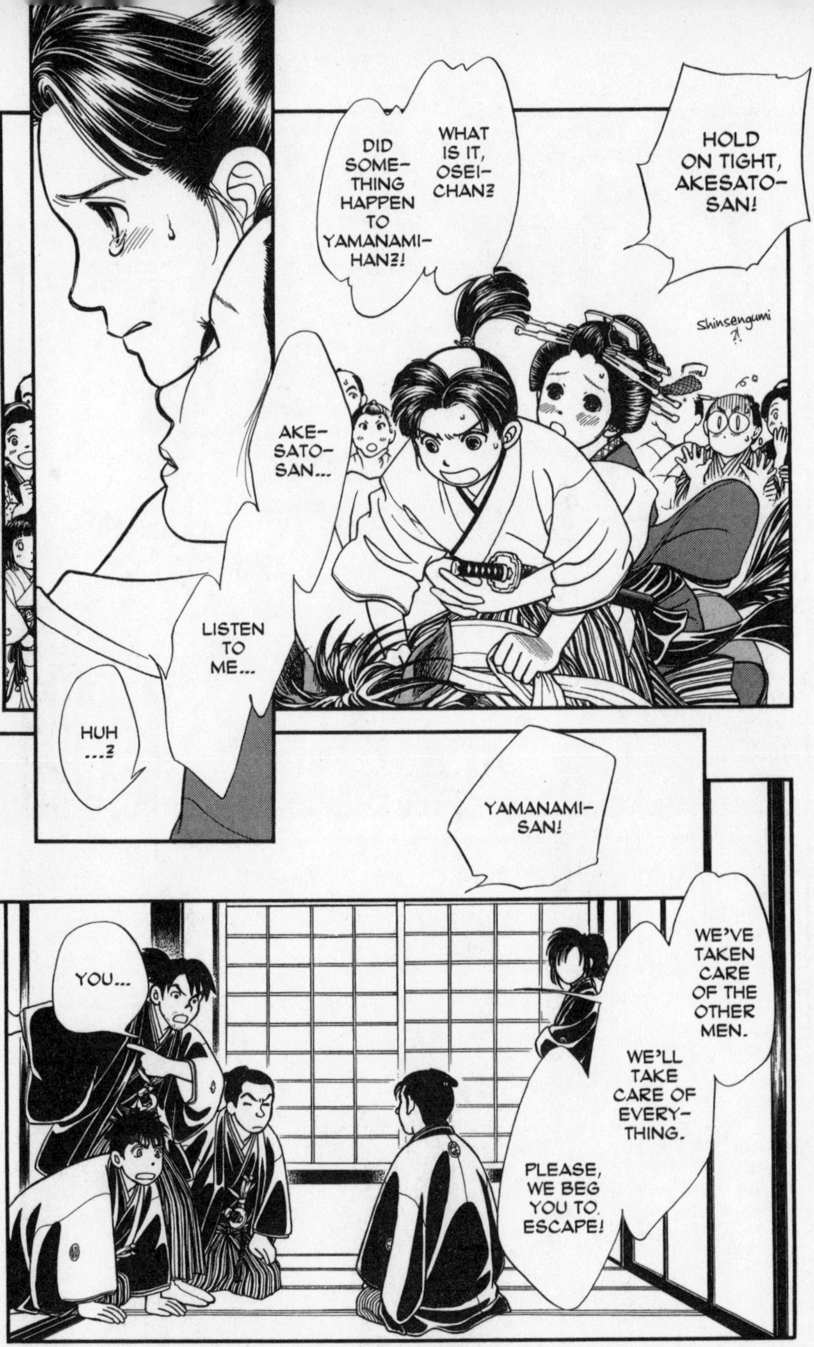
HOLD ON TIGHT, AKESATO-SAN!
WHAT IS IT, OSEI-CHAN?
DID SOME-THING HAPPEN TO YAMANAMI-HAN?!
Shinsengumi ?!
AKE-SATO-SAN...
LISTEN TO ME...
HUH ...?
YAMANAMI-SAN!
WE'VE TAKEN CARE OF THE OTHER MEN.
WE'LL TAKE CARE OF EVERY-THING.
PLEASE, WE BEG YOU TO ESCAPE!
YOU...

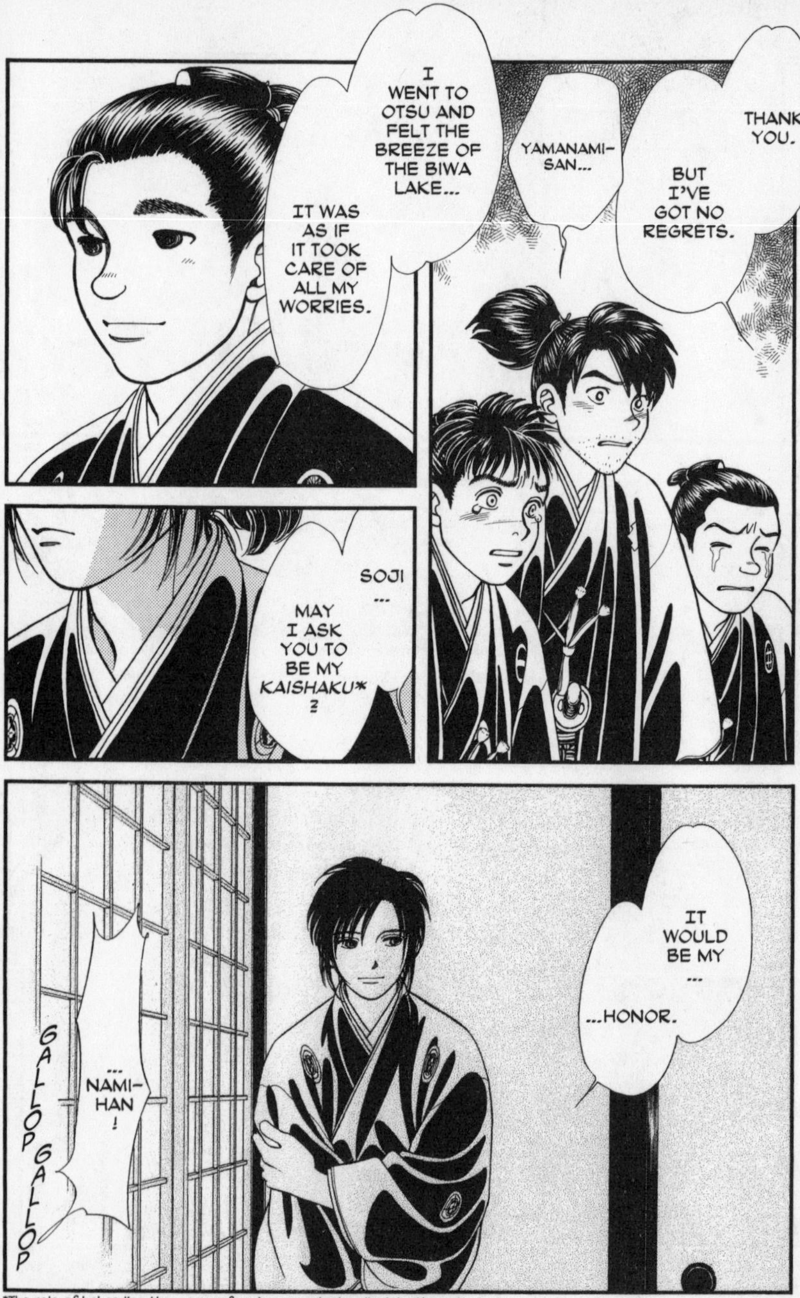
THANK YOU.
BUT I'VE GOT NO REGRETS.
YAMANAMI-SAN...
I WENT TO OTSU AND FELT THE BREEZE OF THE BIWA LAKE...
IT WAS AS IF IT TOOK CARE OF ALL MY WORRIES.
SOJI...
MAY I ASK YOU TO BE MY *KAISHAKU**?
IT WOULD BE MY...
...HONOR.
...NAMI-HAN!
GALLOP GALLOP

*The role of beheading the man performing *seppuku* to alleviate the pain. An important role often given to family or close friends, and a symbol of absolute trust.

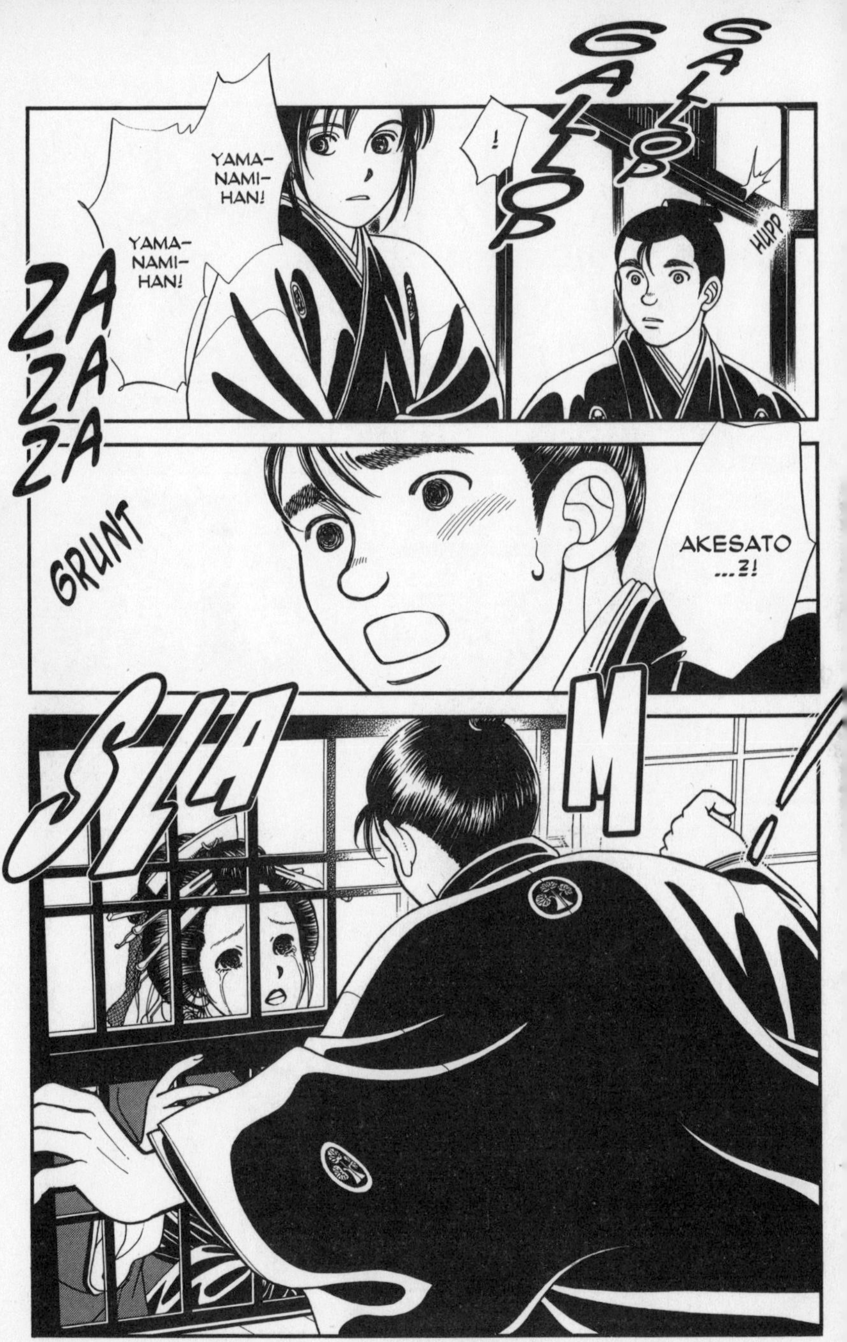
GALLOP GALLOP
!
HUPP
YAMA-NAMI-HAN!
YAMA-NAMI-HAN!
ZAZAZA
AKESATO ...?!
GRUNT
SLAM

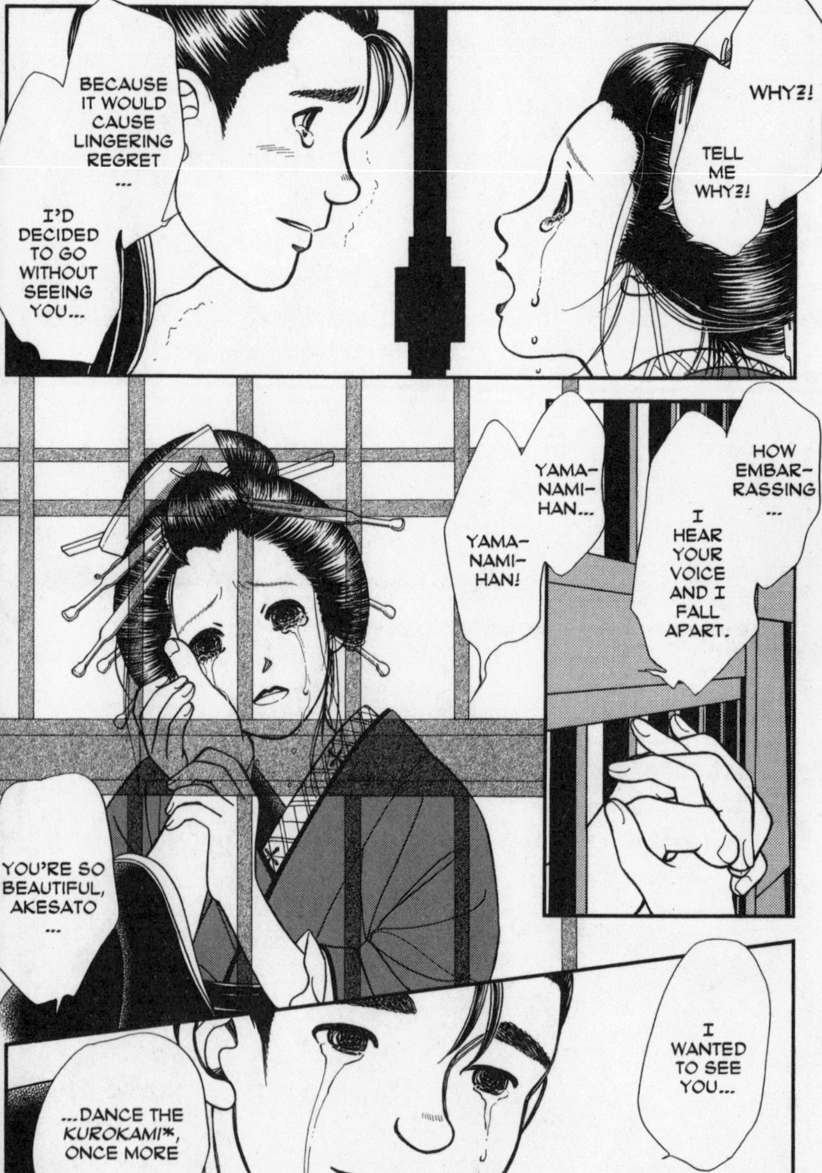
WHY?!
TELL ME WHY?!
BECAUSE IT WOULD CAUSE LINGERING REGRET ...
I'D DECIDED TO GO WITHOUT SEEING YOU...
HOW EMBARRASSING ...
I HEAR YOUR VOICE AND I FALL APART.
YAMA-NAMI-HAN...
YAMA-NAMI-HAN!
YOU'RE SO BEAUTIFUL, AKESATO ...
I WANTED TO SEE YOU...
...DANCE THE *KUROKAMI**, ONCE MORE ...

**Kurokami* literally means black hair, and it is the name of a *samisen* famous song.

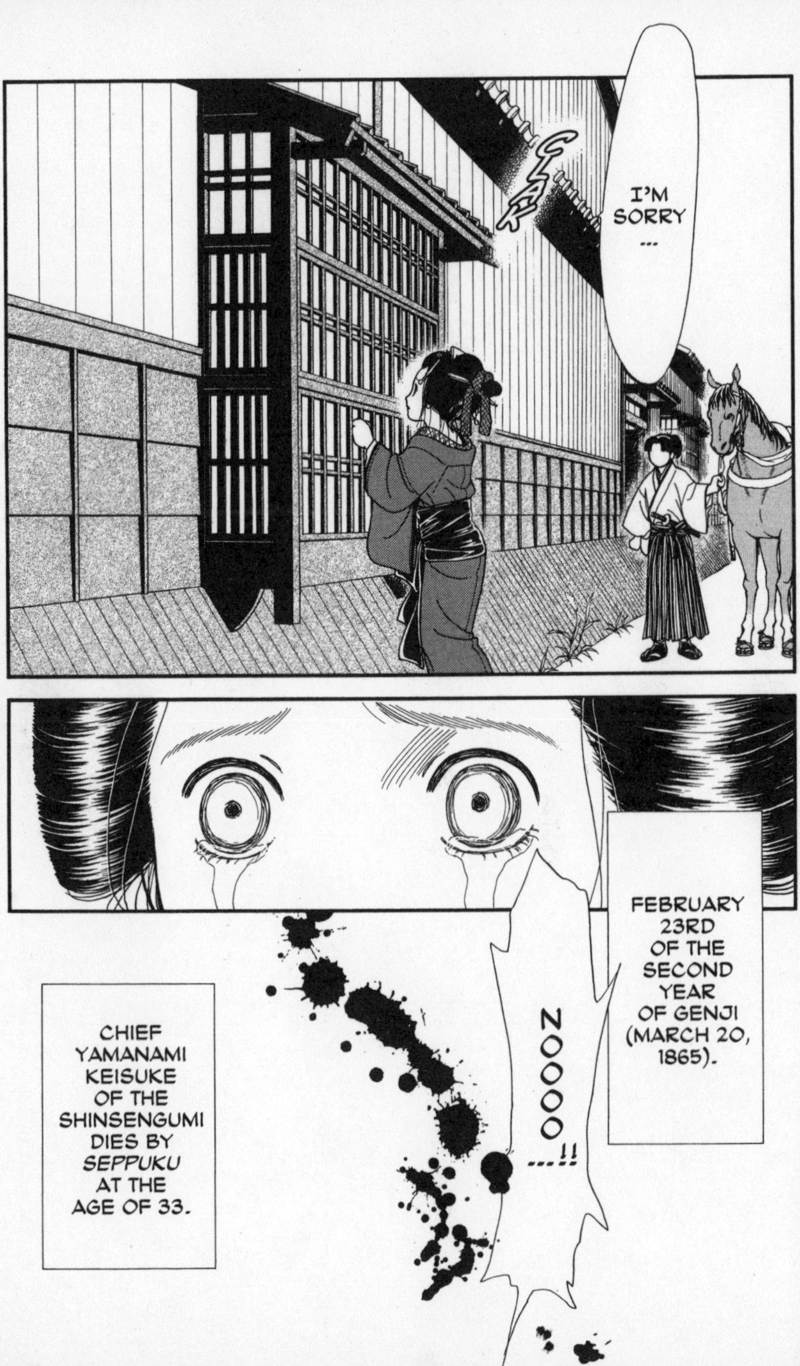
I'M SORRY ---
CLAK
FEBRUARY 23RD OF THE SECOND YEAR OF GENJI (MARCH 20, 1865).
NOOOO---!!
CHIEF YAMANAMI KEISUKE OF THE SHINSENGUMI DIES BY *SEPPUKU* AT THE AGE OF 33.

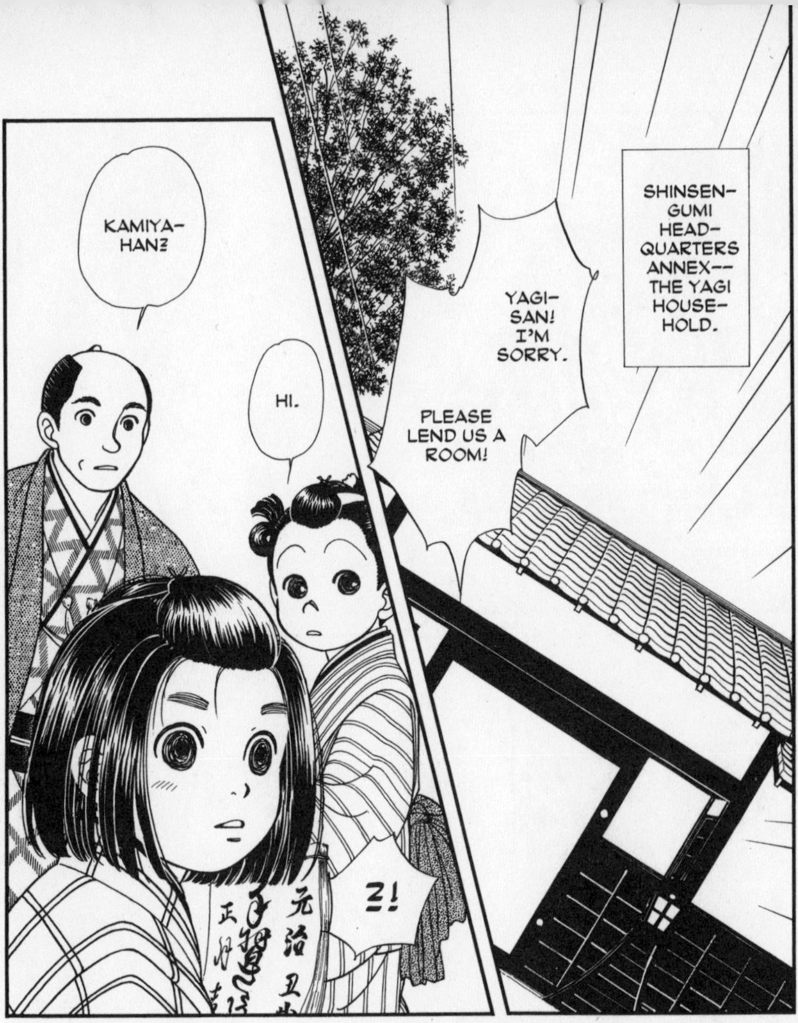
SHINSEN-GUMI HEAD-QUARTERS ANNEX--THE YAGI HOUSE-HOLD.
YAGI-SAN! I'M SORRY.
PLEASE LEND US A ROOM!
KAMIYA-HAN?
HI.
?!

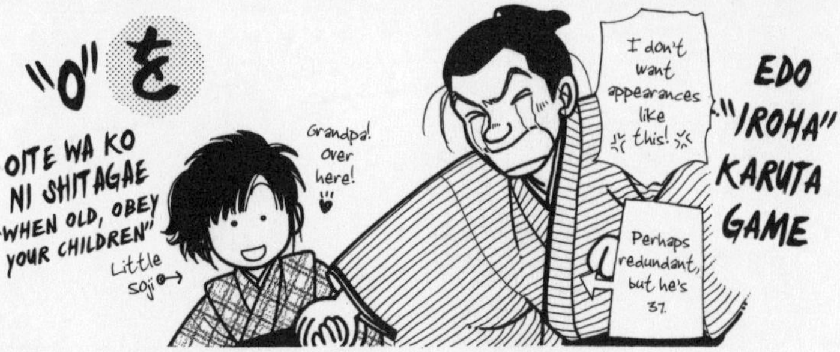
EDO "IROHA" KARUTA GAME
I don't want appearances like this!
Perhaps redundant, but he's 37.
Grandpa! over here!
"O" を
OITE WA KO NI SHITAGAE
"WHEN OLD, OBEY YOUR CHILDREN"
Little Soji

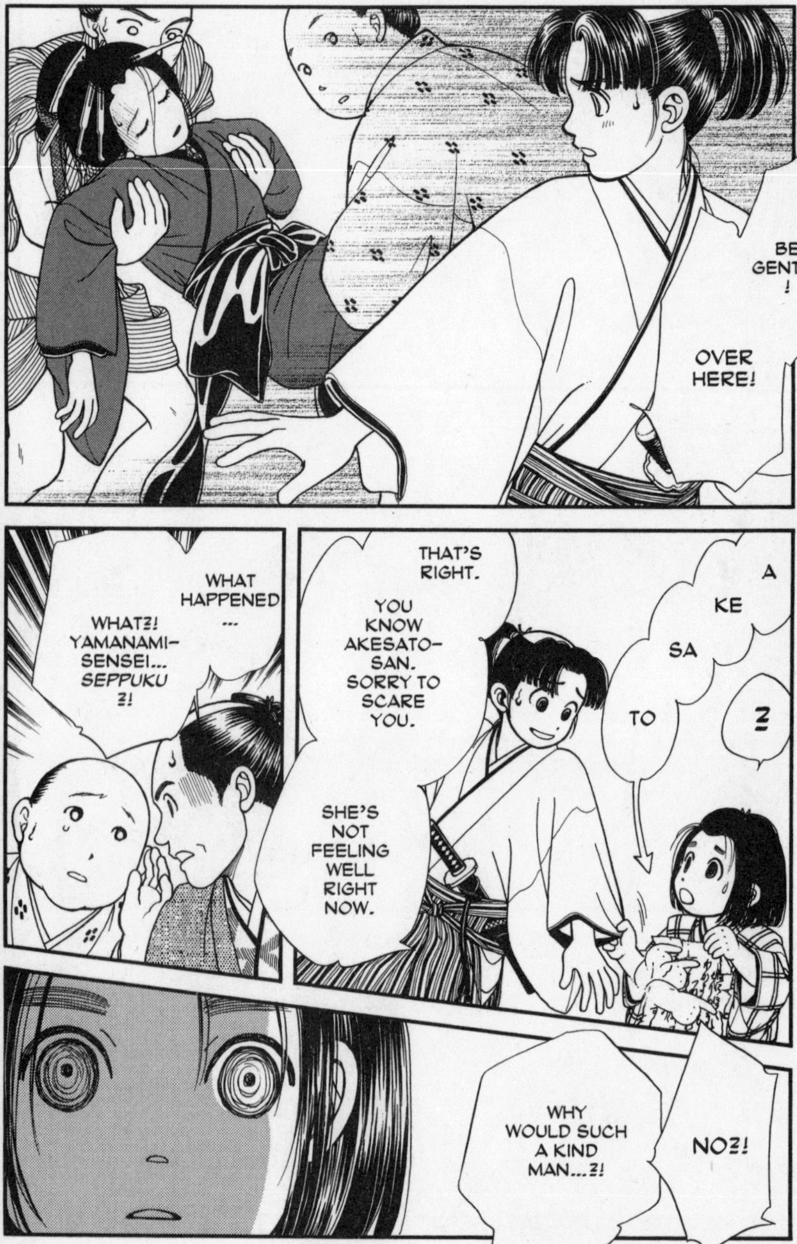
BE GENTLE!
OVER HERE!
A KE SA TO
?
THAT'S RIGHT.
YOU KNOW AKESATO-SAN. SORRY TO SCARE YOU.
SHE'S NOT FEELING WELL RIGHT NOW.
WHAT HAPPENED...
WHAT?! YAMANAMI-SENSEI... SEPPUKU?!
NO?!
WHY WOULD SUCH A KIND MAN...?!

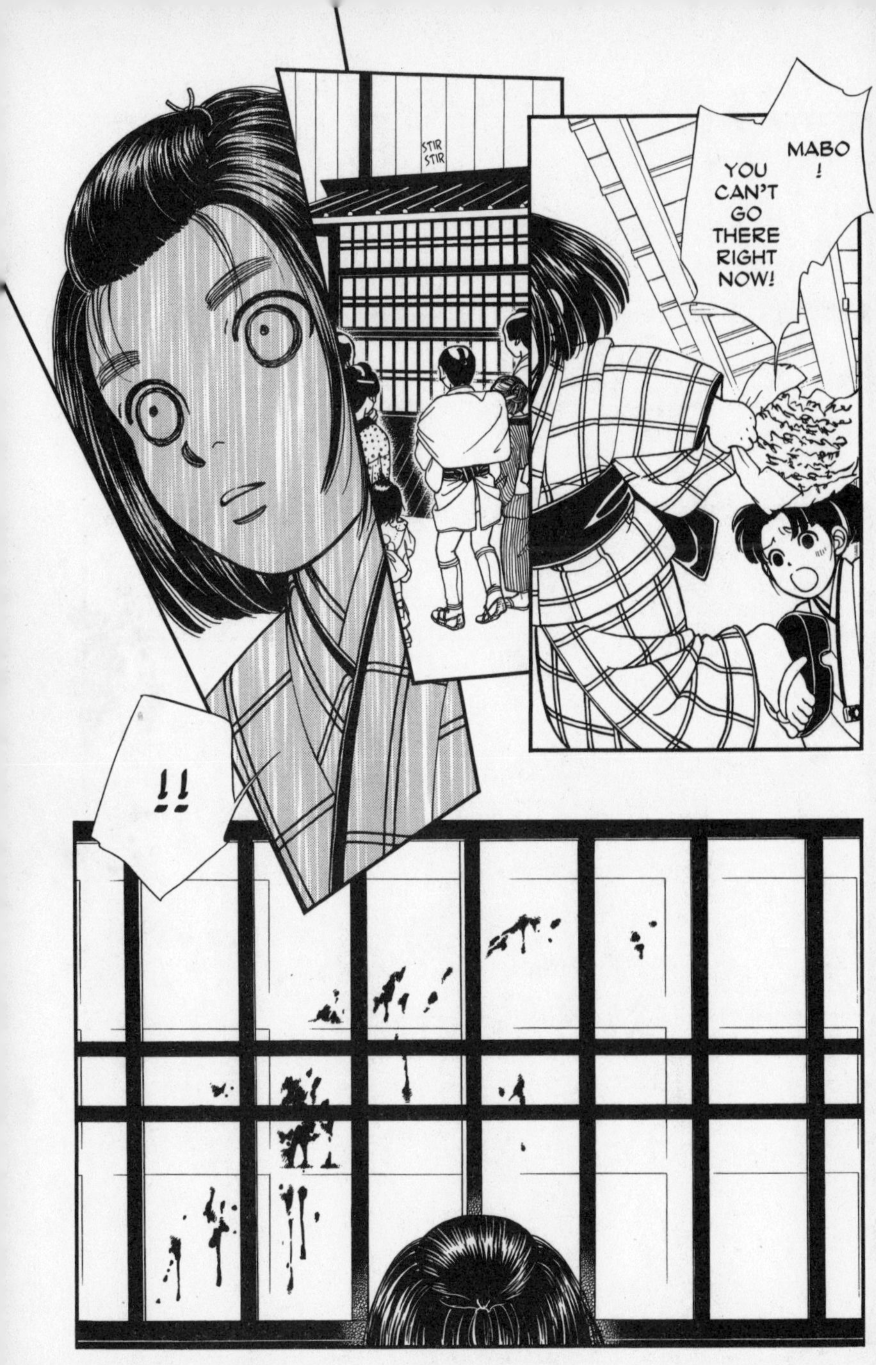
MABO!
YOU CAN'T GO THERE RIGHT NOW!
STIR STIR
!!

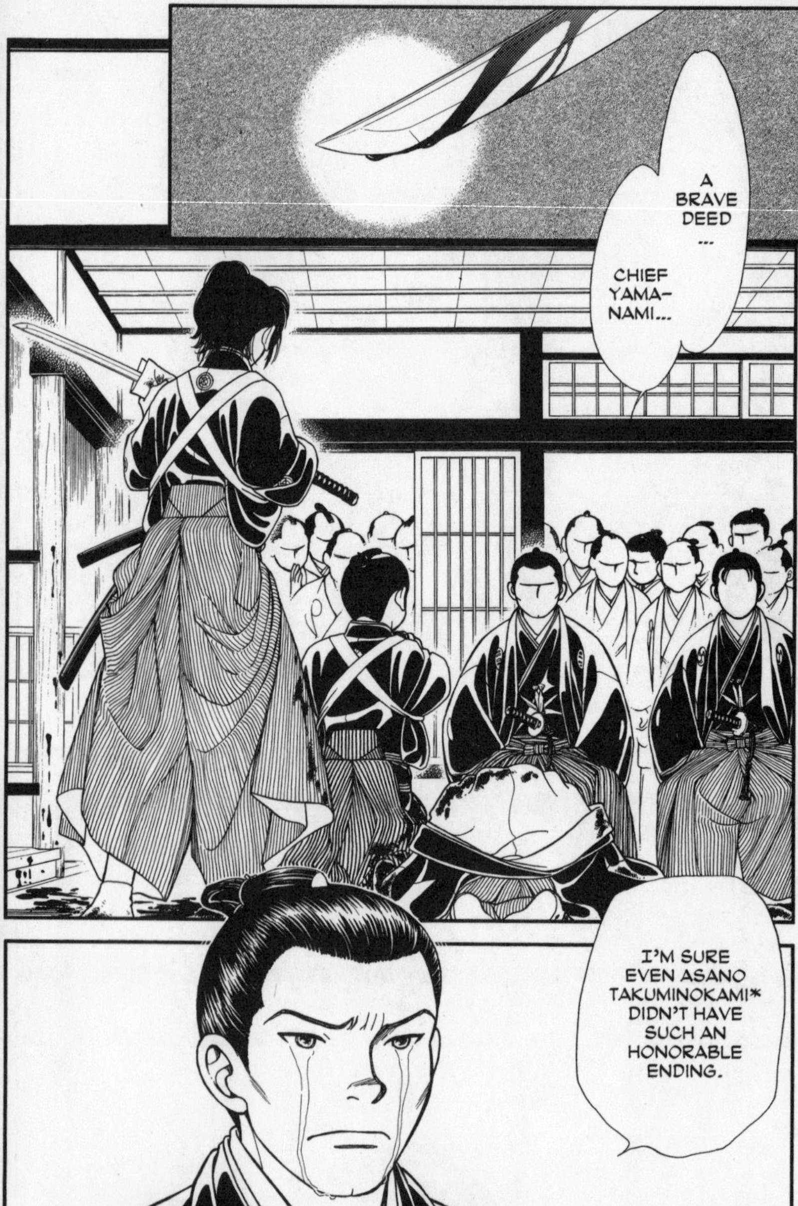
A BRAVE DEED ...
CHIEF YAMA-NAMI...
I'M SURE EVEN ASANO TAKUMINOKAMI* DIDN'T HAVE SUCH AN HONORABLE ENDING.

*The Lord of Ako whose story was told in Chushingura. He wounded Kira Yoshihisa in the Edo Castle and was sentenced to *seppuku*.

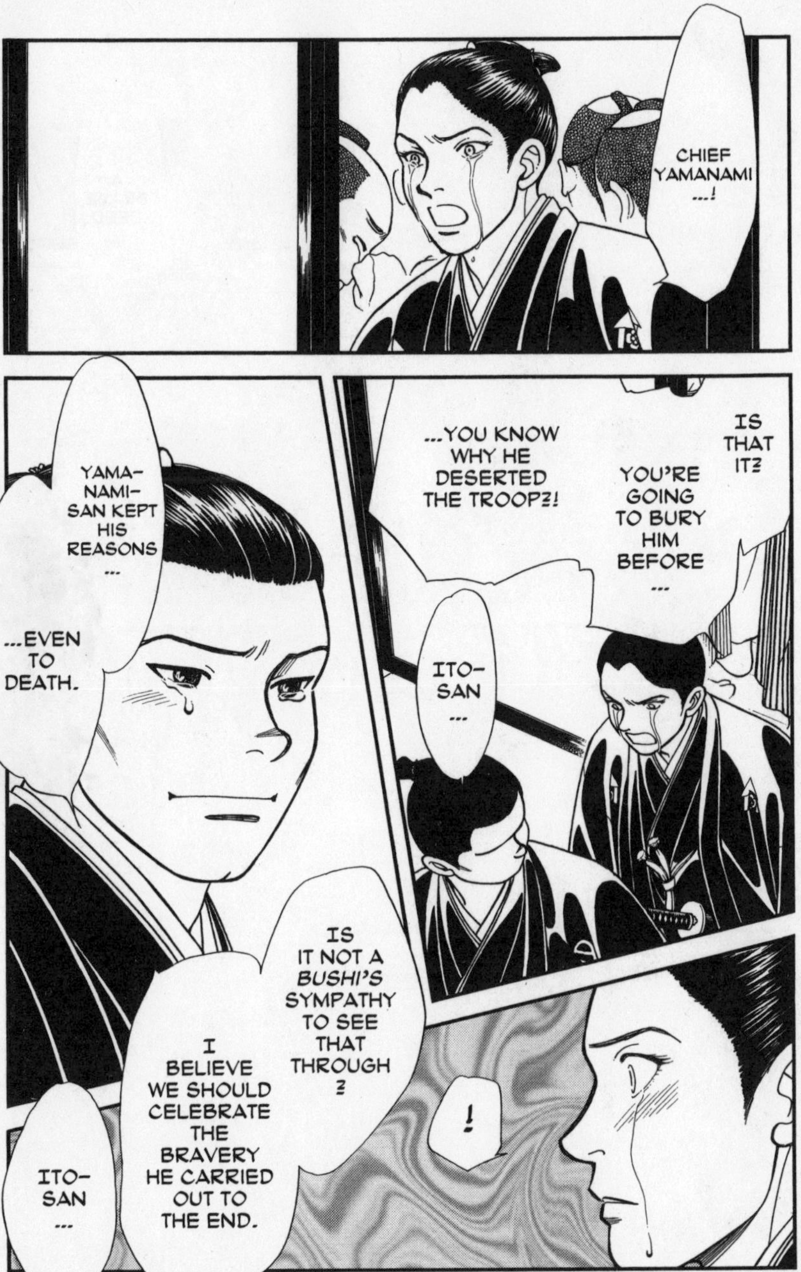
CHIEF YAMANAMI ...!
IS THAT IT?
YOU'RE GOING TO BURY HIM BEFORE ...
...YOU KNOW WHY HE DESERTED THE TROOP?!
ITO-SAN ...
!
YAMANAMI-SAN KEPT HIS REASONS ...
...EVEN TO DEATH.
IS IT NOT A *BUSHI'S* SYMPATHY TO SEE THAT THROUGH?
I BELIEVE WE SHOULD CELEBRATE THE BRAVERY HE CARRIED OUT TO THE END.
ITO-SAN ...

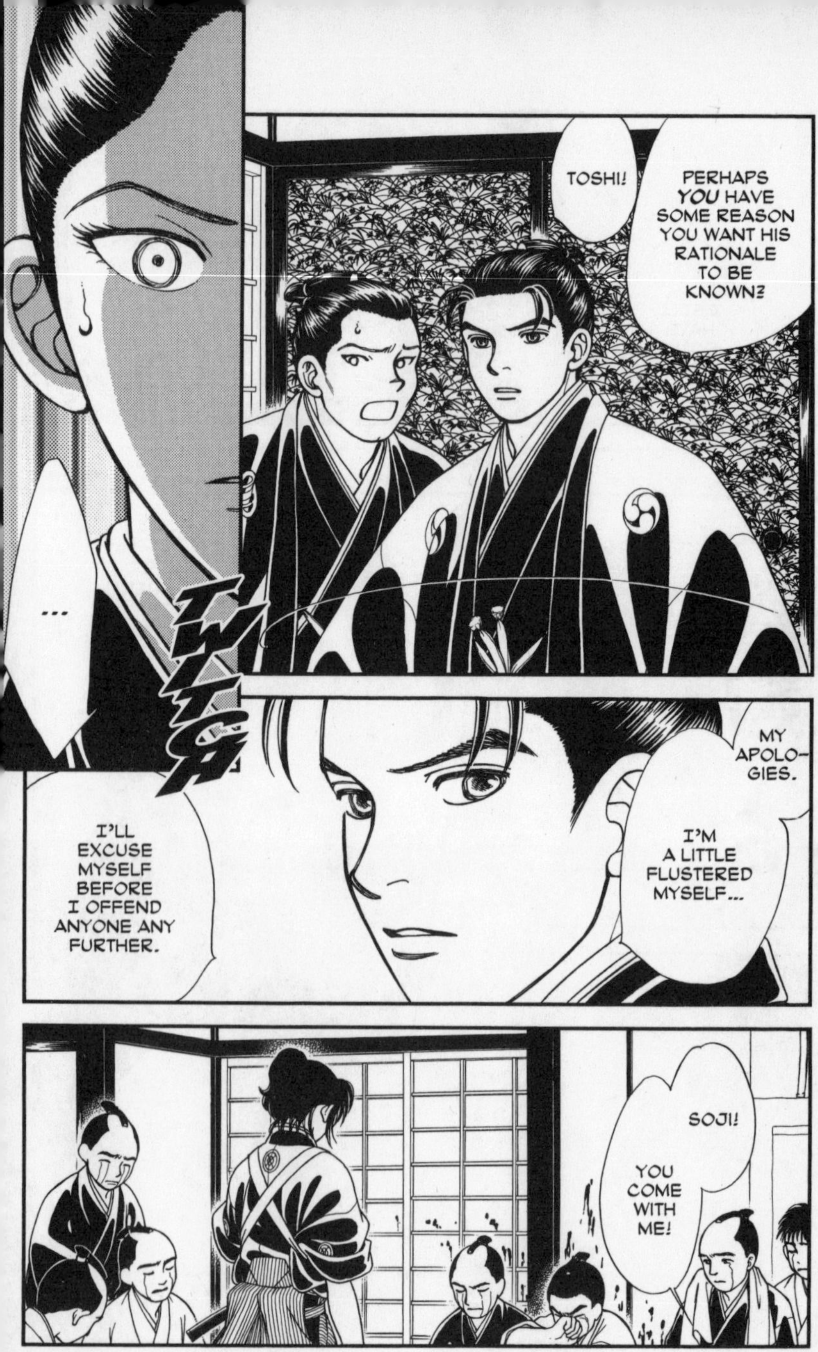
PERHAPS YOU HAVE SOME REASON YOU WANT HIS RATIONALE TO BE KNOWN?
TOSHI!
...
MY APOLOGIES.
I'M A LITTLE FLUSTERED MYSELF...
I'LL EXCUSE MYSELF BEFORE I OFFEND ANYONE ANY FURTHER.
SOJI!
YOU COME WITH ME!

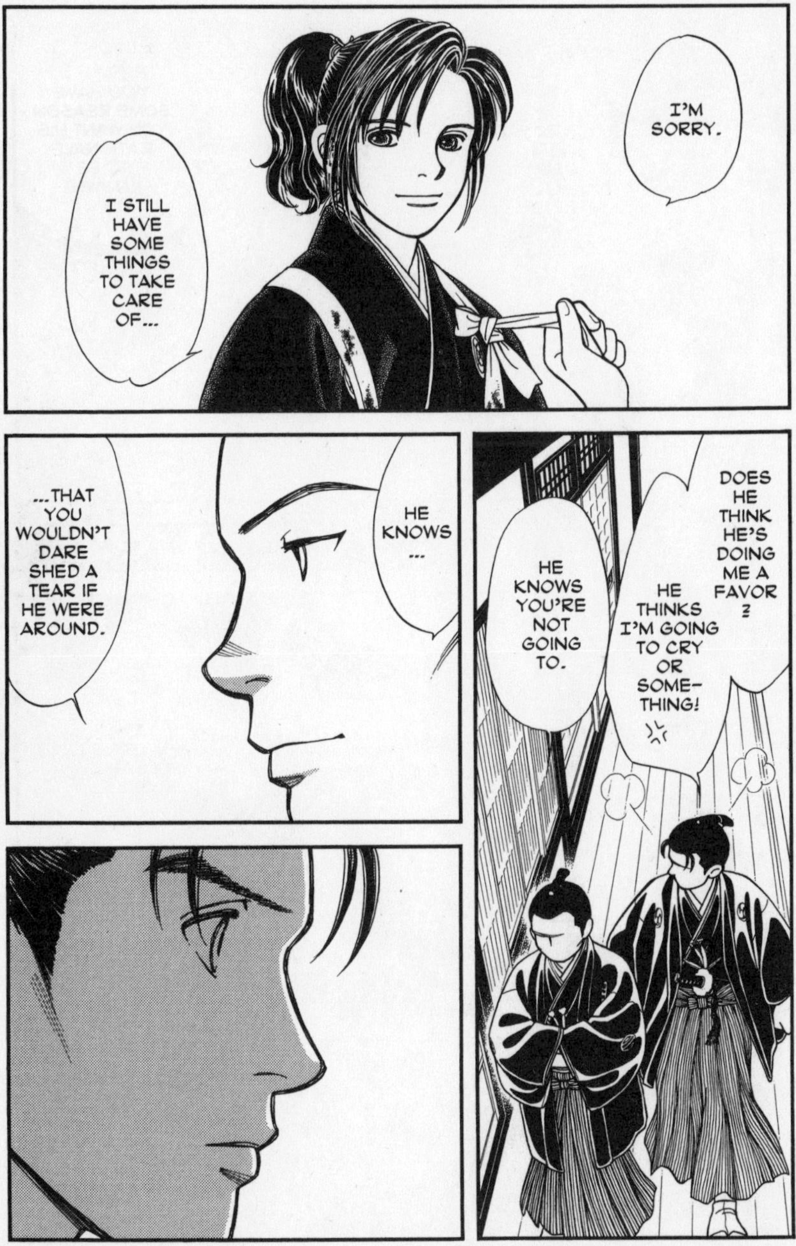
I'M SORRY.
I STILL HAVE SOME THINGS TO TAKE CARE OF...
DOES HE THINK HE'S DOING ME A FAVOR?
HE THINKS I'M GOING TO CRY OR SOME-THING!
HE KNOWS YOU'RE NOT GOING TO.
HE KNOWS...
...THAT YOU WOULDN'T DARE SHED A TEAR IF HE WERE AROUND.

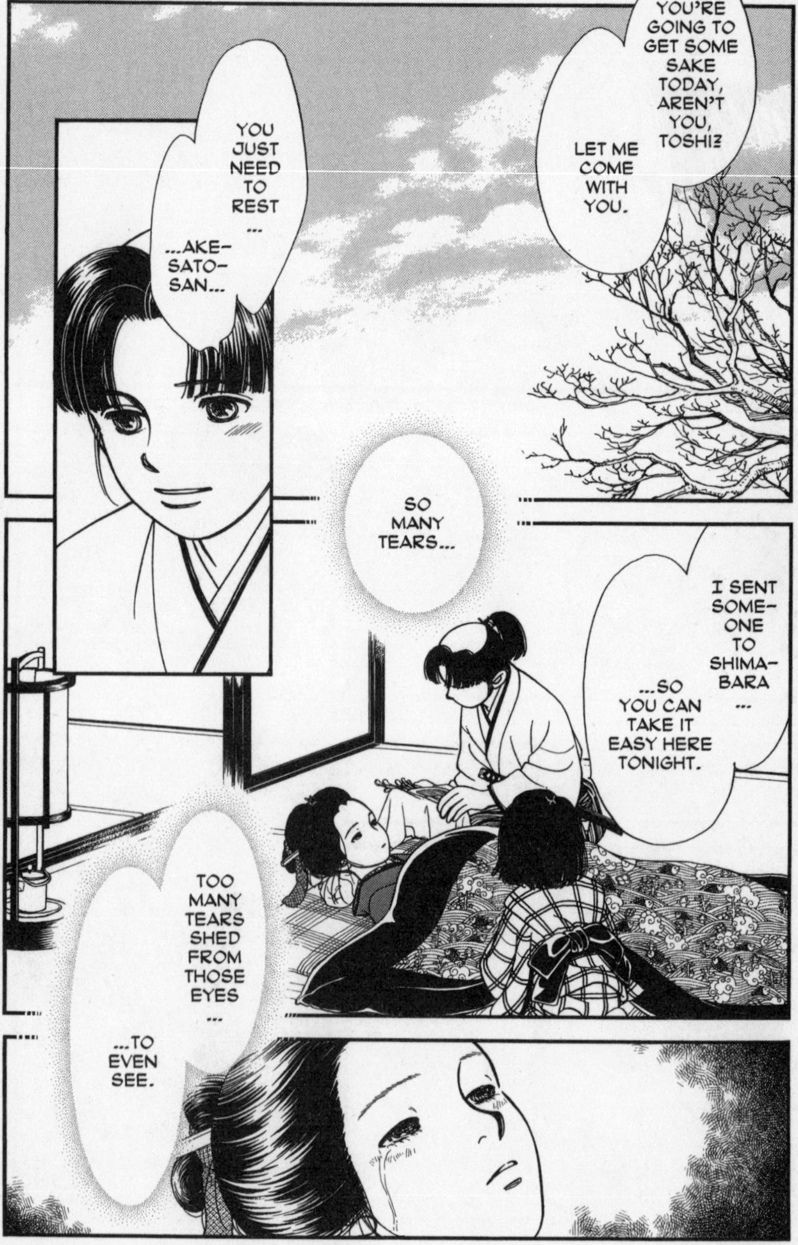
YOU'RE GOING TO GET SOME SAKE TODAY, AREN'T YOU, TOSHI?
LET ME COME WITH YOU.
YOU JUST NEED TO REST ...
...AKE-SATO-SAN...
SO MANY TEARS...
I SENT SOME-ONE TO SHIMA-BARA ...
...SO YOU CAN TAKE IT EASY HERE TONIGHT.
TOO MANY TEARS SHED FROM THOSE EYES ...
...TO EVEN SEE.

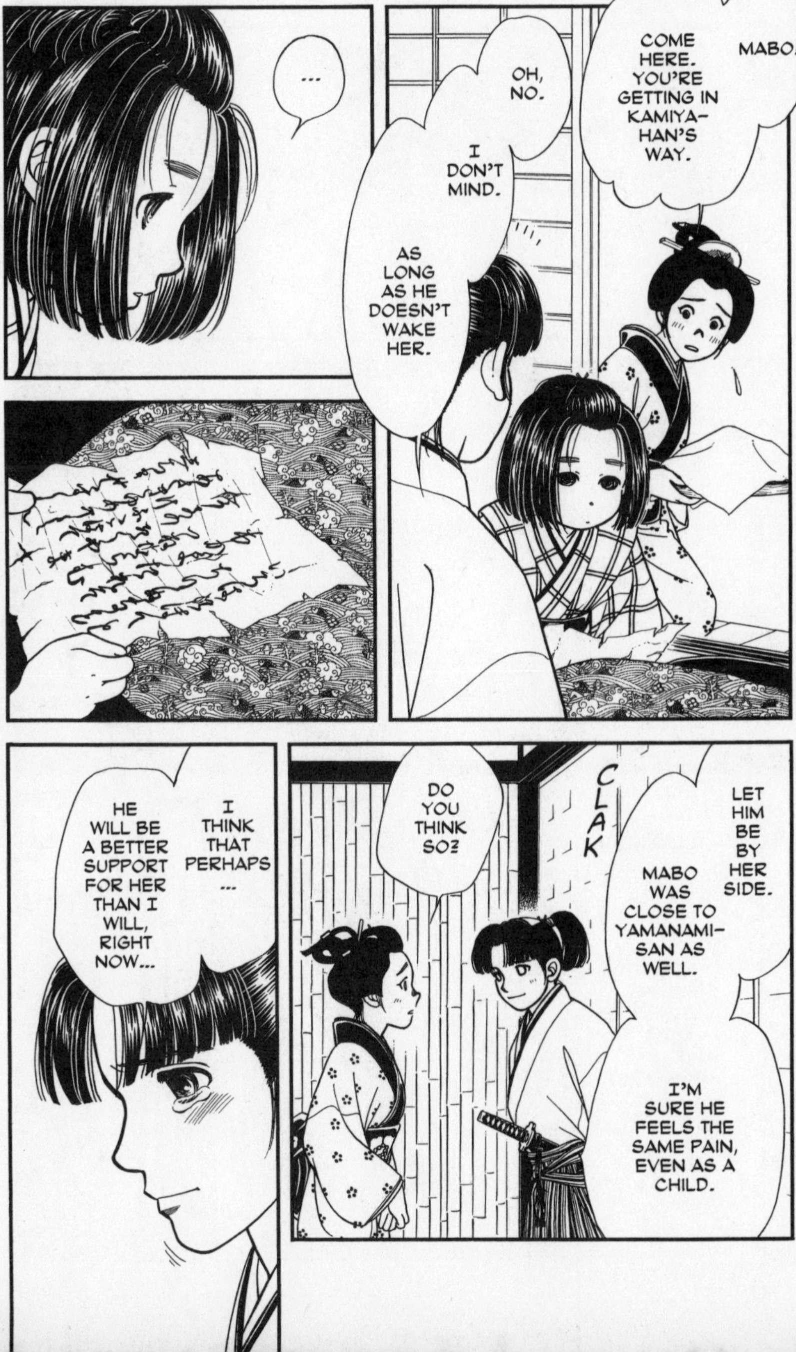
MABO!
COME HERE. YOU'RE GETTING IN KAMIYA-HAN'S WAY.
OH, NO.
I DON'T MIND.
AS LONG AS HE DOESN'T WAKE HER.
...
LET HIM BE BY HER SIDE.
MABO WAS CLOSE TO YAMANAMI-SAN AS WELL.
CLAK
DO YOU THINK SO?
I'M SURE HE FEELS THE SAME PAIN, EVEN AS A CHILD.
I THINK THAT PERHAPS...
HE WILL BE A BETTER SUPPORT FOR HER THAN I WILL, RIGHT NOW...

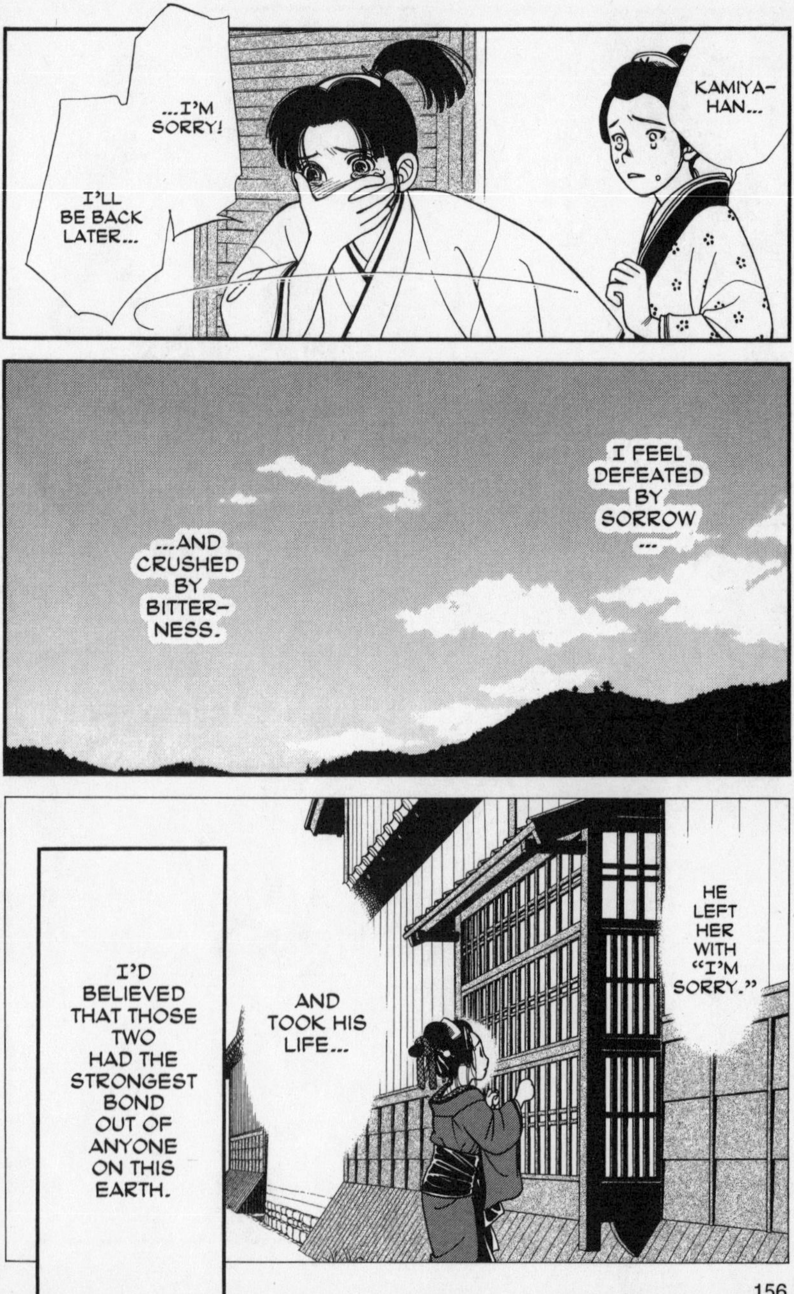
KAMIYA-HAN...
...I'M SORRY!
I'LL BE BACK LATER...
I FEEL DEFEATED BY SORROW...
...AND CRUSHED BY BITTERNESS.
HE LEFT HER WITH "I'M SORRY."
AND TOOK HIS LIFE...
I'D BELIEVED THAT THOSE TWO HAD THE STRONGEST BOND OUT OF ANYONE ON THIS EARTH.

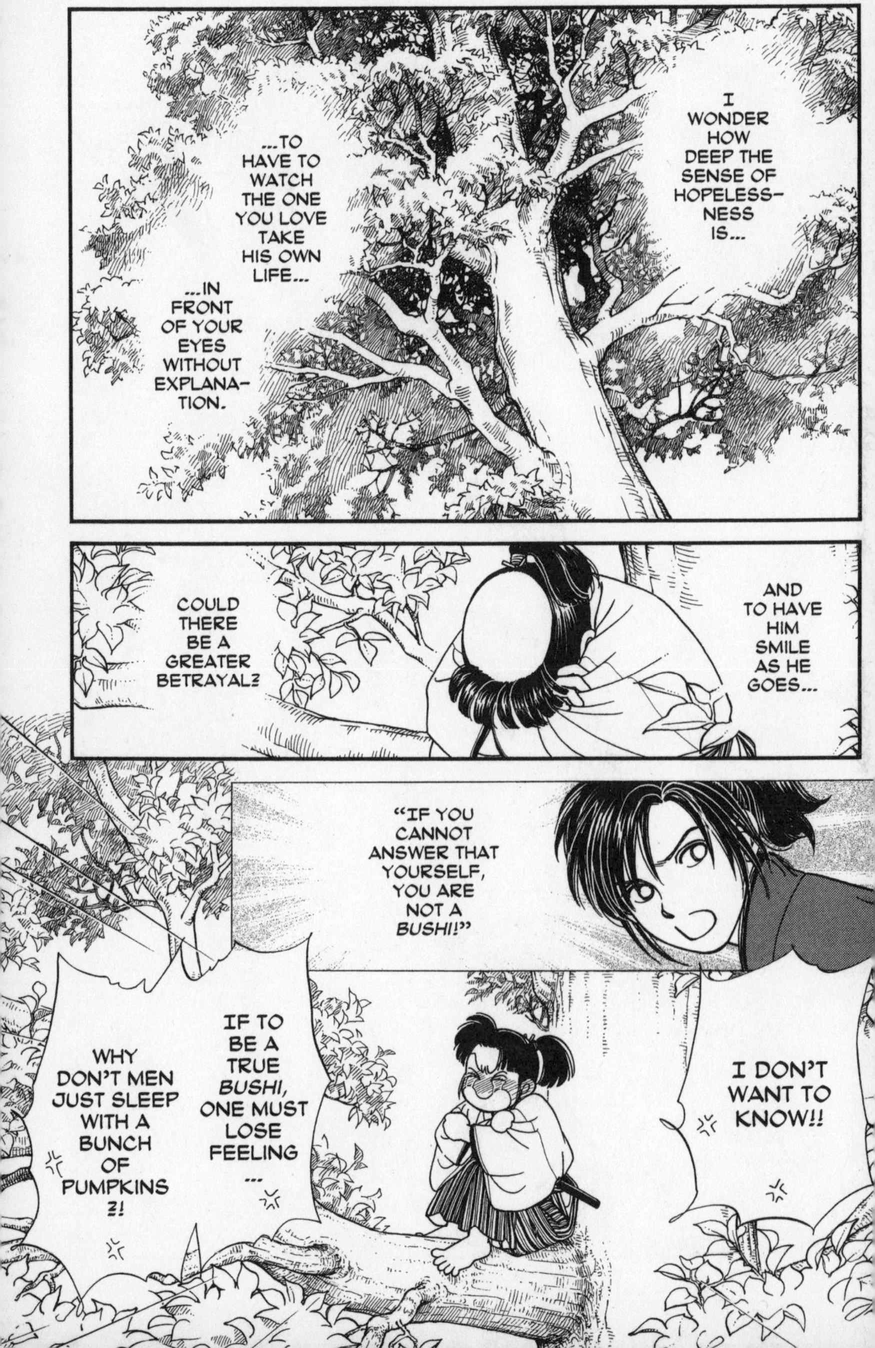
I WONDER HOW DEEP THE SENSE OF HOPELESSNESS IS...
...TO HAVE TO WATCH THE ONE YOU LOVE TAKE HIS OWN LIFE...
...IN FRONT OF YOUR EYES WITHOUT EXPLANATION.
AND TO HAVE HIM SMILE AS HE GOES...
COULD THERE BE A GREATER BETRAYAL?
"IF YOU CANNOT ANSWER THAT YOURSELF, YOU ARE NOT A *BUSHI!*"
I DON'T WANT TO KNOW!!
IF TO BE A TRUE *BUSHI*, ONE MUST LOSE FEELING ...
WHY DON'T MEN JUST SLEEP WITH A BUNCH OF PUMPKINS ?!

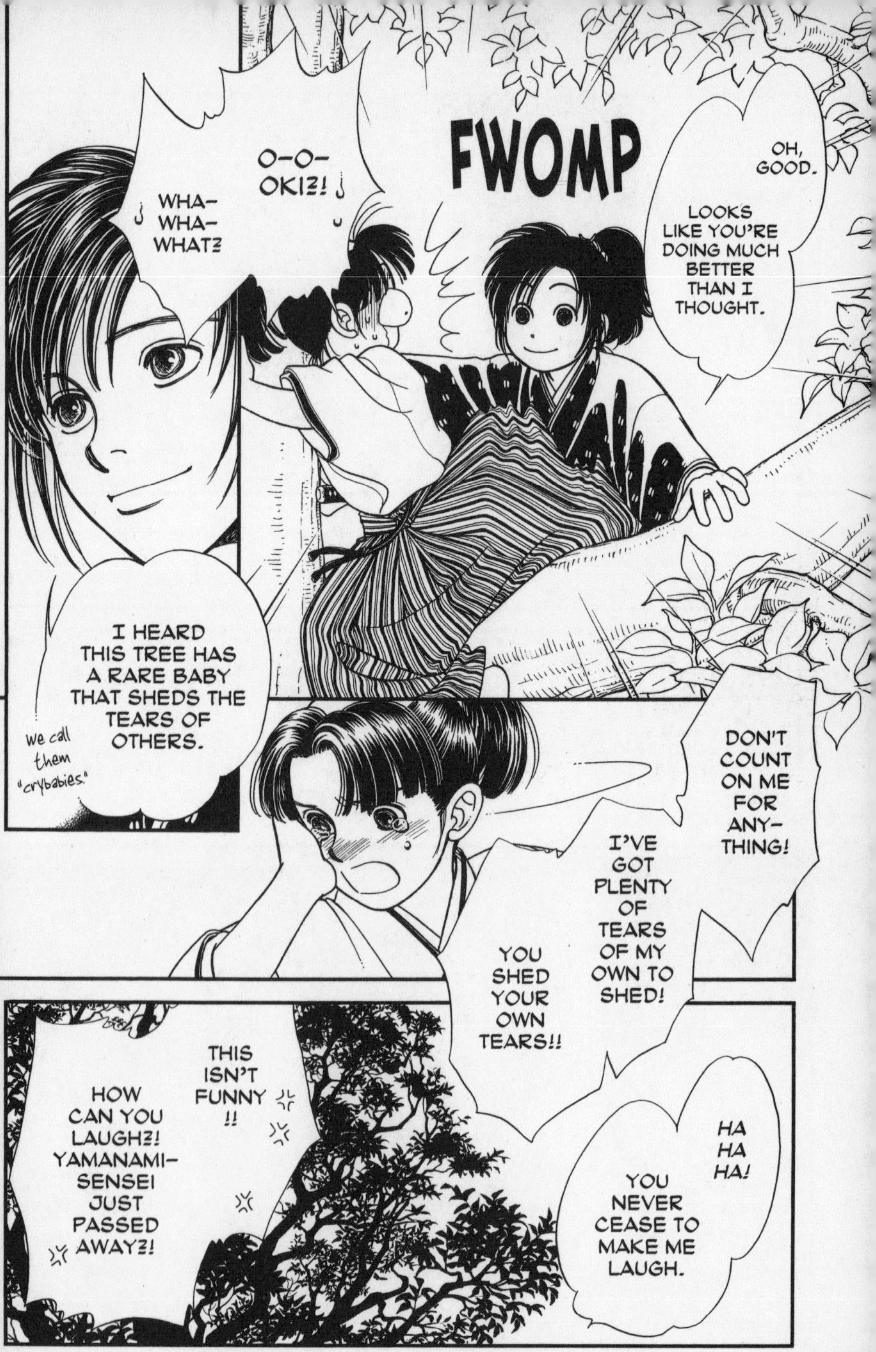
OH, GOOD.
LOOKS LIKE YOU'RE DOING MUCH BETTER THAN I THOUGHT.
FWOMP
O-O-OKI?!
WHA-WHA-WHAT?
I HEARD THIS TREE HAS A RARE BABY THAT SHEDS THE TEARS OF OTHERS.
we call them "crybabies."
DON'T COUNT ON ME FOR ANYTHING!
I'VE GOT PLENTY OF TEARS OF MY OWN TO SHED!
YOU SHED YOUR OWN TEARS!!
HA HA HA!
YOU NEVER CEASE TO MAKE ME LAUGH.
THIS ISN'T FUNNY!!
HOW CAN YOU LAUGH?! YAMANAMI-SENSEI JUST PASSED AWAY?!

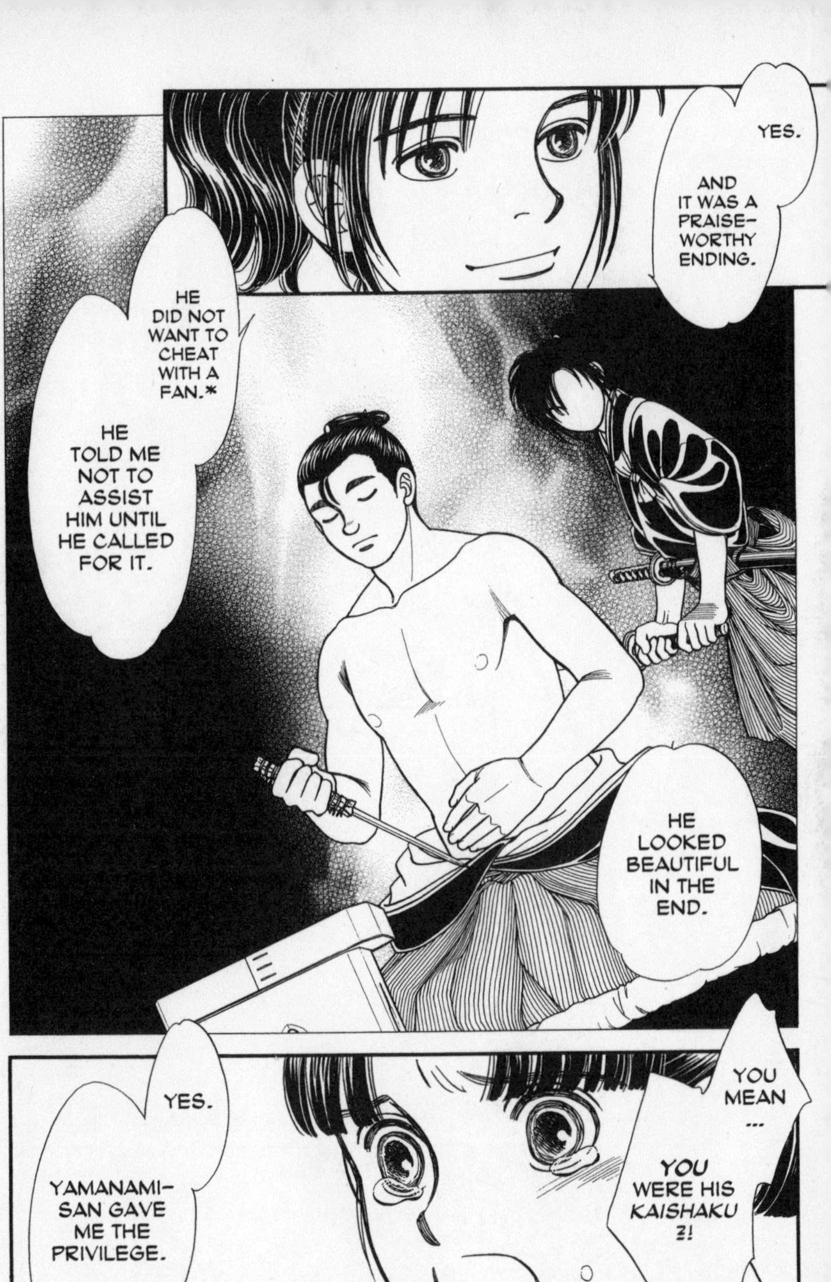
YES.
AND IT WAS A PRAISE-WORTHY ENDING.
HE DID NOT WANT TO CHEAT WITH A FAN.*
HE TOLD ME NOT TO ASSIST HIM UNTIL HE CALLED FOR IT.
HE LOOKED BEAUTIFUL IN THE END.
YOU MEAN ...
YOU WERE HIS KAISHAKU?!
YES.
YAMANAMI-SAN GAVE ME THE PRIVILEGE.

*A ritualistic *seppuku* where men used a fan guised as a knife to pretend as if they were performing *seppuku* but actually had the *kaishaku* take their head for fear of an embarrassing moment caused by pain. In reality, only the very few brave *bushi* actually opted for the real *seppuku*.

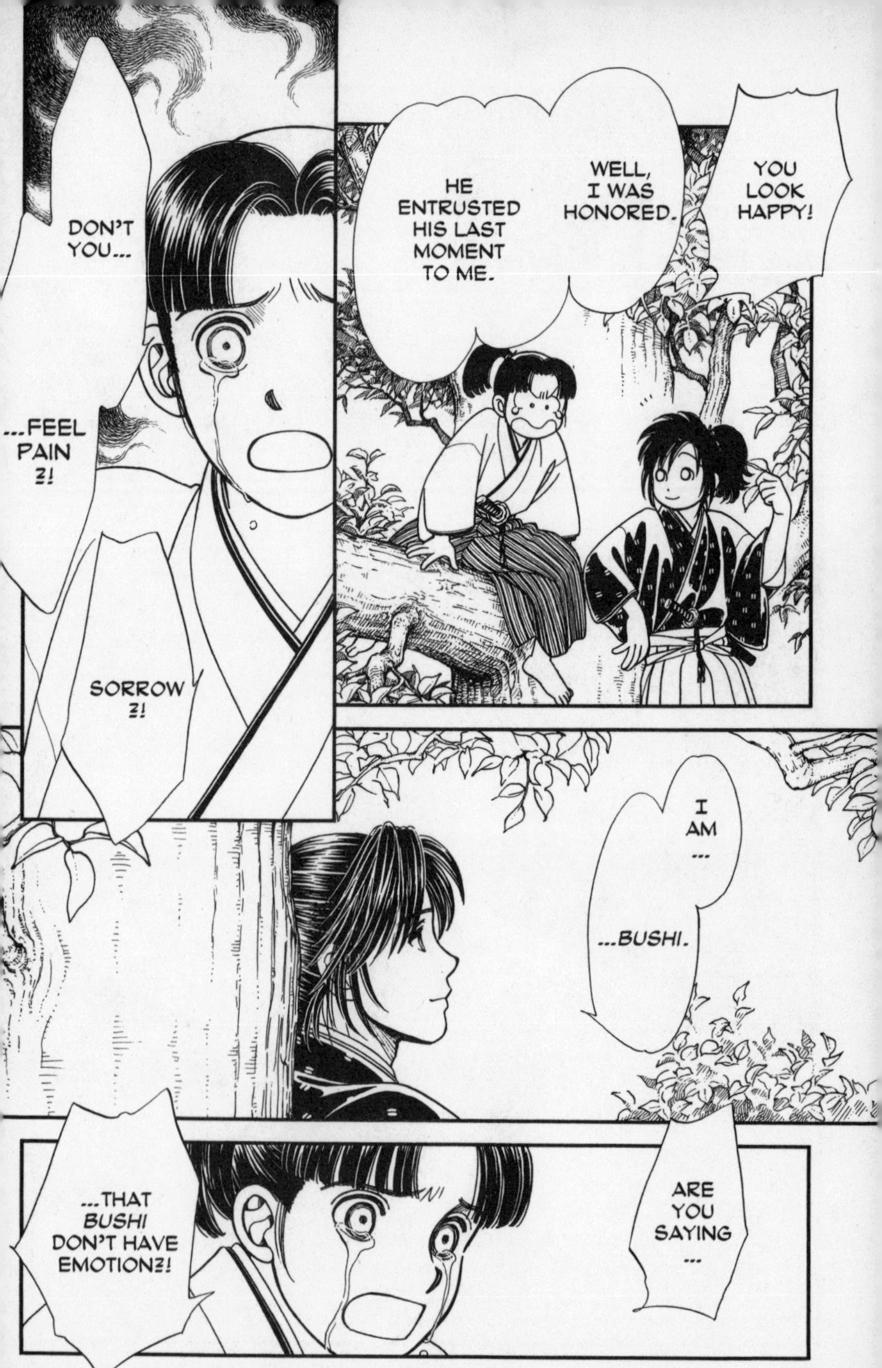
YOU LOOK HAPPY!
WELL, I WAS HONORED.
HE ENTRUSTED HIS LAST MOMENT TO ME.
DON'T YOU...
...FEEL PAIN?!
SORROW?!
I AM ...
...BUSHI.
ARE YOU SAYING ...
...THAT *BUSHI* DON'T HAVE EMOTION?!

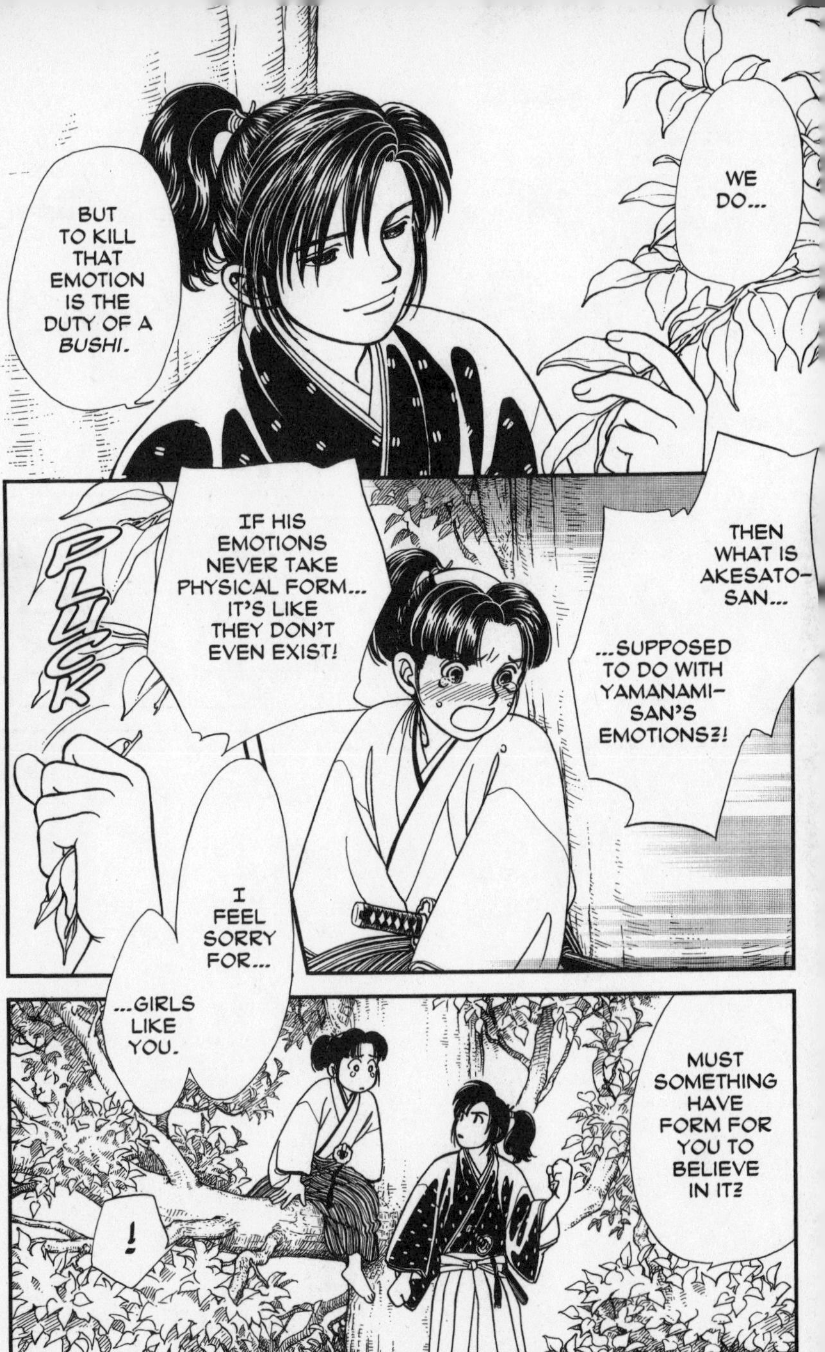
WE DO...
BUT TO KILL THAT EMOTION IS THE DUTY OF A *BUSHI*.
THEN WHAT IS AKESATO-SAN...
...SUPPOSED TO DO WITH YAMANAMI-SAN'S EMOTIONS?!
IF HIS EMOTIONS NEVER TAKE PHYSICAL FORM... IT'S LIKE THEY DON'T EVEN EXIST!
PLUCK
I FEEL SORRY FOR...
...GIRLS LIKE YOU.
MUST SOMETHING HAVE FORM FOR YOU TO BELIEVE IN IT?
!

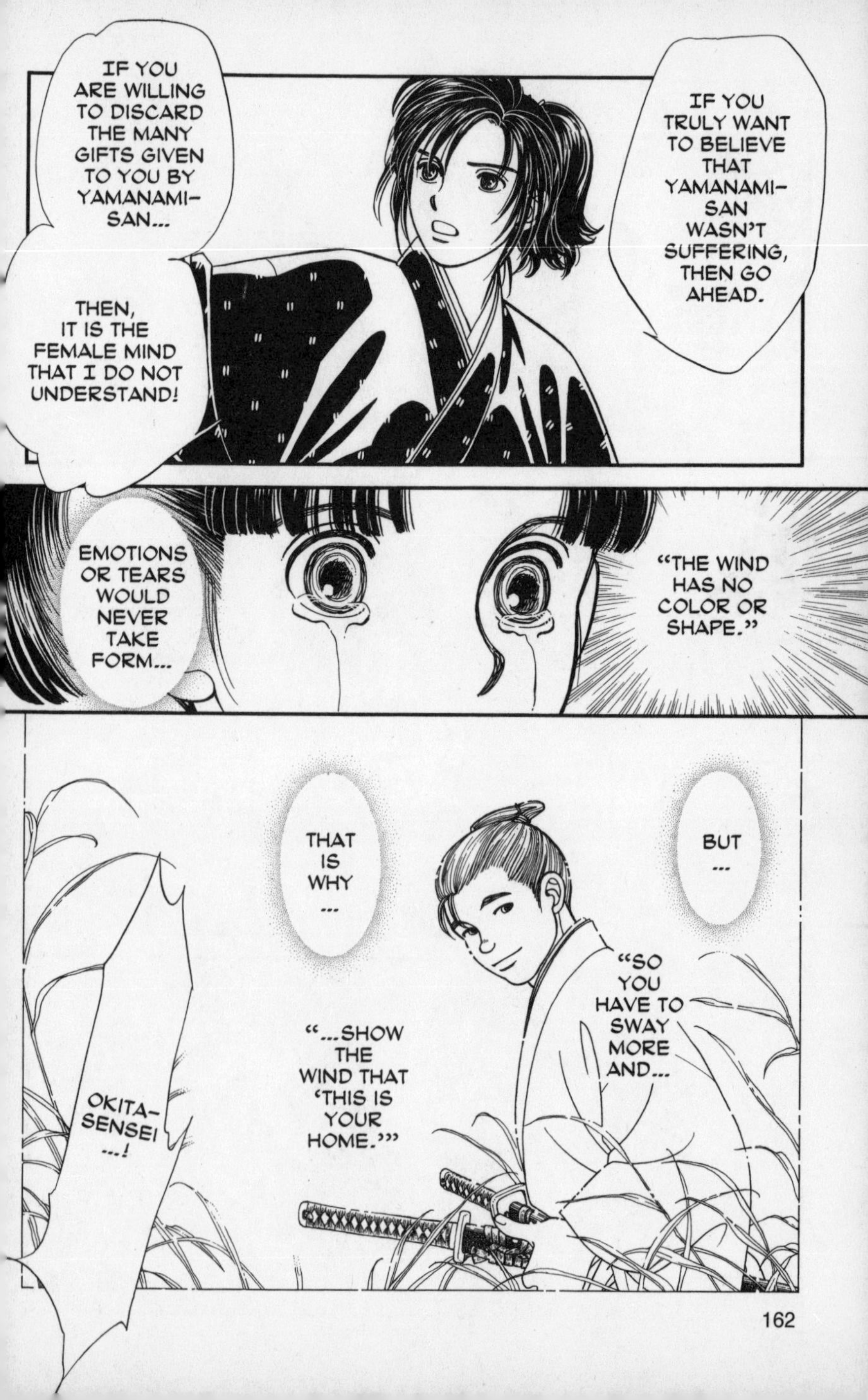
IF YOU TRULY WANT TO BELIEVE THAT YAMANAMI-SAN WASN'T SUFFERING, THEN GO AHEAD.
IF YOU ARE WILLING TO DISCARD THE MANY GIFTS GIVEN TO YOU BY YAMANAMI-SAN...
THEN, IT IS THE FEMALE MIND THAT I DO NOT UNDERSTAND!
"THE WIND HAS NO COLOR OR SHAPE."
EMOTIONS OR TEARS WOULD NEVER TAKE FORM...
BUT...
THAT IS WHY...
"SO YOU HAVE TO SWAY MORE AND...
"...SHOW THE WIND THAT 'THIS IS YOUR HOME.'"
OKITA-SENSEI...!

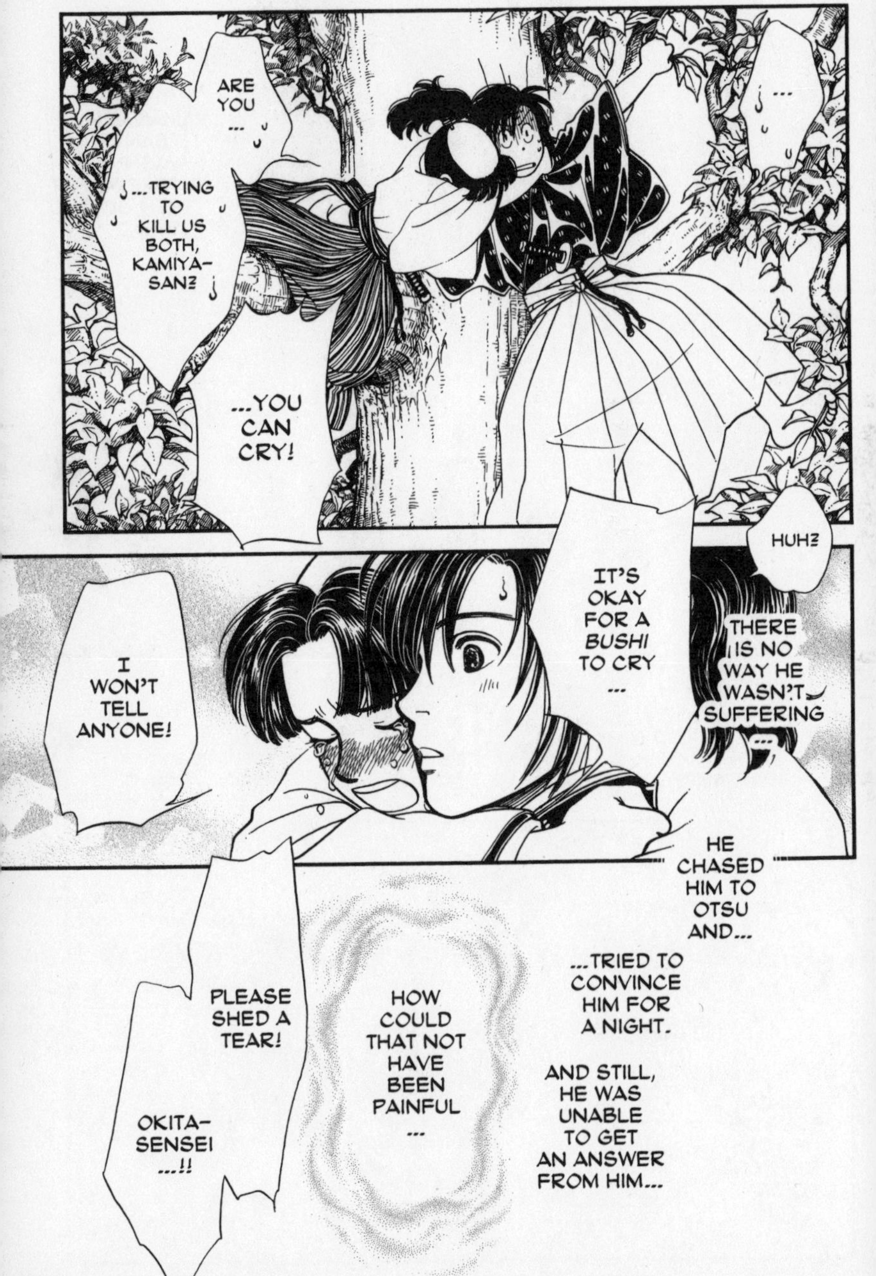
...
ARE YOU ...
...TRYING TO KILL US BOTH, KAMIYA-SAN?
...YOU CAN CRY!
HUH?
THERE IS NO WAY HE WASN'T SUFFERING ...
IT'S OKAY FOR A *BUSHI* TO CRY ...
I WON'T TELL ANYONE!
HE CHASED HIM TO OTSU AND...
...TRIED TO CONVINCE HIM FOR A NIGHT.
AND STILL, HE WAS UNABLE TO GET AN ANSWER FROM HIM...
HOW COULD THAT NOT HAVE BEEN PAINFUL ...
PLEASE SHED A TEAR!
OKITA-SENSEI ...!!

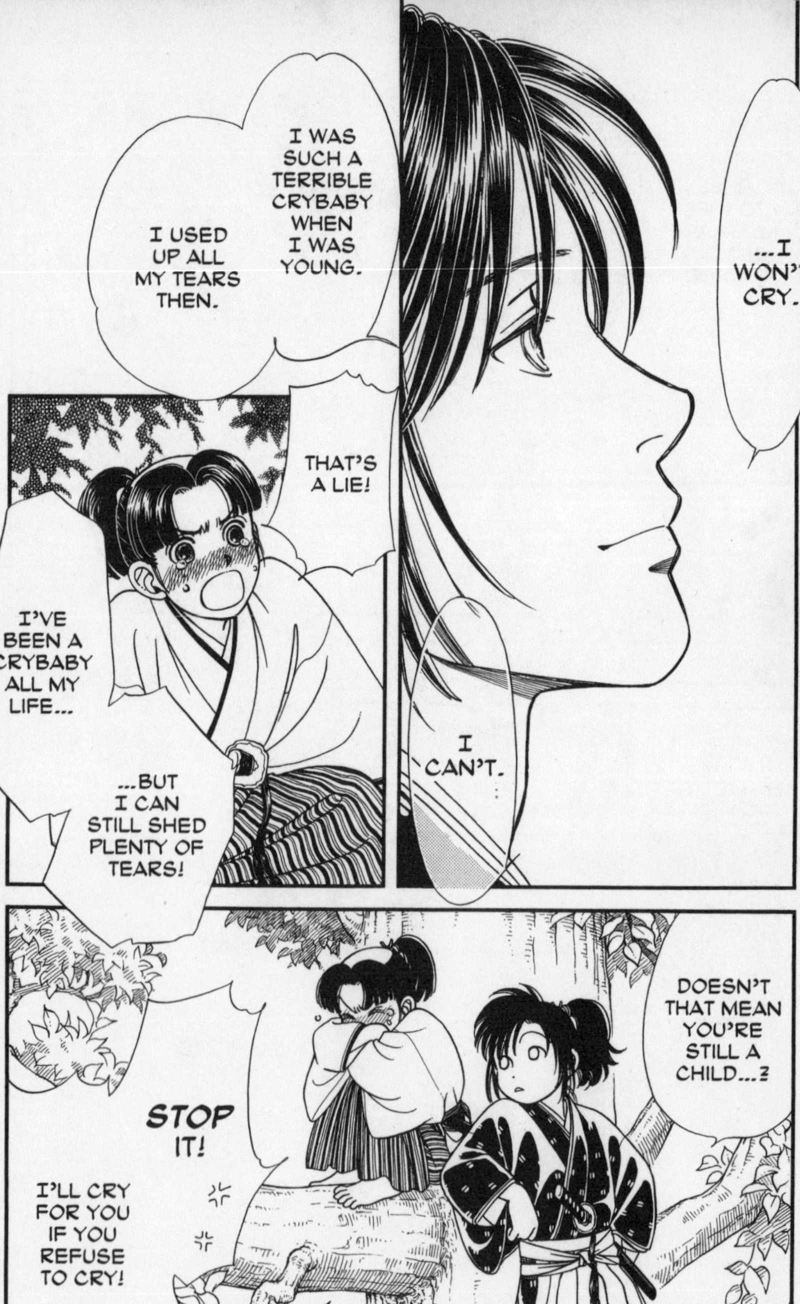
...I WON'T CRY.
I WAS SUCH A TERRIBLE CRYBABY WHEN I WAS YOUNG.
I USED UP ALL MY TEARS THEN.
I CAN'T.
THAT'S A LIE!
I'VE BEEN A CRYBABY ALL MY LIFE...
...BUT I CAN STILL SHED PLENTY OF TEARS!
DOESN'T THAT MEAN YOU'RE STILL A CHILD...?
STOP IT!
I'LL CRY FOR YOU IF YOU REFUSE TO CRY!

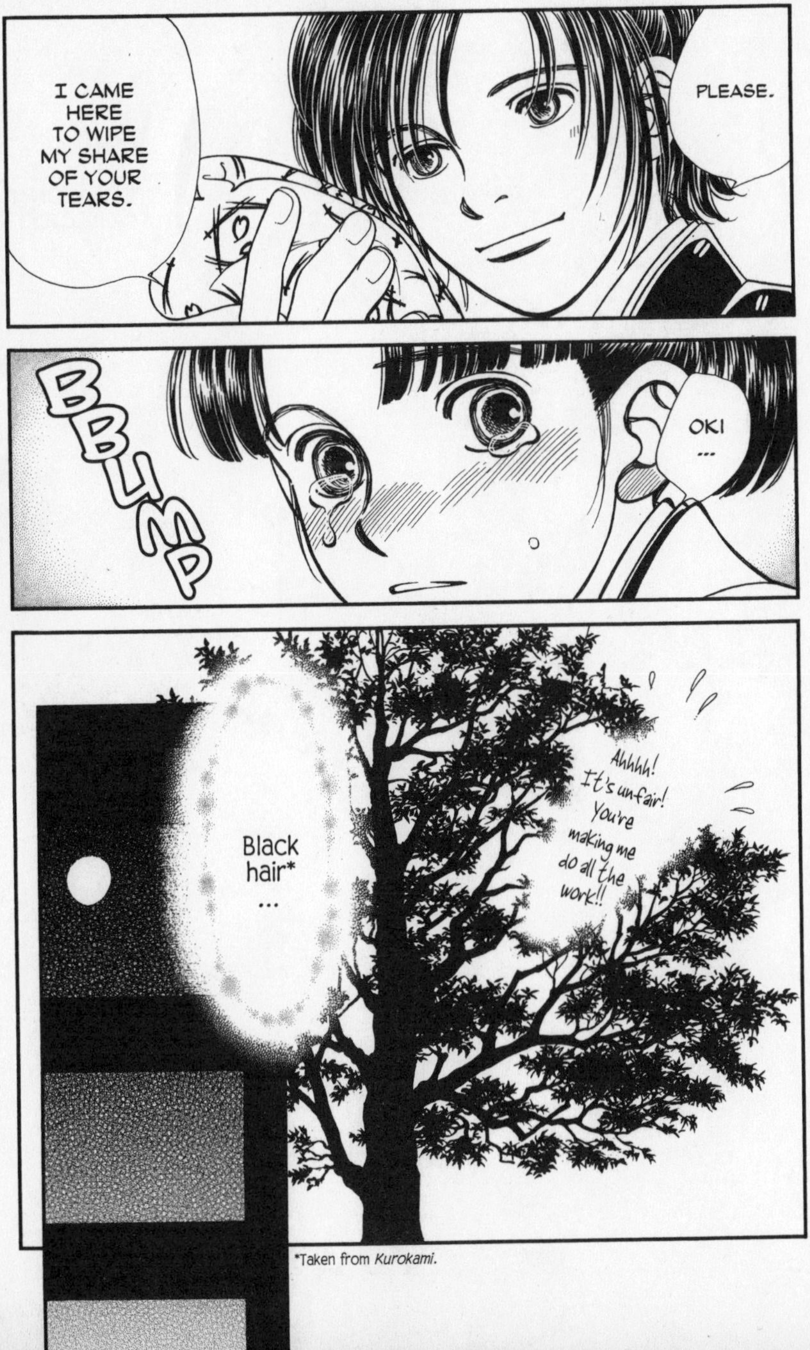
PLEASE.
I CAME HERE TO WIPE MY SHARE OF YOUR TEARS.
OKI ...
BBUMP
Ahhhh! It's unfair! You're making me do all the work!!
Black hair* ...

*Taken from *Kurokami*.

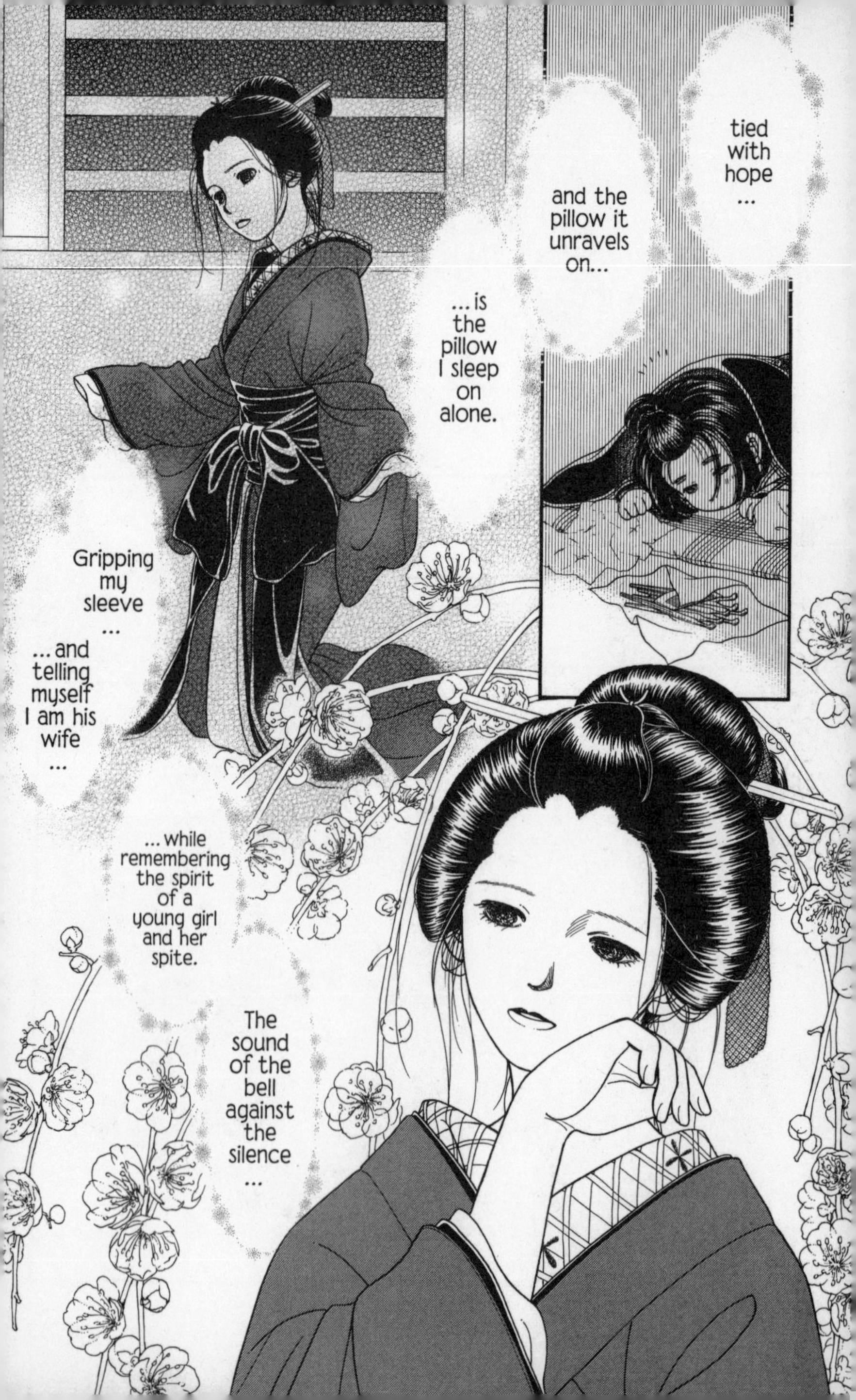
tied with hope ...
and the pillow it unravels on...
... is the pillow I sleep on alone.
Gripping my sleeve ...
... and telling myself I am his wife ...
... while remembering the spirit of a young girl and her spite.
The sound of the bell against the silence ...

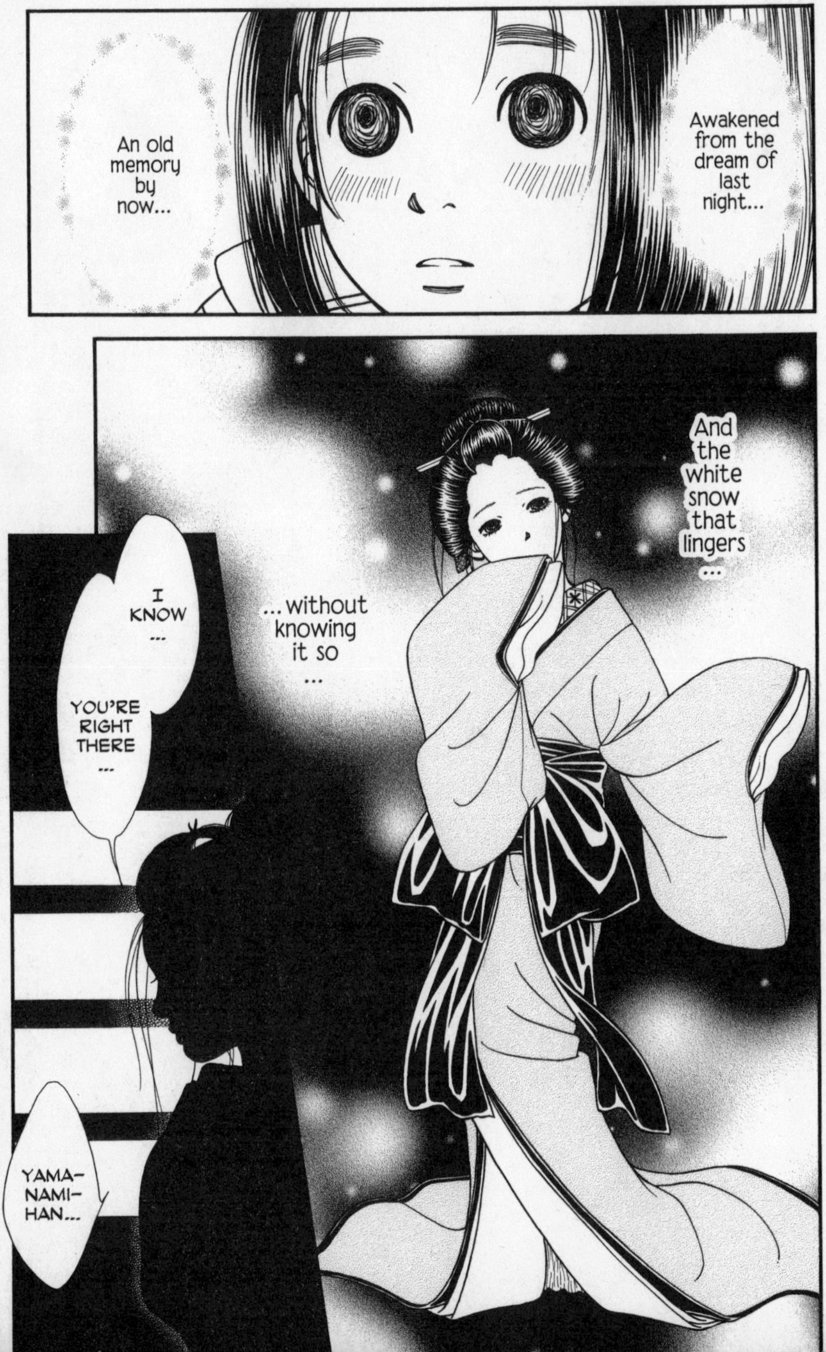
Awakened from the dream of last night...
An old memory by now...
And the white snow that lingers...
...without knowing it so...
I KNOW...
YOU'RE RIGHT THERE...
YAMA-NAMI-HAN...

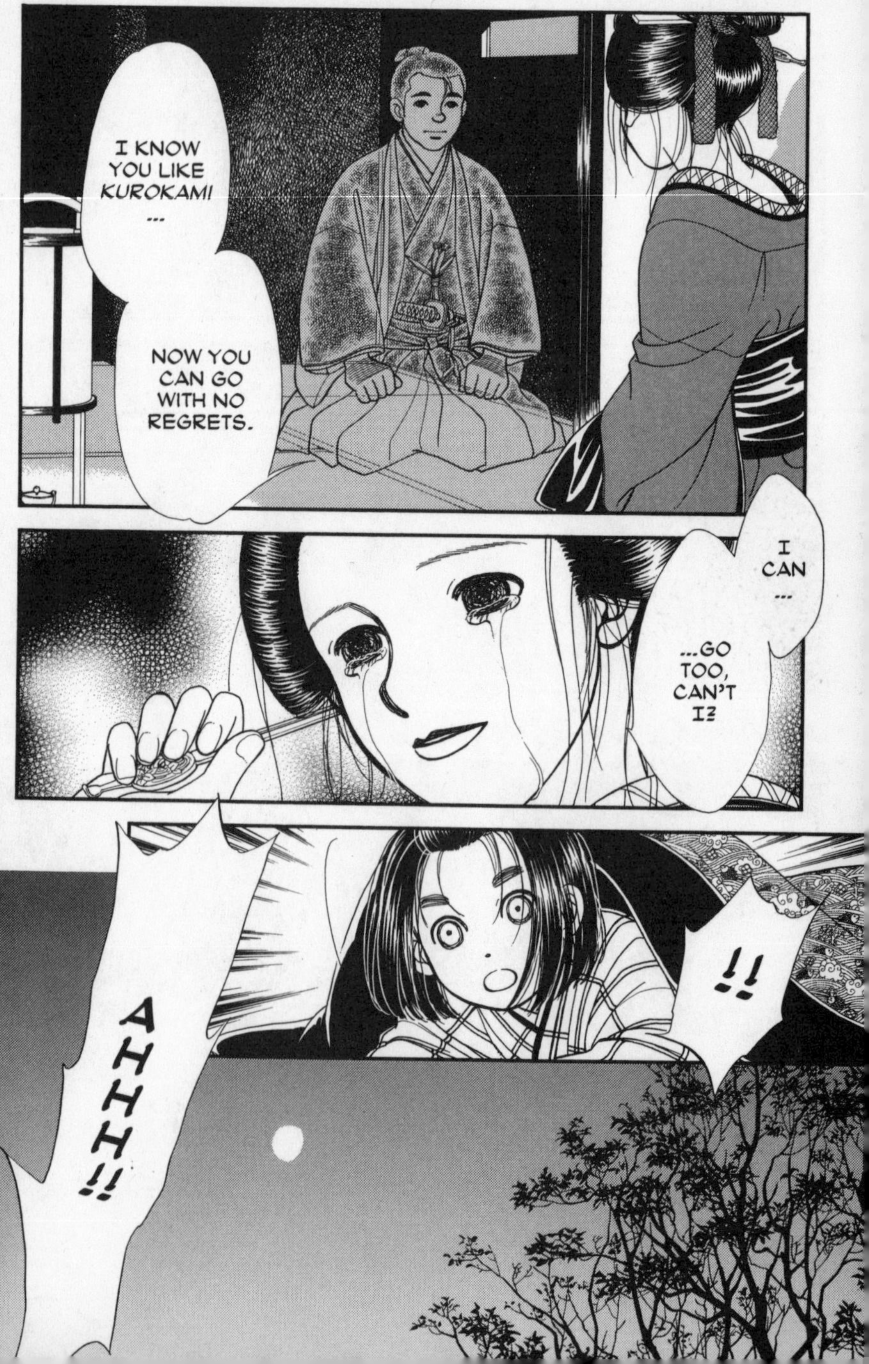
I KNOW YOU LIKE KUROKAMI ...
NOW YOU CAN GO WITH NO REGRETS.
I CAN ...
...GO TOO, CAN'T I?
!!
AHHH!!

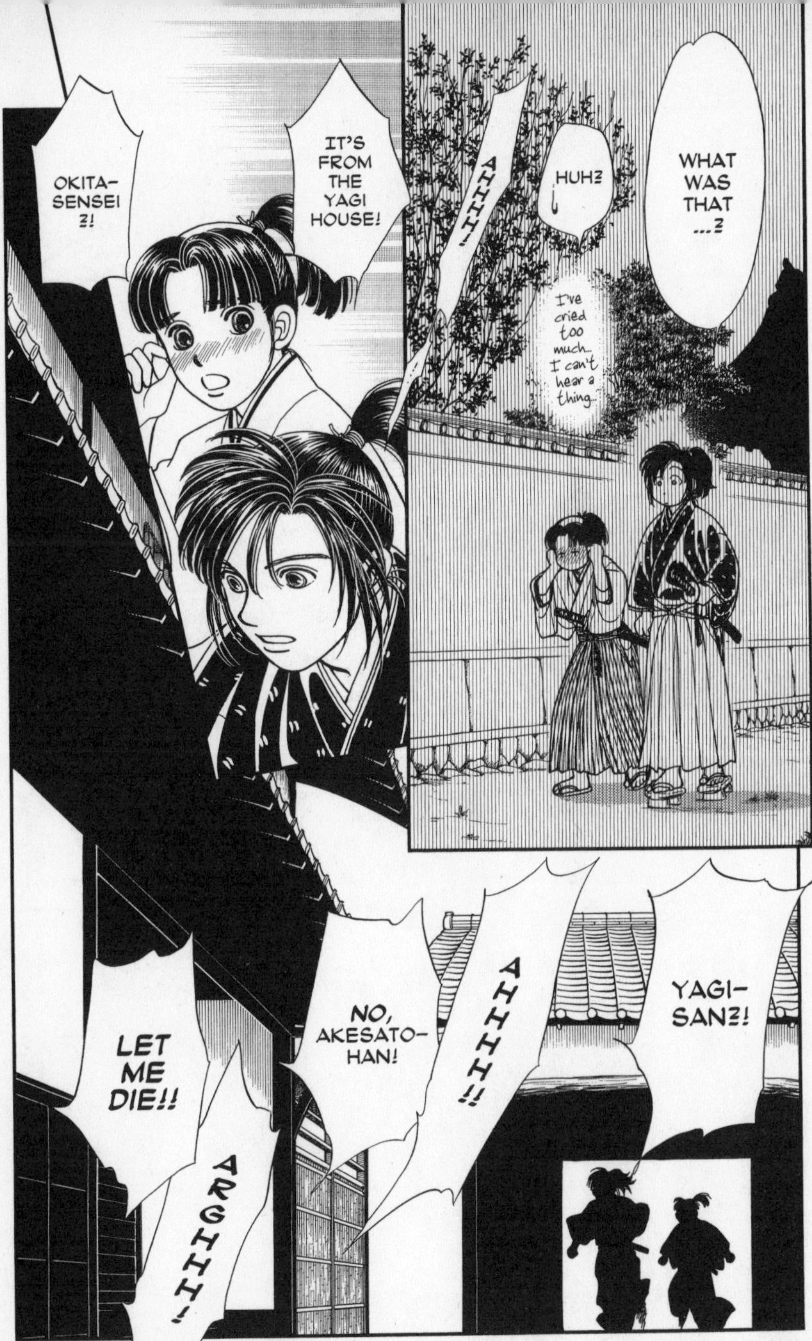
WHAT WAS THAT ...?
HUH?
AHHHH!
I've cried too much... I can't hear a thing...
IT'S FROM THE YAGI HOUSE!
OKITA-SENSEI?!
YAGI-SAN?!
AHHHHH!!
NO, AKESATO-HAN!
LET ME DIE!!
ARGHHH!

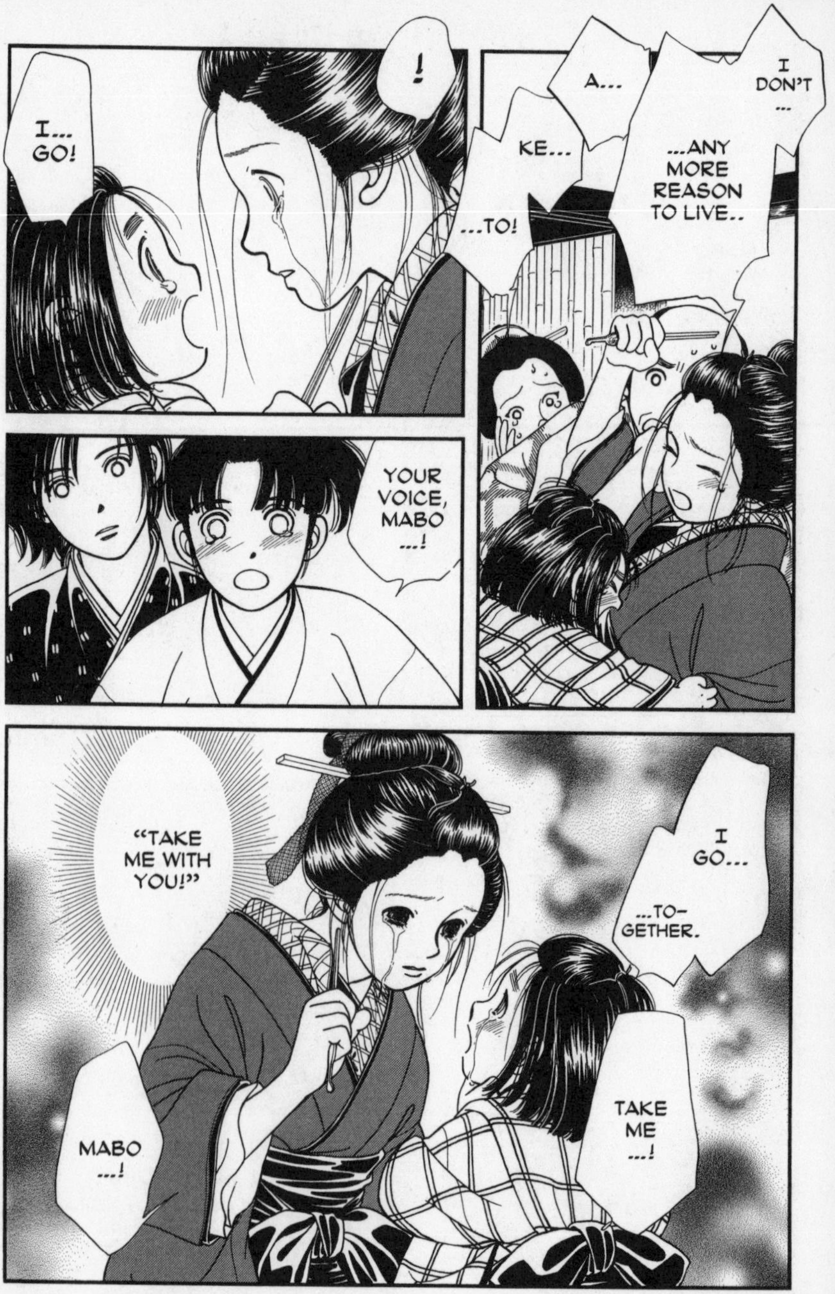

I DON'T ...
...ANY MORE REASON TO LIVE..
A...
KE...
...TO!
!
I... GO!
YOUR VOICE, MABO ...!
I GO...
...TO-GETHER.
"TAKE ME WITH YOU!"
TAKE ME ...!
MABO ...!

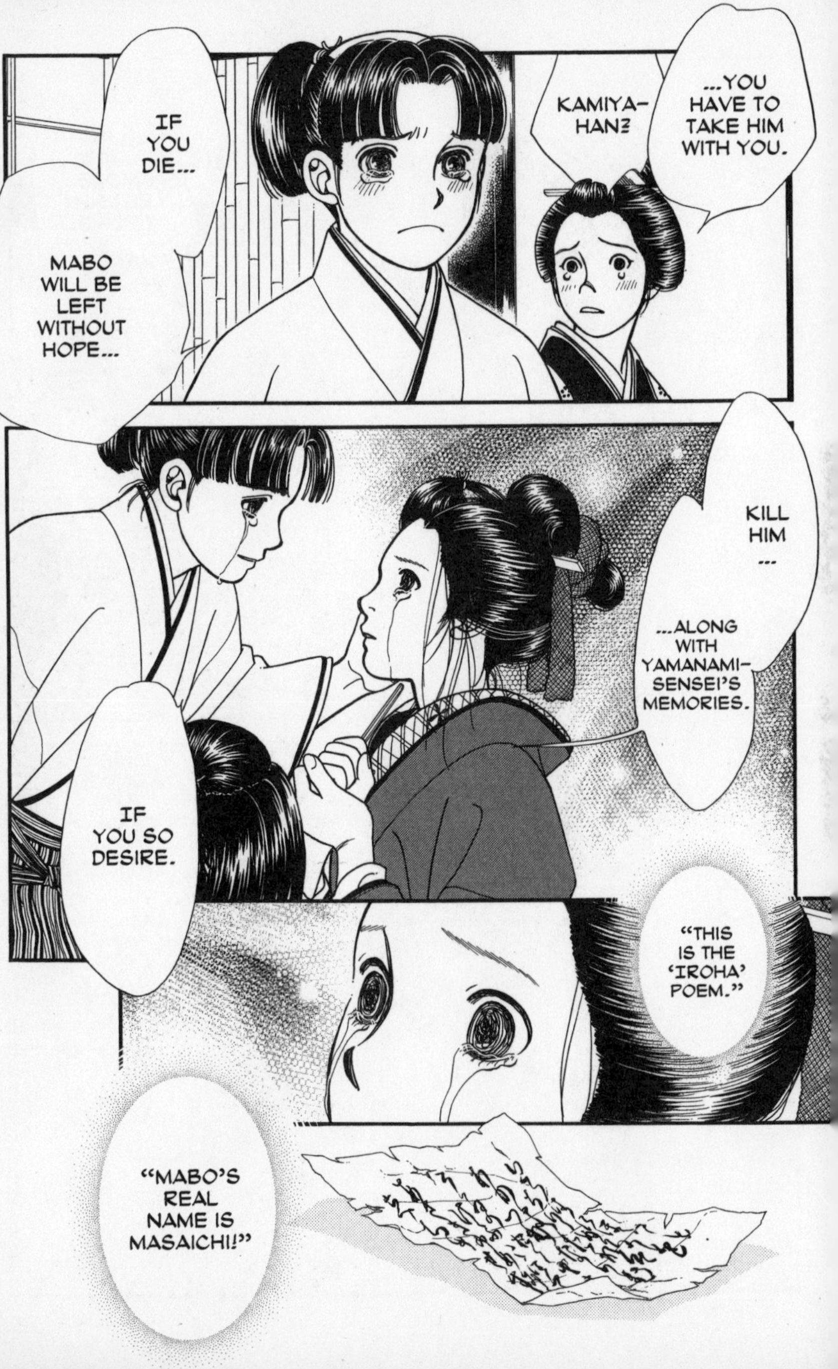

...YOU HAVE TO TAKE HIM WITH YOU.
KAMIYA-HAN?
IF YOU DIE...
MABO WILL BE LEFT WITHOUT HOPE...
KILL HIM ...
...ALONG WITH YAMANAMI-SENSEI'S MEMORIES.
IF YOU SO DESIRE.
"THIS IS THE 'IROHA' POEM."
"MABO'S REAL NAME IS MASAICHI!!"

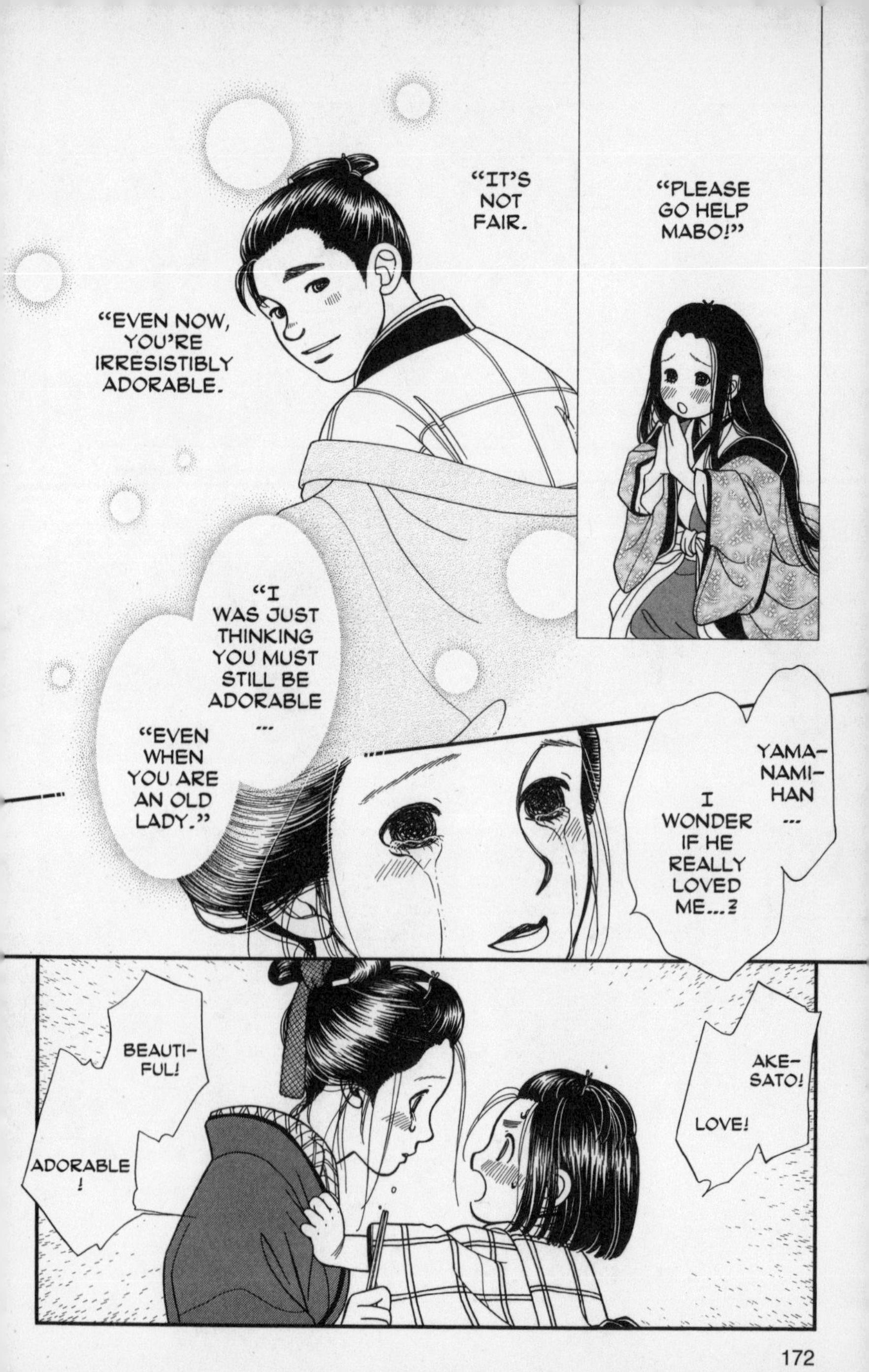

"PLEASE GO HELP MABO!"
"IT'S NOT FAIR.
"EVEN NOW, YOU'RE IRRESISTIBLY ADORABLE.
"I WAS JUST THINKING YOU MUST STILL BE ADORABLE...
"EVEN WHEN YOU ARE AN OLD LADY."
...
YAMA-NAMI-HAN...
I WONDER IF HE REALLY LOVED ME...?
AKE-SATO!
LOVE!
BEAUTI-FUL!
ADORABLE!

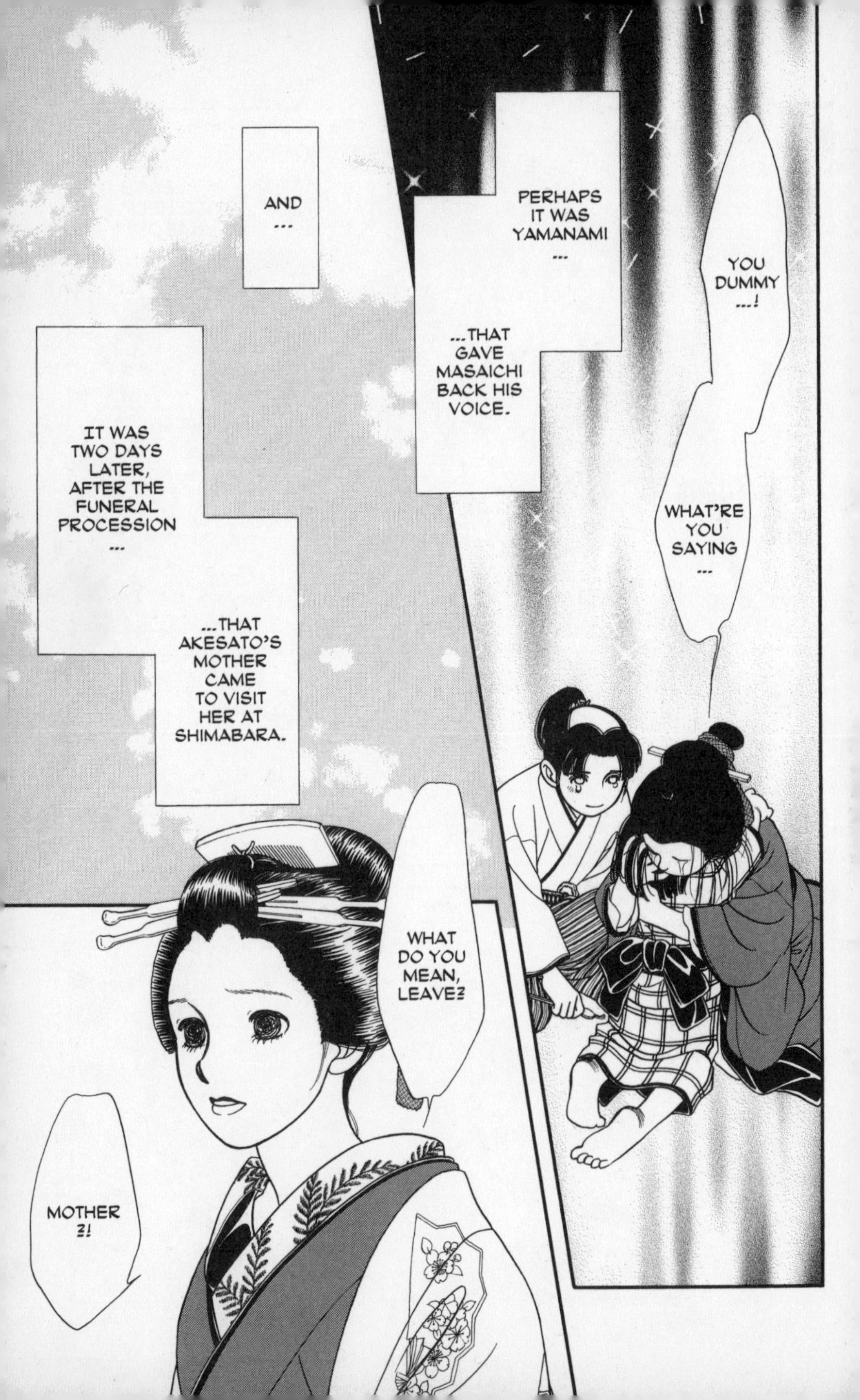
PERHAPS IT WAS YAMANAMI...
...THAT GAVE MASAICHI BACK HIS VOICE.
YOU DUMMY...!
WHAT'RE YOU SAYING...
AND...
IT WAS TWO DAYS LATER, AFTER THE FUNERAL PROCESSION...
...THAT AKESATO'S MOTHER CAME TO VISIT HER AT SHIMABARA.
WHAT DO YOU MEAN, LEAVE?
MOTHER?!

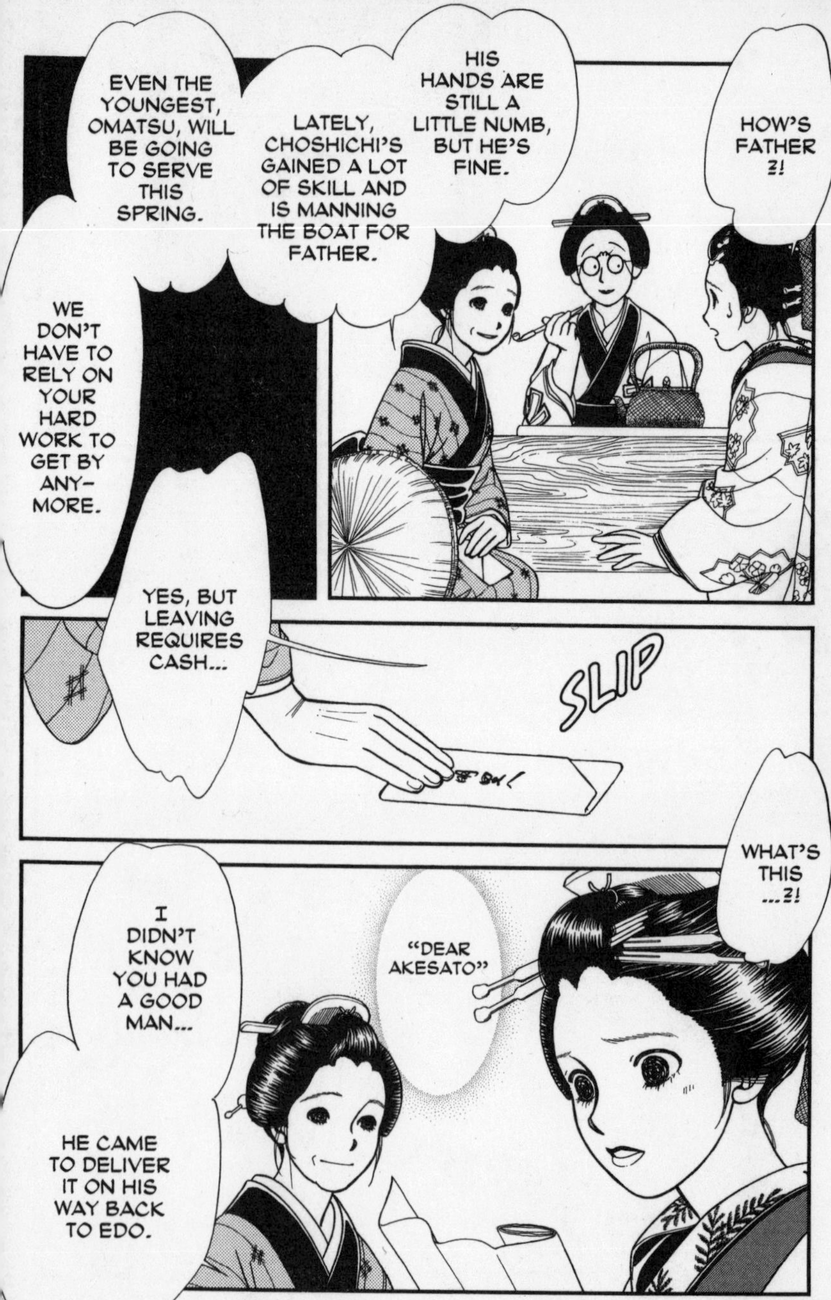
HOW'S FATHER ?!
HIS HANDS ARE STILL A LITTLE NUMB, BUT HE'S FINE.
LATELY, CHOSHICHI'S GAINED A LOT OF SKILL AND IS MANNING THE BOAT FOR FATHER.
EVEN THE YOUNGEST, OMATSU, WILL BE GOING TO SERVE THIS SPRING.
WE DON'T HAVE TO RELY ON YOUR HARD WORK TO GET BY ANY-MORE.
YES, BUT LEAVING REQUIRES CASH...
SLIP
WHAT'S THIS ...?!
"DEAR AKESATO"
I DIDN'T KNOW YOU HAD A GOOD MAN...
HE CAME TO DELIVER IT ON HIS WAY BACK TO EDO.

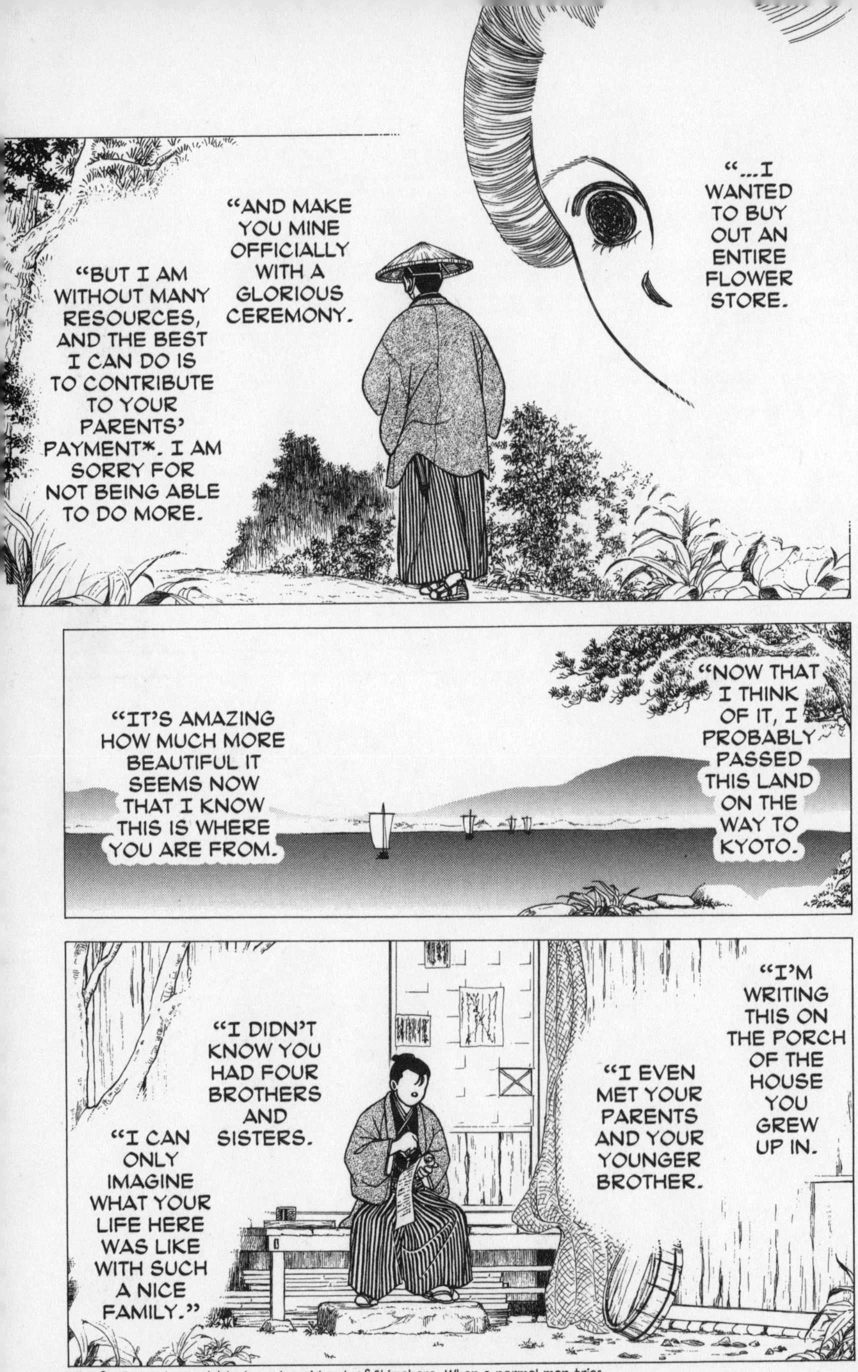
"...I WANTED TO BUY OUT AN ENTIRE FLOWER STORE.
"AND MAKE YOU MINE OFFICIALLY WITH A GLORIOUS CEREMONY.
"BUT I AM WITHOUT MANY RESOURCES, AND THE BEST I CAN DO IS TO CONTRIBUTE TO YOUR PARENTS' PAYMENT*. I AM SORRY FOR NOT BEING ABLE TO DO MORE.
"NOW THAT I THINK OF IT, I PROBABLY PASSED THIS LAND ON THE WAY TO KYOTO.
"IT'S AMAZING HOW MUCH MORE BEAUTIFUL IT SEEMS NOW THAT I KNOW THIS IS WHERE YOU ARE FROM.
"I'M WRITING THIS ON THE PORCH OF THE HOUSE YOU GREW UP IN.
"I EVEN MET YOUR PARENTS AND YOUR YOUNGER BROTHER.
"I DIDN'T KNOW YOU HAD FOUR BROTHERS AND SISTERS.
"I CAN ONLY IMAGINE WHAT YOUR LIFE HERE WAS LIKE WITH SUCH A NICE FAMILY."

*The family must pay debts to get a girl out of Shimabara. When a normal man tries to do so, the funds increases exponentially as he must pay for ceremonies and parties.

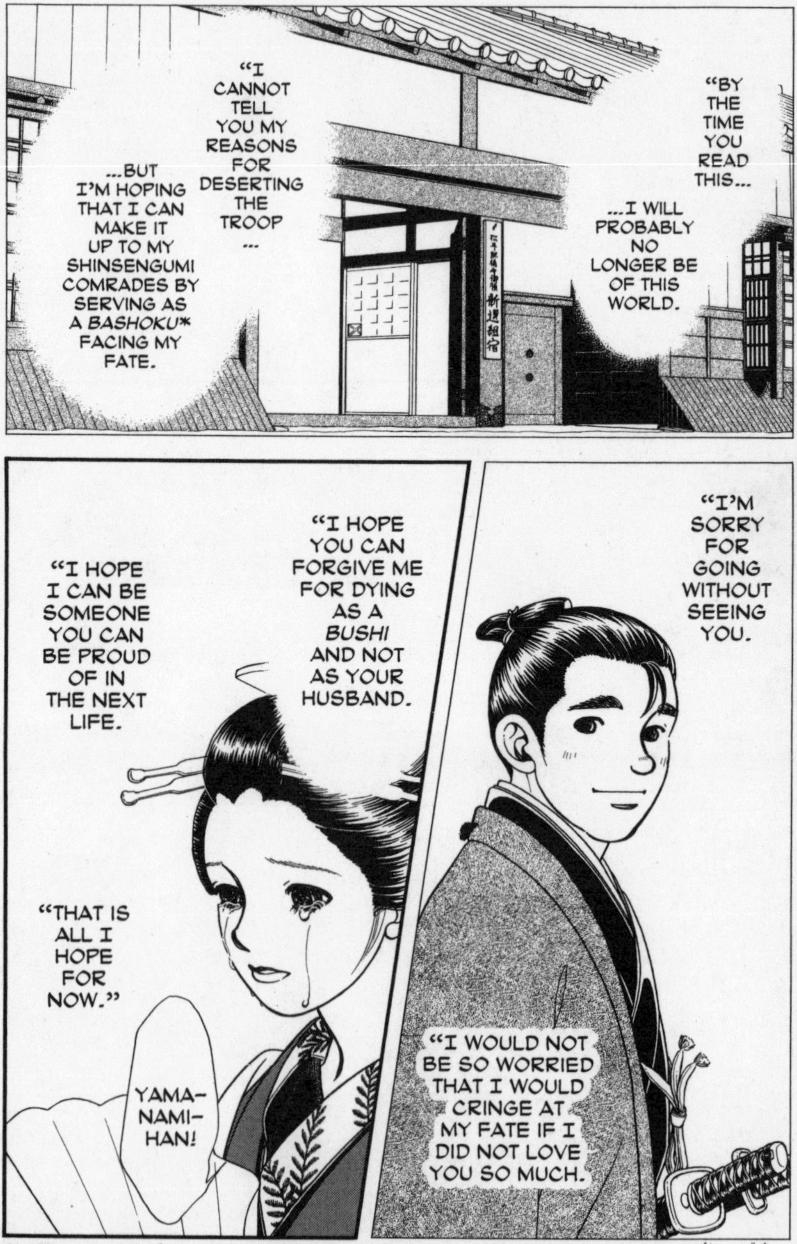
"BY THE TIME YOU READ THIS...
...I WILL PROBABLY NO LONGER BE OF THIS WORLD.
"I CANNOT TELL YOU MY REASONS FOR DESERTING THE TROOP...
...BUT I'M HOPING THAT I CAN MAKE IT UP TO MY SHINSENGUMI COMRADES BY SERVING AS A *BASHOKU** FACING MY FATE.
"I'M SORRY FOR GOING WITHOUT SEEING YOU.
"I WOULD NOT BE SO WORRIED THAT I WOULD CRINGE AT MY FATE IF I DID NOT LOVE YOU SO MUCH.
"I HOPE YOU CAN FORGIVE ME FOR DYING AS A *BUSHI* AND NOT AS YOUR HUSBAND.
"I HOPE I CAN BE SOMEONE YOU CAN BE PROUD OF IN THE NEXT LIFE.
"THAT IS ALL I HOPE FOR NOW."
YAMA-NAMI-HAN!

*A military commander from the Three Kingdoms who was punished for disobeying troop rules, despite being the son of Zhūge Liàng's best friend. It is said that the troop was unified by Liàng's nobility of enforcing regulations on someone he loved dearly.

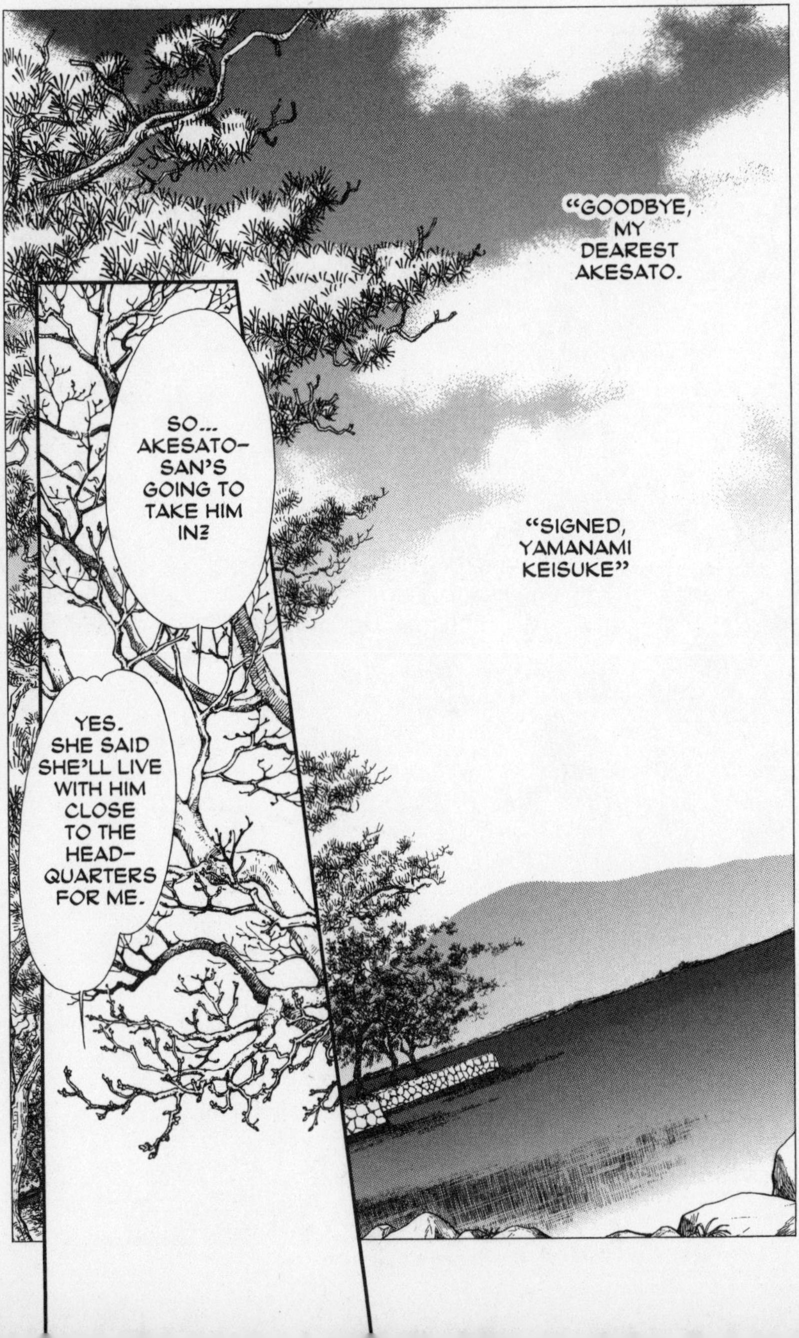
"GOODBYE, MY DEAREST AKESATO.
"SIGNED, YAMANAMI KEISUKE"
SO... AKESATO-SAN'S GOING TO TAKE HIM IN?
YES. SHE SAID SHE'LL LIVE WITH HIM CLOSE TO THE HEAD-QUARTERS FOR ME.

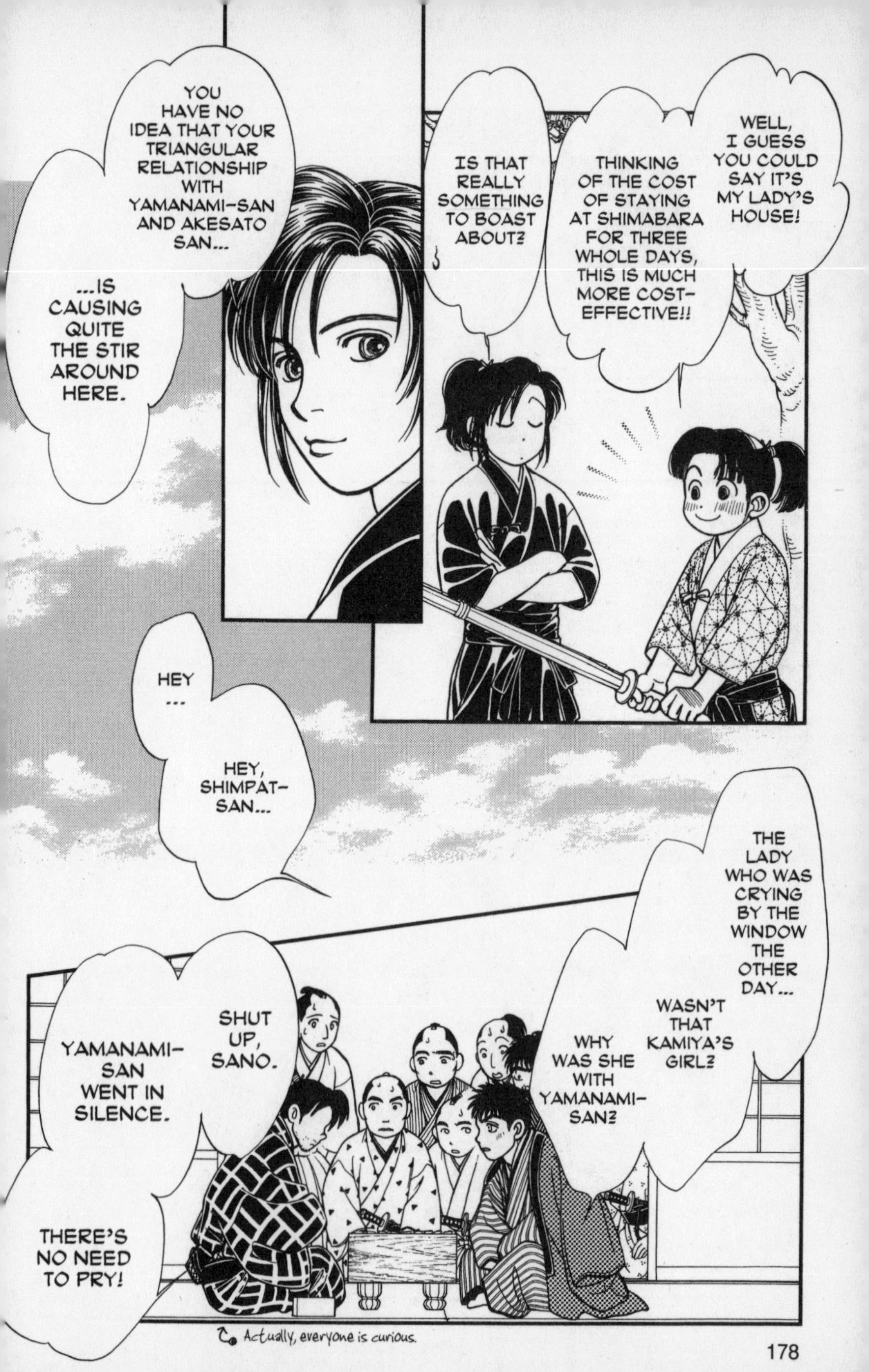
WELL, I GUESS YOU COULD SAY IT'S MY LADY'S HOUSE!
THINKING OF THE COST OF STAYING AT SHIMABARA FOR THREE WHOLE DAYS, THIS IS MUCH MORE COST-EFFECTIVE!!
IS THAT REALLY SOMETHING TO BOAST ABOUT?
YOU HAVE NO IDEA THAT YOUR TRIANGULAR RELATIONSHIP WITH YAMANAMI-SAN AND AKESATO SAN...
...IS CAUSING QUITE THE STIR AROUND HERE.
HEY ...
HEY, SHIMPAT-SAN...
THE LADY WHO WAS CRYING BY THE WINDOW THE OTHER DAY...
WASN'T THAT KAMIYA'S GIRL?
WHY WAS SHE WITH YAMANAMI-SAN?
SHUT UP, SANO.
YAMANAMI-SAN WENT IN SILENCE.
THERE'S NO NEED TO PRY!
Actually, everyone is curious.

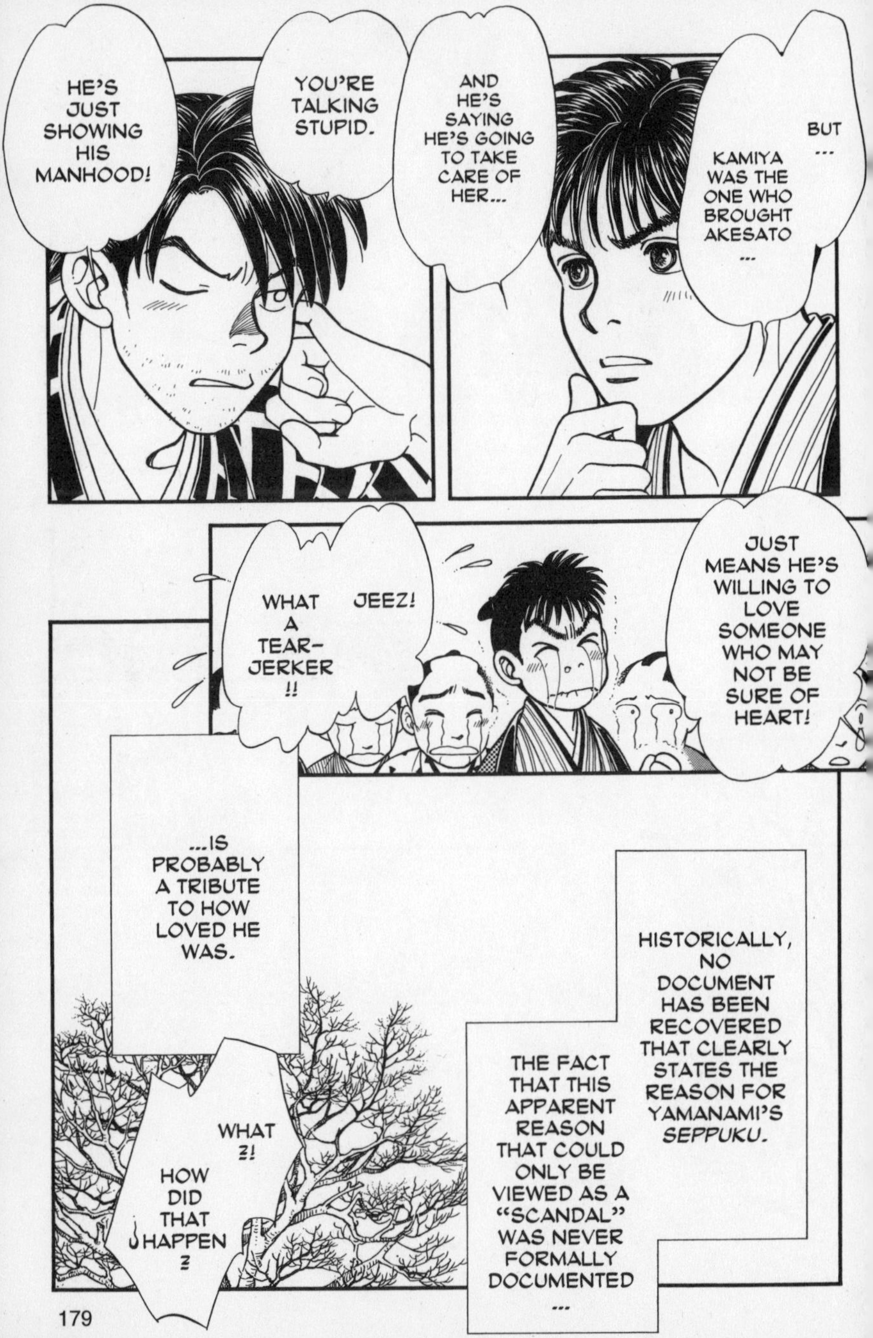
BUT... KAMIYA WAS THE ONE WHO BROUGHT AKESATO...
AND HE'S SAYING HE'S GOING TO TAKE CARE OF HER...
YOU'RE TALKING STUPID.
HE'S JUST SHOWING HIS MANHOOD!
JUST MEANS HE'S WILLING TO LOVE SOMEONE WHO MAY NOT BE SURE OF HEART!
JEEZ! WHAT A TEAR-JERKER!!
HISTORICALLY, NO DOCUMENT HAS BEEN RECOVERED THAT CLEARLY STATES THE REASON FOR YAMANAMI'S *SEPPUKU*.
THE FACT THAT THIS APPARENT REASON THAT COULD ONLY BE VIEWED AS A "SCANDAL" WAS NEVER FORMALLY DOCUMENTED...
...IS PROBABLY A TRIBUTE TO HOW LOVED HE WAS.
WHAT?!
HOW DID THAT HAPPEN?

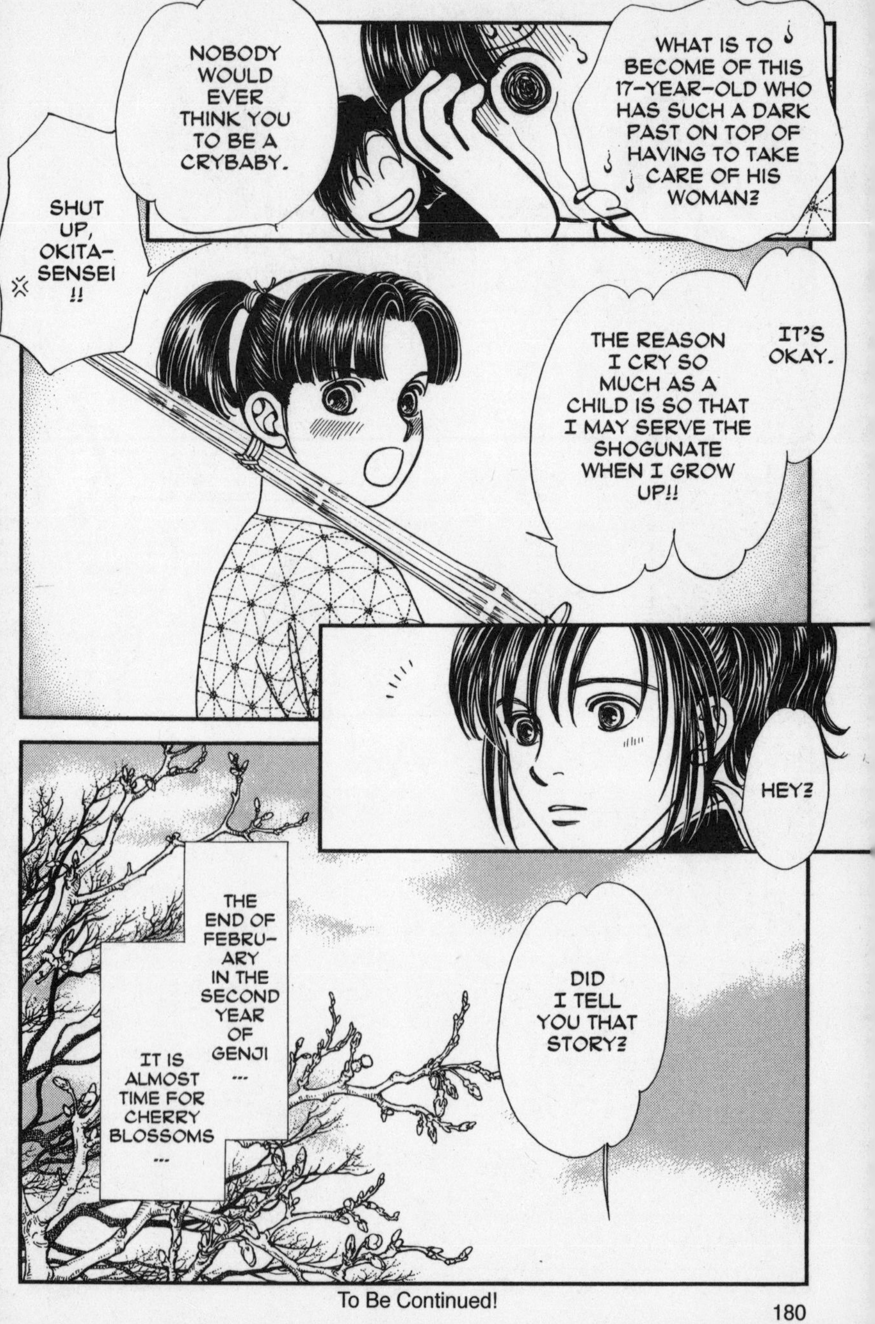
WHAT IS TO BECOME OF THIS 17-YEAR-OLD WHO HAS SUCH A DARK PAST ON TOP OF HAVING TO TAKE CARE OF HIS WOMAN?
NOBODY WOULD EVER THINK YOU TO BE A CRYBABY.
SHUT UP, OKITA-SENSEI!!
IT'S OKAY.
THE REASON I CRY SO MUCH AS A CHILD IS SO THAT I MAY SERVE THE SHOGUNATE WHEN I GROW UP!!
HEY?
DID I TELL YOU THAT STORY?
THE END OF FEBRUARY IN THE SECOND YEAR OF GENJI ...
IT IS ALMOST TIME FOR CHERRY BLOSSOMS ...

To Be Continued!

TAEKO WATANABE PRESENTS

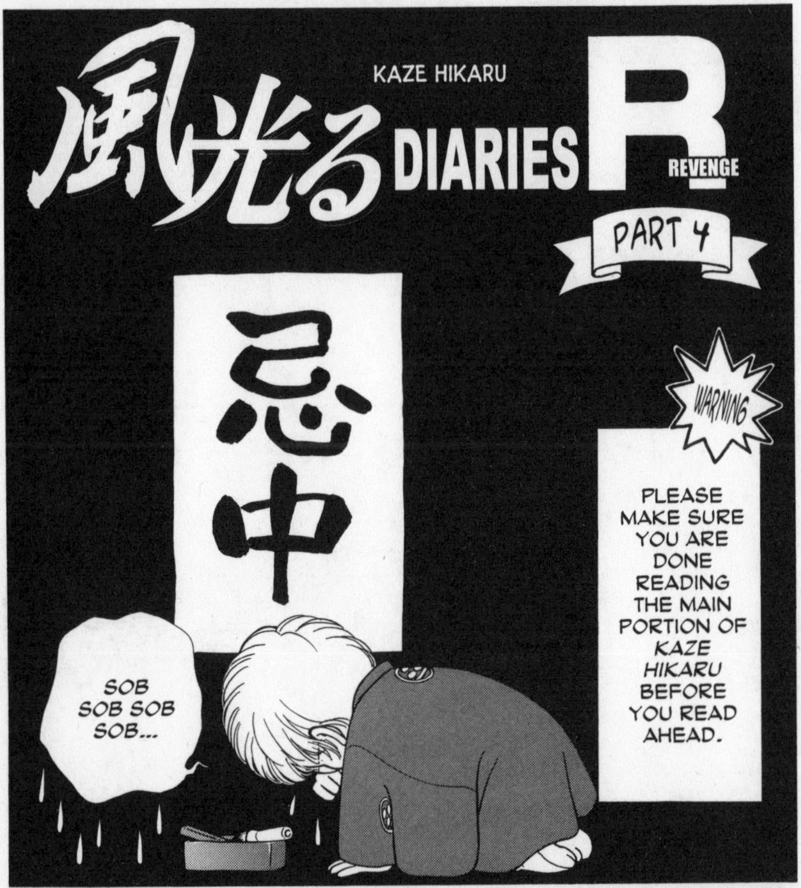
風光る DIARIES R
KAZE HIKARU
REVENGE
PART 4
WARNING
PLEASE MAKE SURE YOU ARE DONE READING THE MAIN PORTION OF KAZE HIKARU BEFORE YOU READ AHEAD.
忌中
SOB SOB SOB SOB...

Sign: Mourning

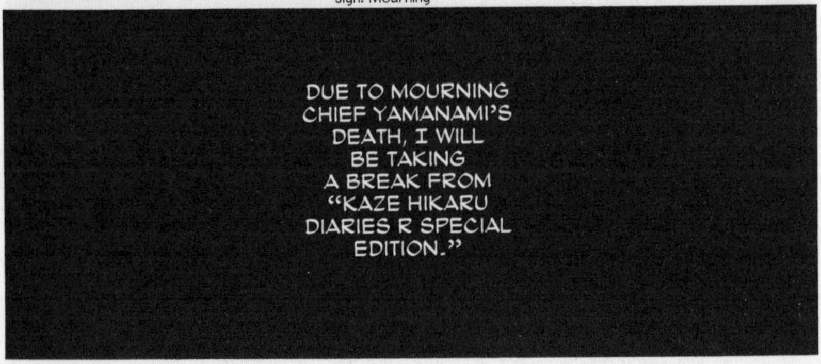
DUE TO MOURNING CHIEF YAMANAMI'S DEATH, I WILL BE TAKING A BREAK FROM "KAZE HIKARU DIARIES R SPECIAL EDITION."

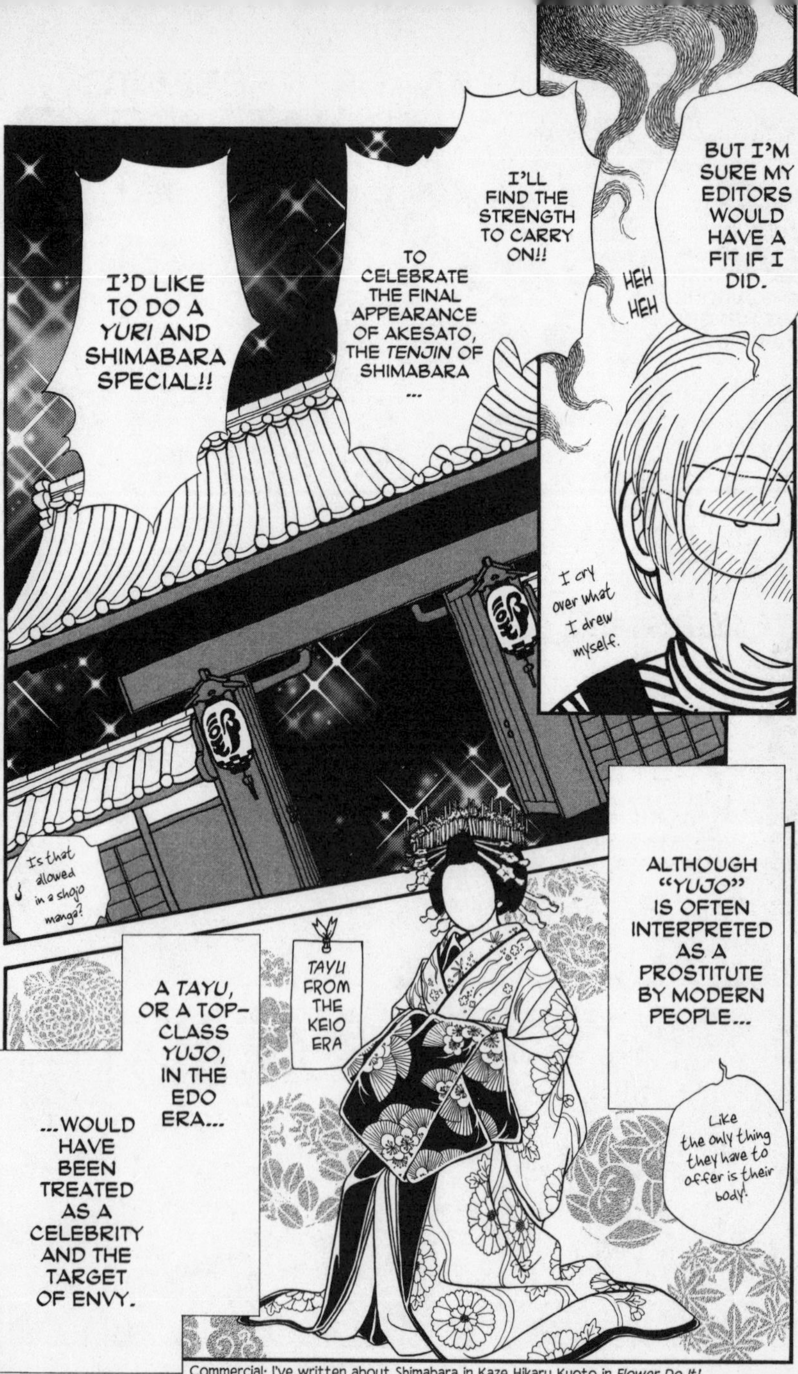
TO CELEBRATE THE FINAL APPEARANCE OF AKESATO, THE *TENJIN* OF SHIMABARA ...
I'D LIKE TO DO A *YURI* AND SHIMABARA SPECIAL!!
Is that allowed in a shojo manga?
BUT I'M SURE MY EDITORS WOULD HAVE A FIT IF I DID.
HEH HEH
I'LL FIND THE STRENGTH TO CARRY ON!!
I cry over what I drew myself.
ALTHOUGH "*YUJO*" IS OFTEN INTERPRETED AS A PROSTITUTE BY MODERN PEOPLE...
Like the only thing they have to offer is their body!
TAYU FROM THE KEIO ERA
A *TAYU*, OR A TOP-CLASS *YUJO*, IN THE EDO ERA...
...WOULD HAVE BEEN TREATED AS A CELEBRITY AND THE TARGET OF ENVY.

Commercial: I've written about Shimabara in Kaze Hikaru Kyoto in *Flower Do It!* See page 191 for details!

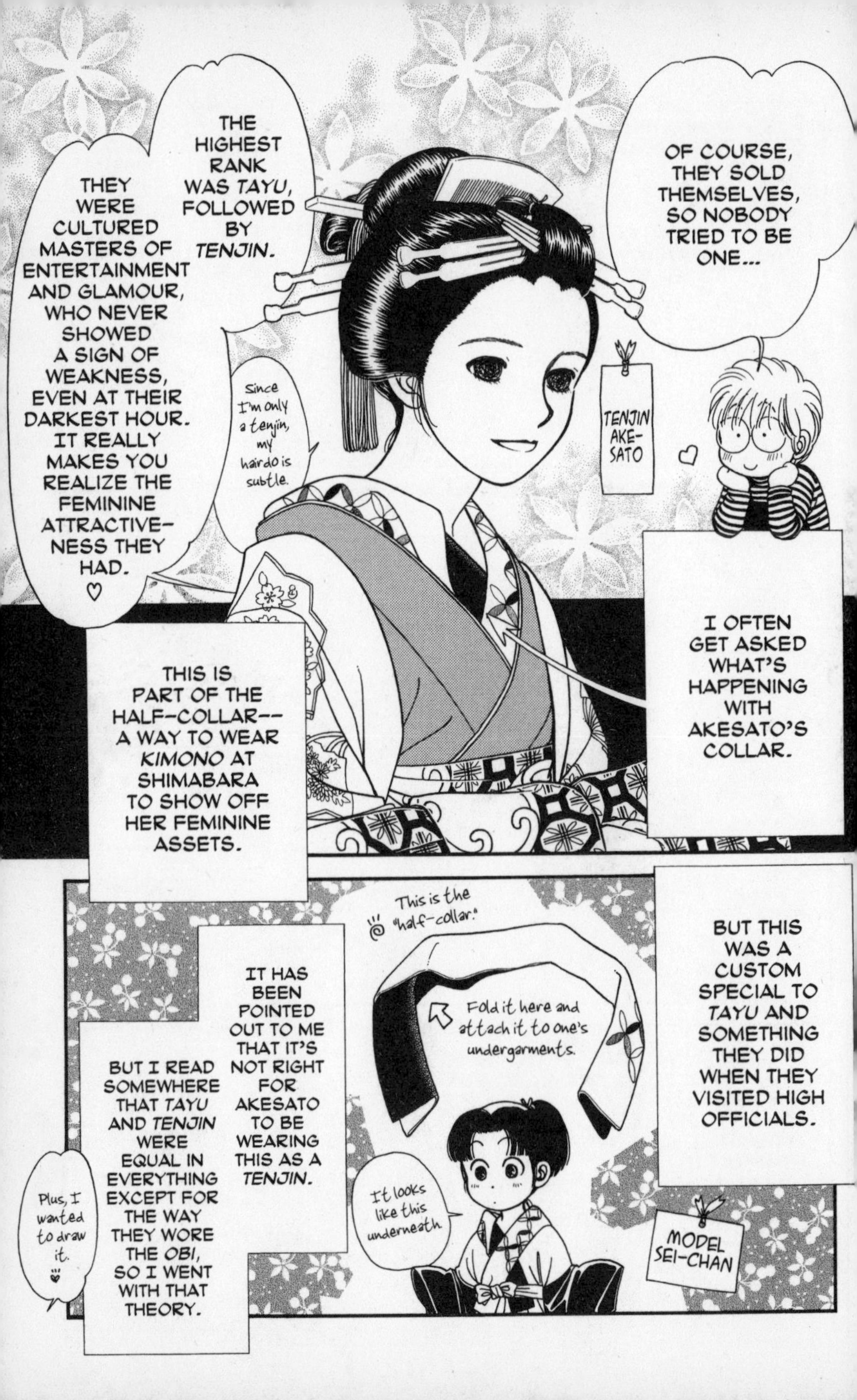

OF COURSE, THEY SOLD THEMSELVES, SO NOBODY TRIED TO BE ONE...
THE HIGHEST RANK WAS TAYU, FOLLOWED BY TENJIN.
TENJIN AKE-SATO
THEY WERE CULTURED MASTERS OF ENTERTAINMENT AND GLAMOUR, WHO NEVER SHOWED A SIGN OF WEAKNESS, EVEN AT THEIR DARKEST HOUR. IT REALLY MAKES YOU REALIZE THE FEMININE ATTRACTIVE-NESS THEY HAD. ♡
Since I'm only a tenjin, my hairdo is subtle.
I OFTEN GET ASKED WHAT'S HAPPENING WITH AKESATO'S COLLAR.
THIS IS PART OF THE HALF-COLLAR-- A WAY TO WEAR KIMONO AT SHIMABARA TO SHOW OFF HER FEMININE ASSETS.
BUT THIS WAS A CUSTOM SPECIAL TO TAYU AND SOMETHING THEY DID WHEN THEY VISITED HIGH OFFICIALS.
This is the "half-collar."
Fold it here and attach it to one's undergarments.
MODEL SEI-CHAN
It looks like this underneath.
IT HAS BEEN POINTED OUT TO ME THAT IT'S NOT RIGHT FOR AKESATO TO BE WEARING THIS AS A TENJIN.
BUT I READ SOMEWHERE THAT TAYU AND TENJIN WERE EQUAL IN EVERYTHING EXCEPT FOR THE WAY THEY WORE THE OBI, SO I WENT WITH THAT THEORY.
Plus, I wanted to draw it.

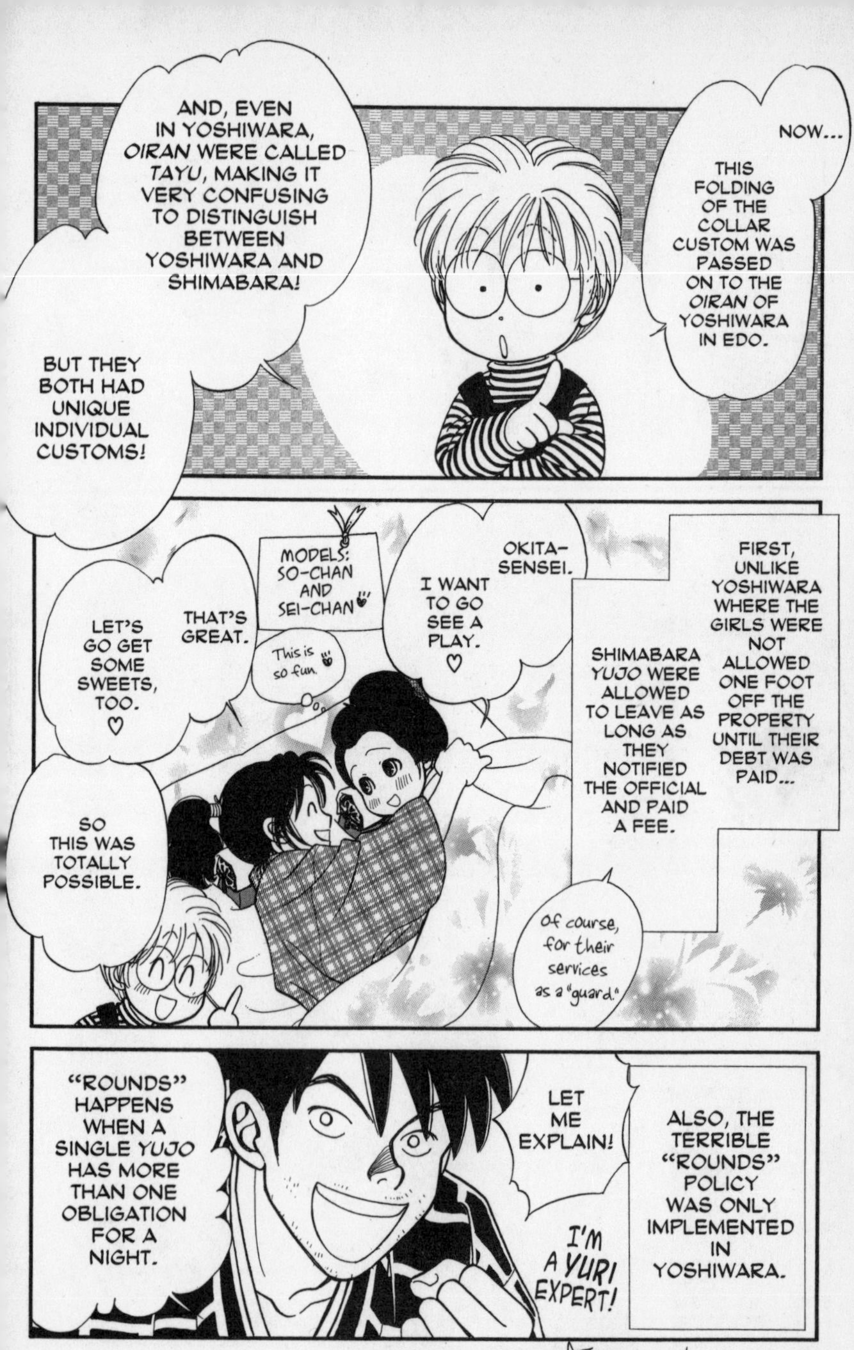
NOW... THIS FOLDING OF THE COLLAR CUSTOM WAS PASSED ON TO THE OIRAN OF YOSHIWARA IN EDO.
AND, EVEN IN YOSHIWARA, OIRAN WERE CALLED TAYU, MAKING IT VERY CONFUSING TO DISTINGUISH BETWEEN YOSHIWARA AND SHIMABARA!
BUT THEY BOTH HAD UNIQUE INDIVIDUAL CUSTOMS!
FIRST, UNLIKE YOSHIWARA WHERE THE GIRLS WERE NOT ALLOWED ONE FOOT OFF THE PROPERTY UNTIL THEIR DEBT WAS PAID...
SHIMABARA YUJO WERE ALLOWED TO LEAVE AS LONG AS THEY NOTIFIED THE OFFICIAL AND PAID A FEE.
OKITA-SENSEI. I WANT TO GO SEE A PLAY. ♡
MODELS: SO-CHAN AND SEI-CHAN
This is so fun.
THAT'S GREAT.
LET'S GO GET SOME SWEETS, TOO. ♡
Of course, for their services as a "guard."
SO THIS WAS TOTALLY POSSIBLE.
ALSO, THE TERRIBLE "ROUNDS" POLICY WAS ONLY IMPLEMENTED IN YOSHIWARA.
LET ME EXPLAIN!
I'M A YURI EXPERT!
"ROUNDS" HAPPENS WHEN A SINGLE YUJO HAS MORE THAN ONE OBLIGATION FOR A NIGHT.
oww!

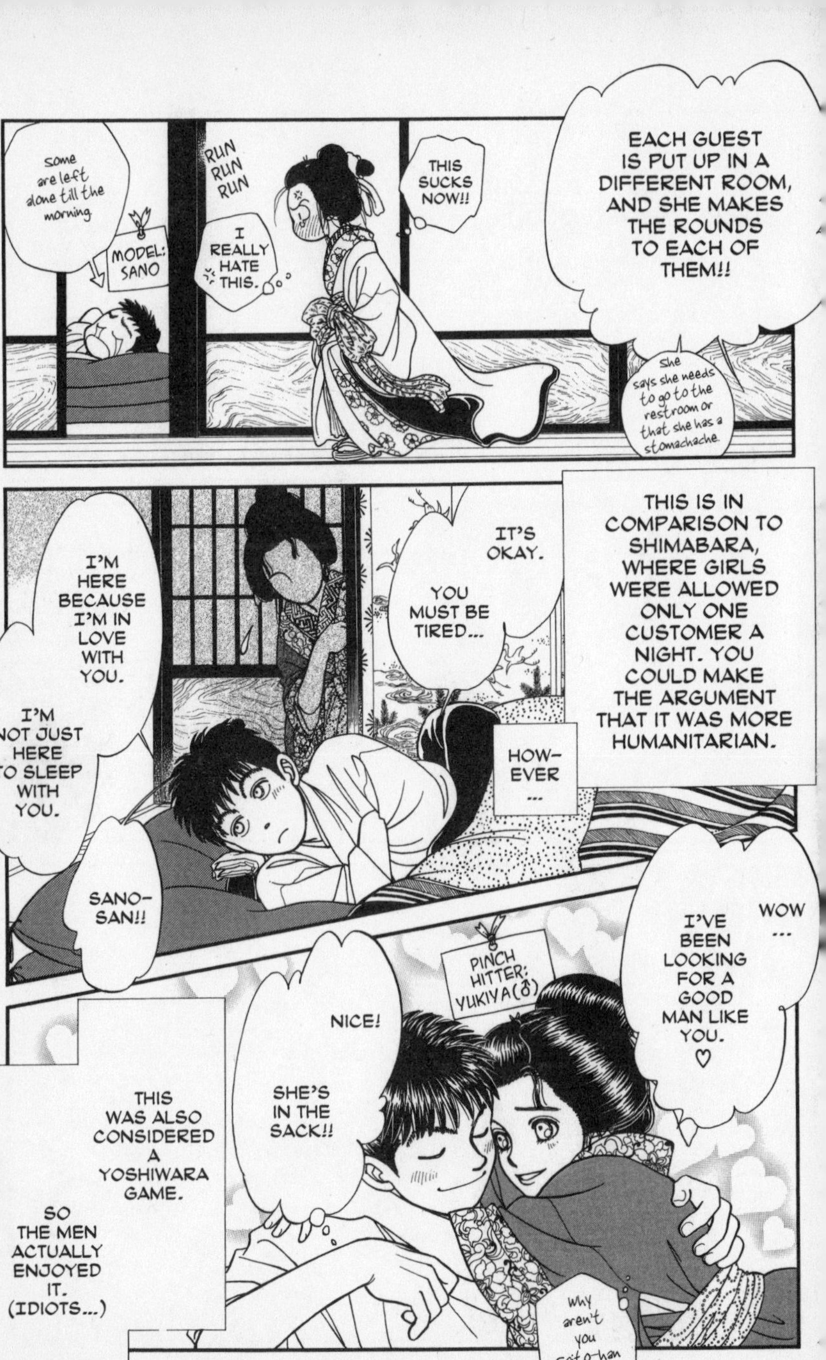
EACH GUEST IS PUT UP IN A DIFFERENT ROOM, AND SHE MAKES THE ROUNDS TO EACH OF THEM!!
She says she needs to go to the restroom or that she has a stomachache.
THIS SUCKS NOW!!
I REALLY HATE THIS.
RUN RUN RUN
Some are left alone till the morning.
MODEL: SANO
THIS IS IN COMPARISON TO SHIMABARA, WHERE GIRLS WERE ALLOWED ONLY ONE CUSTOMER A NIGHT. YOU COULD MAKE THE ARGUMENT THAT IT WAS MORE HUMANITARIAN.
HOW-EVER ...
IT'S OKAY.
YOU MUST BE TIRED...
I'M HERE BECAUSE I'M IN LOVE WITH YOU.
I'M NOT JUST HERE TO SLEEP WITH YOU.
SANO-SAN!!
WOW ...
I'VE BEEN LOOKING FOR A GOOD MAN LIKE YOU. ♡
PINCH HITTER: YUKIYA (♂)
Why aren't you Saito-han ?!
NICE!
SHE'S IN THE SACK!!
THIS WAS ALSO CONSIDERED A YOSHIWARA GAME.
SO THE MEN ACTUALLY ENJOYED IT. (IDIOTS...)

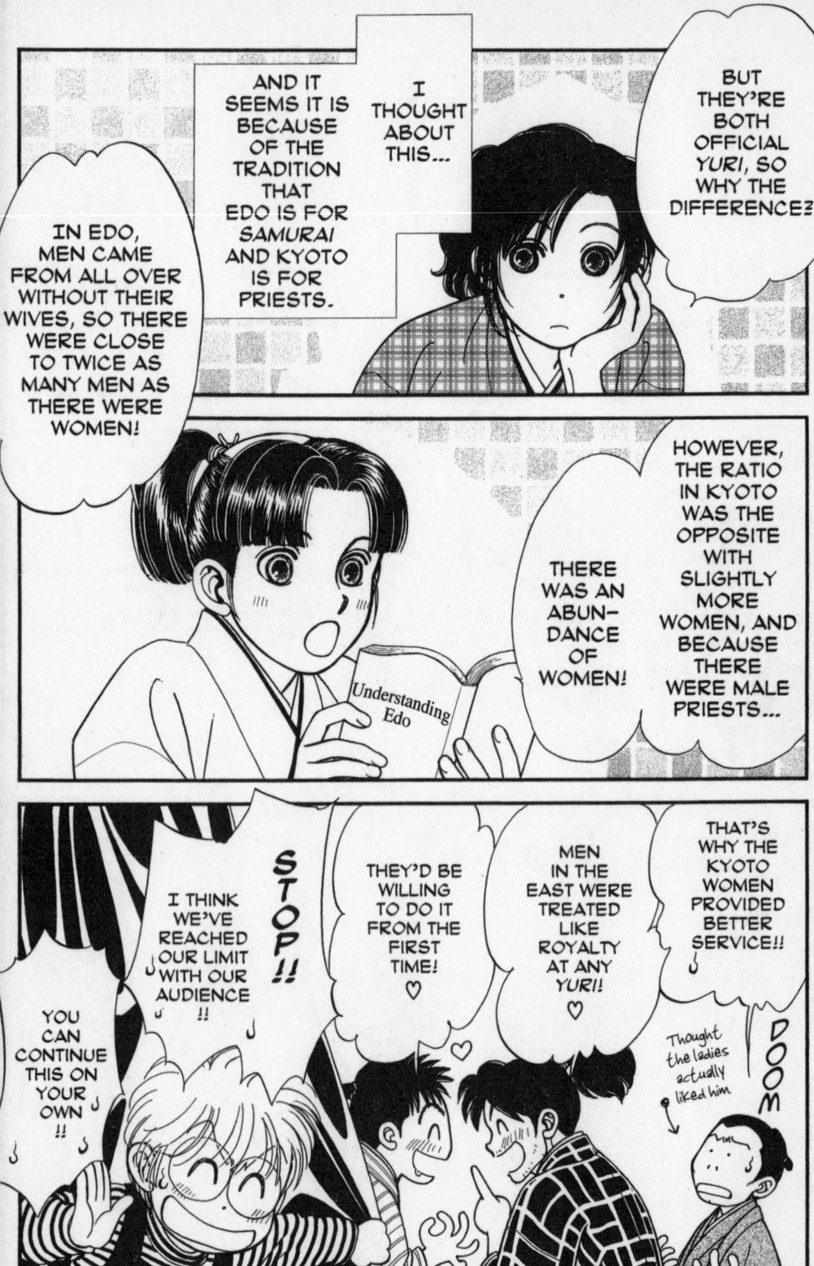

BUT THEY'RE BOTH OFFICIAL YURI, SO WHY THE DIFFERENCE?
I THOUGHT ABOUT THIS...
AND IT SEEMS IT IS BECAUSE OF THE TRADITION THAT EDO IS FOR SAMURAI AND KYOTO IS FOR PRIESTS.
IN EDO, MEN CAME FROM ALL OVER WITHOUT THEIR WIVES, SO THERE WERE CLOSE TO TWICE AS MANY MEN AS THERE WERE WOMEN!
HOWEVER, THE RATIO IN KYOTO WAS THE OPPOSITE WITH SLIGHTLY MORE WOMEN, AND BECAUSE THERE WERE MALE PRIESTS...
THERE WAS AN ABUNDANCE OF WOMEN!
Understanding Edo
THAT'S WHY THE KYOTO WOMEN PROVIDED BETTER SERVICE!!
DOOOM
Thought the ladies actually liked him
MEN IN THE EAST WERE TREATED LIKE ROYALTY AT ANY YURI! ♡
THEY'D BE WILLING TO DO IT FROM THE FIRST TIME! ♡
STOP!!
I THINK WE'VE REACHED OUR LIMIT WITH OUR AUDIENCE!!
YOU CAN CONTINUE THIS ON YOUR OWN!!

Kaze Hikaru Diary R: The End

Decoding Kaze Hikaru

Kaze Hikaru is a historical drama based in 19th century Japan and thus contains some fairly mystifying terminology. In this glossary we'll break down archaic phrases, terms, and other linguistic curiosities for you, so that you can move through life with the smug assurance that you are indeed a know-it-all.

First and foremost, because *Kaze Hikaru* is a period story, we kept all character names in their traditional Japanese form—that is, family name followed by first name. For example, the character Okita Soji's family name is Okita and his personal name is Soji.

AKO-ROSHI:
The ronin (samurai) of Ako; featured in the immortal Kabuki play *Chushingura* (Loyalty), aka *47 Samurai.*

ANI-UE:
Literally, "brother above"; an honorific for an elder male sibling.

BAKUFU:
Literally, "tent government." Shogunate; the feudal, military government that dominated Japan for more than 200 years.

BUSHI:
A samurai or warrior (part of the compound word *bushido*, which means "way of the warrior").

CHICHI-UE:
An honorific suffix meaning "father above."

DO:
In kendo (a Japanese fencing sport that uses bamboo swords), a short way of describing the offensive single-hit strike *shikake waza ippon uchi.*

-HAN:

The same as the honorific –SAN, pronounced in the dialect of southern Japan.

-KUN:

An honorific suffix that indicates a difference in rank and title. The use of *kun* is also a way of indicating familiarity and friendliness between students or compatriots.

MEN:

In the context of *Kaze Hikaru*, *men* refers to one of the "points" in kendo. It is a strike to the forehead and is considered a basic move.

MIBU-ROSHI:

A group of warriors that supports the Bakufu.

NE'E-SAN:

Can mean "older sister," "ma'am," or "miss."

NI'I-CHAN:

Short for *oni'i-san* or *oni'i-chan*, meaning older brother.

OKU-SAMA:

This is a polite way to refer to someone's wife. *Oku* means "deep" or "further back," and comes from the fact that wives (in affluent families) stayed hidden away in the back rooms of the house.

ONI:

Literally "ogre," this is Sei's nickname for Vice-Captain Hijikata.

RANPO:

Medical science derived from the Dutch.

RONIN:
Masterless samurai.

RYO:
At the time, one *ryo* and two *bu* (four bu equaled roughly one ryo) were enough currency to support a family of five for an entire month.

-SAN:
An honorific suffix that carries the meaning of "Mr." or "Ms."

SENSEI:
A teacher, master, or instructor.

SEPPUKU:
A ritualistic suicide that was considered a privilege of the nobility and samurai elite.

SONJO-HA:
Those loyal to the emperor and dedicated to the expulsion of foreigners from the country.

TAMEBO:
A short version of the name Tamesaburo.

YUBO:
A short version of the name Yunosuke.

I was vigorously washing my face in a bath I drew the other day when I caught my right pinky in my nose. I had a very bloody nose... My nose hurt for about three days. This is actually the second time I've done this. ...If you've had the same experience, please write to me. Let's be friends (heh).

Taeko Watanabe debuted as a manga artist in 1979 with her story *Waka-chan no Netsuai Jidai* (Love Struck Days of Waka). *Kaze Hikaru* is her longest-running series, but she has created a number of other popular series. Watanabe is a two-time winner of the prestigious Shogakukan Manga Award in the girls category—her manga *Hajime-chan ga Ichiban!* (Hajime-chan Is Number One!) claimed the award in 1991 and *Kaze Hikaru* took it in 2003.

Watanabe read hundreds of historical sources to create *Kaze Hikaru*. She is from Tokyo.

KAZE HIKARU VOL. II
The Shojo Beat Manga Edition

STORY AND ART BY
TAEKO WATANABE

Translation & English Adaptation/Mai Ihara
Touch-up Art & Lettering/Rina Mapa
Design/Izumi Evers
Editor/Jonathan Tarbox

Editor in Chief, Books/Alvin Lu
Editor in Chief, Magazines/Marc Weidenbaum
VP, Publishing Licensing/Rika Inouye
VP, Sales and Product Marketing/Gonzalo Ferreyra
VP, Creative/Linda Espinosa
Publisher/Hyoe Narita

Printed in Canada

Published by VIZ Media, LLC
P.O. Box 77010
San Francisco, CA 94107

Shojo Beat Manga Edition
10 9 8 7 6 5 4 3 2 1
First printing, November 2008

www.viz.com

store.viz.com

Tell us what you think about Shojo Beat Manga!

Our survey is now available online. Go to:

shojobeat.com/mangasurvey

Help us make our product offerings better!